W9-BIN-067

# Photoshop®
# Elements 13

### FOR
## DUMMIES®
A Wiley Brand

## by Barbara Obermeier
## and Ted Padova

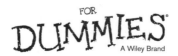

FOR
DUMMIES®
A Wiley Brand

**Photoshop® Elements 13 For Dummies®**

Published by: **John Wiley & Sons, Inc.,** 111 River Street, Hoboken, NJ 07030-5774, www.wiley.com

Copyright © 2014 by John Wiley & Sons, Inc., Hoboken, New Jersey

Published simultaneously in Canada

No part of this publication may be reproduced, stored in a retrieval system or transmitted in any form or by any means, electronic, mechanical, photocopying, recording, scanning or otherwise, except as permitted under Sections 107 or 108 of the 1976 United States Copyright Act, without the prior written permission of the Publisher. Requests to the Publisher for permission should be addressed to the Permissions Department, John Wiley & Sons, Inc., 111 River Street, Hoboken, NJ 07030, (201) 748-6011, fax (201) 748-6008, or online at http://www.wiley.com/go/permissions.

**Trademarks:** Wiley, For Dummies, the Dummies Man logo, Dummies.com, Making Everything Easier, and related trade dress are trademarks or registered trademarks of John Wiley & Sons, Inc. and may not be used without written permission. Photoshop is a registered trademark of Adobe Systems Incorporated. All other trademarks are the property of their respective owners. John Wiley & Sons, Inc. is not associated with any product or vendor mentioned in this book.

LIMIT OF LIABILITY/DISCLAIMER OF WARRANTY: THE PUBLISHER AND THE AUTHOR MAKE NO REPRESENTATIONS OR WARRANTIES WITH RESPECT TO THE ACCURACY OR COMPLETENESS OF THE CONTENTS OF THIS WORK AND SPECIFICALLY DISCLAIM ALL WARRANTIES, INCLUDING WITHOUT LIMITATION WARRANTIES OF FITNESS FOR A PARTICULAR PURPOSE. NO WARRANTY MAY BE CREATED OR EXTENDED BY SALES OR PROMOTIONAL MATERIALS. THE ADVICE AND STRATEGIES CONTAINED HEREIN MAY NOT BE SUITABLE FOR EVERY SITUATION. THIS WORK IS SOLD WITH THE UNDERSTANDING THAT THE PUBLISHER IS NOT ENGAGED IN RENDERING LEGAL, ACCOUNTING, OR OTHER PROFESSIONAL SERVICES. IF PROFESSIONAL ASSISTANCE IS REQUIRED, THE SERVICES OF A COMPETENT PROFESSIONAL PERSON SHOULD BE SOUGHT. NEITHER THE PUBLISHER NOR THE AUTHOR SHALL BE LIABLE FOR DAMAGES ARISING HEREFROM. THE FACT THAT AN ORGANIZATION OR WEBSITE IS REFERRED TO IN THIS WORK AS A CITATION AND/OR A POTENTIAL SOURCE OF FURTHER INFORMATION DOES NOT MEAN THAT THE AUTHOR OR THE PUBLISHER ENDORSES THE INFORMATION THE ORGANIZATION OR WEBSITE MAY PROVIDE OR RECOMMENDATIONS IT MAY MAKE. FURTHER, READERS SHOULD BE AWARE THAT INTERNET WEBSITES LISTED IN THIS WORK MAY HAVE CHANGED OR DISAPPEARED BETWEEN WHEN THIS WORK WAS WRITTEN AND WHEN IT IS READ.

For general information on our other products and services, please contact our Customer Care Department within the U.S. at 877-762-2974, outside the U.S. at 317-572-3993, or fax 317-572-4002. For technical support, please visit www.wiley.com/techsupport.

Wiley publishes in a variety of print and electronic formats and by print-on-demand. Some material included with standard print versions of this book may not be included in e-books or in print-on-demand. If this book refers to media such as a CD or DVD that is not included in the version you purchased, you may download this material at http://booksupport.wiley.com. For more information about Wiley products, visit www.wiley.com.

Library of Congress Control Number is available from the publisher.

ISBN 978-1-118-96464-4 (pbk); ISBN 978-1-118-96465-1 (ebk); ISBN 978-1-118-96470-5 (ebk)

Manufactured in the United States of America

10 9 8 7 6 5 4 3 2 1

# Contents at a Glance

Introduction ...................................................................... 1

Part I: Getting Started with Photoshop Elements 13 ....... 5
Chapter 1: Getting Started with Image Editing ............................................... 7
Chapter 2: Basic Image-Editing Concepts ................................................... 25
Chapter 3: Exploring the Photo Editor ........................................................ 55

Part II: Managing Media ................................................ 79
Chapter 4: Navigating the Organizer ........................................................... 81
Chapter 5: Organizing Your Pictures ........................................................... 99
Chapter 6: Viewing and Finding Your Images ............................................ 121

Part III: Selecting and Correcting Photos .................... 139
Chapter 7: Making and Modifying Selections ............................................. 141
Chapter 8: Working with Layers ................................................................. 171
Chapter 9: Simple Image Makeovers ......................................................... 193
Chapter 10: Correcting Contrast, Color, and Clarity ................................. 227

Part IV: Exploring Your Inner Artist ........................... 259
Chapter 11: Playing with Filters, Effects, Styles, and More ...................... 261
Chapter 12: Drawing and Painting .............................................................. 299
Chapter 13: Working with Type .................................................................. 325

Part V: Printing, Creating, and Sharing ...................... 345
Chapter 14: Getting It on Paper .................................................................. 347
Chapter 15: Sharing Your Work .................................................................. 363
Chapter 16: Making Creations .................................................................... 379

Part VI: The Part of Tens ............................................. 391
Chapter 17: Ten Tips for Composing Better Photos .................................. 393
Chapter 18: Ten More Project Ideas ........................................................... 399

Index .......................................................................... 405

# Table of Contents

*Introduction* .................................................................................................. *1*

About This Book .......................................................................................... 1
Icons Used in This Book ............................................................................. 2
Beyond the Book ........................................................................................ 3
Where to Go from Here .............................................................................. 3

*Part I: Getting Started with Photoshop Elements 13* ........ *5*

**Chapter 1: Getting Started with Image Editing** ...................7

Launching the Photo Editor .................................................................... 7
Making Basic Edits in Quick Mode ......................................................... 9
Sharing a Photo .......................................................................................... 12
Creating Images from Scratch .................................................................. 14
Retracing Your Steps ................................................................................. 17
    Using the History panel ....................................................................... 17
    Reverting to the last save .................................................................... 18
Getting a Helping Hand ............................................................................. 19
Saving Files with Purpose ......................................................................... 21
    Using the Save/Save As dialog box ................................................... 21
    Saving files for the web ....................................................................... 23

**Chapter 2: Basic Image-Editing Concepts** ........................25

Grappling with the Ubiquitous Pixels ..................................................... 26
    Understanding resolution .................................................................... 27
    Understanding image dimensions ...................................................... 30
The Art of Resampling ............................................................................... 30
    Changing image size and resolution .................................................. 31
    Understanding the results of resampling .......................................... 33
Choosing a Resolution for Print or Onscreen ....................................... 34
Go Ahead — Make My Mode! ..................................................................... 35
    Converting to Bitmap mode ................................................................ 36
    Converting to Grayscale mode ........................................................... 38
Understanding File Formats ..................................................................... 42
    File formats at a glance ........................................................................ 47
    Audio and video formats supported in Elements ............................ 49
Getting Familiar with Color ...................................................................... 49
Getting Color Right ..................................................................................... 51
    Color the easy way ............................................................................... 51
    Calibrating your monitor ..................................................................... 51

Choosing a color workspace ............................................................... 52
Understanding how profiles work ...................................................... 53

### Chapter 3: Exploring the Photo Editor. . . . . . . . . . . . . . . . . . . . . . . . .55

Examining the Photo Editor ...................................................................... 55
Examining the image window........................................................ 59
Uncovering the contextual menus................................................. 63
Selecting the tools .......................................................................... 63
Selecting from the Tool Options .................................................... 66
Playing with panels......................................................................... 66
Using the Photo Bin..................................................................................... 69
Creating different views of an image ............................................ 69
Viewing filenames ........................................................................... 70
Using Photo Bin Actions ................................................................ 70
Finding Your Bearings in Guided Mode .................................................... 71
Controlling the Editing Environment ....................................................... 73
Launching and navigating preferences......................................... 74
Checking out all the preferences panes........................................ 75
Customizing Presets..................................................................................... 77

## Part II: Managing Media.................................................. 79

### Chapter 4: Navigating the Organizer. . . . . . . . . . . . . . . . . . . . . . . . .81

Organizing Photos and Media on a Hard Drive ....................................... 82
Adding Images to the Organizer ................................................................ 83
Adding files from folders and removable media......................... 83
Downloading camera images with the Elements Downloader....... 85
Importing additional photos from folders ................................... 87
Getting photos from iPhoto (Mac only)........................................ 88
Navigating the Media Browser.................................................................... 89
Using a Scanner............................................................................................ 90
Understanding image requirements.............................................. 91
Using scanner plug-ins (Windows) ............................................... 92
Scanning on the Mac ....................................................................... 93
Scanning many photos at a time.................................................... 94
Phoning in Your Images .............................................................................. 95
Setting Organizer Preferences ................................................................... 97

### Chapter 5: Organizing Your Pictures. . . . . . . . . . . . . . . . . . . . . . . . .99

Touring the Organizer.................................................................................. 99
Organizing Groups of Images with Tags ................................................ 103
Creating and viewing a tag............................................................ 103
Adding icons to tags....................................................................... 105

Working with custom tags ................................................................ 106
Working with default tags ................................................................ 108
Working with subcategories ............................................................ 109
Sorting photos according to tags .................................................... 109
Rating Images with Stars ...................................................................... 110
Adding Images to an Album .................................................................. 111
Creating an album ............................................................................ 112
Using albums for temporary work .................................................. 113
Editing an album .............................................................................. 114
Finding out more about sharing your albums .............................. 114
Adding People in the Media Browser .................................................. 115
Placing Pictures on Maps ...................................................................... 116
Working with Events .............................................................................. 118

**Chapter 6: Viewing and Finding Your Images . . . . . . . . . . . . . . . . . . .121**
Cataloging Files ...................................................................................... 121
Using the Catalog Manager .............................................................. 122
Working with catalogs ...................................................................... 123
Backing up your catalog .................................................................. 124
Backing up photos and files (Windows) ........................................ 126
Switching to a Different View .............................................................. 126
Viewing Photos in a Slide Show .......................................................... 127
Searching for Photos .............................................................................. 129
Using Search ...................................................................................... 130
Searching for untagged items .......................................................... 130
Searching captions and notes .......................................................... 130
Searching by history .......................................................................... 131
Searching metadata ............................................................................ 131
Searching similarities ........................................................................ 133
Grouping Files That Get in the Way .................................................... 135
Marking files as hidden .................................................................... 135
Stacking 'em up ................................................................................ 135
Creating versions .............................................................................. 137

**Part III: Selecting and Correcting Photos . . . . . . . . . . . . . . . . . . . . 139**

**Chapter 7: Making and Modifying Selections . . . . . . . . . . . . . . . . . . .141**
Defining Selections ................................................................................ 141
Creating Rectangular and Elliptical Selections ................................ 142
Perfecting squares and circles with Shift and Alt
(Option on the Mac) .................................................................... 143
Applying Marquee options ................................................................ 144

Making Freeform Selections with the Lasso Tools....................................146
    Selecting with the Lasso tool...............................................................147
    Getting straight with the Polygonal Lasso tool...........................148
    Snapping with the Magnetic Lasso tool .......................................149
Working Wizardry with the Magic Wand..............................................152
    Talking about Tolerance ....................................................................152
    Wielding the Wand to select............................................................153
Modifying Your Selections ........................................................................154
    Adding to, subtracting from, and intersecting a selection...........154
    Avoiding key collisions .....................................................................155
Painting with the Selection Brush .........................................................156
Painting with the Quick Selection Tool.................................................158
Fine-Tuning with the Refine Selection Brush .......................................160
Working with the Cookie Cutter Tool ....................................................161
Eliminating with the Eraser Tools ..........................................................163
    The Eraser tool...................................................................................163
    The Background Eraser tool..............................................................164
    The Magic Eraser tool .......................................................................165
Using the Select Menu ..............................................................................165
    Selecting all or nothing .....................................................................166
    Reselecting a selection......................................................................166
    Inversing a selection..........................................................................166
    Feathering a selection .......................................................................166
    Refining the edges of a selection ....................................................167
    Using the Modify commands............................................................169
    Applying the Grow and Similar commands....................................169
    Saving and loading selections .........................................................170

**Chapter 8: Working with Layers** ...............................**171**
Getting to Know Layers .............................................................................171
    Converting a background to a layer ...............................................172
    Anatomy of the Layers panel...........................................................173
    Using the Layer and Select menus..................................................175
Working with Different Layer Types ........................................................177
    Image layers........................................................................................177
    Adjustment layers..............................................................................178
    Fill layers.............................................................................................180
    Shape layers .......................................................................................181
    Type layers .........................................................................................182
Tackling Layer Basics ...............................................................................182
    Creating a new layer from scratch...................................................182
    Using Layer via Copy and Layer via Cut ........................................184
    Duplicating layers ..............................................................................184
    Dragging and dropping layers.........................................................184
    Using the Paste into Selection command .....................................185

Moving a Layer's Content...........................................................186
Transforming Layers .................................................................187
Adding Layer Masks .................................................................188
Flattening and Merging Layers.................................................190
    Flattening layers ................................................................191
    Merging layers ...................................................................192

## Chapter 9: Simple Image Makeovers ...........................193

Cropping and Straightening Images .........................................193
    Cutting away with the Crop tool.......................................193
    Cropping with a selection border......................................196
    Straightening images ........................................................196
Recomposing Images ................................................................198
Employing One-Step Auto Fixes................................................200
    Auto Smart Tone ...............................................................200
    Auto Smart Fix...................................................................201
    Auto Levels ........................................................................202
    Auto Contrast ....................................................................203
    Auto Color Correction......................................................203
    Auto Sharpen.....................................................................204
    Auto Red Eye Fix ..............................................................205
Editing in Quick Mode..............................................................206
Fixing Small Imperfections with Tools.....................................210
    Cloning with the Clone Stamp tool...................................210
    Retouching with the Healing Brush..................................212
    Zeroing in with the Spot Healing Brush ...........................214
    Repositioning with the Content-Aware Move tool...........216
    Lightening and darkening with Dodge and Burn tools....217
    Smudging away rough spots...............................................219
    Softening with the Blur tool..............................................221
    Focusing with the Sharpen tool .......................................221
    Sponging color on and off.................................................223
    Replacing one color with another .....................................224

## Chapter 10: Correcting Contrast, Color, and Clarity .............227

Editing Your Photos Using a Logical Workflow .......................228
Adjusting Lighting ....................................................................228
    Fixing lighting with Shadows/Highlights..........................229
    Using Brightness/Contrast................................................230
    Pinpointing proper contrast with Levels ..........................230
Adjusting Color ..........................................................................233
    Removing color casts automatically .................................234
    Adjusting with Hue/Saturation ........................................235
    Eliminating color with Remove Color ..............................236
    Switching colors with Replace Color................................238

Correcting with Color Curves.................................................239
Adjusting skin tones ........................................................241
Defringing layers ............................................................242
Adjusting color temperature with photo filters..........244
Mapping your colors .......................................................245
Adjusting Clarity ......................................................................246
Removing noise, artifacts, dust, and scratches ...........247
Blurring when you need to ............................................248
Sharpening for better focus ..........................................251
Working Intelligently with the Smart Brush Tools ...............254

## Part IV: Exploring Your Inner Artist............................. 259

### Chapter 11: Playing with Filters, Effects, Styles, and More . . . . . . . .261

Having Fun with Filters ..........................................................262
Applying filters ...............................................................262
Corrective or destructive filters ..................................263
One-step or multistep filters.........................................263
Fading a filter ..................................................................264
Selectively applying a filter...........................................264
Working in the Filter Gallery .........................................265
Distorting with the Liquify filter...................................267
Correcting Camera Distortion................................................269
Exploring Element's Unique Filters .......................................271
Creating a comic .............................................................272
Getting graphic................................................................273
Using the Pen and Ink filter...........................................274
Dressing Up with Photo and Text Effects..............................275
Adding Shadows, Glows, and More........................................277
Applying layer styles ......................................................277
Working with layer styles ...............................................279
Mixing It Up with Blend Modes ..............................................280
General blend modes........................................................280
Darken blend modes........................................................281
Lighten blend modes .......................................................282
Lighting blend modes ......................................................283
Inverter blend modes ......................................................284
HSL blend modes .............................................................285
Using Photomerge ...................................................................286
Photomerge Panorama.....................................................286
Photomerge Group Shot ..................................................289
Photomerge Scene Cleaner..............................................291
Photomerge Exposure......................................................292
Photomerge Compose.......................................................295

**Chapter 12: Drawing and Painting** .......................**299**

Choosing Color ................................................299
    Working with the Color Picker ...................................300
    Dipping into the Color Swatches panel.....................301
    Sampling with the Eyedropper tool............................303
Getting Artsy with the Pencil and Brush Tools ...............304
    Drawing with the Pencil tool ....................................304
    Painting with the Brush tool....................................306
    Using the Impressionist Brush ................................307
    Creating your own brush ........................................309
Filling and Outlining Selections ................................310
    Fill 'er up ................................................................310
    Outlining with the Stroke command........................311
Splashing on Color with the Paint Bucket Tool...............312
Working with Multicolored Gradients ..........................313
    Applying a preset gradient ....................................313
    Customizing gradients............................................315
Working with Patterns ............................................317
    Applying a preset pattern .......................................318
    Creating a new pattern ..........................................318
Creating Shapes of All Sorts ....................................319
    Drawing a shape....................................................320
    Drawing multiple shapes .......................................321
    Specifying Geometry options ................................321
    Editing shapes ......................................................323

**Chapter 13: Working with Type** ....................**325**

Understanding Type Basics ......................................325
    Tools....................................................................326
    Modes..................................................................326
    Formats ................................................................327
Creating Point Type................................................327
Creating Paragraph Type..........................................329
Creating Path Type..................................................330
    Using the Text On Selection tool ............................330
    Using the Text On Shape tool................................331
    Using the Text On Custom Path tool........................333
Specifying Type Options..........................................333
Editing Text ..........................................................336
Simplifying Type ....................................................337
Masking with Type ................................................338
Stylizing and Warping Type .....................................340
    Adjusting type opacity ..........................................340
    Applying filters to your type ..................................340
    Painting your type with color and gradients............341
    Warping your type................................................342

## Part V: Printing, Creating, and Sharing ..................... 345

### Chapter 14: Getting It on Paper ........................... **347**
Getting Pictures Ready for Printing ................................................ 348
Working with Color Printer Profiles ............................................... 349
    Printing a photo with the printer managing color ................. 350
    Printing a photo with Elements managing color .................... 356
    Printing a picture package or contact sheet ......................... 358
Getting Familiar with the Print Dialog Box .................................... 360
    Using Page Setup ...................................................................... 362
    Creating transfers, borders, and more with More Options .......... 362

### Chapter 15: Sharing Your Work ........................... **363**
Getting Familiar with the Elements Sharing Options .................... 363
    Planning ahead .......................................................................... 364
    Understanding photo sharing in Elements ............................ 365
Working with Adobe Revel ............................................................... 366
    Knowing what Adobe Revel offers you ................................... 367
    Downloading the Adobe Revel applications .......................... 367
    Understanding the Adobe Revel interface ............................ 368
    Editing a photo with Adobe Revel ......................................... 368
    Sharing photos with Adobe Revel .......................................... 371
    Downloading images from Adobe Revel ................................ 371
Using the Share Panel ...................................................................... 372
    Emailing photos ........................................................................ 373
    Working with Adobe Premiere Elements ................................ 375
    Sharing your photos on social networks ............................... 375

### Chapter 16: Making Creations ............................ **379**
Checking Out the Create Panel ....................................................... 379
Creating Facebook Cover Images .................................................... 380
Grasping Creation-Assembly Basics ............................................... 382
Creating a Slide Show ....................................................................... 386
Creating a PDF Slide Show ............................................................... 388
Making Additional Creations ........................................................... 389

## Part VI: The Part of Tens ............................... 391

### Chapter 17: Ten Tips for Composing Better Photos ........... **393**
Find a Focal Point ............................................................................. 393
Use the Rule of Thirds ...................................................................... 394
Cut the Clutter ................................................................................... 394

Frame Your Shot ............................................................ 395
Employ Contrast ........................................................... 395
Experiment with Viewpoints .................................... 395
Use Leading Lines ........................................................ 396
Use Light ........................................................................ 396
Give Direction ............................................................. 397
Consider Direction of Movement ............................ 398

**Chapter 18: Ten More Project Ideas** . . . . . . . . . . . . . . . . . . . . . . . . .**399**
Screen Savers ............................................................... 399
Flyers, Ads, and Online Auctions ............................ 400
Clothes, Hats, and More ............................................ 402
Posters .......................................................................... 402
Household and Business Inventories ...................... 402
Project Documentation ............................................. 403
School Reports and Projects ..................................... 403
Blogs ............................................................................... 403
Wait — There's More ................................................. 403

*Index* ................................................................. *405*

# Introduction

· · · · · · · · · · · · · · · · · · · · · · · · · · · · · · · · · · · · · · · · · · · · · · · · · · · · · · · · · · · · · · · · ·

*W*e live in a photo world. And Photoshop Elements has become a tool for both professional and amateur photographers who want to edit, improve, manage, manipulate, and organize photos and other media. Considering the power and impressive features of the program, Elements remains one of the best values for your money among computer software applications.

## About This Book

This book is an effort to provide as much of a comprehensive view of a wildly feature-rich program as we can. Additionally, this book is written for a cross-platform audience. If you're a Macintosh user, you'll find all you need to work in Elements 13 for the Macintosh, including support for placing photos on maps and more consistency with Windows features.

As each software product is upgraded to a newer version, you sometimes find a whole bunch of new features that dazzle you and sometimes you find not so many new features but much more improved performance. Photoshop Elements 13 is focused on the latter. You find some new and interesting features such as a few more Guided Edits, a completely new Slideshow tool, a Facebook Profile Creator, Selection Editing, more 16-bit support, Crop suggestions, and Photomerge Compose. However the real power in Photoshop Elements 13 is under the hood and features you don't see such as much improved performance and support for Windows 64-bit operating systems.

Because Photoshop Elements has something for just about everyone, we know that our audience is large and also that not everyone will use every tool, command, or method we describe. We offer many cross-references throughout in case you want to jump around. You can go to just about any chapter and start reading. If a concept needs more explanation, we point you in the right direction for getting some background.

Throughout this book, especially in step lists, we point you to menus for keyboard commands. For accessing a menu command, you may see something like this:

Choose File⇨Get Photos⇨From Files and Folders.

You click the File menu to open its drop-down menu, click the menu command labeled Get Photos, and then choose the command From Files and Folders from the submenu that appears. It's that simple.

We also refer to *context menus,* which jump up at your cursor position and shows you a menu of options related to whatever you're doing at the time. To open a context menu, just right-click the mouse, or Control-click on a Macintosh if you don't have a two-button mouse.

When we mention that keys need to be pressed on your keyboard, the text looks like this:

> Press Alt+Shift+Ctrl+S (Option+Shift+⌘+S on the Macintosh).

In this case, you hold down the Alt key on Windows/the Option key on the Macintosh, then the Shift key, then the Control key on Windows/the ⌘ key on the Macintosh, and then press the S key. Then, release all the keys at the same time.

## Icons Used in This Book

In the margins throughout this book, you see icons indicating that something is important.

This icon informs you that this item is a new feature in Photoshop Elements 13.

Pay particular attention when you see the Warning icon. This icon indicates possible side-effects or damage to your image that you might encounter when performing certain operations in Elements.

This icon is a heads-up for something you may want to commit to memory. Usually, it tells you about a shortcut for a repetitive task, where remembering a procedure can save you time.

A Tip tells you about an alternative method for a procedure, giving you a shortcut, a workaround, or some other type of helpful information.

This icon points out online articles that expand on a topic in this book. To find all this great extra content, point your browser to www.dummies.com/extras/photoshopelements.

 Elements is a computer program, after all. No matter how hard we try to simplify our explanation of features, we can't entirely avoid some technical information. If a topic is a little on the technical side, we use this icon to alert you that we're moving into a complex subject. You won't see many of these icons in the book because we try our best to give you the details in nontechnical terms.

## Beyond the Book

We have online content that you can enjoy in conjunction with this book:

- ✔ **Cheat Sheet:** The cheat sheet for this book includes a detailed look at the Elements photo editing workspace, Tool Panel shortcuts, and tricks for selecting objects, and more.

  www.dummies.com/cheatsheet/photoshopelements

- ✔ **Online articles:** We couldn't fit everything we wanted into this book, so you can find additional content here:

  www.dummies.com/extras/photoshopelements

  A few of the topics covered are organizing and importing photos, dynamically updating saved searches, finding and loading actions, and adjusting brightness/contrast with the Smart Brush tool. But there's much more than these few topics. Be sure to check these out.

## Where to Go from Here

Try to spend a little time reading through the three chapters in Part I. After you know how to edit and save photos, feel free to jump around and pay special attention to the cross-referenced chapters, in case you get stuck on a concept. After exploring Elements' Photo Editor look over Part II, where we talk about organizing and searching photos. If you're ready to jump into more advanced tasks, check out Parts III and IV, where you learn how to make selections; layer images and effects together; add filters and type; and much much more.

We hope you have much success and enjoyment in using Adobe Photoshop Elements 13, and it's our sincere wish that the pages ahead provide you with an informative and helpful view of the program.

# Part I

# Getting Started with Photoshop Elements 13

For Dummies can help you get started with lots of subjects. Visit www.dummies.com to learn more.

## In this part . . .

- ✔ Open the Photo Editor and make quick and easy edits to one of your photos in Quick mode.

- ✔ Choose the right resolution for your image.

- ✔ Select the best file format when you save your image.

- ✔ Tour the Photo Editor interface so that you know how to switch among images and navigate the many panels and options.

# Getting Started with Image Editing

## In This Chapter

▶ Starting the Photo Editor

▶ Opening, editing, sharing, and saving a photo

▶ Creating a new document

▶ Using Undo History

▶ Finding help

▶ Saving your files

*I*mage editing is incredibly fun, especially with a tool like Photoshop Elements, which enables you to modify, combine, and even draw your own images to your imagination's content. To get the most out of Elements, you need to understand some basic technical concepts, but like most people, you probably want to jump in, play around, and basically just get started right away.

You're in luck: In Quick mode, Elements helps you make basic edits to your photos, like revealing your child's face darkened by a baseball cap's shadow or cropping out the gigantic trash can on the left edge of your otherwise perfect landscape shot. In this chapter, we help you jumpstart your image-editing skills by guiding you through Quick mode and how to share photos online, retracing your steps, saving your edits, and more.

## Launching the Photo Editor

Photoshop Elements has two separate components:

✔ **The Organizer** is where you manage photos. It's full of tools for tagging, rating, sorting, and finding your images. Part II helps you start using the Organizer.

  ✔ **The Photo Editor** is where you correct photos for brightness and color, add effects, repair images, and so on.

In this chapter, you work in the Photo Editor to make basic edits to a photo.

Here's how to start Elements and open the Photo Editor:

1. **Double-click the Photoshop Elements shortcut on your desktop or in your Applications folder (Mac) to launch the Elements Welcome screen.**

   *Note:* You have two buttons on the Welcome screen. The first button is Organizer. The other button is Photo Editor.

2. **Click the Photo Editor button shown in the Welcome screen in Figure 1-1.**

   The Photo Editor workspace loads and appears, as shown in Figure 1-2. By default, you see the Quick tab selected at the top of the Photo Editor workspace, which means you're in Quick mode (or right where you want to be for the purposes of this chapter). Quick mode offers a limited number of tools for adjusting brightness, contrast, color, and sharpness.

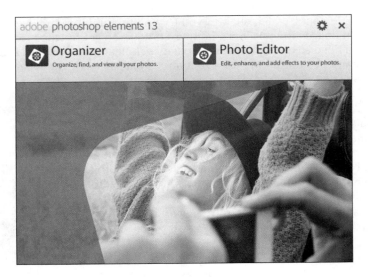

Figure 1-1: The Photoshop Elements Welcome screen.

When you first launch Photoshop Elements, you may see the eLive tab open. Click the Quick tab to see the editing options for Quick mode. See the section, "Getting a Helping Hand," later in this chapter for more about eLive.

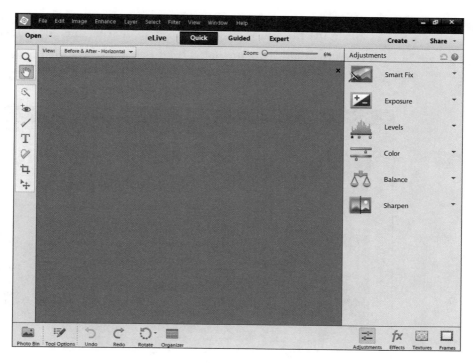

Figure 1-2: The Quick tab is selected.

On the right side of the workspace, you see the Adjustments panel docked in an area dubbed the Panel Bin. When in any one of the three editing modes (Quick, Guided, Expert), you find different panels. On the left side of the workspace, you see a Tools panel. Interacting with the items in the Panel Bin and using tools in the Tools panel provides you an enormous number of options for editing, improving, and stylizing your pictures.

# Making Basic Edits in Quick Mode

For beginning users, the Quick mode in the Photo Editor is both powerful and easy to use. Follow these steps to make some simple changes to an image:

1. **Open the Photo Editor and make sure the Quick tab is selected at the top.**

2. **Choose File⇨Open.**

   If Elements is your default editing application, you can also double-click your photo file in Windows Explorer or the Mac Finder, and the file opens in Elements.

3. **In the Open dialog box that appears, navigate your hard drive to locate the file you want to open, select the file, and click Open.**

4. **From the View drop-down list (in the upper left of the image window), choose Before & After – Horizontal, as shown in Figure 1-3.**

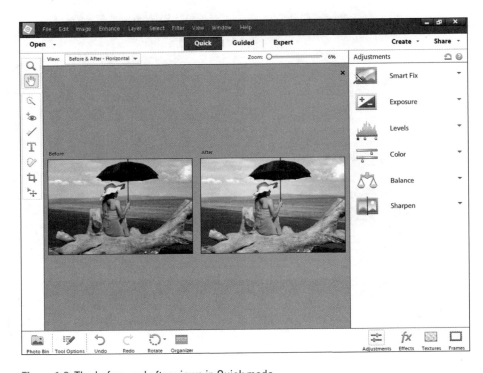

**Figure 1-3:** The before and after views in Quick mode.

5. **Make edits to your photo.**

   Here's an introduction to two simple edits you can make in Quick mode:

   - *Apply a Smart Fix:* Click Smart Fix in the Panel Bin to see the options. To begin with, click Auto at the bottom of the Smart Fix panel and select the After view to see whether you like the changes.

As shown in Figure 1-3, several items are listed in the Panel Bin below the Smart Fix option. Click an item to expand it and move the sliders, or click the thumbnail images to tweak the overall brightness, contrast, and color. In many cases there isn't a right or wrong adjustment. Play with the options to bring it close to your overall vision for the picture. For a more in-depth look at correcting photos in Quick mode, flip to Chapter 10.

- *Crop the photo:* In the Tools panel on the left side of the window, click the Crop tool. You immediately see a rectangle on top of the photo. Move the sides to crop the image to your liking. When finished, click the green check mark, as shown in Figure 1-4, to accept your edit.

When making any one of a huge number of edits to your pictures, you often see icons on top of the image similar to what's shown in Figure 1-4. The green check mark accepts the edit you're making at the time the icons appear. The circle with a diagonal line is the Cancel button. Click this button when you don't want to apply the recent edit.

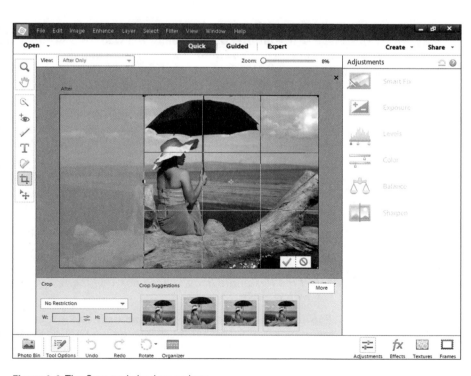

**Figure 1-4:** The Crop tool sized on a photo.

6. **Choose File⇨Save As and, in the Save As dialog box that opens, provide a new name for the photo. Click Save.**

   *Note:* When you use Save As and give your image a new name, you don't destroy your original image. You save a copy of the original with the new edits applied. For more on saving files, see the section "Saving Files with Purpose" later in this chapter.

## Sharing a Photo

After you edit your photo, you can print the photo to share with family and friends or post the photo on a social network.

Because sharing photos on social networks is extremely popular, we introduce you to the Elements sharing features with the following steps, which explain how you can use Elements to share your photo on Facebook:

1. **Prepare the photo you want to upload to Facebook.**

   Typically, digital cameras take photos sized very large — too large for an image that your friends and family will want to download quickly and view via Facebook on a computer screen or a mobile device. To adjust your image so it's the right size and resolution for viewing online, follow these steps:

   a. *Choose Image⇨Resize⇨Image Size.*

   b. *In the Image Size dialog box that appears, enter your desired width (or height).*

   Either Width or Height is fine because the image will maintain correct proportions by choosing either. A width between 6 and 8 inches works well. Click the Pixels drop-down menu next to Width to choose Inches as your unit of measure.

   c. *Type **144** in the Resolution box.* For screen viewing only 72 ppi is fine. However if you want your friends to print the image, 144 is a better choice. You can use either resolution.

   d. *Select the Resample Image check box and then click OK (see Figure 1-5).*

   The image is sized to a workable size for Facebook. In Chapter 2, you take a closer look at what these image-sizing options mean and how to choose the right settings for your prints or online images.

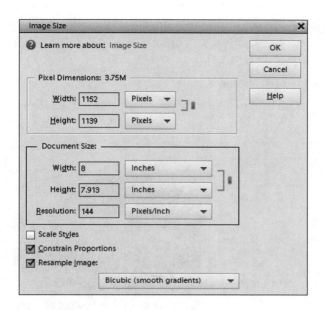

Figure 1-5: Resize an image in the Image Size dialog box.

**2. Choose File➪Save As➪JPEG to save the file as a JPEG.**

Note the location where you save the file on your hard drive. Chapter 2 also explains how to choose the right file format for your images. (JPEG is one of many file formats that Elements supports.)

**3. Click Share in the top-right corner of the workspace to open the Share panel and then choose Facebook from the drop-down list.**

Elements enables you to upload to other services, like Twitter and Flickr, too. For details about the Share panel, flip to Chapter 15.

**4. Authenticate your account.**

A dialog box opens when you choose Facebook in the Share panel, prompting you to authenticate your account. To authenticate your account:

*a. Click Authenticate in the dialog box.*

*b. Fill in the text boxes for your Facebook login and password.*

Your authentication is complete.

5. **Click the Upload button to upload the file.**

   When the file upload is complete, a dialog box opens and prompts you to view the uploaded file.

6. **Click Visit Facebook.**

   Your photo is added to your Facebook account, as shown in Figure 1-6.

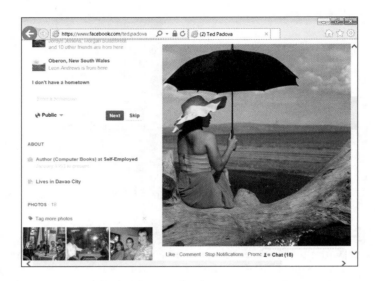

Figure 1-6: An edited photo uploaded to Facebook.

## Creating Images from Scratch

You may want to start from scratch by creating a new document in Elements. New, blank pages have a number of uses:

- ✔ Mix and merge images in a new document, as we explain in Chapter 8.

- ✔ Create a canvas where you can draw and paint, as we explain in Chapter 12.

- ✔ Use the New dialog box to find out a file's size, dimensions, and resolution. You find out why these details are important in Chapter 2.

Follow these steps to create a new document while working in any editing mode:

1. **In the Elements Photo Editor, choose File➪New➪Blank File or press Ctrl+N (⌘+N on the Mac).**

Alternatively, you can choose Open⇨New Blank File in the Photo Editor. The New dialog box opens, as shown in Figure 1-7.

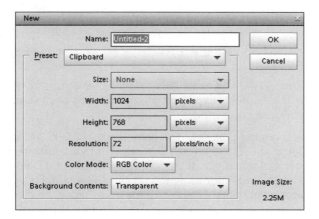

**Figure 1-7:** When you create a new, blank file, the New dialog box opens.

2. **Select the attributes for the new file.**

When you select these attributes, among the things you need to consider is the output you want to use for the image: screen or paper. Files created for the web or for screen views are measured in pixels, and you don't need to specify a resolution. For print, you want to use a measurement other than pixels and you need to specify resolution. We explain how all this works for the relevant settings in the following bulleted list.

You have several options from which to choose:

- *Name:* Type a name for your file.

- *Preset:* Select from a number of sizes.

- *Size:* You can choose a preset size from a long drop-down list. This setting is optional because you can change the file attributes in the other text boxes and drop-down lists.

- *Dimensions (Width/Height):* Values in the Width and Height text boxes are independent; either box can be edited without affecting the other. Adjacent to the values in the Width and Height text boxes, you find drop-down lists that offer many options for units of measure, such as the default units of pixels followed by inches, centimeters (cm), millimeters (mm), points, picas, and columns.

- *Resolution:* Generally speaking, if your image will be printed, choose 300 dpi (dots per inch). If you plan to display your image only on a computer screen or mobile device, choose 72 ppi (pixels per inch). Chapter 2 explains the details about how resolution works.

- *Color Mode:* You most likely want to leave this at the default of RGB. Chapter 2 explains when you might want to use the other available color modes.

- *Background Contents:* You have three choices: White, Background Color, and Transparent. The selection you make results in the color of the blank image. If you choose Background Color, the current background color assigned on the Tools panel is applied to the background. See Chapter 12 for information on changing background color. If you choose Transparent, the blank image is the digital version of a sheet of acetate, and the image is created as a layer. Chapter 8 explains how you work with layers.

- *Image Size:* This value (displayed in the lower-right corner of the dialog box) dynamically changes when you change the Width, Height, and Resolution values. The Image Size value tells you how much file space is required to save the uncompressed file.

3. **Click OK after setting the file attributes to create the new document.**

Sometimes you may want to copy a selection to the Clipboard and convert the Clipboard information to an image. Be sure you have copied some image data to the Clipboard. In Elements, choose File➪New➪Image from Clipboard. The data on the Clipboard appears in a new document window.

After you create a new image, try playing with the different brushes and painting tools, just to experiment and get a feel for how they work. For example, click a brush on the Tools panel and then click and drag to paint in the image window. Or jump to Chapter 12, where we help you start using the drawing and painting tools.

# *Retracing Your Steps*

In Elements, Undo is a favorite command for both beginners and experienced users alike. If you don't like a change to your image, you simply choose Edit⇨Undo or press the keyboard shortcut Ctrl+Z (⌘+Z on the Mac).

Because trial and error (and thus undoing your work) is so important to making your image look just right, Elements also offers ways to undo that are much more sophisticated than simply reverting to the last view. In the following sections, we introduce you to these more sophisticated tools.

## *Using the History panel*

On the History panel, you see a record of your changes in an editing session. And from this record, you can undo your changes from any step in an editing sequence. To work with the History panel, you must be in Expert mode. After you click Expert at the top of the Photo Editor, here's how undoing with the History panel works:

1. **To open the panel, choose Window⇨History.**

   The History panel displays a record of each step you made in the current editing session, as shown in Figure 1-8.

2. **To undo one or more edits, click any item on the History panel.**

   Elements reverts your image to that last edit. All edits that follow the selected item are grayed out.

3. **If you want to bring back the edits, click any grayed-out step on the panel.**

   Elements reinstates your edits up to that level.

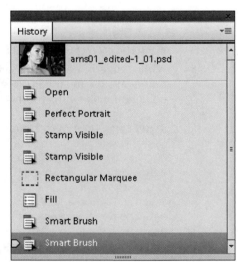

**Figure 1-8:** The Undo History panel.

All your steps are listed on the History panel as long as you remain in Elements and don't close the file. When the file is closed, all history information is lost.

Storing all this editing history can affect Elements' performance. If your computer slows to a snail's pace when you're using Elements, check out the following options:

- ✔ **Choose Edit➪Clear➪History.** Elements flushes all the recorded history and frees up some precious memory, which often enables you to work faster. Just be sure you're okay with losing all the history in the History panel thus far.

- ✔ **Eliminate Clipboard data from memory.** To do so, choose Edit➪Clear Clipboard or Edit➪Clear➪All.

- ✔ **Restore the number of history states stored to the default of 50.** In Chapter 3, we show you how to increase the number of history states via Elements preferences. You can ratchet this number up to 1,000 if you like. But realize that the more history states you record, the more memory Elements requires.

## Reverting to the last save

While you edit photos in Elements, plan on saving your work regularly. Each time you save in an editing session, the History panel preserves the list of edits you make until you hit the maximum number or close the file.

If you save, then perform more edits, and then want to return to the last saved version of your document, Elements provides you with a quick, efficient way to do so. If you choose Edit➪Revert, Elements eliminates your new edits and takes you back to the last time you saved your file.

When you choose Revert, *Revert* appears in the History panel. You can eliminate the Revert command from the History panel by right-clicking (Windows) or Ctrl-clicking (on a Mac with a one-button mouse) the Revert item and choosing Delete from the contextual menu that appears.

# Getting a Helping Hand

You probably bought this book because you're not a fan of sifting through help files and want an expert guide to image editing. We share everything a beginner needs to get started in Elements, but Elements is too sophisticated a program to cover completely in the pages we have here. You may also need some quick help if you don't have this book nearby.

Whenever you need a hand, know that you can find valuable help information quickly and easily within Elements itself. If you're stuck on understanding a feature, ample help documents are only a mouse click away and can help you overcome some frustrating moments.

Your first stop is the Help menu, where you can find several commands that offer information:

- **Photoshop Elements Help:** Choose Help➪Photoshop Elements Help or press the F1 key (Windows) or the Help key (on a Mac with an extended keyboard) to open the Elements Help file. You can type a search topic and press Enter to display a list of search results.

- **Key Concepts:** While you read this book, if we use a term that you don't completely understand, choose Help➪Key Concepts. A web page opens in your default web browser and provides many web pages with definitions of terms and concepts.

- **Support:** This menu command launches your default web browser and takes you to the Adobe website (www.adobe.com), where you can find information about Elements, problems reported by users, and some workaround methods for getting a job done. You can find additional web-based help information by clicking Photoshop Elements Online and Online Learning Resources. The vast collection of web pages on Adobe's website offers you assistance, tips and techniques, and solutions to many problems that come with editing images. Be sure to spend some time browsing these web pages.

- **Video Tutorials:** Choose Help➪Video Tutorials to open a web page where videos for common tasks are hosted on Adobe's website.

- **Forum:** Choose Help➪Forum to explore user comments and questions with answers to many common problems.

Tooltips can be another helpful resource. While you move your cursor around tools and panels, pause a moment before clicking the mouse. A slight delay in your actions produces a *tooltip,* which is a small box that describes the item your mouse is pointing to. Elements provides this sort of dynamic help when you pause the cursor before moving to another location.

When you launch the Organizer or Photo Editor for the first time, you may see the eLive tab selected by default. eLive, shown in Figure 1-9, is a new feature in Elements that offers you help, tutorial assistance, and information related to updates. When you first begin to explore Elements, take a look at the various options you have for learning more about the program.

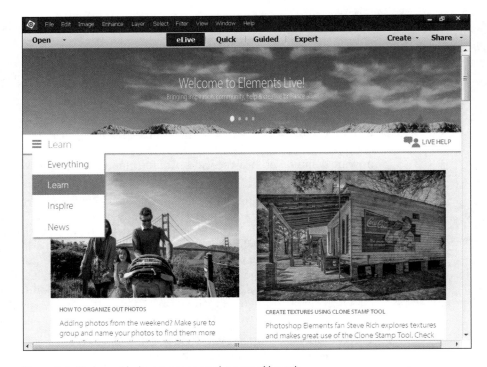

Figure 1-9: Find great help resources on the new eLive tab.

eLive has three separate categories and a View All category (called Everything) where all options are shown in the eLive window. You select a category by opening the drop-down menu from the left side of the window. Here you find:

- **Learn:** Click this item to learn various techniques in editing photos.

- **Inspire:** Click this item to view some inspirational creations.

- **News:** Click this tab to view updated Elements news items such as updates and announcements.

The eLive tab shows updated information as Adobe posts it. The interface is web-based and new updates to the individual items occur routinely. Be sure to explore eLive to keep updated with new ideas and announcements.

# Saving Files with Purpose

When you save a file after editing it, you might save the file in the same file format, or change the format to suit your photo service center's specifications or to ensure your image downloads quickly on a website.

When you save, Elements also enables you to take advantage of special features, such as saving different versions of a file or including your edited file in the Organizer as well as saving it to your hard drive.

This section is your guided tour of the Save dialog box (or Save As dialog box if you're saving a file for the first time) and the Save for Web dialog box. In Chapter 2, you find a detailed explanation of how to choose a file format when you save.

## Using the Save/Save As dialog box

In most any program, the Save (or Save As) dialog box is a familiar place where you make choices about the file to be saved. With Save As, you can save a duplicate copy of your image or save a modified copy and retain the original file. However, if you're planning to upload your final image to the web, skip the familiar Save (or Save As) dialog box and see the next section, "Saving files for the web."

To use the Save (or Save As) dialog box, choose File➪Save for files to be saved the first time, or choose File➪Save As for any file, and a dialog box then opens.

As a matter of good practice, when you open an image, choose File➪Save As for your first step in editing a photo. Save with a new filename to make a copy and then proceed to edit the photo. If you don't like your editing results, you can return to the original, unedited photo and make another copy for editing.

The standard navigational tools you find in any Save dialog box appear in the Elements Save/Save As dialog box. Here are two standard options you find in the Elements Save/Save As dialog box:

- **Filename:** This item is common to all Save (Windows) or Save As (Mac) dialog boxes. Type a name for your file in the text box.

- **Format:** From the drop-down list, you choose file formats. We explain the formats that Elements supports in Chapter 2.

A few options make the Photoshop Elements Save/Save As dialog box different from other Save dialog boxes that you might be accustomed to using. The Save Options area in the Save As dialog box provides these choices:

- **Include in the Elements Organizer:** If you want the file added to the Organizer, select this check box. (For more information about using the Organizer, see Part II.)

- **Save in Version Set with Original:** You can edit images and save a version of your image, but only in Quick mode. When you save the file from Quick mode, this check box is enabled. Select the box to save a version of the original, which appears in the Organizer.

- **Layers:** If your file has layers, selecting this check box preserves the layers.

- **As a Copy:** Use this option to save a copy without overwriting the original file.

- **Color:** Color profiles help you maintain accurate color, and this box controls your image's color profile. Select the box for ICC (International Color Consortium) Profile. Depending on which profile you're using, the option appears for sRGB or Adobe RGB (1998). When the check box is selected, the profile is embedded in the image. Chapter 2 introduces color profiles in more detail, and Chapter 14 explains how to use color profiles with your prints.

✓ **Thumbnail (Windows only):** If you save a file with a thumbnail, you can see a miniature representation of your image when viewing it in folders or on the desktop. If you select Ask When Saving in the Saving Files preferences, the check box can be enabled or disabled. If you select an option for Never Save or Always Save in the Preferences dialog box, this box is enabled or disabled (grayed out) for you. You need to return to the Preferences dialog box if you want to change the option.

## Saving files for the web

The Save for Web command helps you prepare photos to show on the web or just onscreen. To use this command, make sure you're in Expert mode. Then choose File➪Save for Web. In the Save for Web dialog box that opens (see Figure 1-10), you see your original image on the left, and the result of making changes for file format and quality settings on the right.

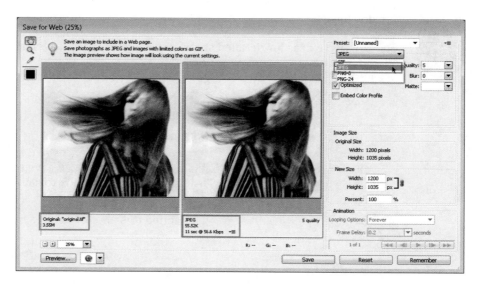

**Figure 1-10:** The Save for Web dialog box.

The standard rule with web graphics is to find the smallest file size for an acceptable image appearance. In the Save for Web dialog box, you have many choices for reducing file size. Notice in Figure 1-9 that you see the original image with the file size reported below the image on the left. After choosing JPEG for the file type, you can see that the image size is reduced from the original 3.55MB to 55.52K. (See Chapter 2 for details about choosing a file type.)

You can also use the Quality item that appears to the right of the drop-down list to adjust the final quality of the saved file. Here, you need to find the right balance between quick download times and image appearance. Just keep an eye on the preview image as well as the download time information for your optimized file.

For the most accurate viewing, set the zoom size to 100 percent. In the lower-left corner of the dialog box, you can choose zoom levels from the drop-down list or just type a value in the field box. If your chosen settings noticeably degrade your image quality, you can easily discern the loss when viewing at a 100-percent view.

Working in the Save for Web dialog box is a matter of making choices and viewing the results. Toggle the different file type choices and make adjustments for quality. If you see image degradation, change to a different quality setting or file format. Always look at the file-size item reported below the image on the right and try to find the lowest file size that produces a good-looking image.

See our web extras for detailed steps on saving files for the web at www.dummies.com/extras/photoshopelements.

# 2

# Basic Image-Editing Concepts

## In This Chapter

▶ Understanding and changing resolution

▶ Resampling images

▶ Understanding color modes

▶ Working with file formats

▶ Understanding color

*W*hen you open a picture in Photoshop Elements, you're looking at a huge mass of pixels. These *pixels* are tiny, colored squares, and the number of pixels in a picture determines the picture's *resolution*.

This relationship between pixels and resolution is important for you to understand in all your Elements work. You'll find the concepts covered in this chapter especially helpful when creating selections (as we explain in Chapter 7), printing files (Chapter 14), and sharing files (Chapter 15).

Additionally, you need to understand *color modes,* which are also represented as collections of pixels. Color modes are important when you're using tools in the Tools panel and Panel Bin and printing and sharing files. Basically, you want to choose a color mode for your image that is best suited for print or onscreen and the type of image you have (a photo with lots of colors versus a line drawing with only a few colors, for example).

Like resolution and color modes, the file format in which you save an image often depends on your desired output — print or screen — so this chapter concludes with an introduction to choosing a file format. This chapter helps you under-stand the basics of working with resolution, color modes, and file formats that are essential to great results in your final images. We talk about changing resolution by resizing images, converting color modes, and saving the results in different file formats.

## Grappling with the Ubiquitous Pixels

Most digital images are composed of millions of tiny, square pixels. Each pixel has one, and only one, color value. The arrangement of the pixels of different shades and colors creates an optical illusion when you view an image onscreen. For example, black-and-white pixels might create the impression that you're looking at something gray — not at tiny black-and-white squares.

Just about everything you do in Elements has to do with changing pixels:

- Surrounding pixels with selection tools to select what appear to be objects in your image
- Making pixels darker or lighter to change contrast and brightness
- Changing shades and tints of pixels for color correction
- Performing a variety of other editing tasks

An image made of pixels is a *raster image*. If you open a file in Elements that isn't made of pixels, you can let Elements *rasterize* the data. In other words, Elements converts other data to pixels if the document wasn't originally composed of pixels.

Images not made of pixels are typically *vector images*. You can also have vector content in an Elements file. Text added with the Type tool, for example, is a vector object. When you save an Elements file with the Text layer intact or save it as a Photoshop PDF file, the vector data is retained. We talk more about vector data in Chapter 13. For this chapter, you just need to focus on raster data.

To use most of the tools and commands in Elements, you must be working on a raster image file. If your data isn't rasterized, many tools and commands are unavailable.

The pixels in an image determine an image's resolution and dimensions, as we explain in the following sections.

## Understanding resolution

The number of pixels in an image file determines the image's resolution, which is measured in pixels per inch (ppi). For example:

- ✔ If you have 300 pixels across a 1-inch horizontal line, your image resolution is 300 ppi.

- ✔ If you have 72 pixels across 1 inch, your image resolution is 72 ppi.

Image resolution is critical to properly outputting files in the following instances:

- ✔ **Printing images:** The optimal resolution for print is 300 ppi. If the image resolution is too low, the image prints poorly. If the resolution is too high, you waste time processing all the data that needs to be sent to your printer.

- ✔ **Showing images onscreen:** The best resolution for onscreen images is 72 ppi. Onscreen resolution is lower than print to match typical screen resolutions (also called *display resolution*). Just as images have resolution inherent in their files, your computer monitor displays everything you see in a fixed resolution. Computer monitors display images at 72 ppi (or 85 or 96 ppi or higher). That's all you get. What's important to know is that you can always best view photos on your computer monitor at a 72-ppi image size in a 100 percent view.

Newer devices, such as smartphones and tablets, have screens with higher resolutions. You can find device display resolutions from 150 ppi to more than 300 ppi on a variety of devices. When you design for a specific display, it's important to know the device display-resolution capabilities before you start working in Elements.

To see how image resolution and screen resolution combine and impact what you see onscreen, look at Figure 2-1. You see an image reduced to 50 percent and then at different zoom sizes. When the size changes, the monitor displays your image at different resolutions. For example, if you view a photo with a resolution of 72 ppi and reduce the size to 50-percent view on your monitor, the resolution on the monitor appears as though the photo is at 144 ppi. When the size is 100 percent, the image resolution is the same as the monitor resolution. Table 2-1 provides a closer look at these differences in resolution.

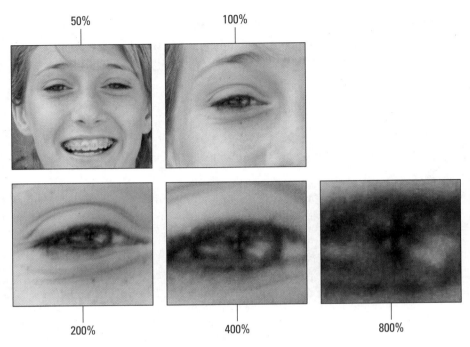

Figure 2-1: The same image is viewed at different zoom levels.

| Table 2-1 | How Image and Display Resolutions Affect What You See Onscreen | | |
|---|---|---|---|
| **Image Resolution** | **Display Resolution** | **Zoom Level** | **How Image Appears Onscreen** |
| 72 ppi | 72 ppi | 100% | Image appears onscreen at its actual resolution, so the onscreen display is the same as what you'd see if you printed the image. The print won't be crisp, however, because the resolution is too low for print. A low resolution looks fine on a monitor but not on paper. |

| Image Resolution | Display Resolution | Zoom Level | How Image Appears Onscreen |
|---|---|---|---|
| 72 ppi | 72 ppi | 50% | Image appears smaller onscreen, as though it has a higher image resolution (144 ppi, or twice the resolution that it actually has). |
| 72 ppi | 72 ppi | 200% | Image appears larger onscreen, as though it has a lower image resolution (36 ppi, or half of its actual resolution). The display needs to simulate "spreading out" the pixels to make the image appear bigger. |
| 300 ppi | 72 ppi | 100% | Image appears larger onscreen than it will in print, because the monitor can display only 72 ppi. A print of this image will look clear and crisp, because 300 ppi is the ideal resolution for prints. |
| 300 ppi | 72 ppi | 50% | Image appears smaller onscreen but will print larger than the monitor view. |
| 300 ppi | 72 ppi | 200% | Image appears larger onscreen but will print smaller than the monitor view. |

This relationship between the image resolution and viewing the image at different zoom levels is an important concept to grasp. If you grab an image off the web and zoom in on it, you may see a view like the 800-percent view shown in Figure 2-1. If you acquire a digital camera image, you may need to zoom out to a 16-percent view to fit the entire image in the image window.

The reason that these displays vary so much is because of image resolution. That image you grabbed off a web page might be a 2-inch-square image at 72 ppi, and that digital camera image might be a 10-x-12-inch image at 240 ppi. To fill the entire window with the web image, you need to zoom in on the file. When you zoom in, the image appears as though it's reduced in resolution.

When you zoom into or out of an image, you change the resolution as it appears on your monitor. *No resolution changes are made to the file.* The image resolution remains the same until you use one of the Elements tools to reduce or increase the image resolution.

### Understanding image dimensions

Image dimensions involve the physical size of your file. If the size is 4 x 5 inches, for example, the file can be any number of different resolution values. After the file is open in Elements, you can change the dimensions of the image, the resolution, or both.

When you change only the dimensions of an image (not the number of pixels it contains), an inverse relationship exists between the physical size of your image and the resolution. When image size is increased, resolution decreases. Conversely, when you raise resolution, you reduce image size.

## The Art of Resampling

In some cases, images are too large, and you need to reduce their resolution and physical size. In other cases, you might need a higher resolution to output your images at larger sizes. This method of sizing — changing the size, as well as the number of pixels — is dubbed *resampling* an image. Specifically, reducing resolution is *downsampling,* and raising resolution is *upsampling.*

Here's a quick example to clarify the benefit of resampling. Say you have a photo taken with a digital single-lens reflex (SLR) camera, which takes pretty high-resolution photos. The photo could easily have a resolution of 300 dpi and dimensions of 14 x 10 inches. If you just want to make a few color corrections in Elements and then make 7-x-5-inch prints for your family members, resampling the file keeps the file size manageable for both your computer's memory and for uploading to a printing service. Because you decreased the photo's dimensions, the photo still maintains the resolution you need for a high-quality photo print (that is, 300 dots per inch; dpi). If you just changed the photo's dimensions without resampling, the photo's resolution would almost double, making for an unnecessarily large file.

Use caution when you resample images; when you resample, you either toss away pixels or manufacture new pixels. To protect your images during resampling, work on a copy of your image, instead of the original file.

## Changing image size and resolution

You can change an image's size and resolution in a couple of different ways. One method is cropping images. You can use the Crop tool with or without resampling images. For more information on using the Crop tool, see Chapter 9. Another method is using the Image Size dialog box, which you use in many of your editing sessions in Elements.

To resample an image with the Image Size dialog box, follow these steps:

1. **Choose Image➪Resize➪Image Size.**

   Alternatively, you can press Ctrl+Alt+I (⌘+Option+I on the Mac). The Image Size dialog box opens, as shown in Figure 2-2.

   The Pixel Dimensions area in the Image Size dialog box shows the file size (in this example, 12.1M). This number is the amount of space the image takes up on your hard drive. The width and height values are fixed unless you select the Resample Image check box at the bottom of the dialog box.

2. **In the Document Size area, redefine dimensions and resolution.**

   The options are

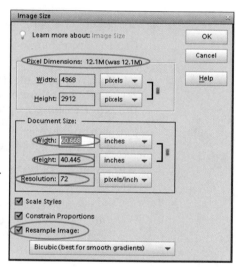

Figure 2-2: The Image Size dialog box.

   • *Width:* Type a value in the text box to resize the image's width. Then press Tab to move out of the field and implement the change. From the drop-down list to the right of the text box, you can choose a unit of measure: percent, inches, centimeters, millimeters, points, picas, or columns.

- *Height:* The Height options are the same as the Width.

  If you keep the sizing proportional, you typically edit either the Width or Height text box, but not both. When you alter either width or height, the resolution changes inversely.

- *Resolution:* Type a value in the text box to change resolution and then press Tab to commit the change. After you edit the resolution, the Width and Height values are changed inversely (if the Constrain Proportions check box is selected).

3. **(Optional) If you're okay with resampling your image to get the desired size, select the Resample Image check box.**

   With this check box selected, you can change dimensions and pixels at the same time, which results in either reducing or increasing the number of pixels. When the check box is deselected, the values for dimensions are linked; changing one value automatically changes the other values.

   Before you resample your image, however, be sure to check out the following section, "Understanding the results of resampling."

4. **(Optional) If you select the Resample Image check box, choose a resampling method from the drop-down list below it and/or select the other resample options above it.**

   In the drop-down list, you find different choices for resampling. See Table 2-2 for details on each method.

   When you select the Resample Image check box, the two check boxes above it become active. Here's what they do:

   - *Scale Styles:* Elements has a Styles panel from which you can add a variety of different style effects to images. (See Chapter 11 for details.) When you apply a style, such as a frame border, the border appears at a defined width. When you select the Scale Styles check box and then resize the image, the Styles effect is also resized. Leaving the check box deselected keeps the style at the same size while the image is resized.

   - *Constrain Proportions:* By default, this check box is selected, and you should leave it that way unless you want to intentionally distort an image.

5. **When you're done selecting your options, click OK to resize your image.**

| Table 2-2 | Resampling Methods | |
|-----------|--------------------|---|
| *Method* | *What It Does* | *Best Uses* |
| Nearest Neighbor | This method is fastest, and the results produce a smaller file size. | This method is best used when you have large areas of the same color. |
| Bilinear | This method produces a medium-quality image. | You might use this option with grayscale images and line art. |
| Bicubic | This method is the default and provides a good-quality image. | Unless you find better results by using any of the other methods, leave the default at Bicubic. |
| Bicubic Smoother | This method improves on the Bicubic method, but you notice a little softening of the edges. | If sharpness isn't critical and you find Bicubic isn't quite doing the job, try this method. It tends to work best if you have to upsample an image. |
| Bicubic Sharper | This method produces good-quality images and sharpens the results. | Downsample high-resolution images that need to be output to screen resolutions and web pages. |

## Understanding the results of resampling

As a general rule, reducing resolution is okay, but increasing resolution isn't. If you need a higher-resolution image and you can go back to the original source (such as rescanning the image or reshooting a picture), try (if you can) to create a new file that has the resolution you want instead of resampling in Elements. In some cases, upsampled images can be severely degraded. Regardless of whether you upsample or downsample an image, always save a copy of the photo under a new filename.

If you take a picture with a digital camera and want to add the picture to a web page, the image needs to be sampled at 72 ppi. In most cases, you visit the Image Size dialog box, select the Resample Image check box, add a width or height value, and type **72** in the Resolution text box. What you end up with is an image that looks great on your web page but still downloads quickly. In Figure 2-3, you can see an image that was downsampled in Elements from over 14 inches horizontal width.

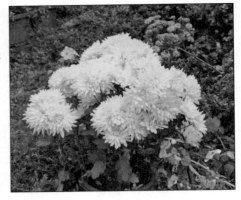

Figure 2-3: Downsampling images most often produces satisfactory results.

If you start with an image that was originally sampled for a web page and you want to print a large poster, you can forget about using Elements or any other image editor. Upsampling low-resolution images often turns them the sort of mush shown in Figure 2-4.

You might wonder whether upsampling can be used for any purpose. In some cases, yes, you can upsample with some satisfactory results. You can achieve better results with higher resolutions of 300 ppi and more if the resample size isn't extraordinary. If all else fails, try applying a filter to a grainy, upsampled image to mask the problem. Chapter 11 has the details on filters.

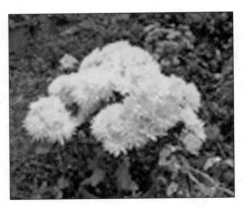

Figure 2-4: Upsampling low-resolution images often produces severely degraded results.

## Choosing a Resolution for Print or Onscreen

The importance of resolution in your Elements work is paramount to printing files. Good ol' 72-ppi images can be forgiving, and you can get many of your large files scrunched down to 72 ppi for websites and slide shows. For a nice-looking print, you need a much higher resolution. Many different printing output devices exist, and their resolution requirements vary.

For your own desktop printer, plan to print a variety of test images at different resolutions and on different papers. You can quickly determine the best file attributes by running tests. When you send files to service centers, ask the technicians what file attributes work best with their equipment.

White does not print as a color. When you use white, it appears transparent on your prints and the color appears the same as the paper color you're using.

For a starting point, look over the recommended resolutions for various output devices listed in Table 2-3.

| Table 2-3 | Resolutions and Printing | |
|---|---|---|
| *Output Device* | *Optimum* | *Acceptable Resolution* |
| Desktop laser printers | 300 ppi | 200 ppi |
| Desktop color inkjet printers | 300 ppi | 180 ppi |
| Large-format inkjet printers | 150 ppi | 120 ppi |
| Professional photo lab printers | 300 ppi | 200 ppi |
| Desktop laser printers (black and white) | 170 ppi | 100 ppi |
| Magazine quality — offset press | 300 ppi | 225 ppi |
| Screen images (web, slide shows, and video) | 72 ppi | 72 ppi |
| Tablet devices and smartphones | 150+ ppi | 150 ppi |

# Go Ahead — Make My Mode!

Regardless of what output you prepare your files for, you need to consider color mode and file format. In the section "Getting Familiar with Color" later in this chapter, we talk about RGB (red, green, and blue) color mode. You'll likely use the RGB mode most of the time: RGB is what you use to prepare color files for printing on your desktop color printer or to prepare files for photo-service centers. It's also the mode most commonly used for color images displayed onscreen.

You can also use color modes other than RGB. If you start with an RGB color image, menu options in Elements enable you to convert to a different color mode. Photoshop Elements uses an *algorithm* (a mathematical formula) to convert pixels from one mode to another. In some cases, the conversion that's made via a menu command produces good results, and in other cases, a method other than a menu command works better.

In the following sections, we introduce the modes that are available in Elements, discuss when changing an image's color mode can be useful, and explain how to convert from RGB to the mode of your choice: bitmap, grayscale, or indexed color.

Another mode you may have heard of is CMYK. Although CMYK mode isn't available in Photoshop Elements, you should be aware of what it is and the purposes of CMYK images. CMYK, commonly referred to as *process color,* contains percentages of cyan, magenta, yellow, and black colors. This mode is used for commercial printing. If you design a magazine cover in Elements and send the file to a print shop, the file is ultimately converted to CMYK. Also note that most desktop printers use different ink sets within the CMYK color space. CMYK is a narrower color space than RGB, which means there are fewer colors in CMYK. Therefore using CMYK inks on printers may often display some shifts in colors between the prints and the screen images.

## Converting to Bitmap mode

Bitmap mode is most commonly used in printing line art, such as black-and-white logos, illustrations, or black-and-white effects that you create from your RGB images. Also, you can scan your analog signature as a bitmap image and import it into other programs, such as the Microsoft Office applications. If you're creative, you can combine bitmap images with RGB color to produce interesting effects.

When you combine images with different color modes into a single file, the images need to be in the same mode. (A file can have only one mode.) So, if you create an image in Bitmap mode and want to combine it with an RGB image, you need to convert the bitmap files to grayscale or color first. If you convert to grayscale, Elements takes care of converting grayscale to RGB mode.

As an example of an effect resulting from combining grayscale and color images, look over Figure 2-5. The original RGB image was converted to a bitmap and then saved as a different file. The bitmap was converted to grayscale and dropped on top of the RGB image. After you adjust the opacity, the result is a grainy effect with desaturated color.

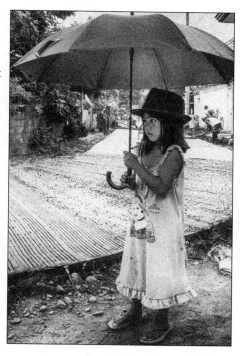

You can acquire Bitmap mode images directly in Elements when you scan images that are black and white. Illustrated art, logos, or your signature might be the kinds of files you scan directly in Bitmap mode. Additionally, you can convert your images to Bitmap mode.

Converting RGB color to bitmap is a two-step process. You need to first convert to grayscale and then convert from grayscale to bitmap. If you select the Bitmap menu command while in RGB color, Elements prompts you to convert to grayscale first.

**Figure 2-5:** You can create some interesting effects by combining the same image from a bitmap file and an RGB file.

The Elements Bitmap mode isn't the same as the Windows `.bmp` file format. In Elements, Bitmap mode is a color mode. A Windows `.bmp` file can be an RGB color mode image, a Grayscale color mode image, or a Bitmap color mode image.

To convert from RGB mode to Bitmap mode, do the following:

1. **In the Photo Editor workspace, open an image that you want to convert to Bitmap mode in either Expert or Quick mode.**

2. **Choose Image⇨Mode⇨Bitmap.**

   If you start in RGB mode (which is generally the case), Elements prompts you to convert to grayscale.

3. **At the prompt click OK.**

   The Bitmap dialog box opens and provides options for selecting the output resolution and a conversion method.

4. **Select a resolution.**

   By default, the Bitmap dialog box, as shown in Figure 2-6, displays the current resolution. You can edit the Output box and resample the image or accept the default. See the section "The Art of Resampling," earlier in this chapter, for more on changing image resolutions.

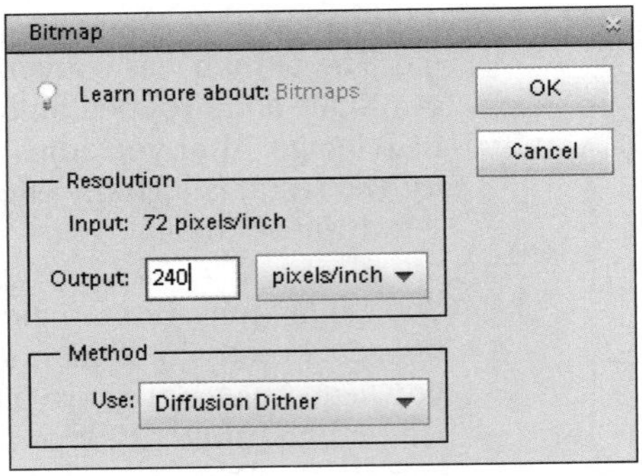

5. **From the Use drop-down list, choose a method for converting an RGB image to a bitmap image.**

   Your options are as follows:

   - 50% Threshold
   - Pattern Dither
   - Diffusion Dither

   Figure 2-7 shows the effect each method creates.

6. **Click OK to convert your image to Bitmap mode.**

Figure 2-6: Type a resolution for your output and choose the conversion method from the Use drop-down list.

## Converting to Grayscale mode

Grayscale images have black-and-white pixels and any one of an additional 254 levels of gray. By converting an RGB image to grayscale, you can make a color image look like a black-and-white photo.

You can convert an image to grayscale in one of three ways, but remember that one of these methods isn't as good as the others. We recommend that you avoid converting to grayscale by choosing Image➪Mode➪Grayscale. When Elements performs this conversion, it removes all the color from the pixels, so you lose some precious data during the conversion and can't regain the color after conversion. If you were to convert an image to grayscale, save the file, and delete the original from your hard drive or memory card, the color image would be lost forever. You could save a secondary file, but this method can add a little confusion and require some more space on your hard drive.

The following two sections explain better ways to create a grayscale image.

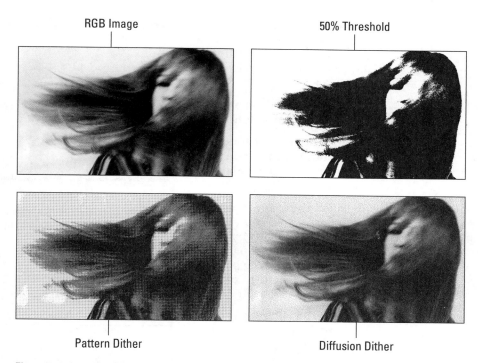

RGB Image

50% Threshold

Pattern Dither

Diffusion Dither

**Figure 2-7:** An original RGB image converted to bitmap by using 50% Threshold, Pattern Dither, and Diffusion Dither.

### Desaturating a layer

You don't *have* to give up your color data when you convert to grayscale. As an alternative to using the menu command for converting images to grayscale, follow these steps:

1. **Open an RGB image in Elements in Expert Mode.**

2. **Duplicate a layer.**

    The default Panel Bin contains the Layers panel. In this panel, click the icon in the upper-right corner. From the pop-up menu, choose Duplicate Layer. (A *layer* is like a clear sheet of acetate that you can draw on, only it's digital. For information on working with layers, see Chapter 8.) In this example, we duplicated the layer, adjusted the duplicate layer, and duplicated again to create a third layer.

    You can also duplicate a layer by dragging the layer name to the New Layer icon at the top of the Layers panel.

3. **Choose Enhance⇨Adjust Color⇨Adjust Hue/Saturation to open the Hue/Saturation dialog box, as shown in Figure 2-8.**

Alternatively, you can press Ctrl+U (⌘+U on the Mac).

4. **Drag the Saturation slider to the far left to desaturate the image on the selected layer and then click OK.**

All color disappears, but the brightness values of all the pixels remain unaffected. (For more information on using the Hue/Saturation dialog box and the other Adjust Color commands, see Chapter 10.)

5. **Turn off the color layer by clicking the eye icon in the Layers panel.**

In the Layers panel, you see three layers, as shown in Figure 2-9. The top layer in RGB color is hidden from view (notice the diagonal line through the eye icon). The second layer is grayscale. You don't need to turn off the color layer to print the file in grayscale, but turning it off can help you remember which layer you used the last time you printed or exported the file.

Following the preceding steps provides you with a file that contains both RGB and grayscale information. If you want to print the color layer, you can turn off the grayscale layer. If you need to exchange files with graphic designers, you can send the layered file, and then the design professional can use both the color image and the grayscale image.

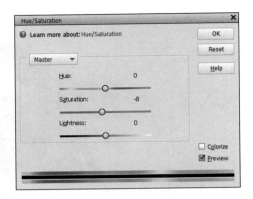

Figure 2-8: Open the Hue/Saturation dialog box and move the Saturation slider to the far left to eliminate color.

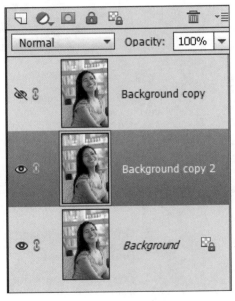

Figure 2-9: The Layers panel shows the grayscale and color layers. You can turn layers on or off by clicking the eye icon.

The other advantage of converting RGB color to grayscale by using the Hue/ Saturation dialog box is that you don't disturb any changes in the brightness values of the pixels. Moving the Saturation slider to desaturate the image affects only the color. The luminance and lightness values remain the same.

### Choosing the Convert to Black and White command

A menu command exists for converting color images to black and white. Choose Enhance⇨Convert to Black and White in either Expert or Quick mode to get to the Convert to Black and White dialog box, as shown in Figure 2-10.

This dialog box contains these controls for adjusting brightness and contrast in images that you convert to grayscale:

- ✔ **Select a Style list:** Select one of the presets and, as you make adjustments, keep your eye on the dynamic preview in the After thumbnail area.

- ✔ **Adjust Intensity area:** Move the sliders until you get the result you like.

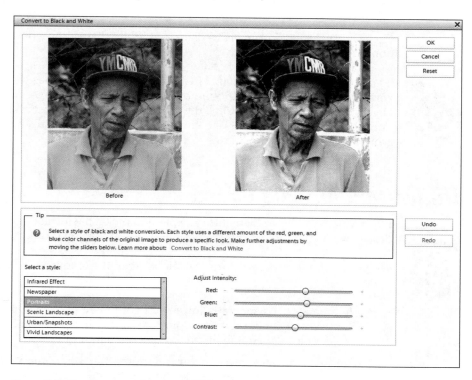

**Figure 2-10:** The Convert to Black and White dialog box.

---

## Converting web graphics to Indexed Color mode

Indexed Color is a mode you use occasionally with web graphics. When saving indexed color images, sometimes you can create file sizes smaller than RGB. These small index-color images are ideal for using in website designs because the smaller the file size, the faster a page downloads to the visitor's browser.

If you have files composed of artwork, such as logos, illustrations, and drawings, you may find that the appearance of index colors is no different from the same images in RGB mode. If that's the case, you can keep the indexed color image and use it for your web pages.

To convert RGB images to indexed color, choose Image➪Mode➪Indexed Color; the Indexed Color dialog box opens. Several options are available to you, and fortunately, you can preview the results while you make choices. Get in and poke around, and you can see the options applied in the image window. To see the benefit of Indexed Color mode, save your image in the GIF or PNG-8 format, which we explain in the section "Understanding File Formats," later in this chapter. Also, you find details about saving images for the web online at www.dummies.com/extras/photoshopelements.

---

Click OK to close the Convert to Black and White dialog box when you're done.

If you want to keep your original RGB image in the same file as the grayscale version, duplicate the background by choosing Duplicate Layer from the Layers panel's More menu. Click the background and choose Enhance➪ Convert to Black and White. The conversion is applied only to the background, leaving the copied layer in your original color mode.

## *Understanding File Formats*

When you save files in Elements, you need to pick a file format in the Format drop-down list found in both the Save and Save As dialog boxes.

When you choose from the format options, keep the following information in mind:

- **File formats are especially important when you exchange files with other users.** Each format has a purpose, and other programs can accept or reject files depending on the format you choose.

- **Whether you can select one format or another when you save a file depends on the color mode, the bit depth, and whether layers are present.** If a format isn't present in the Format drop-down list when you attempt to save a file, return to one of the edit modes and perform some kind of edit, such as changing a color mode or flattening layers, in order to save the file in your chosen format.

*Bit-depth* is the measure of bits in each sample. As an example, JPEG photos are 8-bits. When shooting in a camera raw file format, you can capture 16 or even 32 bits of data. Think of higher bit depths as having more data. As such, when you edit a photo having higher bit depths, such as 16-bits, you apply edits in a much less destructive manner.

Elements provides you a long list of file formats, many of which are out-dated. Although many different file formats are available, use only a few. Figure 2-11 shows the open Format drop-down list you see in the Save or Save As dialog box.

In the following sections, we explain the formats you find in Elements.

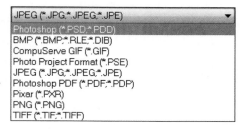

Figure 2-11: The drop-down list of file formats that Elements supports.

### Photoshop (*.PSD, *.PDD)

This format is the native file format for both Photoshop and Photoshop Elements. The format supports saving all color modes and bit depths, and you can preserve layers. Use this format when you want to save in a native format or exchange files with Photoshop users. Also use it for saving files that you need to return to for more editing. When you save layers, any text you add to layers can be edited when you return to the file. (See Chapter 13 for more information on adding text to an image.)

### BMP (*.BMP, *.RLE, *.DIB)

The term *bitmap* can be a little confusing. You have both a file format type that's bitmap and a color mode that's bitmap.

The bitmap *format* supports saving in all color modes and in all bit depths. The Bitmap color mode, which we cover in the section "Converting to Bitmap mode," earlier in this chapter, only supports images that are 1-bit and in black-and-white.

Use the bitmap format when you want to add images to system resources, such as wallpaper for your desktop. Bitmap is also used with many programs. If you can't import images in other program documents, try to save them as BMP files.

### CompuServe GIF (*.GIF)

When CompuServe was the host for our email accounts, Barb was a college coed, and Ted had a mustache and wore a green leisure suit. We exchanged files and mail on 300-baud modems. Later, in 1977, CompuServe developed GIF (Graphics Interchange Format) to exchange files between mainframe computers and the ever-growing number of users working on Osborne, Kaypro, Apple, and Radio Shack TRS-80 computers.

If you choose to use the GIF format, don't save the file using the File⇨Save or File⇨Save As command. Instead, choose File⇨Save for Web, as we explain online at www.dummies.com/extras/photoshopelements.

### Photo Project Format (*.PSE)

Use this option when you create a project in Elements and want to save the file as a project. See Chapter 16 for details about creating projects.

### JPEG (*.JPG, *.JPEG, *.JPE)

JPEG (Joint Photographic Experts Group) is perhaps the most common file format now in use. That's in large part because of smaller file sizes that make web viewing and exchanging files much easier. You can use JPEG files for prints or share them online via a web page or email attachment. Creative professionals wouldn't dream of using the JPEG format in design layouts, but everyone else uses the format for all kinds of documents.

You need to exercise some caution when you're using the JPEG format. JPEG files are compressed to reduce file size, so you can scrunch an image of several megabytes into a few hundred kilobytes. When you save a file with JPEG compression, however, you experience data loss. You might not see this on your monitor, or it might not appear noticeably on photo prints if you're using low compression while preserving higher quality. However, when you save with maximum compression, more pixels are tossed away, and you definitely notice image degradation.

When you save, open, and resave an image in JPEG format, each new save degrades the image more. If you need to submit JPEG images to photo labs for printing your pictures, keep saving in the Photoshop PSD file format until you're ready to save the final image. Save in JPEG format when you want to save the final file for printing, and use a low compression with high quality.

When you select JPEG for the format and click Save, the JPEG Options dialog box opens, as shown in Figure 2-12. You choose the amount of compression by typing a value in the Quality text box or by moving the slider below the Quality text box. The acceptable range is from 0 to 12 — 0 is the lowest quality and results in the highest compression, and 12 is the highest quality that results in the lowest amount of compression.

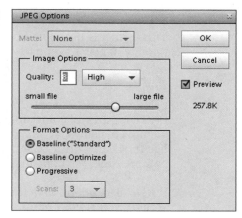

Figure 2-12: When saving in JPEG format, choose the amount of compression you want to apply to the saved image.

Notice that you also have choices in the Format Options area of the JPEG Options dialog box. The Progressive option creates a progressive JPEG file commonly used with web browsers. This file type shows progressive quality while the file downloads from a website. The image first appears in a low-quality view and shows higher-resolution views until the image appears at full resolution when it's completely downloaded in your browser window.

### Photoshop PDF (*.PDF, *.PDP)

Adobe PDF (Portable Document Format) is designed to maintain document integrity and exchange files between computers. PDF is one of the most popular formats, and you can view it in the free Adobe Reader program available for installation by downloading it from the Adobe website. On the Mac, you can also view PDFs in Apple's Preview application or the QuickLook feature of OS X.

PDF is all over the place in Elements. When you jump into Organize mode and create slide presentations, cards, and calendars, for example, you can export your documents as PDF files. When you save in Photoshop PDF format, you can preserve layers and text. Text is recognizable in Adobe Reader (or other Acrobat viewers), and you can search text by using the Reader's Find and Search tools.

PDF files can be printed, hosted on websites, and exchanged with users of Windows, Mac, Unix, and Linux. All in all, this format is well suited for all the files you create in Elements that contain text, layers, and transparency, and for when you want to exchange files with users who don't have Elements or Photoshop.

### Pixar (*.PXR)

This format is used for exchanging files with Pixar workstations. In all likelihood, you may never use this format.

### PNG (*.PNG)

PNG (Portable Network Graphics) is another format used with web pages. PNG supports all color modes, 24-bit images, and transparency. One disadvantage of using PNG is that color profiles can't be embedded in the images, like they can with JPEG. An advantage, however, is that PNG uses lossless compression, resulting in images without degradation.

PNG is also an option in the Save for Web dialog box. Choose File➪Save for Web to export your photos as PNG.

When saving images for the web, if you have an image with just a few colors such as a logo, try the GIF or PNG-8 format. If you need transparency in an image, you need to use either GIF or PNG-24. Quite often you'll find PNG-24 results in the best-looking image. You find out more about saving images for display online at www.dummies.com/extras/photoshopelements.

### TIFF (*.TIF, *.TIFF)

TIFF (Tagged Image File Format) is the most common format used by graphic designers. TIFF is generally used for importing images in professional layout programs, such as Adobe InDesign and QuarkXPress, and when commercial photo labs and print shops use equipment that supports downloading TIFF files directly to their devices. (***Note:*** Direct downloads are used in lieu of opening a Print dialog box.)

Inasmuch as creative professionals have used TIFF for so long, a better choice for designers using a program such as Adobe InDesign is saving in the native Photoshop PSD file format. This requires a creative professional to save only one file in native format without bothering to save both native and TIFF formats.

TIFF, along with Photoshop PSD and Photoshop PDF, supports saving layered files and works in all color modes. When you save in TIFF format, you can also compress files in several different compression schemes, but compression with TIFF files doesn't lose data unless you choose a JPEG compression.

When you choose TIFF from the Format drop-down list and click Save in the Save/Save As dialog box, the TIFF Options dialog box opens, as shown in Figure 2-13.

In the Image Compression area, you have these choices:

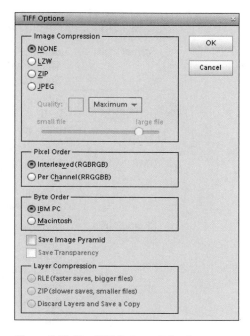

Figure 2-13: The TIFF Options dialog box.

- ✔ **NONE:** Selecting this option results in no compression. You use this option when sending files to creative professionals for creating layouts in programs such as Adobe InDesign. (None of the three compression schemes listed next is recommended for printing files to commercial printing devices.)

- ✔ **LZW:** This lossless compression scheme results in much lower file sizes without destroying data.

- ✔ **ZIP:** ZIP is also a lossless compression scheme. You can favor ZIP compression over LZW when you have large areas of the same color in an image.

- ✔ **JPEG:** JPEG is lossy and results in the smallest file sizes. Use JPEG here the same as when you apply JPEG compression with files saved in the JPEG format.

Leave the remaining items in the dialog box at defaults and click OK to save the image.

## File formats at a glance

Although we've been working with Photoshop (which saves in the same formats listed in this section) since 1989, we have never used all the formats available in Photoshop Elements. At most, you'll use maybe three or four of these formats.

You don't need to remember all the formats and what they do. Just pick the ones you use in your workflow, mark Table 2-4 for reference, and check it from time to time until you have a complete understanding of how files need to be prepared in order to save them in your desired formats. If you happen to receive a file from another user in one of the formats you don't use, come back to the description in this chapter when you need details about how the format is used.

**Table 2-4  File Format Attributes Supported by Photoshop Elements**

| Format | Color Modes Supported | Embed Profiles* Supported | Bit Depth Supported** | Layers Supported |
|---|---|---|---|---|
| Photoshop PSD, PDD | Bitmap, RGB, Indexed, Grayscale | Yes | 1, 8, 24, H | Yes |
| BMP | Bitmap, RGB, Indexed, Grayscale | No | 1, 8, 24, H | No |
| CompuServe GIF*** | Bitmap, RGB, Indexed, Grayscale | No | 1, 8 | No |
| JPEG | RGB, Grayscale | Yes | 8, 24 | No |
| Photoshop PDF | Bitmap, RGB, Indexed, Grayscale | Yes | 1, 8, 24, H | Yes |
| Pixar | Bitmap, RGB, Indexed, Grayscale | No | 1, 8, 24, H | No |
| PNG | Bitmap, RGB, Indexed, Grayscale | No | 1, 8, 24, H | No |
| TIFF | Bitmap, RGB, Indexed, Grayscale | Yes | 8, 24, H | Yes |

*Embedding profiles is limited to embedding either sRGB IEC61966-2.1 or AdobeRGB (1998).*

*** The letter H in Column 4 represents higher-bit modes, such as 16- and 32-bit images, which you might acquire from scanners and digital cameras. See Chapter 5 for more information on higher-bit images.*

**** CompuServe GIF doesn't support saving layers, although it supports saving layers as frames. You use the frames when creating an animated GIF file to be used for web pages.*

## Audio and video formats supported in Elements

In addition to the image formats listed in Table 2-4, Elements supports audio and video files. The support is limited to adding and viewing audio and video files in the Organizer and printing the first frame in a video file. Other kinds of edits made to audio and video files require special software for audio and video editing.

Audio files can be imported in slide shows, as we explain in Chapter 16. The acceptable file formats for audio files are MP3, WAV, QuickTime, and WMA. If you have audio files in another format, you need to convert the file format. For these kinds of conversions, you can search the Internet for *shareware audio-conversion program.*

Video files can also be imported in slide shows, as we discuss in Chapter 16. Elements supports the WMV (Windows) and Apple QuickTime (Mac) video formats. As with audio files, if videos are saved in other formats (too numerous to mention), you need to convert the video format to a format acceptable to Elements. For video-conversion utilities, you can also find shareware and freeware programs to do the job. Search the Internet for *video converter.*

# Getting Familiar with Color

In this section, you find some fundamental principles to make your work in Elements easier when you're editing color images.

Your first level of understanding color is to understand what RGB is and how it works. *RGB* stands for *red, green,* and *blue.* These are the primary colors in the computer world. Forget about what you know about primary colors in an analog world; computers see primary colors as RGB. RGB color is divided into *color channels.* Although you can't see the individual channels in Elements, you still need to understand just a little about color channels.

When you see a color *pixel* (a tiny square), the color is represented as different levels of gray in each channel. This may sound confusing at first, but stay with us for just a minute. When you have a color channel, such as the red channel, and you let all light pass through the channel, you end up with a bright red. If you screen that light a little with a gray filter, you let less light pass through, thereby diluting the red color. This is how channels work. Individually, they all use different levels of gray that permit up to 256 levels of light to pass through them. When you change the intensity of light in the different channels, you ultimately change the color.

Each channel can have up to 256 levels of gray that mask out light. The total number of possibilities for creating color in an RGB model is achieved by multiplying the values for each channel ($256 \times 256 \times 256$). The result is more than 16.7 million; that's the total number of colors a computer monitor can display in RGB color.

This is all well and good as far as theory goes, but what does that mean in practical terms? Actually, you see some of this information in Elements' tools and dialog boxes. As an experiment, open a file in Elements and choose Enhance⇨Adjust Lighting⇨Levels; the Levels dialog box shown in Figure 2-14 opens.

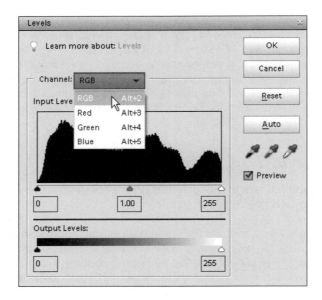

Figure 2-14: The Levels dialog box.

Notice that the Channel drop-down list shows you Red, Green, and Blue as individual channels, as well as a composite RGB selection. Furthermore, the Output Levels area shows you values ranging from 0 on the left to 255 on the right. Considering that 0 is a number, you have a total of 256 different levels of gray.

What's important is that you know that your work in color is related to RGB images that comprise three different channels. There are 256 levels of gray that can let through or hold back light and change brightness values and color. See Chapters 9 and 10 for more on using tools, such as levels, to adjust color in this way.

# Getting Color Right

In Elements, when it comes to color, the challenge isn't understanding color theory or definitions, but rather matching the RGB color you see on your computer monitor as closely as possible to your output. *Output* can be a printout from a color printer or a screen view on a web page.

We say match "as closely as possible" because you can't expect to achieve an exact match. You have far too many printer and monitor variables to deal with. However, if you properly manage color, you can get a very close match.

To match color between your monitor and your output, you need to first calibrate your monitor and then choose a color workspace profile. In the following sections, you can find all the details.

## Color the easy way

The upcoming sections are complex and require some dedicated effort to follow the descriptions. If you're interested in sharing photos only onscreen (that is, on your own website or on Flickr, Facebook, Twitter, and so on) and you plan to leave the printing to others, you don't need to bother with color correction and going through a maze of steps to get the color perfected. In that case, you can skip the technical stuff in the following sections.

The only consideration you need to make is your overall monitor brightness. If your monitor displays images darker or lighter than other computers viewing your images, you need to follow the upcoming sections and understand how to adjust your overall monitor brightness.

## Calibrating your monitor

Your monitor needs to be calibrated to adjust the gamma and brightness; correct any color tints or colorcasts; and generally get your monitor to display, as precisely as possible, accurate colors on your output. You can choose among a few tools to adjust monitor brightness. These tools range from a low-cost hardware device that sells for less than $100 to expensive calibration equipment of $3,000 or more — or you can skip the hardware and use tools provided by OS X or Windows.

*Gamma* is the brightness of midlevel tones in an image. In technical terms, it's a parameter that describes the shape of the transfer function for one or more stages in an imaging pipeline.

We skip the costly high-end devices and software utilities that don't do you any good and suggest that you make, at the very least, one valuable purchase for creating a monitor profile: a hardware profiling system. On the low end, some affordable devices go a long way toward helping you adjust your monitor brightness and color balance, with prices ranging from $60 to $100. The best way to find a device that works for you is to search the Internet for hardware descriptions, dealers, and costs. You'll find items such as the ColorVision Spyder2express ($100) and Pantone huey Pro ($99), to name just a couple.

On LCD/LED monitors, you need to adjust the hardware controls to bring your monitor into a match for overall brightness with your photo prints. Be certain to run many test prints and match your prints against your monitor view to make the two as similar as possible.

You have a lot to focus on when calibrating monitors and getting the color right on your monitor and your output. We talk more about color prints in Chapter 14.

## Choosing a color workspace

After you adjust your monitor color by using a hardware profiling system, your next step is to choose your color workspace. In Elements, you have a choice between two workspace colors: either sRGB or Adobe RGB (1998). You access your color workspace settings by choosing Edit⇨Color Settings. The Color Settings dialog box opens, as shown in Figure 2-15.

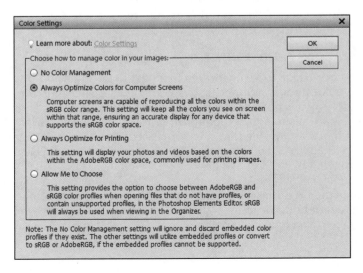

**Figure 2-15:** The Color Settings dialog box.

The Color Settings dialog box gives you these options:

- **No Color Management:** This choice turns off all color management. Don't choose this option for any work you do in Elements. When using No Color Management, you need to work with files that have color profiles embedded in the photos. Most likely you won't use these types of photos. For information on when you might use the No Color Management option, see Chapter 14.

- **Always Optimize Colors for Computer Screens:** Selecting this radio button sets your workspace to sRGB. sRGB color is used quite often for viewing images on your monitor, but this workspace often results in the best choice for color printing, too. Many color printers can output all the colors you can see in the sRGB workspace. In addition, many photo services we talk about in Chapter 16 prefer this workspace color.

- **Always Optimize for Printing:** Selecting this option sets your color workspace to Adobe RGB (1998). The color in this workspace has more available colors than you can see on your monitor. If you choose this workspace, be certain that your printer is capable of using all the colors in this color space.

- **Allow Me to Choose:** When you select this option, Elements prompts you for a profile assignment when you open images that contain no profile. This setting is handy if you work back and forth between screen and print images.

## Understanding how profiles work

You probably created a monitor color profile when you calibrated your monitor. You probably also selected a color profile when you opened the Color Settings dialog box and selected your workspace color. When you start your computer, your monitor color profile kicks in and adjusts your overall monitor brightness and corrects for any colorcasts. When you open a photo in Elements, color is converted automatically from your monitor color space to your workspace color.

At print time, you use another color profile to output your photos to your desktop color printer. Color is then converted from your workspace color to your printer's color space. In Chapter 14, we show you how to use color profiles for printing. For now, just realize that each of these color profiles, and using each one properly, determines whether you can get good color output.

# Exploring the Photo Editor

*In This Chapter*

▶ Examining the Editor workspace

▶ Using the Photo Bin

▶ Working in Quick mode and Guided mode

▶ Launching preferences

▶ Customizing the presets

*P*hotoshop Elements has two workspaces: the Organizer, which we discuss in Chapter 4, and the Photo Editor we introduce in Chapter 1. You manage and arrange your photos in the Organizer, and you edit photos in the Photo Editor.

In this chapter, we continue our discussion of the Photo Editor so that you can refine your photo-editing skills. You discover the Photo Editor's workspace in depth and how to access the Photo Editor's three editing modes: Expert, Quick, and Guided.

## Examining the Photo Editor

Before you begin editing photos, you'll find it helpful to look over the Photo Editor and figure out how to move around the workspace. When the Photo Editor is in Expert mode, you find the following (as labeled in Figure 3-1):

A. **Menu bar:** Like just about every other program you launch, Elements supports drop-down lists. The menus are logically constructed and identified to provide commands for working with your pictures (including many commands that you don't find supported in tools and on panels). A quick glimpse at the menu names gives you a hint of what might be contained in a given menu list. Throughout this book, we point you to the menu bar whenever it's helpful. Most of the menu commands you find in Elements 13 are the same as those you found in earlier versions of Elements.

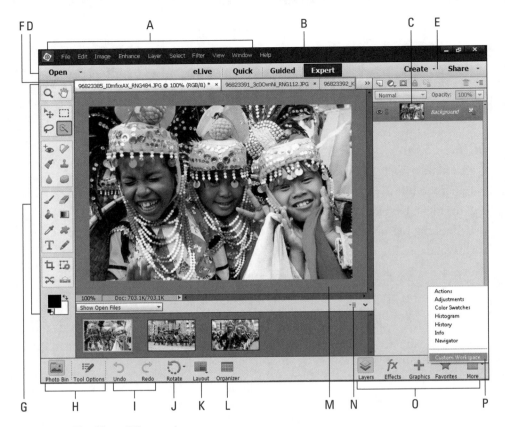

**Figure 3-1:** The Photo Editor workspace.

**B. Photo Editor modes:** The Photo Editor has three modes. The Expert mode is shown in Figure 3-1. You find an introduction to Quick mode in Chapter 1 and a more detailed look at Quick mode in Chapter 9. An introduction to Guided mode appears later in this chapter. Parts III and IV cover all the different features of Expert mode, including making selections, creating composites from several images, drawing, adding text, and exploring creative flourishes with filters and effects.

**C. Panel Bin:** Figure 3-1 shows the Layers panel. You change panels by clicking the icons at the bottom of the Panel Bin. (The icons are described in item O.) *Creations* (things you make) are also contained in the Panel Bin when you click the Create button (item E).

**D. Open menu:** When you have several files open in the Photo Editor, the Open menu is one way to switch among these files. To use this menu, click Open and from the drop-down list, choose the image you want to move to the foreground. *Note:* The Open menu also offers you an option to create a new, blank file.

In Figure 3-1, three files are open, indicated by the tabs at the top of the image window. You can also place an open file in the foreground in the image window in these other ways:

- Click a tab at the top of the image window to move the image to the foreground (item F).

- Click a photo in the Photo Bin (see item H).

- Open the Window menu and choose a photo.

**E. Create and Share menus:** When you open the Create menu and choose an option, you leave the current editing mode. For example, when in Expert mode, choose Create➪Photo Collage, and all the options that were available in the Photo Editor temporarily disappear when the Creation Wizard opens. To return to the Photo Editor, complete the creation or cancel the wizard. The Share menu works similarly and offers options for sharing your images. (Chapter 15 focuses on the Share menu, and Chapter 16 guides you through the options on the Create menu.)

**F. Photo tabs:** Multiple photos opened in the Photo Editor appear in different tabs at the top of the window by default.

In technical-speak, this is a *docked* position, where the photos are docked in the image window. You can click a tab and drag it down to *undock* the photo. However, you must change a preference setting to undock the windows. (See "Controlling the Editing Environment," later in this chapter, for more on changing preferences.) Doing so makes the photo appear as a *floating window.* You might want to float windows when copying and pasting image data between two or more photos. You can also view all open files in a floating window without changing preferences by choosing All Floating from the Layout pop-up menu (item K).

**G. Tools panel:** Here you find the Photo Editor toolbox, where you click a tool and apply an edit to the photo. See "Selecting the tools" and Selecting from the Tool Options" later in this chapter.

**H. Photo Bin/Tool Options:** Figure 3-1 shows the Photo Bin open. (See item H for more on the Photo Bin.) Click the Tool Options button, and a set of Tool Options replaces the Photo Bin. You can also open the Tool Options by clicking a tool in the Tools panel.

Tool Options enable you to specify how the selected tool works. For example, the Tool Options for the Brush tool, as shown in Figure 3-2, enable you to select from a few different brush styles, set the size of your brush, and much more. (You discover how the specific tools work in the relevant chapters later in this book. For example, you find out how the Brush tool works in Chapter 12, which covers drawing and painting.)

Each tool in the Tools panel supports various tool options. To return to the Photo Bin, click the Photo Bin button at the bottom left of the window.

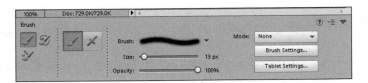

**Figure 3-2:** Tool Options provide more editing features for tools selected in the Tools panel.

**I. Undo/Redo:** These commands are so useful, they have this extra prominent place in the Photo Editor interface. (See Chapter 1 for other tools that help you undo or redo your work.) Click the respective tool for Undo or Redo. You can also press Ctrl+Z (⌘+Z on the Mac) for Undo and Ctrl+Y (⌘+Y) for Redo.

**J. Rotate:** Click the arrow to open a pop-up menu and choose the Clockwise or Counterclockwise tool to rotate the photo you see in the image window.

**K. Layout:** When you have multiple photos open in the Photo Editor, the Layout pop-up menu enables you to choose how the photos display in the image window (such as rows, columns, as a grid, and so on). To return to the tabbed view, choose Default from the Layout pop-up menu.

**L. Organizer:** Click the Organizer button to return to the Organizer, which we introduce in Chapter 4. Elements makes it very easy for you to toggle back and forth between the Organizer and the Photo Editor by clicking the respective buttons at the bottom of the windows.

**M. Image window:** In this window, you view a photo you want to edit. Likewise, you can view multiple photos you want to edit.

**N. Photo Bin Options menu:** Click this icon to open a pop-up menu of tasks, such as making creations from photos selected in the Photo Bin and printing selected photos.

**O. Panel Bin icons:** Click an icon at the bottom of the Panel Bin to display a different panel. Your choices are the Layers panel, the Effects panel, the Graphics panel, and the Favorites panel. These panels are docked in the Panel Bin by default and can't be removed (unless you choose Custom Workspace (item P). We talk more about these panels in the later section, "Playing with panels."

**P. Panels Options menu:** To open additional panels, click the right-pointing arrow to open a pop-up menu of choices. The panels you open from the Panel Options menu appear as floating windows and can't be docked in the Panel Bin.

Notice at the bottom of the pop-up menu you find Custom Workspace. When you click Custom Workspace, you can move panels around and dock or undock them in the Panel Bin.

The description of the Photo Editor workspace is brief in this chapter. Most of the options you have for using tools, panels, and menu commands are discussed in later chapters. For now, try to get a feel for what the Photo Editor provides and how to move among many of the Photo Editor features.

## Examining the image window

Not surprisingly, the image window's tools and features are most useful when an image is open in the window. To open an image in the image window, as shown in Figure 3-3, follow these steps:

1. **Choose File⇨Open.**

   The standard Open dialog box appears; it works like any ordinary Open dialog box that you find in other applications.

   You can always click one or more photos in the Organizer and click the Editor button to open the selected photos in the Photo Editor.

2. **Navigate your hard drive (by using methods you know to open folders) and then select a picture.**

   If you haven't yet downloaded digital camera images or acquired scanned photos and want an image to experiment with, you can use a sample image. Both your operating system and Photoshop Elements typically provide sample images:

   - On your operating system, sample images are typically found in your Pictures folder that's one of the default folders in both Windows and OS X installations.

   - Elements installs some nice sample images that you can play with. On a Windows computer, look in the following folder:

     ```
     Program Files/Adobe/Photoshop Elements 13\Sample
     Files
     ```

     On a Mac, look in this folder:

     ```
     Applications/Adobe Photoshop Elements 13/Support
     Files/Tutorials
     ```

3. **Select a picture and click Open.**

   The photo opens in a new image window in Elements.

You can open as many image windows in Elements as your computer memory can handle. When each new file is opened, a thumbnail image is added to the Photo Bin at the bottom of the workspace (refer to Figure 3-1).

Notice that in Figure 3-1, filenames appear as tabs above the image window. Additionally, photo thumbnails appear in the Photo Bin. To bring a photo forward, click the filename in a tab or double-click a thumbnail in the Photo Bin. To close a photo, click the X adjacent to the filename or choose File➪Close.

Here's a look at important items in the image window, as shown in Figure 3-3:

- ✓ **Filename:** Appears above the image window for each file open in the Photo Editor.

- ✓ **Close button:** Click the X to the right of the filename to close the file. (On the Mac, click the red button in the upper-left corner.)

- ✓ **Scroll bars:** These become active when you zoom in on an image. You can click the scroll arrows, move the scroll bar, or grab the Hand tool in the Tools panel and drag within the window to move the image.

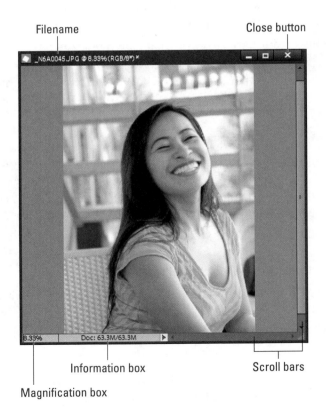

Filename         Close button

Information box   Scroll bars

Magnification box

Figure 3-3: The image window displays an open file within the Elements workspace.

*For Mac users:* If you don't see scroll bars on your Finder windows, open the System Preferences by clicking the System Preferences icon on the Dock. In General Preferences, click Always in the Show Scroll Bars section.

✔ **Magnification box:** See at a glance how much you've zoomed in or out.

✔ **Information box:** You can choose what information this readout displays by choosing one of the options from the pop-up menu, which we discuss in more detail later in this section.

When you're working on an image in Elements, you always want to know the physical image size, the image resolution, and the color mode. (We explain these terms in more detail in Chapter 2.) Regardless of which menu option you select from the status bar, you can quickly glimpse these essential stats by clicking the Information box (not the right-pointing arrow but the box itself), which displays a pop-up menu like the one shown in Figure 3-4.

✔ **Size box:** Enables you to resize the window. If you move the cursor to the box, a diagonal line with two opposing arrows appears. When the cursor changes, drag in or out to size the window smaller or larger, respectively.

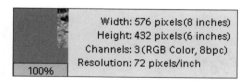

Figure 3-4: Click the readout on the status bar to see file information.

You can also resize the window by dragging any corner in or out when the image is undocked and not viewed as a tab (see item D in the section "Examining the Photo Editor.")

Now that you're familiar with the overall image window, we want to introduce you to the Information box's pop-up menu, which enables you to choose what details appear in the Information box. Click the right-pointing arrow to open the menu, as shown in Figure 3-5.

Here's the lowdown on the options you find on the pop-up menu:

✔ **Document Sizes:** Shows you the saved file size. For information on file sizes and resolutions, see Chapter 2.

✔ **Document Profile:** Shows you the color profile used with the file. Understanding color profiles is important when printing files. Turn to Chapters 2 and 14 for more information on using color profiles.

✔ Document Sizes
Document Profile
Document Dimensions
Current Selected Layer
Scratch Sizes
Efficiency
Timing
Current Tool

Figure 3-5: From the pop-up menu on the status bar, choose commands that provide information about your file.

- **Document Dimensions:** When selected, this option shows you the physical size in your default unit of measure, such as inches.

- **Current Selected Layer:** When you click a layer in the Layers panel and choose Current Selected Layer, the layer name appears as the readout.

- **Scratch Sizes:** Displays the amount of memory on your hard drive that's consumed by all documents open in Elements. For example, 20M/200M indicates that the open documents consume 20 megabytes and that a total of 200 megabytes are available for Elements to edit your images. When you add more content to a file, such as new layers, the first figure grows while the second figure remains static. If you find that Elements runs slowly, check your scratch sizes to see whether the complexity of your file is part of the problem. If so, you might clear some of your history (see Chapter 1) or merge a few layers (see Chapter 8) to free up space.

- **Efficiency:** Indicates how many operations you're performing in RAM, as opposed to using your *scratch disk* (space on your hard drive). When the number is 100 percent, you're working in RAM. When the number drops below 100 percent, you're using the scratch disk.

  If you continually work below 100 percent, it's a good indication that you need to buy more RAM to increase your efficiency.

- **Timing:** Indicates the time it took to complete the last operation.

- **Current Tool:** Shows the name of the tool selected from the Tools panel.

Why is this information important? Suppose you have a great photo you want to add to your Facebook account and you examine the photo to find the physical size of 8 x 10 inches at 300 pixels per inch (ppi). You also find that the saved file size is over 20MB. At a quick glance, you know you want to resize or crop the photo to perhaps 4 x 6 inches at 72 ppi. (Doing so drops the file size from over 20MB to around 365K.) Changing the resolution dramatically reduces the file size. We cover file sizes and changing the physical dimensions of your photos in Chapter 2. For now, realize that the pop-up menu shows you information that can be helpful when preparing files for print and display.

Don't worry about trying to understand all these terms. The important thing to know is that you can visit the pop-up menu and change the items at will during your editing sessions.

## Uncovering the contextual menus

*Contextual menus* are common to many programs, and Photoshop Elements is no exception. They're those little menus that appear when you right-click, offering commands and tools related to whatever area or tool you right-clicked.

The contextual menus are your solution when you're in doubt about where to find a command on a menu. You just right-click an item, and a pop-up menu opens.

Because contextual menus provide commands respective to the tool you're using or the object or location you're clicking, the menu commands change according to the tool or feature you're using and where you click at the moment you open a contextual menu. For example, in Figure 3-6, you can see the contextual menu that appears after we create a selection marquee and right-click that marquee in the image window. Notice that the commands are all related to selections.

> Deselect
> Select Inverse
> Feather...
> Refine Edge...
>
> Layer via Copy
> Layer via Cut
> New Layer...
>
> Free Transform
> Transform Selection
>
> Fill Selection...
> Stroke (Outline) Selection...
>
> Last Filter

**Figure 3-6:** A contextual menu for selections.

## Selecting the tools

More often than not, clicking a tool on the Tools panel is your first step in editing operations. (If you're not familiar with the Tools panel, refer to Figure 3-1.) In panel hierarchy terms, you typically first click a tool on the Tools panel and then use another panel to fine-tune how the tool will work.

Sometimes, when you select a tool in the Tools panel, you find additional tools in the Tool Options area. For example, you may click the Marquee Rectangle tool in order to access the Elliptical Marquee tool in the Tool Options, directly below the image window. Figure 3-7 shows how the Magic Wand tool is the current tool in the Tools panel. The Quick Selection tool, the Selection Brush tool, and the Magic Wand tool are all in the Tool Options. See the following section for more about the Tool Options area.

Keep in mind that if you don't find a tool in the Tools panel, look in the Tool Options for additional tools within a tool group.

Magic Wand tool

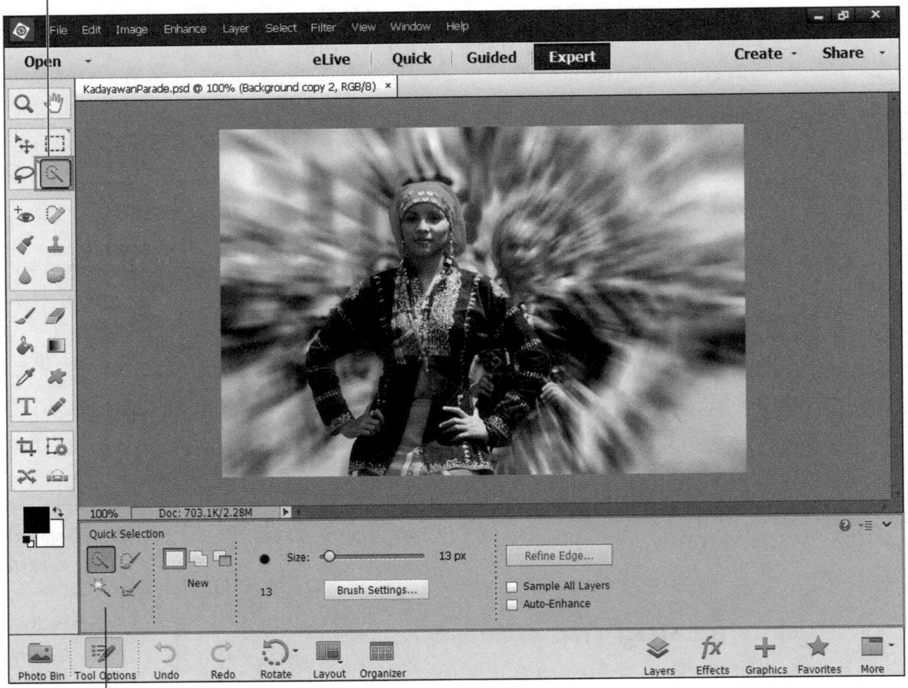

![Screenshot of Photoshop Elements 13 interface showing a photo with the Quick Selection tool options]

Other selection tools in Tool Options

**Figure 3-7:** Additional tools within a tool group are available in the Tool Options.

You can easily access tools in Elements by pressing shortcut keys on your keyboard. For a quick glance at the key that selects each tool in the Tools panel, look over Figure 3-8.

The following tips can help you find your way around the Tools panel with keyboard shortcuts:

- ✔ **To select tools within a tool group by using keystrokes, press the respective key to access the tool.** For example, press the L key to select the next tool — the Magnetic Lasso tool. Press L again and repeatedly press the shortcut key to step through all tools in a given group.

- ✔ **Whether you have to press the Shift key to select tools is controlled by a preference setting.** To change the default setting so that you don't have to press Shift, choose Edit⇨Preferences⇨General or press Ctrl+K. (Choose Photoshop Elements 13⇨Preferences⇨General or press ⌘+K on the Mac.) Then, in the General Preferences, deselect the Use Shift Key for Tool Switch check box.

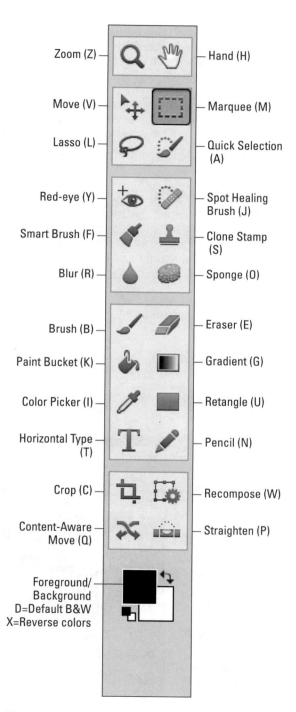

**Figure 3-8:** The Tools panel with keystroke equivalents to access a tool from the keyboard.

> ✔ **The shortcuts work for you at all times, except when you're typing text with the cursor active inside a text block.** Be certain to click the Tools panel to select a tool when you finish editing text or click the Commit green check mark to end using the Text tool.

The tools are varied, and you may find that you don't use all the tools in the Tools panel in your workflow. Rather than describe the tool functions here, we address the tools in the rest of this book as they pertain to the respective Elements tasks.

## Selecting from the Tool Options

When you click a tool on the Tools panel, the Tool Options appears at the bottom of the workspace and offers you choices specific to the selected tool. (Refer to Figure 3-8, which shows the Quick Selection tool options.) In addition to providing you choices for selecting tools within a tool group, you can adjust settings for a selected tool.

In Figure 3-8, you see choices for adjusting the Magic Wand tolerance, a button to refine the edge, and choices for adding and subtracting from selections or creating a new selection.

You can find many of these fine-tuning adjustments in the Tool Options for most of the tools you select in the Tools panel.

## Playing with panels

The panels are where you control features such as layers, effects, and more. In the Photo Editor, you open these panels in the Panel Bin:

> ✔ **Layers:** The Layers panel displays all the layers you've added to a photo. We talk much more about layers in Chapter 8. For now, look at how the different panels are designed. In the Layers panel, you find various tools at the top-left corner and an icon with horizontal lines in the top-right corner (as shown in Figure 3-9).
>
> When you click the icon at the top right, a pop-up menu appears. In Figure 3-10, you see menu items supporting the tasks you perform in the Layers panel.

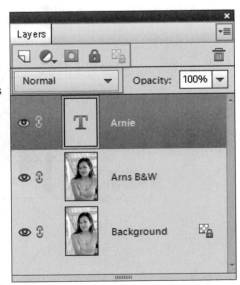

Figure 3-9: The Layers panel contains tools, a menu icon, and a pop-up menu.

✔ **Effects:** At the bottom of the Panel Bin, click the fx button to open the Effects panel. The Effects panel contains menus and tabs for applying a number of different effects to your pictures. You simply double-click the effect you want when you edit the photo. We cover applying effects in Chapter 11.

✔ **Graphics:** The Graphics panel contains several menus where you can choose among a huge assortment of graphic illustrations that can also be applied to your photos. For more information on using the Graphics panel, see Chapter 16.

✔ **Favorites:** The Favorites panel also contains a number of graphic images. You can also select items from the Effects and the Graphics panel and then add them to the Favorites panel.

✔ **Additional panels:** Click the down-pointing arrow at the bottom of the Panel Bin, and a pop-up menu opens, allowing you to choose additional panels. The Layers, Effects, Graphics, and Favorites panels are docked in the Panel Bin and can't be removed. The panels you open from the pop-up menu shown in Figure 3-11 open as floating panels. These are your options:

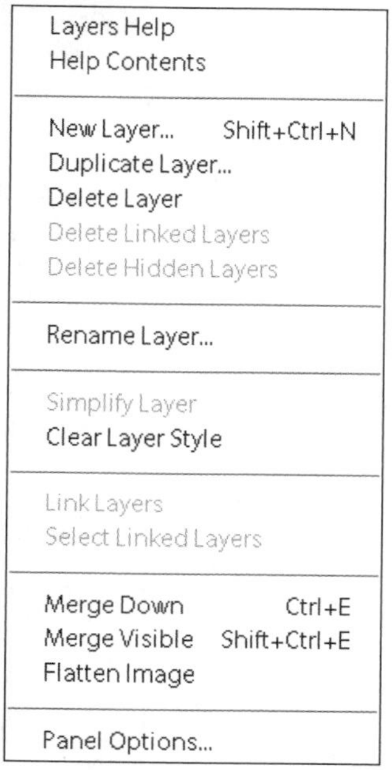

| |
| --- |
| Layers Help |
| Help Contents |
| |
| New Layer...        Shift+Ctrl+N |
| Duplicate Layer... |
| Delete Layer |
| Delete Linked Layers |
| Delete Hidden Layers |
| |
| Rename Layer... |
| |
| Simplify Layer |
| Clear Layer Style |
| |
| Link Layers |
| Select Linked Layers |
| |
| Merge Down             Ctrl+E |
| Merge Visible     Shift+Ctrl+E |
| Flatten Image |
| |
| Panel Options... |

**Figure 3-10:** The Layers panel pop-up menu.

• *Actions:* Actions enable you to automate a series of edits to your pictures. In Figure 3-12, you can see the Actions that are supported when you open the Text Effects presets. As with other panels, a pop-up menu is supported, and it offers Load, Replace, Reset, and Clear options so you can modify Actions.

| |
| --- |
| Actions |
| Adjustments |
| Color Swatches |
| Histogram |
| History |
| Info |
| Navigator |
| |
| Custom Workspace |

Layers    Effects    Graphics    Favorites    More

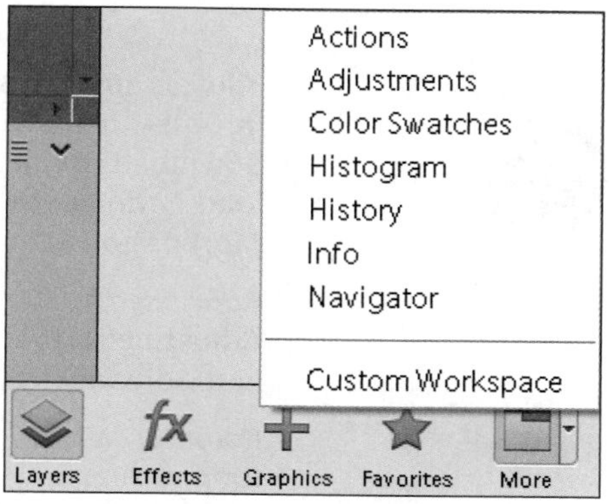

**Figure 3-11:** Click the down-pointing arrow to display a menu where you can open additional panels.

Elements 13 still doesn't support recording your own series of editing steps and capturing the steps as an Action. However, most of the Actions that are created in Adobe Photoshop can be loaded in Elements.

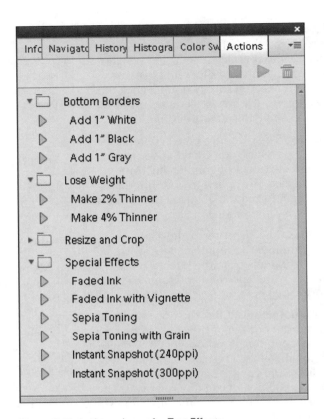

Figure 3-12: Actions shown for Text Effects.

TIP

You can find a number of free downloadable Actions on the Internet. Just search for *Photoshop Actions* and explore the many downloads available to you. For step-by-step details on how to load Actions, see our web extras at www.dummies.com/extras/photoshopelements.

- *Adjustments:* The Adjust-ments panel works only when you have an Adjustment layer. For details about using the Adjustments panel and Adjustment layers, see Chapter 10.

- *Color Swatches:* This panel displays color swatches you might use for coloring and painting that we cover in Chapter 12.

- *Histogram:* Open this panel to display a histogram of the photo in the foreground. We talk more about histograms in Chapters 9 and 10.

- *History:* Choose this item to display the Undo History panel. For more on using the Undo History panel, see the section about retracing your steps in Chapter 1.

- *Info:* The Info panel provides readouts for different color values and physical dimensions of your photos.

- *Navigator:* The Navigator panel helps you zoom in and move around on a photo in the image window.

- *Custom Workspace:* When you choose Custom Workspace, you can dock and undock panels. This option enables you to configure a custom workspace to your liking.

✓ **Create/Share panel:** These panels also exist in the Organizer. Click Create at the top right of the Panel Bin to open the Create panel in the Photo Editor. In both the Photo Editor and the Organizer, the Create panel is used for making a number of creations such as calendars, photo books, greeting cards, photo collages, and more. The Share panel contains many options for sharing your photos. We talk more about making creations in Chapter 16, and we cover using the Share panel in Chapter 15.

When you open the additional panels as floating windows, the panels are docked in a common floating window. You can drag a panel out of the docked position and view it as a separate panel or move it to the docked panels.

When you open a panel in either the Organizer or the Photo Editor, you find other options available from tools, drop-down lists, and a menu you open by clicking the icon with horizontal lines in the top-right corner of the panel.

## Using the Photo Bin

The Photo Bin displays thumbnail views of all your open images. You can immediately see a small image of all the pictures you have open at one time, as shown earlier in Figure 3-1. You can also see thumbnail views of all the different views you create for a single picture. Find out all the details in the following sections.

If you want to rearrange the order of the thumbnails in the Photo Bin, you can click and drag any thumbnail to the left or right.

### Creating different views of an image

What? Different views of the same picture, you say? Yes, indeed. You might create a new view when you want to zoom in on an area for some precise editing and then want to switch back to a wider view. Here's how you do it:

1. **Double-click a thumbnail image in the Photo Bin.**

   You must have a photo open in the Photo Editor. The photo you double-click in the Photo Bin appears in the image window as the active document.

2. **Choose View⇨New Window for *<filename>*.**

   Note that *<filename>* is the name of the file in the image window.

3. **Zoom to the new view.**

   A new view appears for the active document, and you see another thumbnail image added to the Photo Bin.

   To zoom quickly, click the Zoom tool in the Tools panel and then click a few times on the picture in the image window to zoom in to the photo.

4. **Double-click the thumbnails in the Photo Bin to toggle views of the same image.**

   Double-click the original thumbnail to see the opening view; double-click the other thumbnail to see the zoomed view.

## Viewing filenames

By default, photos open and are displayed in the Photo Bin without the associated filenames. If you want the name of each file shown in the Photo Bin, open a contextual menu on a photo in the Photo Bin and choose Show Filenames.

## Using Photo Bin Actions

On the Photo Bin Actions menu, you find handy tasks that you can perform on photos open in the Photo Editor. Click the Photo Bin Options menu to display the menu commands, as shown in Figure 3-13.

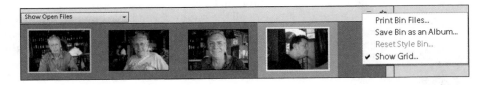

Show Open Files

Print Bin Files...
Save Bin as an Album...
Reset Style Bin...
✔ Show Grid...

**Figure 3-13:** Open the Photo Bin Options pop-up menu to display various actions you can perform on pictures open in the Photo Bin.

Here's what each Photo Bin Action does:

- ✔ **Print Bin Files:** Select the files in the Photo Bin that you want to print and then choose Print Bin Files. The selected files open in the Print dialog box where you can make photo prints of the selected images.

- ✔ **Save Bin as an Album:** You can add photos to an existing album or you can create a new album. You can do many wonderful things with Photo Albums, and we cover it all in Chapter 17.

✔ **Reset Style Bin:** Resets the Style Bin images when you're performing a Photomerge style match. (To find out more about Photomerge, see Chapter 11.)

✔ **Show Grid:** By default, no divider lines appear between photos in the Photo Bin. When you choose Show Grid, divider lines appear between the photos.

# Finding Your Bearings in Guided Mode

Guided mode is a marvelous editing feature in Elements. To access Guided mode, click the Guided tab near the top of the Photo Editor workspace.

*Guided mode,* as the name implies, is a guided process for performing various editing tasks. When you open the Guided panel, you find a list of edits, as shown in Figure 3-14. Not all editing tasks are contained in the Guided panel, but what you have available is an impressive list of many tasks you perform often.

If you used Photoshop Elements prior to version 13, you'll notice the Guided panel has changed. The panel opens with several topics listed. Click a topic such as Photo Effects (as shown in Figure 3-14) and the list expands to display different photo effects.

Elements 13 offers three new items in Guided mode:

✔ **B&W Selection** helps you turn just part of a photo into a black-and-white image, as shown in Figure 3-15.

✔ **Noir Edit** takes you through the steps for highlighting a selective color (red, green, yellow, and blue).

✔ **Black and White** enables you to choose different levels of contrast when you convert color to black and white.

To use the Selective Black and White effect, follow these steps:

1. **With an image open in the Photo Editor, click Guided and then in the Guided Photo Edit panel, click Photo Effects. When the panel expands click Selective Black and White.**

2. **Click the B&W Selection Brush button.**

3. **Drag the brush over the area you want to convert to black and white.**

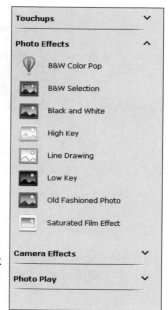

Figure 3-14: Click the Guided tab to open the Guided Photo Edit panel.

4. **(Optional) Click B&W Detail Brush to refine the selection.**

5. **Click Done.**

This example is quite simple because you have only a few steps to follow. However, even the more complicated items in Guided mode offer you step-by-step instructions you can easily follow to create a final result.

The best way to discover what results you can achieve is to open photos and apply various edits using the Guided panel. Some of the more complicated options, such as creating Out of Bounds effects, offer you a link to online video tutorials to help you further simplify the process.

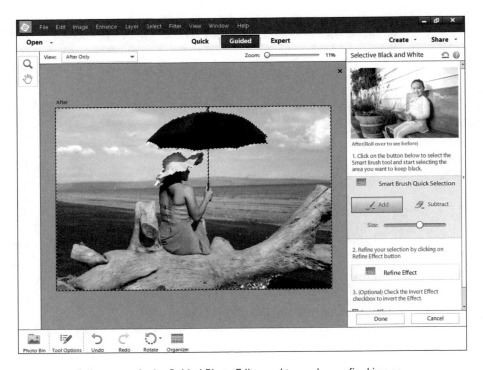

Figure 3-15: Follow steps in the Guided Photo Edit panel to produce a final image.

Some items, such as Picture Stack, require using multiple images. Load up the Photo Bin with photos and apply the effects to multiple images.

You have effects that can help improve images that might otherwise be uninteresting photos. Experiment with the Lomo effect (which is similar to cross-processing film), Old Fashioned Photo effect, Saturated Slide Film effect, and

Soft Focus effect. For a new creative experience, use the Puzzle effect that was introduced in Elements 12 or some of the new Guided Edits in Elements 13, such as the Noir effect.

For portraiture, the Perfect Portrait item in the Touchups group offers an easy way to improve portrait-type images, as shown in Figure 3-16.

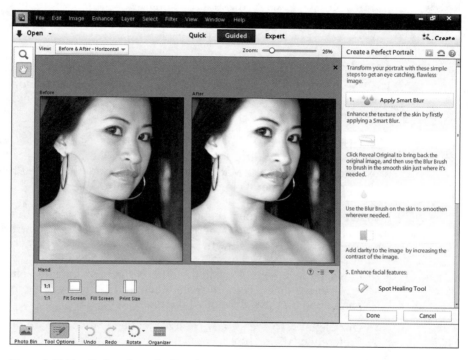

**Figure 3-16:** The Perfect Portrait effect is a set of easy steps to help you improve portraits.

# Controlling the Editing Environment

Opening Elements for the first time is like moving into a new office. Before you begin work, you need to organize the office. At minimum, you need to set up the desk and computer before you can do anything. In Elements terms, the office organization consists of specifying preference settings. *Preferences* are settings that provide a means to customize your work in Elements and to fine-tune the program according to your personal work habits.

In the following sections, we explain the preference options that you most likely want to adjust. If you need more detail about a preference option than the following section provides, look at the help documents we discuss in Chapter 1.

Elements has two Preferences dialog boxes: one in the Photo Editor workspace and another in the Organizer workspace. The following sections cover the Preferences dialog box that you open when in the Photo Editor, whether you're using Windows or the Mac. See Chapter 4 for details about Organizer preferences.

## Launching and navigating preferences

The Photo Editor's Preferences dialog box organizes all the options into several panes. By default, when you open the Preferences dialog box, you see the General pane.

To open the Preferences dialog box, choose Edit⇨Preferences⇨General (or Photoshop Elements Editor⇨Preferences⇨General on the Mac). Alternatively, press Ctrl+K (⌘+K on the Mac). Using either method opens the Preferences dialog box to the General pane, as shown in Figure 3-17.

In Figure 3-17, you see items on both the left and right sides of the dialog box that are common to all preferences panes. Here's a quick introduction to what these items are and how they work:

- ✔ **Panes list:** Elements lists all the different panes along the left side of the Preferences dialog box. Click an item in the list to make the respective pane open on the right side of the dialog box.

- ✔ **OK:** Click OK to accept any changes made in any pane and dismiss the Preferences dialog box.

- ✔ **Cancel:** Click Cancel to return to the same settings as when you opened a pane and to dismiss the dialog box.

- ✔ **Reset:** Clicking the Reset button returns the dialog box to the same settings as when you opened the dialog box. The dialog box stays open for you to set new settings.

- ✔ **Prev:** Move to the previous pane.

- ✔ **Next:** Move to the next pane. Alternatively, you can jump to another pane by pressing Ctrl+(1 through 9) in Windows or pressing ⌘+(1 through 9) on the Mac.

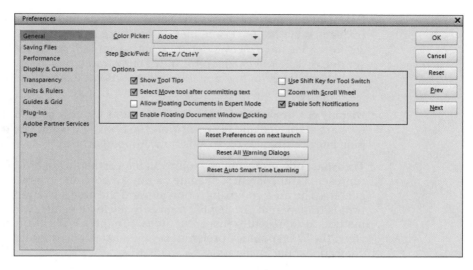

Figure 3-17: The General pane in the Preferences dialog box.

Of particular importance in the General tab are the items you see for Allow Floating Documents in Expert Mode and Enable Floating Document Window Docking. As we discuss earlier in this chapter (See "Examining the image window"), select these check boxes if you want to undock the document windows from the tabs.

## Checking out all the preferences panes

The settings in the Preferences dialog box are organized into different panes that reflect key categories of preferences. The following list briefly describes the types of settings you can adjust in each preferences pane:

- **General preferences,** as the name implies, apply to general settings you adjust for your editing environment.

- **Saving Files preferences** relate to options available for saving files. You can add extensions to filenames, save a file with layers or flatten layers (as we explain in Chapter 8), save files with image previews that appear when you're viewing files as icons on your desktop (Windows), and save with some compatibility options. On the Mac, the Finder generates thumbnails automatically, so you don't need to specify thumbnails in a Save dialog box.

- ✔ **Performance preferences** is the pane where you find history states (explained in Chapter 1) and memory settings, such as scratch disk settings. (See the nearby sidebar "What's a scratch disk?" for more on scratch disks.) You can monitor how your scratch preferences are working in the image window. See the earlier section, "Examining the image window," for details.

- ✔ **Display & Cursors preferences** offer options for how certain tool cursors are displayed and how you view the Crop tool when you're cropping images. Chapter 9 explains how cropping works.

- ✔ **Transparency preferences** require an understanding of how Elements represents transparency. Imagine painting a portrait on a piece of clear acetate. The area you paint is opaque, and the area surrounding the portrait is transparent. To display transparency in Elements, you need some method to represent transparent areas. (Chapter 7 has more details.) Open the Transparency preferences and make choices for how transparency appears in Elements.

- ✔ **Units & Rulers preferences** let you specify settings for ruler units, column guides, and document preset resolutions.

- ✔ **Guides & Grid preferences** offer options for gridline color, divisions, and subdivisions. A *grid* shows you nonprinting horizontal and vertical lines. You use a grid to align objects, type, and other elements. You can snap items to the gridlines to make aligning objects much easier. You can drag guides (sometimes called *guidelines*) from the ruler and position them between gridlines.

- ✔ **Plug-Ins preferences** include options for selecting an additional Plug-Ins folder. Plug-ins are third-party utilities that work with Elements. For example, you can find plug-ins that offer editing features not found in Elements, many different adjustments for brightness/contrast and color correction, and some nifty special effects. There are many free plug-ins you can find on the Internet by searching for *Photoshop Elements Plug-Ins*.

- ✔ **Adobe Partner Services** enable you to control whether Elements automatically checks for new services, clears the online stored data, and resets your account information for all services.

- ✔ **Type preferences** provide options for setting text attributes. You have options for using different quote marks, showing Asian characters, showing font names in English, and previewing font sizes.

## What's a scratch disk?

Assume that you have 1GB of free RAM (your internal computer memory), and you want to work on a picture that consumes 1.25GB of hard drive space. Elements needs to load all 1.25GB of the file into RAM. Therefore, an auxiliary source of RAM is needed for you to work on the image. Elements uses your hard drive. When a hard drive is used as an extension of RAM, this source is a *scratch disk*.

If you have more than one hard drive connected to your computer, you can instruct Elements to use all hard drives, and you can select the order of the hard drives that Elements uses for your extension of RAM. All disks and media sources appear in a list as 1, 2, 3, 4, and so on.

*Warning:* Don't use USB 1.1 external hard drives or other drives that have connections slower than USB 2.0, Thunderbolt, or FireWire. Using slower drives slows Elements' performance. Most drives made in the last decade are USB 2.0, so you only need to worry about this if your drive is very old.

## Customizing Presets

Part of the fun of image editing is choosing brush tips, swatch colors, gradient colors, and patterns to create the look you want. To get you started, Elements provides you with a number of preset libraries that you can load and use when you want. For example, you can load a Brushes library to acquire different brush tips that you can use with the Brush tool and the Eraser tool. But you're likely to want to customize the preset libraries at least a little bit, too.

You can change libraries individually in respective panels where the items are used. For example, you can change color swatch libraries on the Color Swatches panel or choose brush-tip libraries in the Tool Options. Another way you can change libraries is to use the Preset Manager dialog box, as shown in Figure 3-18.

We cover using the presets in Chapter 12, which is where you can find out how to use the many presets that Elements provides. The important thing to note here is that you can change the presets according to your editing needs.

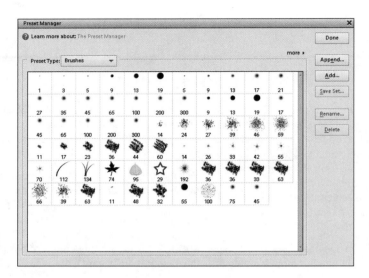

**Figure 3-18:** The Preset Manager dialog box provides a central area where you can change libraries.

To open the Preset Manager dialog box, choose Edit⇨Preset Manager. The available options in the dialog box are

- **Learn More About: The Preset Manager:** Click the blue Preset Manager hyperlinked text to open the Help document and find out more about managing presets.

- **Preset Type:** Open the drop-down list to choose from Brushes, Swatches, Gradients, and Patterns.

- **More:** The More drop-down list lists the viewing options. You can view the library items as text lists or as thumbnail views.

- **Done:** Any changes you make in the Preset Manager are recorded and saved when you click Done.

- **Append:** Click the Append button to append a library to the existing library open in the Preset Manager.

- **Add:** Click this button to open another library. Elements allows you to choose from several libraries for each preset type.

- **Save Set:** You can save any changes you make in the Preset Manager as a new library. If you make a change, use this option so that you don't disturb the original presets.

- **Rename:** Each item in a library has a unique name. If you want to rename an item, click the thumbnail in the Preview pane, click Rename, and then type a new name in the dialog box that appears.

- **Delete:** Click an item in the Preview window and click Delete to remove the item from the library.

# Part II
# Managing Media

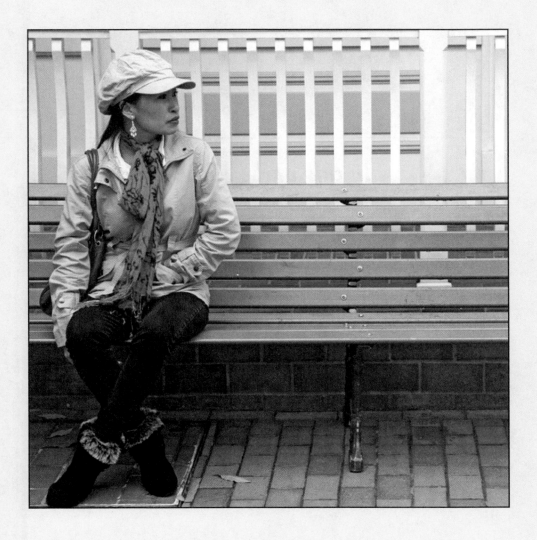

Find detailed steps on how to create albums at www.dummies.com/extras/
photoshopelements.

# In this part . . .

- ✔ Discover the basic features of the Organizer interface.

- ✔ Import images from your computer, camera, scanner, or Adobe Revel into the Organizer.

- ✔ Tag images with keywords, faces, places, or events so you can easily find images.

- ✔ View your pictures in the Media Browser and change views.

- ✔ Use the Organizer's search features to pinpoint the images you need.

# Navigating the Organizer

## In This Chapter

▶ Organizing your photos on your computer

▶ Importing photos into the Organizer

▶ Exploring the Media Browser

▶ Scanning photos and artwork

▶ Acquiring photos from cellphones

▶ Using Preferences

**D**o you treasure your color-coded filing system and own a special sock drawer organizer? Or are you more inclined to hand your accountant a plastic grocery sack of statements and receipts to sort out for you when tax-filing season comes around?

We're not here to judge. Whatever your organizational style, you'll like the Elements Organizer. The Organizer gives you myriad ways to tag and rate your images, but it also provides tools that automate some of the work.

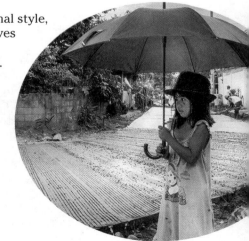

Before you get started with all the organizational tools, you need to import images into the Elements Organizer. That's what this chapter is all about.

You have many ways to import a picture into Elements. We walk you through an easy method for importing images from cameras and card readers into the Organizer. We also help you import images from CDs, DVDs, a scanner, or your phone.

# Organizing Photos and Media on a Hard Drive

Photos and media hog most of the available storage space on the average consumer's computer. If you're anything like us, you grab a ton of photos and videos with your digital camera, smartphone, and maybe a tablet, too. Even if you faithfully transfer images from all these different sources to your computer, you can end up with a real mess of photos — all with inscrutable filenames such as `DS603_Azb42.jpg`.

If all the photos on your hard drive are organized into folders, you'll have an easier time managing those photos in the Elements Organizer. We recommend you organize your image files in folders before you start working with Elements.

How you label your folders is a personal choice. You may want to name the folders by year and use subfolders for organizing photos by events, locations, photo content, and so on. In Figure 4-1, you can see just one example of how you might organize your photos on a hard drive.

After you organize your photos into folders, you can use the Organizer to import files from folders, as we explain later, in the section "Adding files from folders and removable media."

If your image files gobble up too much space on your computer's hard drive, we recommend storing all your photos on an external drive instead. Fortunately, the price of large-capacity drives is well within the reach of most people who own a computer, digital camera, or smartphone. Depending on how many photos you take (or image files you create), look for a 1TB to 3TB USB drive that attaches to your computer. Use the drive only for your photos, videos, and other media, and don't copy other data files to it. When all your image and media files are in one place, keeping them organized on that drive becomes much easier.

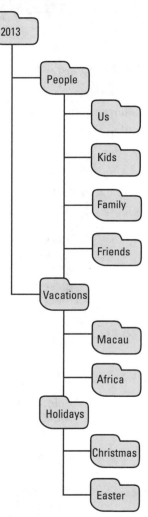

**Figure 4-1:** Organize photos and media in folders and subfolders on your hard drive.

For detailed steps on importing and organizing your photos, see our web extras at www.dummies.com/extras/photoshopelements.

# Adding Images to the Organizer

To use the Elements Organizer, you need to import the images first to your computer's hard drive and then into the Organizer.

You have several options for downloading photos from your camera and other devices to your computer:

- ✔ Using AutoPlay Wizards for Windows and Assistants on the Mac
- ✔ Importing photos directly from iPhoto if you use a Mac
- ✔ Using the Photoshop Elements Downloader

The built-in downloaders from your operating system attempt to make your life easier, but in reality, it may be more difficult to struggle with a downloader application and later organize files in folders (as we recommend earlier in this chapter).

Perhaps the easiest method for transferring photos from a camera or card reader is to cancel out of the operating system's downloader application or any camera-specific applications and just stay with the tools that Photoshop Elements provides you.

The following sections introduce you to the tools available for adding images to the Organizer. If you've already organized images on your hard drive or other media into folders, the Get Files from Folders command (as we explain in the first section) can help. If images are still on your camera, the Elements Downloader enables you to download images from your camera into the folder where you want to keep the images, using whatever folder organization system you've created; the Elements Downloader also imports the images into the Organizer at the same time.

## Adding files from folders and removable media

Most people have photos on their computer's hard drive, as well as on removable media, such as CDs or maybe even a USB flash drive. Adding images from your hard drive to the Organizer is easy. If you have a source, such as a USB flash drive or a CD, you copy files from the source to the drive where you store photos. Or you can copy files into the Organizer directly from the removable media.

The following steps explain how to import images from your hard drive into the Organizer Media Browser:

1. **Click the Import button in the top-left corner of the Organizer to open the drop-down list and choose From Files and Folders.**

   Alternatively, you can choose File⇨Get Photos and Videos⇨From Files and Folders.

   The Get Photos and Videos from Files and Folders dialog box opens, as shown in Figure 4-2.

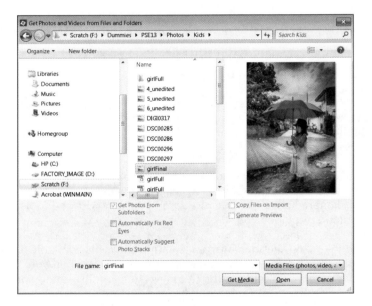

**Figure 4-2:** The Get Photos and Videos from Files and Folders dialog box.

2. **Browse your hard drive for the photos you want to add.**

   You can navigate your computer and any connected external drives or media in the left-hand pane. (For example, you've connected a USB drive of photos or loaded a CD of images into your CD drive.) The contents of the selected drive or folder appear in the middle pane of the dialog box.

If you're importing photos directly from the external device, by default, the Get Photos and Videos from Files and Folders dialog box copies your media to your hard drive when you click the Get Media button. You can deselect the Copy Files on Import check box so that only thumbnail images will appear in the Media Browser. To edit a photo, you have to reconnect the CD or DVD to your computer. If you elect to copy the images, the photos are available for editing each time you start a new Elements session.

3. **Select the files or a folder that you want to import.**

   You can import individual images, a single folder of photos, or a folder and all its subfolders.

4. **Click the Get Media button.**

When you add files to the Organizer, the image thumbnails are links to the files stored on your drive. They aren't the complete image data.

## Downloading camera images with the Elements Downloader

Import photos from your camera to the Organizer as follows:

1. **Insert a media card from a camera or attach a camera to your computer via a USB port.**

   We recommend using a media card instead of attaching your camera, in case the battery is low on your camera. (If the battery runs out, the import stops.) If you have a media card for your camera, take it out and insert it into a card reader that you attach to your computer via a USB port or a built-in card reader in your computer.

2. **If you see an Autoplay Wizard on Windows or a dialog box for importing photos into iPhoto on the Mac, cancel out of the dialog box and let Elements control your import. Otherwise, skip to Step 3.**

3. **In Elements, open the Organizer workspace and choose Import⇨From Files and Folders. Or choose File⇨Get Photos and Videos from Camera or Card Reader.**

   The Elements Organizer – Photo Downloader opens, as shown in Figure 4-3.

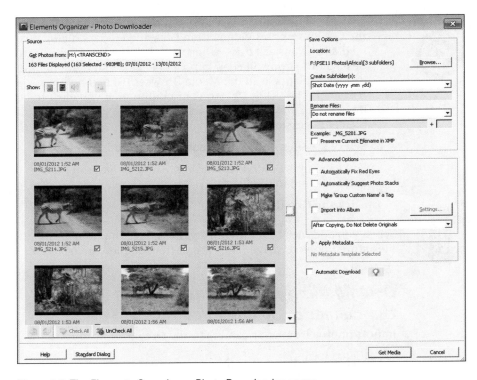

Figure 4-3: The Elements Organizer – Photo Downloader opens.

**4. From the Get Photos From drop-down list at the top of the dialog box, choose your media card.**

**5. Click the Browse button and locate the folder on your drive to which you want to copy the photos.**

If you don't click the Browse button and select a folder, all files copied to your hard drive are copied to the User Pictures folder. This is the default for Photoshop Elements. If you use an external hard drive to store your photos, you'll want to copy photos to the external drive. When you select a folder, select the one that fits the overall folder organizational structure for your images so your image files stay organized.

You can leave the rest of the settings at the defaults or rename the photos here. You can also take care of file renaming in the Organizer later. Don't delete the photos from your card just in case you delete some photos in the Organizer and want to retrieve them. After you're certain everything in Elements is to your liking, you can later delete photos by using your camera.

There's an Advanced dialog box for the Downloader that you access by clicking the Advanced Dialog button. In the Advanced settings, you can make choices for things like correcting for red-eye, creating photo stacks, and editing photo data that we call metadata. (We explain this in Chapter 6.) Because you can handle all these tasks in Elements, just leave the Advanced settings at their defaults.

6. **Import photos by clicking the Get Media button in the Photo Downloader dialog box.**

   Elements adds the photos to the Organizer, and you eventually see thumbnail images in the Organizer's Media Browser after the upload completes.

## Importing additional photos from folders

Suppose you have your folders organized and photos copied to various folders. You take some more pictures of family members and want to add these photos to a folder you already have labeled as Family. To add pictures to a folder on your hard drive, follow these steps:

1. **Copy photos from a CD, a media card, or an external media drive to your hard drive.**

   In this example, we want to copy photos to a folder we have labeled Family.

2. **In the Organizer, choose File⇨Get Photos and Videos⇨From Files and Folders.**

   The Get Photos and Videos from Files and Folders dialog box opens.

3. **Select the folder on your hard drive where you copied the new photos.**

   In this case, we select the folder labeled Family.

4. **Click the Get Media button.**

   The Getting Media dialog box appears, and the photos are added to the Organizer.

5. **Click OK in the Getting Media dialog box.**

   Photoshop Elements is smart enough to import only new images into the Organizer, as shown in Figure 4-4. Any images you previously imported from a given folder are listed in the Getting Media dialog box, and you're informed that the old images will not be imported.

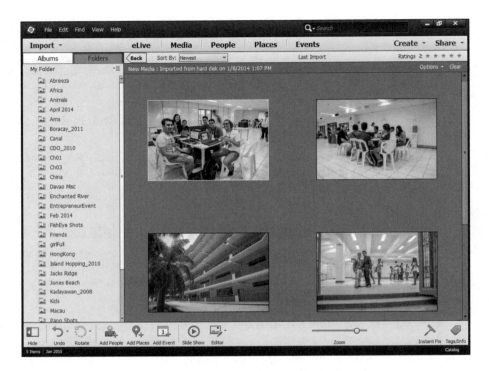

Figure 4-4: Only new photos added to a folder are imported in the Organizer.

## Getting photos from iPhoto (Mac only)

Mac users may want to use both Apple's iPhoto and Elements. If you're familiar with iPhoto and enjoy using it, you may want to view and manage photos, albums, and events in iPhoto, but still use the more powerful editing tools in Elements to edit your pictures.

If you want to convert an iPhoto library to the Elements Organizer, choose File⇨Get Photos and Videos⇨From iPhoto. Your photos are imported into the Organizer and appear in the Media Browser.

If you want to edit photos in Elements directly from iPhoto, take these steps:

1. **Open iPhoto⇨Preferences.**

   The Preferences dialog box appears.

2. **Click the Advanced icon at the top (see Figure 4-5) and then choose In Application from the Edit Photos drop-down list.**

   The Open dialog box appears.

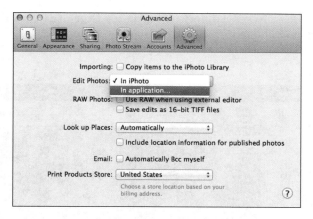

**Figure 4-5:** In iPhoto, click Advanced and choose In Application to select the Elements Editor.

3. **Navigate your hard drive and locate Adobe Photoshop Elements 13.**

# Navigating the Media Browser

When you add photos to the Organizer, the photos and any additional media appear as thumbnails in the central portion of the Organizer — known as the *Media Browser*.

After files are imported into the Organizer, you see just those photos you imported in the Media Browser. Similarly, when you click a folder in the Import panel, only the photos within the selected folder display in the Media Browser. To see all the photos in your catalog, click the All Media button at the top of the Media Browser.

The Import panel is the list of folders on the left. You can collapse the panel to provide more viewing area in the Media Browser. Just click the Hide Panel button in the lower-left corner of the Organizer workspace. (See Figure 4-6.)

The Import panel offers two different views.

✔ **List view:** By default, you see the folder List view that shows all folders imported in alphabetical order. If you have photos in subfolders, the Folder List view doesn't reflect the hierarchy for how your photos are organized on your hard drive.

> ✔ **Tree view:** To see a different view in the Organizer, click the drop-down menu and choose View as Tree, and you change the Import panel view to the hierarchy view, as shown in Figure 4-6.

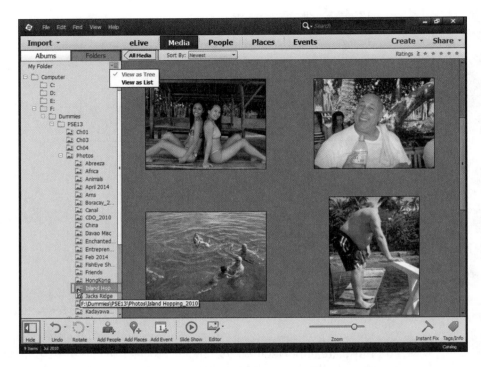

**Figure 4-6:** Photos displayed in a Tree view in the Import panel.

If you have a touchscreen monitor or device, you can swipe photos to view them one at a time.

If you don't see the details below the photos or the photos don't appear in grid view, press Ctrl+D (⌘+D) to change the Media Browser view.

## Using a Scanner

Scanners connect through the same ports as cameras and card readers — typically either the USB or FireWire port. Low-end scanners sold now are typically USB devices.

Even the lowest-end scanners provide 14-bit scans that help you get a little more data in the shadows and highlights. As with a digital camera, a scanner's price is normally in proportion with its quality.

## Understanding image requirements

All scanning software provides you with options for determining resolution and color mode before you start a new scan. Chapter 2 introduces you to choosing a resolution and color mode.

You should decide what output you intend to use and choose your resolution based on that output. Some considerations include the following:

- ✔ **Scan the artwork or photo at the size and resolution for the final output.** If you have a 3-x-5 photo that needs to be 1.5 x 2.5 inches on a web page, scan the original with a 50-percent reduction in size at 72 ppi (the desired resolution for images on the web).

- ✔ **Size images with the scanner software.** If you have a 4-x-6 photo that needs to be output for prepress and commercial printing at 8 x 12 inches, scan the photo at 4 x 6 inches at 600 ppi (a resolution that's large enough to increase the image size to 200 percent and still have a 300 dpi [dots per inch] image, which is the desired resolution for a print).

- ✔ **Scan properly for line art.** *Line art* is 4-bit black and white only and should be used for scanning not only black-and-white artwork but also text. When you print line art on a laser printer or prepare files for commercial printing, the line art resolution should match the device resolution. For example, printing to a 600 dpi laser printer requires 600 ppi for a 4-bit line-art image.

- ✔ **Scan grayscale images in color.** In some cases, it doesn't matter, but with some images and scanners, you can get better results by scanning grayscale images in RGB (red, green, and blue) color and converting to grayscale as we explain in Chapter 2.

- ✔ **Scan in high-bit depths.** If your scanner is capable of scanning in 14- or 32-bit, by all means, scan at the higher bit depths to capture the most data. See Chapter 2 for more information about working with higher-bit images.

## Using scanner plug-ins (Windows)

Generally, when you install your scanner software, a standalone application and a plug-in are installed to control the scanning process. *Plug-ins* work inside other software programs, such as Photoshop Elements. When you're using the plug-in, you can stay right in Elements to do all your scanning. Here's how it works:

1. **After installing a new scanner and the accompanying software, open the Organizer.**

2. **Press Ctrl+K to open the Preferences dialog box.**

   The Preferences dialog box opens.

3. **Click Scanner in the left column and adjust the Scanner preferences, such as choosing your scanner, setting the quality, and choosing a target destination for your scans.**

When the Preferences dialog box displays your scanner, you know that the connection is properly set up and you're ready to scan. Here's how to complete your scan:

1. **In the Organizer, choose File⇨Get Photos⇨From Scanner (Windows).**

2. **In the Get Photos from Scanner dialog box that appears (as shown in Figure 4-7), make your choices and then click OK.**

   Here you can choose your scanner in the Scanner drop-down list, a location on your hard drive for saving the scanned images, a quality setting, and an option to automatically correct red-eye.

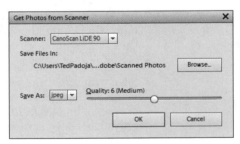

Figure 4-7: Make choices in the Get Photos from Scanner dialog box and click OK.

   Elements may churn a bit, but eventually your scanner software window appears atop the Organizer, as you can see in Figure 4-8. The window is the scanner software provided by your scanner manufacturer. (Your window will look different from Figure 4-8 unless you use the same scanner we use.)

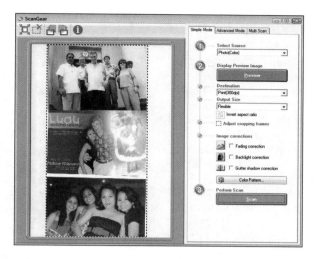

**Figure 4-8:** When you scan from within Elements, your scanner software window loads on top of the Elements workspace.

3. **Preview the scan.**

   Regardless of which software you use, you have similar options for creating a preview; selecting resolution, color mode, and image size; scaling; and other options. If you click the Preview button, you see a preview before scanning the photo(s).

4. **Adjust the options according to your output requirements and the recommendations made by your scanner manufacturer.**

5. **When everything is ready to go, click the Scan button.**

   The final image drops into an Elements image window.

## Scanning on the Mac

Photoshop Elements doesn't support scanning on the Mac as it does for Windows. On the Mac, you have a few options:

- ✔ **Scanner software:** You can use your scanner software and open the resulting scan in the Elements Photo Editor.

- ✔ **Image Capture:** With Image Capture (found in your Applications folder), you can complete a scan and open the file directly in Elements. Image Capture provides options for saving scans as JPEG, TIFF, PNG, or PDF. Quite often you'll find best results when saving as PNG.

## Scanning many photos at a time

If you have several photos to scan, you can lay them out on the scanner platen and perform a single scan to acquire all images in one pass. Arrange the photos to scan on the glass and set up all the options in the scanner window for your intended output. When you scan multiple images, they form a single scan, as you can see in Figure 4-9.

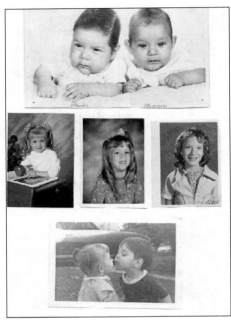

After you scan multiple images, Elements makes it easy for you to separate each image into its own image window, where you can save the images as separate files. In the Photo Editor, choose Image➪Divide Scanned Photos to make Elements magically open each image in a separate window while your original scan remains intact. The images are neatly tucked away in the Photo Bin, where you can select them for editing, as shown in Figure 4-10. (For more information on using the Photo Editor and working with the Photo Bin, see Chapter 3.)

**Figure 4-9:** You can scan multiple images with one pass.

When scanning multiple images and using the Divide Scanned Photos command, be sure to keep your photos on the scanner bed aligned vertically, horizontally, and parallel to each other as best you can. Doing so enables Elements to do a better job of dividing and straightening your photos.

If you close one of the images that were divided, Elements prompts you to save the image. Only the scan was saved when you started the process. You still need to save the divided scans.

After dividing the images, choose File➪Close All. Elements closes all files that have been saved and individually prompts you to save all unsaved images.

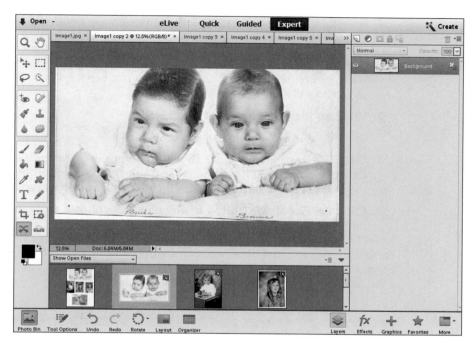

**Figure 4-10:** The scan is split.

# Phoning in Your Images

You can acquire images from cellphones, iPhones, iPods, iPads, and a variety of different handheld devices. As a matter of fact, you can do quite a bit with uploading, downloading, and preparing photos for handheld devices.

If you want to add images from a cellphone to the Organizer or open images in one of the editing modes, you need to copy files to your hard drive via a USB or Bluetooth connection or download an email attachment of the photos if your phone can use email.

Follow these steps after copying files to your hard drive:

1. **Choose File⇨Get Photos and Video⇨From Files and Folders.**

   The Elements Organizer – Photo Downloader dialog box opens (refer to Figure 4-11).

2. **Locate the folder into which you copied the files and add them to your Organizer.**

   Or you can open them in one of the editing modes.

   With an iPhone, iPod touch, or iPad, you can use the Photo Downloader to transfer media.

3. **Hook up the device with a USB cable.**

   The Photo Downloader opens automatically.

4. **Click the Browse button, as shown in Figure 4-11, to open the Select Directory to Store Files window and select a destination folder. Click the Select Folder Button to identify where the photos are saved.**

5. **Click the Get Media button to download the photos to your computer.**

For iPhone, iPod touch, and iPad, you can also hook up your device via a USB cable and choose File⇨Get Photos and Videos⇨From Camera or Card Reader. Elements recognizes the device, and the Photo Downloader opens, giving you options for importing all photos or selected images.

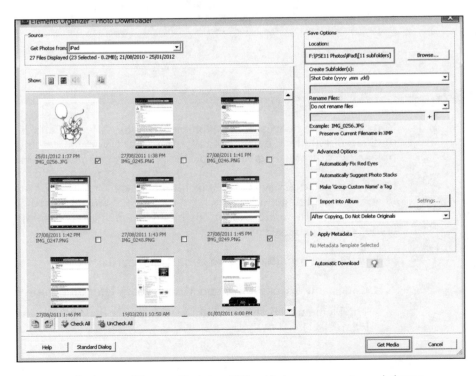

**Figure 4-11:** Hook up an iPhone or iPad via a USB cable to your computer and choose File⇨Get Photos and Videos⇨From Camera or Card Reader.

To upload Elements creations and edited photos to your iPhone, iPad, or iPod touch, use Apple's iTunes:

1. **In iTunes, choose File⇨Add Files to Library.**

2. **Select the images and videos from a folder on your hard drive that you want to upload to the device.**

   When uploading photos to an iPhone or iPad, use only the formats these devices support, such as JPEG, TIFF, GIF, and PNG.

3. **Hook up the iPhone or iPad and then click the Photos and/or Videos tab at the top of the iTunes window.**

4. **Select the check box for each item you want to upload and then click the Sync button.**

   Your files are uploaded to your device while the sync is in progress.

You can bypass iTunes with the iPad by using the Camera Connection Kit, provided by Apple for $29.95. The kit supports only SD cards, but you can attach many different types of card readers to the USB port on the Camera Connection Kit and use other media cards. Copy files from the Organizer to the media card and use it as you would use an external media source to share photos back and forth between your computer and the iPad.

# Setting Organizer Preferences

Throughout this book we often refer to making some choices in the application Preferences. The Organizer and the Photo Editor have a set of preferences that you open by choosing Edit⇨Preferences (Windows) or Photoshop Elements Organizer⇨Preferences (Mac). There are several panels in each set of preferences. You click an item in the left pane and options for the respective item appear in the right pane. After making your choices, click OK and the preferences remain for all subsequent sessions in the Organizer.

Many preference items are self-explanatory. Where you need some detail on making a preference choice, refer to the Adobe Help file you can find by choosing Help⇨Elements Organizer Help.

# Organizing Your Pictures

**In This Chapter**

▶ Creating and organizing keyword tags

▶ Rating your images

▶ Working with albums

▶ Adding People tags

▶ Placing images on maps

▶ Working with Events

**D**ownloading a bunch of media cards filled with photos and leaving them in folders distributed all over your hard drive is like having a messy office with papers stacked haphazardly all over your desk. Trying to find a file, even with all the great search capabilities we cover in Chapter 6, can take you as much time as sorting through piles of papers. What you need is a good file-management system.

In this chapter, we talk about tagging photos, organizing and annotating files, creating versions and stacks, creating photo albums, and performing other tasks so that you can quickly sort through large collections of photos. Be certain to take some time to understand the organizational methods that Elements offers and keep your files organized when you copy them to your hard drive. Sharpening your photo-management skills enables you to easily find photos you want to edit, add photos to a new creation, or share photos with friends and family.

## Touring the Organizer

To help you start using the Organizer's photo-management tools, we begin this chapter about more Organizer tasks by first offering a glimpse at the Organizer workspace.

Figure 5-1 shows you an Organizer view. The various items in the Organizer include the following:

**A. Menu bar:** The Organizer menus appear in the top-left section of the menu bar. In Windows, the menus belong to the application. On the Mac, the menu bar is part of the operating system's menus.

**B. All Media/Sort By:** When you click a folder as you see in item J, the thumbnail images shown in the Media Browser (item V) display only those photos within the selected folder. Figure 5-1 shows the Canal folder selected. If you click the All Media button, you leave the selected folder and see all photos from all folders in the Media Browser. Next to the All Media button is a Sort By drop-down list where you can sort the thumbnails in the Media Browser according to Newest, Oldest, and Batches of photos that you imported.

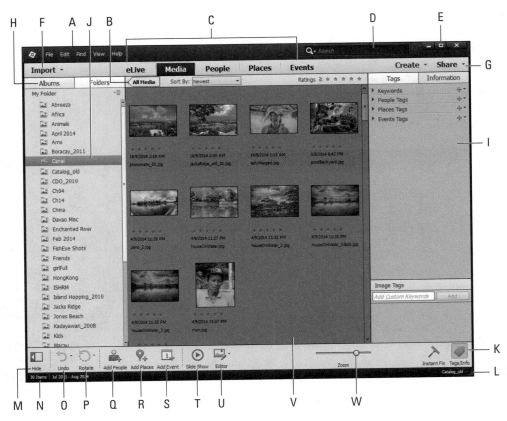

**Figure 5-1:** The Organizer workspace.

**C. Media/People/Places/Events:** At the top of the Organizer window, you find four tabs:

- *Media:* The first tab is Media. Click the Media tab to display thumbnails of photos either in a folder or in the entire catalog. (See Chapter 6 for more on catalogs.)

- *People:* Click this tab to display photos where you have tagged faces, as we discuss later in this chapter.

- *Places:* Click this tab, and a Google map appears in the Panel Bin. You can tag photos according to map coordinates by using Google maps. Click the Add Places button (item R) to tag an image with a place on the map. See Chapter 6 for more on adding places.

- *Events:* Click this tab to display photos that have been tagged as Events. To tag a photo with an event, click the Add Event button (item S). See the section "Working with Events" later in this chapter.

We talk more about tagging photos later in this chapter, in the section "Organizing Groups of Images with Tags."

**D. Search:** Any photos you have tagged with keywords can be searched. Type the search criteria, such as the name of a person you have tagged with the People tag in the text box, and then press Enter/Return or click the magnifying-glass icon.

**E. Features buttons:** In Windows, you find Maximize, Minimize, and Close buttons in the top-right corner of the Organizer. On the Mac, in the top-left corner you find Close, Minimize to Dock, and Maximize.

**F. Import:** From the drop-down menu, you can choose to import photos from Files and Folders, Camera or Card Reader, or Scanner. Another option enables you to search your hard drive.

**G. Create/Share:** These two items are drop-down lists. You choose a menu item that takes you either to the Photo Editor or a wizard where you work step-by-step to complete a task. For more information on making creations, see Chapter 16. For more information on sharing photos, see Chapter 15.

**H. Albums/Folders tabs:** Click Albums to view any Photo Albums you have created. Click Folders to display a folder view as shown in Figure 5-1.

**I. Panel Bin:** Within the Panel Bin, you find various panels that are docked. By default, you see Tags, Information, and Image Tags. The section "Organizing Groups of Images with Tags," later in this chapter, has details about using the panels.

**J. Folders view:** Click a Folder name to display just the photos within the respective folder. Click All Media to display all images from all folders.

**K. Instant Fix/Tags Info:** Click the Instant Fix button, and you see the same panel in the Organizer that opens when you select Quick mode in the Photo Editor. We explain Quick mode in Chapter 1. The nice thing about having the Quick mode options in the Organizer is that you don't need to open files in the Photo Editor to apply some edits to your photos. Click Tags/Info to display the Tags and Information tabs in the panel bin.

**L. Catalog Name:** Here, you see the name of the current open catalog.

**M. Hide:** Click this button to hide the left panel. If you click this button and the Tags/Info button (item K), you can hide both panels. Doing so provides you a maximum viewing area for the photo thumbnails.

**N. Status bar:** The bottom of the Organizer window provides information. On the left, you see the number of items in your catalog and the date you created the catalog. On the far right, you see the name of your catalog.

**O. Undo/Redo:** Click the tiny arrow, and a pop-up menu displays Undo and Redo. Choose an item to undo or redo your last action.

**P. Rotate:** When you click the arrow, you can choose to rotate a photo clockwise or counterclockwise. To use either tool, you must first select a thumbnail in the Media Browser.

**Q. Add People:** Later in this chapter, we talk about adding people when you import photos in the Media Browser. Elements does a nice job of recognizing people, but it has a hard time with profile shots, tilted heads, and photos where people are not easily recognized.

Double-click a photo to zoom into it and click the Add People button. A new rectangle appears in the photo that you can move to position and add a name.

**R. Add Places:** When you click Add Places, a window opens atop the Organizer. A filmstrip appears at the top of the window, displaying files currently shown in the Media Browser. Below the filmstrip is a large map where you can assign map locations to the photos you select in the filmstrip.

**S. Add Event:** Add Event is yet another item that helps you organize your photos. You can add tags for people, places, and then events to help narrow down a large collection of photos. Each of these items can be sorted by clicking the respective tab at the top of the Organizer.

**T. Slide Show:** Slide Show provides an onscreen view of all the photos you have open in the Media Browser. You can sort photos according to tags, click Slide Show, and sit back and watch the photos scroll on your computer monitor.

**U. Editor:** Click to return to the Photo Editor.

**V. Media Browser:** Shows thumbnail displays of your images.

**W. Zoom:** Adjust the slider to see thumbnails larger or smaller.

This overall description of the Organizer can be helpful when you perform tasks related to the Organizer. Earmark this page and use it as a reference to quickly identify items contained in the Organizer.

# Organizing Groups of Images with Tags

*Tags* are a great way to organize your files. After you acquire your images in the Organizer, as we discuss in Chapter 4, you can tag images according to the dates when you took the pictures, the subject matter, or some other categorical arrangement, so that the images are easy to sort.

The Organizer's Tags panel helps you tag your photos and gives you the flexibility to customize your tags.

The Tags panel is divided into four categories: Keywords, People Tags, Places Tags, and Events Tags (see Figure 5-2).

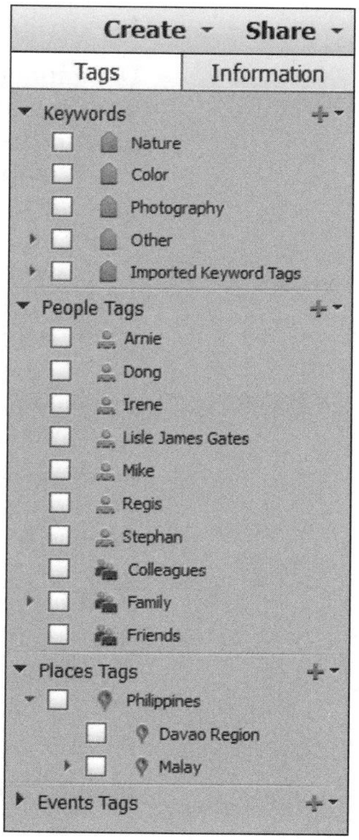

The Organizer helps you organize your photos into these four main categories, and each category has a drop-down list you can use to create new tags and add new subcategories. In the following sections, you can find out how to create and manage tags.

## Creating and viewing a tag

To create a new tag and add tags to photos, follow these steps:

**1. Open photos in the Organizer.**

See Chapter 4 for details about opening images in the Organizer.

Figure 5-2: The Tags panel in the Organizer.

2. **To create a new tag, choose which category you want to use (Keywords, People Tags, Places Tags, or Events Tags) and then click the plus (+) icon next to that category to open a drop-down list.**

3. **From the drop-down list, choose an option:**

   - *Keywords:* Choose New Keyword Tag.

   - *People Tags:* Choose New Person.

   - *Places Tags:* Choose Add a New Place.

   - *Events Tags:* Choose Add an Event.

   When you add a new Keyword tag, the Create Keyword Tag dialog box opens, as shown in Figure 5-3, where you can add information about the tag attributes.

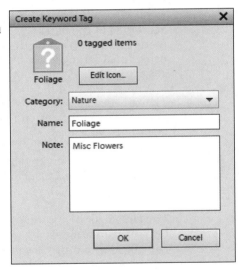

   Depending on what category you choose, the information you fill into the dialog box varies. For example, when you add a new tag in the Keywords category, the Create Keyword Tag dialog box provides options for editing the tag icon, specifying a category, typing a name, and adding comments. If you add a People tag, you type a person's name and choose a group such as family, friends, and so on. If you add a Places tag, you can choose to map the location. If you add an Event tag, you type the tags for the event, choose dates, and add a description. Hence, the attributes change according to the type of tag you create.

Figure 5-3: The Create Keyword Tag dialog box.

In our example, we add a new tag to the Keywords category.

4. **Specify a category.**

   Click the Category drop-down list and choose one of the preset categories listed in the menu. (See the section "Working with subcategories" for instructions on customizing categories.)

5. **Type a name for the tag in the Name text box and add a note to describe the tag.**

   You might use the location where you took the photos, the subject matter, or other descriptive information for the note.

6. **Click OK.**

   You return to the Organizer.

7. **In the Organizer, select the photos to which you want to add tags.**

   Click a photo and Shift-click another photo to select photos in a group. Click a photo and Ctrl-click (⌘-click) different photos scattered around the Organizer to select nonsequential photos.

8. **To add a new tag to a photo, first click the plus (+) symbol in the Tags panel to name a new tag, as shown in Figure 5-4. After a tag has been created, drag photos to the tag to tag them.**

   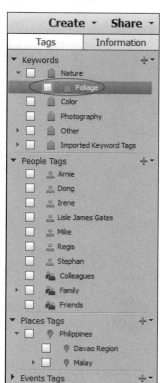

   Alternatively, you can drag a tag to the selected photos.

   When you release the mouse button, the photos are tagged.

   The checkbox adjacent to the tag name is used to display all photos with the respective tag in the Media Browser.

9. **Repeat Steps 2–8 to create tags for all the images you want to organize.**

Tags help you in many ways as we explain later in this chapter in the sections, "Sorting photos according to tags" and "Creating an album." The more you become familiar with tagging photos, the more opportunities you have for sorting and finding photos and adding found photos to albums. We encourage you to play with the Tags panel and explore creating tags and tagging photos in each of the different categories.

## Adding icons to tags

By default, Elements provides a set of icons displayed adjacent to all tag names. You can change the icon appearance to match a view similar to one of the photos you tag for a given keyword.

Figure 5-4: The Tags panel after adding a tag in the Keywords category.

If you want to add an image to the tag icon, you can handle it in a few ways. Perhaps the most reliable is to edit the tag as follows:

1. **Right-click a tag in the Tags panel and choose Edit.**

   The Edit Keyword Tag dialog box opens.

2. **Click the Edit Icon button.**

   The Edit Keyword Tag Icon dialog box opens, as shown in Figure 5-5.

3. **Select an image for the tag icon.**

   Click the Import button to import an image for the icon. Or click the left and right arrows to scroll through all the images with this tag and choose one for an icon.

   Additionally, you can click the Find button to open a window displaying thumbnail images of all the photos with this tag.

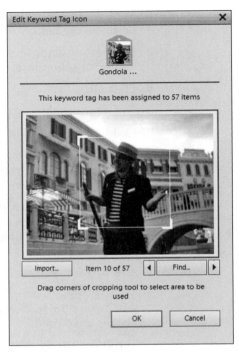

Figure 5-5: The Edit Keyword Tag Icon dialog box enables you to add or change a tag icon.

4. **(Optional) Crop the image by moving handles on the rectangle displayed in the Edit Keyword Tag Icon dialog box.**

5. **Click OK when you finish editing the icon.**

   The icon displays in the Tags panel.

To view the icons appearing in the Tags panel with the custom appearance you add in the Edit Keyword Tag Icon dialog box, you need to view the Tags panel with Large Icons. See the next section, "Working with custom tags," to change the view.

## Working with custom tags

We refer to *custom tags* as those tags you create in the Tags panel. Elements offers you a number of preset tags that you can use to tag your photos, and we refer to those as the *default tags*. In this section, we look at creating and editing custom tags.

You can manage tags by using menu commands from the Tags panel drop-down list (click the down arrow adjacent to one of the + icons) and other commands from a contextual menu that you open by right-clicking a tag on the Tags panel.

In the Tags panel drop-down list, you can access these commands:

- **New Keyword Tag:** Create a new tag, as we describe in the steps in the preceding section.

- **New Sub-Category:** A *subcategory* is a tag nested inside another tag. Create a subcategory by choosing New Sub-Category from the New menu; a dialog box opens, prompting you to type a name for the new subcategory. As an example of how you'd use tags and subcategories, you might have a tag named Uncle Joe's Wedding. Then you might create subcategories for Bride Dressing Room, Ceremony, Family Photos, Reception, and so on.

- **New Category:** Choose New Category to open a dialog box that prompts you to type a name for the new category. By default, you can find pre-defined category names for People, Places, Events, and Other. If you want to add your own custom categories, use this menu command.

- **Edit:** Choose Edit to open the Edit Keyword Tag dialog box. This dialog box appears exactly the same as the Create Keyword Tag dialog box (refer to Figure 5-3).

- **Import Keyword Tags from File:** If you export a tag, the file is written as XML (eXtensible Markup Language). When you choose From File, you can import an XML version of a tags file. This can be helpful if you've spent a lot of time tagging files, create a new catalog, import photos, and then import the tags associated with the photos.

- **Save Keyword Tags to a File:** You can save tags to a file that you can retrieve with the Import Keyword Tags from File command. This option is handy when you open a different catalog file and want to import the same collection names created in one catalog file to another catalog file. (See Chapter 6 for more information.)

- **Collapse All Keyword Tags:** Tags appear in lists that can be collapsed and expanded. An expanded list shows you all the subcategory tags. Choose Collapse All Keyword Tags to collapse the list.

- Expand All Keyword Tags: This command expands a collapsed list.

- Show Large Icons: Click this option to display the tag icons larger in the Tags panel. When you change the view to large icons, you see the custom edits you make when editing an icon.

Tags are saved automatically with the catalog you work with. By default, Elements creates a catalog and automatically saves your work to it. If you happen to create another catalog, as we explain in Chapter 6, your tags disappear. Be aware of which catalog is open when you create tags in order to return to them.

## Working with default tags

When you create a custom tag, you can modify its appearance. With the default tags that Elements provides, you can make some changes to the tags' appearances, but in limited ways. For example, you cannot add a custom image for the tag icon. However, you can modify the names for the preset tags, and you can add custom subcategories.

To edit a preset category tag, follow these steps:

1. **On one of the predefined categories, right-click and choose Edit.**

   The Edit Category dialog box opens, as shown in Figure 5-6.

2. **Click the Choose Color button to change the color of the tag icon.**

3. **To choose an icon for the preset category, move the scroll bar horizontally and click the icon you want to use.**

   You're limited to the images Elements provides you for displaying icons on the predefined categories.

4. **Click OK when you're done.**

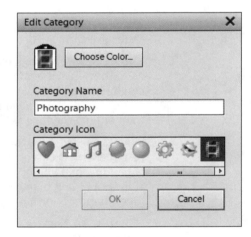

Figure 5-6: In the Edit Category dialog box, you can make some changes to the tag icon.

## Working with subcategories

A category tag is at the top of the tag hierarchy. As we mention earlier, there are four main categories. Below a category, you can add subcategories, and each subcategory can have subcategories below it. For example, you may want to create separate tags for different people in the People Tags category. You can't use custom icons, and you're restricted to using the icons provided by Elements, as shown in Figure 5-6. Here's how to add a new category and subcategory:

1. **From one of the Tags panel drop-down lists (+ icon), choose New Category.**

   In this case, we're working with People Tags, so we clicked Family and then clicked the plus (+) icon to add a new tag name. The Create Sub-Category Name dialog box then opens.

2. **Provide a name in the Sub-Category Name dialog box and choose a group from the Parent Group or Sub-Category drop-down list.**

   In our example we add two new subcategories to the Family tag.

3. **Click OK and repeat these steps until you create all the subcategories you want.**

   Notice that you don't have options for creating custom icons or for adding icons provided by Elements. All the subcategory icons are predefined for you, as shown in Figure 5-7, where a few different subcategories appear on the People Tags panel.

## Sorting photos according to tags

Tagging photos is useless unless you have a way to view the photos according to their tags. The Organizer makes it easy to view your tagged photos. Simply click the check box next to a tag name (the check box occupies a tiny pair of binoculars when checked). The Media Browser view changes to show you all the photos that have been tagged with the respective tag name, as shown in Figure 5-8.

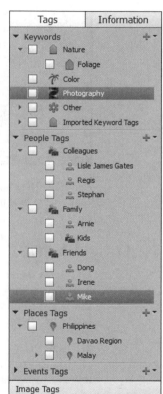

**Figure 5-7:** The Family tag now has two new subcategory tags of its own.

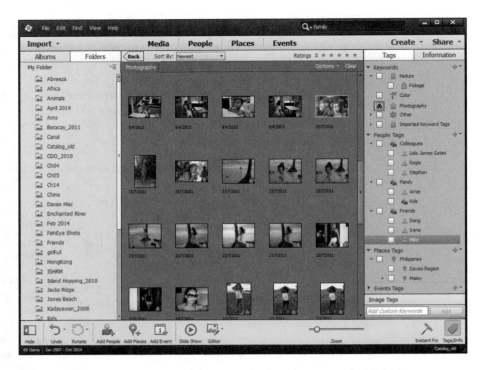

Figure 5-8: The Media Browser displays photos that have been tagged with the item you check in the Tags panel.

## Rating Images with Stars

You can rate photos in the Organizer by assigning images a number of stars, from one to five. You might have some photos that are exceptional, which you want to give five-star ratings, whereas poor photos with lighting and focus problems might be rated with one star.

To assign a star rating to a photo, select a photo in the Media Browser and click a star in the Information panel, as shown in Figure 5-9. One star is the lowest rating, and five stars is the highest.

After assigning star ratings to photos, you can sort photos according to their ratings. For example, click a star that appears in the Ratings at the top of the Media Browser. (See Figure 5-9.) If you click the third star, all photos rated with three, four, and five stars appear in the Media Browser. If you click the fifth star, only those photos rated with five stars appear in the Media Browser.

Click a star to rate the selected photo.

Click to sort photos by star rating.

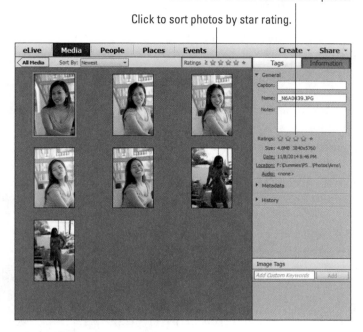

Figure 5-9: Rating photos with stars in the Information panel.

Be certain to click the star value in the Information panel when rating a photo with a star rating. If you click a star next to the Ratings label at the top of the Media Browser, Elements thinks you want to sort photos in the Media Browser according to star rating.

## Adding Images to an Album

Albums offer another way to organize your images. You can use albums to store photos that meet a specific set of criteria. For example, you might use your tags and star ratings to easily find all the five-star photos of your family. Or use your Events and Places tags to find all the photos you took at a conference in Paris. However, the photos you put in an album don't need to be tagged or starred. When you need a folder for a special stash of digital photos, the Organizer's albums feature is there for you.

## Creating an album

With albums and star ratings, you can further break down a collection into groups that you might want to mark for printing, sharing, or onscreen slide shows.

To create an album, follow these steps:

1. **Sort photos in the Media Browser to determine what photos you want to include in a new album.**

   In our example, we clicked the third star to sort photos ranked with three or more stars.

2. **Click the plus (+) icon next to Albums at the top of the left panel, as shown in Figure 5-10. From the drop-down list, choose New Album.**

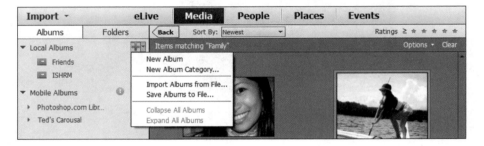

Figure 5-10: Click the plus (+) icon to open the drop-down list and then choose New Album.

3. **Name the new album.**

   In the Panel Bin, you see the Add New Album panel. Type a name for the album in the Name text box, as shown in Figure 5-11.

   If you didn't sort files in Step 1, you can do so now or simply pick and choose which photos to add to the new album from photos appearing in your catalog.

4. **Drag photos from the Media Browser to the Content tab in the Add New Album panel, as shown in Figure 5-11.**

   If photos are sorted and you want to include all photos in the Media Browser, press Ctrl+A/⌘+A to select all the photos or choose Edit➪Select All. After the files are selected, drag them to the Content pane in the Add New Album panel. (See Figure 5-11.)

If you don't have files sorted, click one or more photos and drag them to the Content pane. Repeat dragging photos until you have all photos you want to include in your new album.

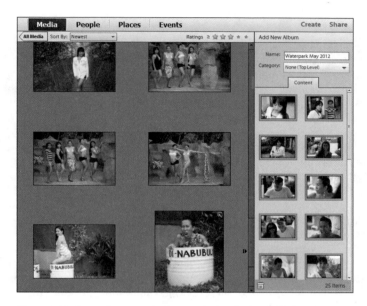

Figure 5-11: Drag photos to the items window in the Add New Album Content panel.

5. **Click Done at the bottom of the panel.**

   Your new album now appears listed in the Albums category on the Import panel.

That's it! Your new album is created, and the photos you dragged to the album are added to it. You can display all the photos within a given album in the Media Browser by clicking the album name in the Albums panel.

Creating multiple albums uses only a fraction of the computer memory that would be required if you wanted to duplicate photos for multiple purposes, such as printing, web hosting, sharing, and so on.

## Using albums for temporary work

You can add an album for temporary work and then delete the album when you no longer need it.

For instance, you may want to explore some of the creation and sharing items in the Create and Share panels. Before you peruse the options, create an album and add photos to it. Then proceed to use the sharing feature that interests you. When you finish, right-click to open a contextual menu and choose Delete *<album name>*.

### Editing an album

After creating an album, you may want to change the album name, add more photos to an album, delete some photos from an album, change the album category, or make some other kind of edit.

Your first step in performing any kind of edit to an album is to look at the left side of the Organizer. In the Import panel, you see a list of albums under the Albums category. To edit an album, right-click the album name and choose Edit. After clicking Edit, the album appears in the Panel Bin on the right side of the Organizer, much like you see in Figure 5-11.

Other commands are available in the context menu you open from an album name in the Import panel. You can rename an album, delete an album, explore some export options, share an album, and add more media to your album.

If you want to use the context menu commands, you must close the Add New Album panel in the Panel Bin. While this panel is open, you cannot open a context menu on an album name. Click either Done or Cancel to close the Add New Album panel in the Panel Bin.

### Finding out more about sharing your albums

An album is a starting point for many exciting things you can do with a collection of photos. Albums help you assemble a collection of photos that can be viewed on many devices and shared with others. Later in this book, we explore many ways you can share your albums with friends, family, and even the world, if you like:

- ✔ Host albums online for others to view your photos.
- ✔ Save the albums to a file on your hard drive.
- ✔ Organize an album for sharing photos with others on Adobe Revel.
- ✔ View albums as slide shows.

Chapter 15 gives you the details on all these sharing tricks, except the last bullet. To find out how to view albums as slide shows, see Chapter 16.

# Adding People in the Media Browser

For most people, the most enjoyable pictures are those of family and friends. You may take photos of landscapes and wonderful places, but quite often you'll ask someone to stand in front of the Coliseum, Louvre, Grand Canyon, or other notable landmark.

For just that reason, Photoshop Elements makes it easy for you to identify, sort, and view pictures with people.

You know that you can add folders of pictures to the Organizer to help manage photos. After you add new pictures to the Organizer, you can select a folder in the Import panel and label all the people in the photos. Elements makes it easy to label people's faces:

1. **Select the folder in the Import panel and click the Add People icon at the bottom of the Organizer.**

   If you have several photos in a folder, Elements prompts you in a dialog box to confirm your action.

2. **Click OK if you see the prompt.**

   The People Recognition – Label People window opens. You see the words *Who Is This?* below each photo.

3. **Click the Who Is This? text and type the name of the individual, as shown in Figure 5-12.**

   That's it! After you label the photos, you can easily search, sort, and locate photos with specific people. You can even download your Facebook friends list to the Organizer to help simplify labeling people.

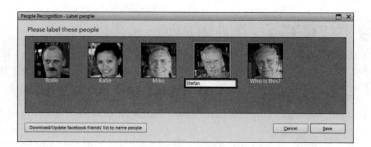

Figure 5-12: Type the name of the individual below each photo.

TIP

Elements is very good at recognizing people, but it's not perfect. Elements has particular difficulty with recognizing profile shots as photos of people. The good news, though, is that even if Elements doesn't recognize that people are in a photo, you can still tag it. To add People tags when you aren't prompted to do so, take these steps:

1. **Double-click a photo in the Media Browser.**

   You must first double-click a photo before proceeding. When you double-click a photo, the Mark Face tool appears in the Tools panel at the bottom of the Organizer, as shown in Figure 5-13.

2. **Click the Mark Face button.**

   Elements adds a new rectangle that you can move and resize.

3. **Move the rectangle to a person that hasn't been tagged and click the Who Is This? text box.**

4. **Type the person's name and click the check mark adjacent to the text box (shown in Figure 5-13) to confirm your action.**

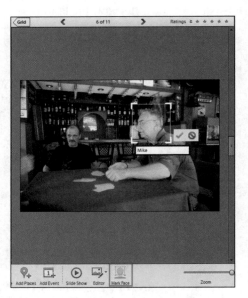

Figure 5-13: Double-click a photo in the Media Browser, and the Mark Face tool appears in the bottom Tools panel.

## Placing Pictures on Maps

You may take vacations to interesting places and want to sort photos according to the location where the photos were shot. You can easily place photos on geospatial maps.

To see how easy placing photos on maps is, do the following:

1. **Click photos in the Media Browser that you want to add to a new place.**

2. **Click the Add Places icon at the bottom of the Media Browser.**

   The Organizer changes to the Add Places window.

**3. Search for a location.**

In the search text box at the top of the Google map, type the name of a location that you want to assign photos. The Google map offers some suggestions in a drop-down list below the search text box. Click the area on the map to which you want to assign photos.

**4. Select photos to assign to locations.**

At the top, you can click individual photos. Or hold down the Ctrl (or ⌘) key and click to add more photos to a selection. If you want to add all photos to a given location, open the drop-down list in the top-right corner and choose Select All. (See Figure 5-14.)

**5. Click the check mark to assign the photos to the location.**

The selected photos are now assigned to the specified location. At the bottom of the window is a check box for Show Existing Pins on Map. When you check the box, all places that have been added are displayed with a readout indicating the number of photos assigned to the location(s).

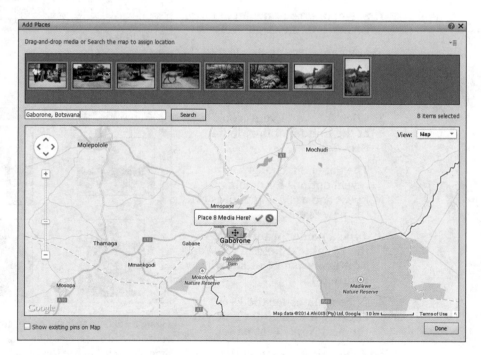

**Figure 5-14:** Click the Add Places icon at the bottom of the Media Browser to open the Add Places window.

If you want to sort photos according to location, choose Find⏵Using Advanced Search. The Organizer view changes, and notice that a column for Places appears. All photos assigned to places are listed in this column. You can easily select the check boxes to find photos assigned to a given place or select multiple check boxes to find photos from several places.

# Working with Events

You may have photos taken at special occasions or during holidays. You can add more organization opportunities to your Organizer management by assigning photos to different Events.

An *Event* can be any function of your choosing, such as a Christmas party, a ski trip, or an anniversary celebration. To create an Event and assign photos to it, do the following:

1. **Select photos in the Media Browser in the Organizer.**

   You can select photos in folders, select from an All Media view, or use any sort order you choose.

2. **Click the Add Event icon at the bottom of the Media Browser.**

   The Panel Bin changes to reveal options for naming an Event and assigning photos to the new Event.

3. **Type a name for the Event in the Event text field in the Add New Event panel, as shown in Figure 5-15.**

4. **Choose dates for the Event by clicking the calendar icons in the Add New Event panel.**

5. **Type a description in the Description text box.**

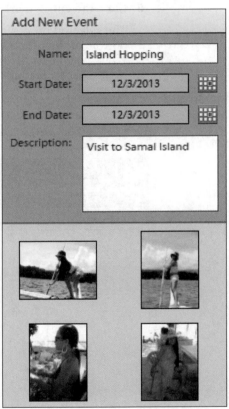

Figure 5-15: Type an Event name, choose the start and end dates, type a description, and drag photos to the Add New Event panel to assign photos to a new Event.

6. **Add photos to the Event.**

   Drag the selected photos to the panel.

7. **Click Done.**

   The photos are now assigned to an Event. To view events, click the Events tab at the top of the Organizer. You see collections of photos if you added several Events, with the first photo in the Event appearing on top. To view all photos, double-click the Event thumbnail you want to view.

# 6

# Viewing and Finding Your Images

*In This Chapter*

▶ Working with catalogs

▶ Switching to different views

▶ Viewing slide shows

▶ Searching for your photos

▶ Grouping your files in stacks

*P*hoto organization begins with adding images to a catalog. By default, the Organizer creates a new catalog for you (so you might not even notice the presence of your catalog without reading this book). As your catalog grows with the addition of more files, you'll want to discover ways to search and use a given set of images for a project.

In this chapter, we begin by talking about catalogs and then look at how to view and organize your pictures in the Organizer and the Media Browser. We show how the many options help speed up your work in Photoshop Elements. Before tackling this chapter, get familiar with the Organizer — Chapter 4 offers a brief glimpse of the Organizer and looks at a few different views; Chapter 5 explains how to tag photos and create photo albums in the Organizer.

## Cataloging Files

When you import files in the Organizer, all your files are saved automatically to a catalog. The files themselves aren't really saved to the catalog; rather, links from the catalog to the individual files are saved. In Elements, *links* are like pointers that tell the catalog where to look for a file. When you add and delete files within the Organizer, the catalog is updated continually.

After you import files in the Organizer, the Organizer maintains a link to the media. If you move the media on your hard drive, the link is broken. You need to reestablish the link by opening the file in the Photo Editor. The Find Offline Drives – Edit dialog box opens so that you can reconnect the file by browsing for its new location.

Your default catalog is titled *My Catalog* by the Organizer. As you add photos in the Organizer, your default catalog grows and may eventually store thousands of photos. At some point, you may want to create one or more additional catalogs to store photos. You may want to use one catalog for your family's and friends' photos and another for business or recreational activities. You may want to create separate catalogs for special purposes such as business, family, social networking, or other kinds of logical divisions.

## Using the Catalog Manager

Catalogs are created, deleted, and managed in the Catalog Manager. To access the Catalog Manager, choose File⇨Manage Catalogs. The Catalog Manager opens, as shown in Figure 6-1.

To keep your photos organized and your catalog files small, you can start a completely new catalog before you import photos. Follow these steps:

1. **Choose File⇨Manage Catalogs and click the New button in the Catalog Manager dialog box, as shown in Figure 6-1.**

2. **When the New Catalog dialog box opens, type a name for the new catalog in the File Name text box.**

3. **(Optional) If you want to add the free music files that installed with Elements, select the Import Free Music into All New Catalogs check box.**

   We recommend selecting the Import Free Music into All New Catalogs and Import Music Files check box. The Organizer ships with free music files that you can use in a variety of projects. See Chapter 16 for more on making creations.

4. **Click Save to create the new catalog.**

5. **Choose File⇨Get Photos and Videos⇨From Files and Folders to add files to the new catalog.**

   The Get Photos and Videos from Files and Folders dialog box opens.

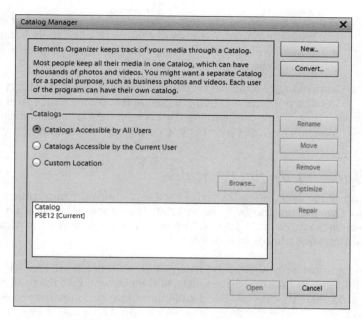

Figure 6-1: The Catalog Manager dialog box.

6. **Navigate your hard drive and select the photos you want to add. After you identify all the files, click Open.**

   The selected photos are added to your new collection of media contained in the catalog.

## Working with catalogs

After you create different catalogs for your images, the following tips for working with catalogs will come in handy:

- ✔ **Understanding how you want to organize your photos before creating your first catalog:** Unfortunately, Elements doesn't provide you with a command to split large catalogs into smaller ones. However, if you've created a large catalog and want to split it into two or more separate catalogs, you can manually add new photos to a new catalog and delete photos from the older catalog.

- ✔ **Switching to a different catalog:** When you need to open a different catalog file, choose File⇨Manage Catalogs and select the name of the catalog you want to open. Click Open at the bottom of the dialog box to open the selected catalog. The Organizer window changes to reflect files contained in that catalog.

✔ **Fixing a corrupted catalog:** Notice the Repair button in Figure 6-1. If you can't see thumbnail previews of images or open them in one of the editing modes, your catalog file might be corrupted. Click the Repair button to try to fix the problem.

✔ **Improving catalog performance:** When catalogs get sluggish, you might need to optimize a catalog to gain better performance. You should regularly optimize your catalog (by clicking the Optimize button in the Catalog Manager) to keep your catalog operating at optimum performance.

## Backing up your catalog

Computer users often learn the hard way about the importance of backing up a hard drive and the precious data they spent time creating and editing. We can save you that aggravation right now, before you spend any more time editing your photos in Elements.

We authors are so paranoid when we're writing a book that we back up our chapters on multiple drives, CDs, and DVDs when we finish them. The standard rule is that if you spend sufficient time working on a project and it gets to the point where redoing your work would be a major aggravation, it's time to back up files.

When organizing your files, adding keyword tags, creating albums, and creating stacks and version sets, you want to back up the catalog file in case it becomes corrupted. Fortunately, backing up catalogs is available to both Windows and Mac users; however, backing up to a CD or DVD from within Elements is available only on Windows.

Here's how you can use Elements to create a backup of your catalog:

1. **Choose File⇨Backup Catalog to open the Backup Catalog Wizard.**

   This wizard has two panes that Elements walks you through to painlessly create a backup of your files.

2. **Select the source to back up.**

   The first pane in the Backup Catalog to CD, DVD, or Hard Drive Wizard offers two options:

   • *Full Backup:* Select this radio button to perform your first backup or write files to a new media source.

   • *Incremental Backup:* Select this radio button if you've already performed at least one backup and you want to update the backed-up files.

3. **Click Next and select a target location for your backed-up files, as shown in Figure 6-2.**

   Active drives, including CD/DVD drives (on Windows) or external hard drives attached to your computer or mounted network drives available to your computer, appear in the Select Destination Drive list. Select a drive, and Elements automatically assesses the write speed and identifies a previous backup file if one was created.

   The total size of the files to copy is reported in the wizard. This information is helpful so that you know whether more than one CD or DVD is needed to complete the backup (on Windows) or a backup drive has enough space to complete the backup.

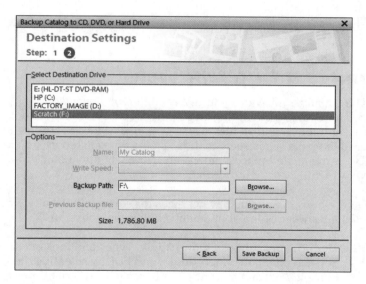

Figure 6-2: The wizard provides options for selecting the destination media for the backup.

4. **If you intend to copy files to your hard drive or to another hard drive attached to your computer, click the Browse button and identify the path.**

   If you use a media source, such as a CD or DVD (Windows only), Elements prompts you to insert a disc and readies the media for writing.

5. **Click Done.**

   The backup commences. Be certain to not interrupt the backup. It might take some time, so just let Elements work away until you're notified that the backup is complete.

## Backing up photos and files (Windows)

With files stored all over your hard drive, manually copying files to a second hard drive, CD, or DVD would take quite a bit of time. Fortunately, Elements makes finding files to back up a breeze.

Choose File⇨Copy/Move to Removable Drive and then, in the dialog box that opens, select the Move Files check box and click Next. Select a hard drive or a CD/DVD drive, type a name for the backup folder, and click OK. Elements goes about copying all files shown in the Organizer to your backup source.

Mac users don't have an option for backing up photos from the Organizer to CDs or DVDs. On the Mac, you can create a burn folder in the Finder, select all photos in the Organizer, and drag the selected files to the burn folder. Click the Burn button, and the files are copied to a CD or DVD.

# Switching to a Different View

The Organizer provides you several different viewing options. In Chapter 4, you find out about viewing files in the Media Browser and look at viewing recent imports and all files. You can also view files according to a timeline, certain media types such as those media types listed in the View⇨Media Types menu, and places and events. Here you find a quick tour of the View menu.

On the View menu, you have choices for sorting files that are displayed in the Media Browser. Some of the menu choices you have are

- **Media Types:** Choose View⇨Media Types and look over the submenu. You can eliminate video, audio, and PDF by selecting the respective items if you want to view just photos in the Media Browser. Likewise, you can eliminate photos and explore the other choices by selecting or deselecting the submenu items.

- **Hidden Files:** If files are hidden, you can view all files by choosing View⇨Hidden Files, and then you can choose (in the submenu) to view All Files, view Hidden Files, or (if files are in view) to hide Files.

- **Details:** By default, file details, such as file creation dates and star ratings, are hidden. You can show file details by choosing View⇨Details or pressing Ctrl+D/⌘+D.

- **File Names:** By default, the filenames of the photos appearing in the Media Browser are hidden. You can show filenames by choosing View⇨File Names.

✔ **Timeline:** Choose View➪Timeline, and a horizontal bar opens at the top of the Organizer. A slider appears on the bar that you can drag left and right to select a time when your photos were taken. In Figure 6-3, you can see the timeline, details, and filenames.

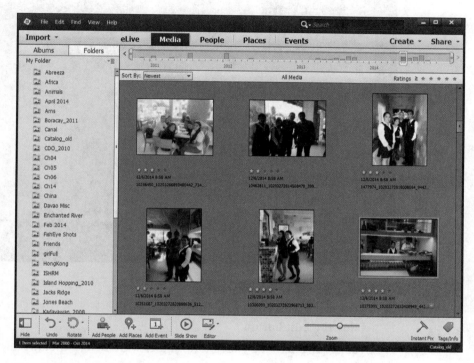

**Figure 6-3:** The Media Browser displaying a timeline, file details, and filenames.

# Viewing Photos in a Slide Show

Elements 13 offers a new Slide Show option. The new Slide Show view is intended for a quick and easy viewing of your selected photos with a fixed transition and options for exporting the slide show to a movie file. Here's how it works:

1. **Select photos in the Organizer and click the Slide Show button.**

   You open the photos in a slide show view, as shown in Figure 6-4.

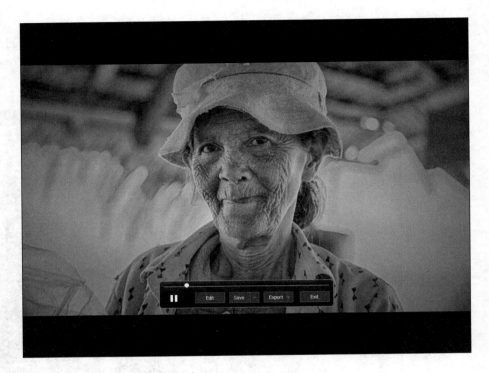

Figure 6-4: The default slide show view.

2. **Click the Edit button.**

   You are taken to the Slideshow Builder window, shown in Figure 6-5.

3. **Use the options in the Slideshow Builder to create your slide show.**

   You can try out the themes, add audio and captions, and insert text slides. The Speed menu offers different options that affect the pace of your slide show. Click the Preview button to see how your edits and selections work. You can continue to make edits and preview your slide show until you're happy with the result.

4. **Click the Export button to export your slideshow to a movie file that you can share.**

   You can open the Export menu from either the first Slide Show screen or when in the Slideshow builder. There are two options available for exporting:

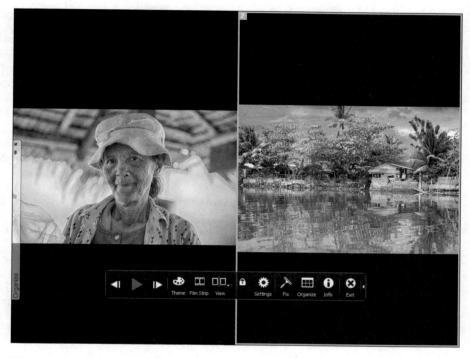

**Figure 6-5:** The Slideshow Builder enables you to add and delete photos from your slide show.

- You can choose Export to a Local Disk (that is, save the file to your computer's hard drive) and choose from one of three video export options.

- You can choose to export a movie file direct to your Facebook account.

We cover the video export options and uploading to Facebook thoroughly in Chapter 15.

## Searching for Photos

When you're looking for a photo, but aren't quite sure how you filed it away, the Elements search options are a great tool. You probably remember some detail that can help you find the photo or photos you're looking for. In Elements, you'll likely find a search tool that can look for that specific detail or details so that you locate your photo in no time.

## Using Search

Before we explore the many options you have from menu commands on the Find menu, look at the Media Browser. At the top, you find a text box and magnifying glass. You type search criteria in the text box and press Enter or Return to search through your catalog and find matches for your criteria. If you click the magnifying glass to open a drop-down list, you find more options to narrow your search.

This search feature in Elements is very powerful. Not only can you search for a single criterion (such as searching for a person's name), but you can take advantage of Boolean expressions to narrow your search — the AND, OR, and NOT expressions all work. For example, you can search for *Jack AND Jill,* and only photos having both those names in the image metadata, tags, and file-names are returned. Likewise, you can search for *Jack OR Harry NOT Jill,* and photos of either Jack or Harry are returned but not any photos containing Jack and Jill or Harry and Jill.

To get a feel for how you use Boolean expressions, play around with the Search text box and experiment a little. When you become familiar with this powerful search feature in the Organizer, you'll find yourself reaching for the Search text box before going to the many menu commands on the Find menu.

### Searching for untagged items

You can tag files with a number of different criteria, as we explain in Chapter 5. When tags are added to images, you can sort files according to tag labels. We also cover sorting by tag labels in Chapter 5. For now, look at the Find menu and notice the Untagged Items command.

 If you haven't added tags to some items and want to show only the untagged files so that you can begin to add tags, choose Find➪Untagged Items or press Ctrl+Shift+Q on Windows or ⌘+Shift+O on the Mac. Elements displays all files without tags in the Media Browser, so you can easily see which photos need to be tagged.

### Searching captions and notes

Captions and notes are added in the Information panel. When captions or notes are added to files, you can search for the caption name, contents of a note, or both. To search caption names and notes, follow these steps:

1. **Make sure you have media added to the Organizer.**

   See Chapter 4 for details.

2. **Add captions and/or notes.**

   If you don't have any files tagged with captions or notes, you need to add them in the Information panel. Open the Information panel and type captions and notes in the respective text boxes.

3. **Choose Find⇨By Caption or Note.**

   The Find by Caption or Note dialog box opens, as shown in Figure 6-6.

4. **In the Find Items with Caption or Note text box, type the words you want to locate and choose to match all or part of the word or words you typed.**

   Options in the dialog box are

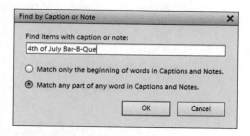

Figure 6-6: In the Find by Caption or Note dialog box, specify search criteria.

   - *Match Only the Beginning of Words in Captions and Notes:* Select this radio button when you know that your caption or note begins with words you type in the text box.

   - *Match Any Part of Any Word in Captions and Notes:* Select this radio button if you're not sure whether the text typed in the box is used at the beginning of a caption or note, or whether it's contained within the caption name or note text.

5. **Click OK.**

   The results appear in the Organizer.

## Searching by history

Searching *history* is searching for chronologically ordered information about operations performed on your media, such as printing, emailing, sharing, and so on. Elements keeps track of what you do with your photos when you perform a number of different tasks. You can search for files based on their file history by choosing Find⇨By History. Select the options you want on the By History submenu, and Elements reports files found on date searches that meet your history criteria.

## Searching metadata

*Metadata* includes information about your images that's supplied by digital cameras, as well as custom data you add to a file. Metadata contains descriptions of the image, such as your camera name, the camera settings you used to take a picture, copyright information, and much more.

Metadata also includes some of the information you add in Elements, such as keyword tags, albums, People tags, and so on. You can combine various metadata items in your search, such as keyword tags, camera make and model, f-stop, ISO setting, and so on. Searching for metadata might be particularly helpful when you have photos taken during an event by several family members and friends. In this example, you might want to isolate only those photos taken with a particular camera model.

To search metadata, follow these steps:

1. **Choose Find⇨By Details (Metadata) in the Organizer.**

   The Find by Details (Metadata) dialog box, shown in Figure 6-7, opens.

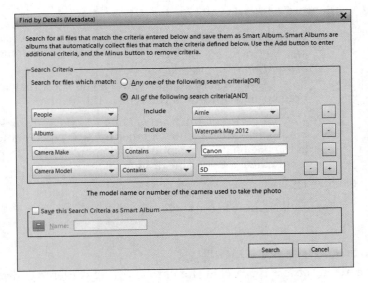

Figure 6-7: Choose Find⇨By Details (Metadata) in the Organizer to open the dialog box in which metadata are specified.

2. **Choose to search for one criterion or all your criteria by selecting a radio button.**

   The first two radio buttons in the dialog box offer choices for Boolean OR and Boolean AND. In other words, do you want to search for one item *or* another, or to search for one item *and* another. The results can be quite different depending on the criteria you identify in the menus below the radio buttons.

3. **Choose an item from the first menu (we used People in Figure 6-6) and then choose to include or exclude the item. Next fill in the third column.**

   How you fill in the third column depends on your selections in the first two columns.

   Items are listed as menus in horizontal rows. The third column can be a menu or a text box, as shown in Figure 6-6.

4. **(Optional) To add criteria (in our example, we use four items for our search), click the plus (+) symbol.**

   Another row is added to the dialog box, and you select your choices as explained in Step 3.

5. **After identifying your search criteria, click Search.**

   The media matching the criteria is shown in the Media Browser.

## Searching similarities

We discuss tagging people in Chapter 5. When you have people tagged, you can easily click the People tab at the top of the Organizer and locate all the people you have tagged.

### Searching visually similar photos

Elements also lets you search photos for visual similarities. You may have group shots, architecture, animal life, and so on and want to search for photos containing objects that are visually similar.

To search for photos with visual similarities, choose Find⇨By Visual Searches, Visually Similar Photos and Videos, Objects within Photos, and Duplicate Photos.

### Searching duplicates

You may have a number of photos that are duplicates or are very close to being duplicate images. You might want to locate duplicates or near-duplicate images and delete some from your catalog or stack the photos. (See "Stacking 'em up," later in this chapter.) Searching for duplicates is a two-step process:

1. **Choose Find⇨By Visual Searches⇨Visually Similar Photos and Videos.**

2. **Choose Find⇨By Visual Searches menu and choose Duplicate Photos.**

Photos that are visually similar appear in horizontal rows. Notice the Stack button on the right side of the figure. Click Stack, and the photos are stacked.

If you want to delete photos, click a photo and then click the Remove from Catalog button at the bottom of the window.

### Searching objects

You may want to stack or delete photos that contain similar objects, such as buildings, automobiles, trees, groups of people, and so on. To search for objects, follow these steps:

1. **Choose Find⇨By Visual Searches⇨Visually Similar Photos and Videos.**

2. **Search again and choose Objects within Photos from the By Visual Searches submenu.**

   A rectangle appears for selecting a photo that contains the object you want to search.

3. **Move the rectangle and resize it so it surrounds the object you're looking for, as shown in Figure 6-8.**

4. **Click the Search Object button**

   Elements displays its search results.

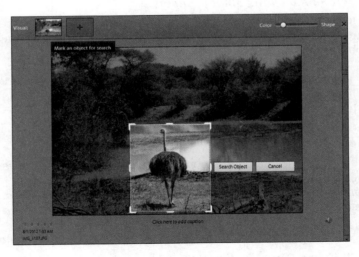

Figure 6-8: Mark the object you want to search and then click the Search Object button.

# Grouping Files That Get in the Way

Elements offers a few ways to organize images that are getting in the way. You can hide files, stack files, or create versions, as we explain in the following sections.

## Marking files as hidden

With a simple menu command, you can mark selected files in the Organizer as *hidden*. Select files you want to hide, and, from either the Edit menu or a contextual menu, choose Visibility⇨Mark as Hidden. To see the files you mark for hiding, return to the same Visibility menu and choose Show Hidden. Essentially, you remove the check mark for Show Hidden, which results in the files being hidden. To easily toggle between showing and hiding files marked for hiding, choose View⇨Hidden Files.

## Stacking 'em up

Think of a *stack* of images as like a stack of cards that's face-up: You see only the front card, and all the other cards are hidden behind that card. Stacks in the Organizer work the same way. You hide different images behind a foreground image. At any time, you can sort the images or display all images in the stack in the Organizer.

To create a stack, follow these steps:

1. **In the Organizer, select several photos.**

   You can select any number of photos. However, you can't stack audio or movie files.

2. **Choose Edit⇨Stack⇨Stack Selected Photos.**

   Elements stacks your photos. The first image you select remains in view in the Media Browser. In the upper-right area, an icon that looks like a stack of cards appears on the image thumbnail when you've stacked some images.

3. **Double-click the photo to open the stack in the Media Browser.**

   You find the stack icon in the top-right corner, as shown in Figure 6-9.

In Figure 6-9 (top of the figure), you see an arrow icon to the right of a stack. Click the arrow, and the stack expands. A left-pointing arrow (bottom of Figure 6-9) appears on the right of the last image in a stack. Click this arrow, and the stack is collapsed.

Closed Stack

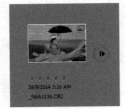

Open Stack

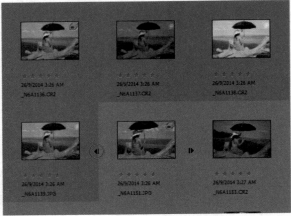

Figure 6-9: Viewing a stack in the Media Browser.

After you stack a group of images, you can use the Stack submenu commands to manage the photos. Click a stack to select it and then choose Edit⇨Stack. The available submenu commands are as follows:

- Automatically Suggest Photo Stacks
- Stack Selected Photos
- Unstack Photos
- Expand Photos in Stack
- Collapse Photos in Stack
- Flatten Stack

When you flatten a stack, all photos except for the top photo are deleted from the catalog but not from your hard drive.

> ✒ Remove Photo from Stack
>
> ✒ Set as Top Photo

To view all stacks in the Media Browser in expanded form, choose View⇨ Expand All Stacks. Using this command doesn't require you to individually select stacks in the Media Browser before expanding them.

## Creating versions

*Versions* are similar to stacks, but you create versions from only one file. You can edit an image and save both the edited version and the original as a version set. Also, you can make additional edits in either editing mode and save to a version set. To create a version set, follow these steps:

1. **Select an image by clicking it in the Media Browser.**

2. **Apply an edit.**

   For example, right in the Organizer, you can correct some brightness problems in your image. Click Instant Fix to open the Instant Fix panel and click one of the tools in the panel. See Chapter 9 for more details on using the Instant Fix tools or any other editing tool.

3. **Save the edited file in a version set.**

   Choose File⇨Save As. In the Save As dialog box under Save Options, select Save in Version Set with Original.

4. **View the items in the version set by clicking the image in the Media Browser and choosing Edit⇨Version Set⇨Expand Items in Version Set.**

   Elements automatically creates a version set for you when you apply the Instant Fix to the file. The Media Browser shows two thumbnail images — one representing the original image and the other representing the edited version.

5. **To open the original image in the Photo Editor, select the image in the Media Browser, and then click the Editor button.**

6. **Edit the image in Expert mode.**

   You can choose from many different menu commands to edit the image. For example, change the color mode to Indexed Color by choosing Image⇨Mode⇨Indexed Color, as we explain in Chapter 2.

7. **Save a version by choosing File⇨Save As.**

8. **In the Save Options area of the Save As dialog box, select the Include in the Organizer and Save in Version Set with Original check boxes.**

   Chapter 2 also explains the options for saving files.

9. **Click Save.**

   The edits made in the Photo Editor are saved as another version in your version set.

After you create a version set, you find additional submenu commands that you can use to manage the version set. Choose Edit⇨Version Set or right-click a version set and then choose Version Set.

# Part III
# Selecting and Correcting Photos

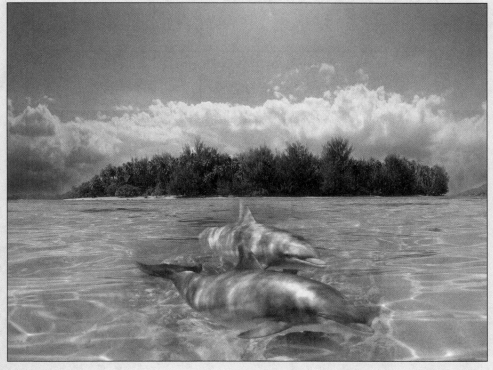

©istockphoto/meltonmedia Image #1779174, tomh1000 Image #1281272

Visit www.dummies.com/extras/photoshopelements to find guided steps for correcting your images.

## In this part . . .

✔ Change, optimize, perfect, and combine images into composite designs.

✔ Select image content and then alter that content for a variety of purposes, such as correcting the color, changing the appearance, and extracting the content so that you can add it to other photos.

✔ Correct an image's contrast, brightness, and color irregularity.

✔ Convert one color mode to another.

# 7

# Making and Modifying Selections

## In This Chapter

▶ Creating selections with the Lasso tools, Magic Wand, and more

▶ Using the Cookie Cutter tool

▶ Rubbing away pixels with the Eraser tools

▶ Saving and loading your selections

*I*f all you want to do is use your photos in all their unedited glory, feel free to skip this chapter and move on to other topics. But if you want to occasionally pluck an element out of its environment and stick it in another or apply an adjustment to just a portion of your image, this chapter's for you.

Finding out how to make accurate selections is one of those skills that's well worth the time you invest. In this chapter, we cover all the various selection tools and techniques. We also give you tips on which tools are better for which kinds of selections. But remember that you usually have several ways to achieve the same result. Which road you choose is ultimately up to you.

## Defining Selections

Before you dig in and get serious about selecting, let us clarify for the record what we mean by "defining a selection." When you *define* a selection, you specify which part of an image you want to work with. Everything within a selection is considered selected. Everything outside the selection is unselected. After you have a selection, you can then adjust only that portion, and the unselected portion remains unchanged. Or you can copy the selected area into another image altogether. Want to transport yourself out of your background and onto a white, sandy beach? Select yourself out of that backyard BBQ photo, get a stock photo of the tropical paradise of your choice, and drag and drop yourself onto your tropics photo with the Move tool. It's that easy.

When you make a selection, a dotted outline — dubbed a *selection border,* an *outline,* or a *marquee* — appears around the selected area. Elements, the sophisticated imaging program that it is, also allows you to partially select pixels, which allows for soft-edged selections. You create soft-edged selections by feathering the selection or by using a mask. Don't worry: We cover these techniques in the section "Applying Marquee options," later in this chapter.

For all the selection techniques described in this chapter, be sure that your image is in Expert mode in the Photo Editor and not in Quick or Guided modes or in the Organizer.

# Creating Rectangular and Elliptical Selections

If you can drag a mouse, you can master the Rectangular and Elliptical Marquee tools. These are the easiest selection tools to use, so if your desired element is rectangular or elliptical, by all means, grab one of these tools.

The Rectangular Marquee tool, as its moniker states, is designed to define rectangular (including square) selections. This tool is great to use if you want to home in on the pertinent portion of your photo and eliminate unnecessary background.

Here's how to make a selection with this tool:

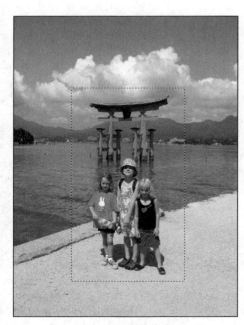

1. **Select the Rectangular Marquee tool from the Tools panel.**

   The tool looks like a dotted square. You can also press M to access the tool. If the tool isn't visible, press M.

2. **Drag from one corner of the area you want to select to the opposite corner.**

   While you drag, the selection border appears. The marquee follows the movement of your mouse cursor.

3. **Release your mouse button.**

   You have a completed rectangular selection, as shown in Figure 7-1.

**Figure 7-1:** Use the Rectangular Marquee tool to create rectangular selections.

The Elliptical Marquee tool is designed for elliptical (including circular) selections. This tool is perfect for selecting balloons, clocks, and other rotund elements.

Here's how to use the Elliptical Marquee:

1. **Select the Elliptical Marquee tool from the Marquee flyout menu on the Tools panel.**

   The tool looks like a dotted ellipse. You can also press M to access this tool if it's visible; if it isn't, press M.

2. **Position the crosshair near the area you want to select and then drag around your desired element.**

   With this tool, you drag from a given point on the ellipse. While you drag, the selection border appears.

3. **When you're satisfied with your selection, release the mouse button.**

   Your elliptical selection is created, as shown in Figure 7-2. If your selection isn't quite centered around your element, simply move the selection border by dragging inside the border.

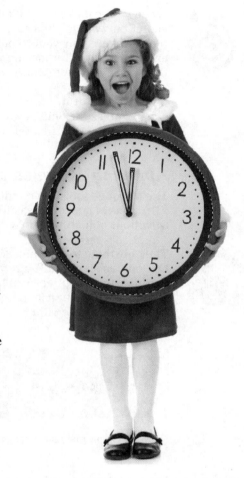

©istockphoto.com/sjlocke Image #14312433

**Figure 7-2:** The Elliptical Marquee tool is perfect for selecting round objects.

You can move a selection while you're making it with either of the Marquee tools by holding down the spacebar while you're dragging.

## Perfecting squares and circles with Shift and Alt (Option on the Mac)

Sometimes you need to create a perfectly square or circular selection. To do so, simply press the Shift key after you begin dragging. After you make your selection, release the mouse button and then release the Shift key. You can also set the aspect ratio to 1:1 in the Tool Options.

When you're making an elliptical selection, making the selection from the center outward is often easier. To draw from the center, first click the mouse button where you want to position the center, press Alt (Option on the Mac), and then drag. After making your selection, release the mouse button and then release the Alt (Option on the Mac) key.

If you want to draw from the center outward *and* create a perfect circle or square, press the Shift key as well. After you make your selection, release the mouse button and then release the Shift+Alt (Shift+Option on the Mac) keys.

## Applying Marquee options

The Marquee tools offer additional options when you need to make precise selections at specific measurements. You also find options for making your selections soft around the edges.

The only thing to remember is that you must select the options in the Tool Options, as shown in Figure 7-3, before you make your selection with the Marquee tools. Options can't be applied after the selection has already been made. The exception is that you can feather a selection after the fact by choosing Select⇨Feather.

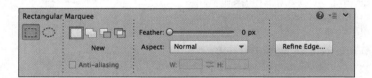

Figure 7-3: Apply Marquee settings in the Tool Options.

Here are the various Marquee options available to you:

- **Feather:** Feathering creates soft edges around your selection. The amount of softness depends on the value, from 0 to 250 pixels, that you enter by adjusting the slider. The higher the value, the softer the edges, as shown in Figure 7-4. Very small amounts of feathering can be used to create subtle transitions between selected elements in a collage or for blending an element into an existing background. Larger amounts are often used when you're combining multiple layers so that one image gradually fades into another. If you want a selected element to have just a soft edge without the background, simply choose Select⇨Inverse and delete the background. See more on inversing selections in the "Modifying Your Selections" section, later in this chapter. For more on layers, see Chapter 8.

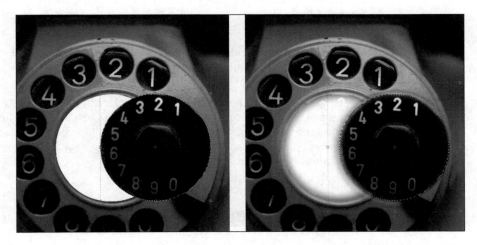

©istockphoto.com/cobalt Image #1275827

Figure 7-4: Feathering creates soft-edged selections.

Don't forget that those soft edges represent partially selected pixels.

✔ **Anti-aliasing:** Antialiasing barely softens the edge of an elliptical or irregularly shaped selection so that the jagged edges aren't quite so obvious. An antialiased edge is always only 1 pixel wide. We recommend leaving this option chosen for your selections. Doing so can help to create natural transitions between multiple selections when you're creating collages.

✔ **Aspect:** The Aspect drop-down list contains three settings:

- *Normal:* The default setting, which allows you to freely drag a selection of any size.

- *Fixed Ratio:* Lets you specify a fixed ratio of width to height. For example, if you enter **3** for width and **1** for height, you get a selection that's three times as wide as it is high, no matter what the size.

- *Fixed Size:* Lets you specify desired values for the width and height. This setting can be useful when you need to make several selections that must be the same size.

✔ **Width (W) and Height (H):** When you choose Fixed Ratio or Fixed Size from the Aspect drop-down list, you must also enter your desired values in the Width and Height text boxes. To swap the Width and Height values, click the double-headed arrow button between the two measurements.

✔ **Refine Edge:** For details on this great option, see "Refining the edges of a selection," later in this chapter.

The default unit of measurement in the Width and Height text boxes is pixels (px), but that doesn't mean that you're stuck with it. You can enter any unit of measurement that Elements recognizes: pixels, inches (in), centimeters (cm), millimeters (mm), points (pt), picas (pica), or percentages (%). Type your value and then type the word or abbreviation of your unit of measurement.

## Making Freeform Selections with the Lasso Tools

You can't select everything with a rectangle or an ellipse. Life is just way too freeform for that. Most animate, and many inanimate, objects have undulations of varying sorts. Luckily, Elements anticipated the need to capture these shapes and provided the Lasso tools.

The Lasso tools enable you to make any freehand selection you can think of. Elements generously provides three types of Lasso tools:

✔ Lasso

✔ Polygonal

✔ Magnetic

Although all three tools are designed to make freeform selections, they differ slightly in their methodology, as we explain in the sections that follow.

To use these tools, all that's really required is a steady hand. You'll find that the more you use the Lasso tools, the better you become at your tracing technique. Don't worry if your initial lasso selection isn't super-accurate. You can always go back and make corrections by adding and deleting from your selection. To find out how, see the section "Modifying Your Selections," later in this chapter.

If you find that you really love the Lasso tools, you may want to invest in a digital drawing tablet and stylus. This device makes tracing (and also drawing and painting) on the computer more comfortable. It better mimics pen and paper, and many users swear that they'll never go back to a mouse after trying it out. This is especially handy for laptop users. Accurately drawing on a trackpad can make you downright cranky.

## Selecting with the Lasso tool

Using the Lasso tool is the digital version of tracing an outline around an object on a piece of paper. It's that easy. And you have only three choices in the Tool Options — Feather, Antialias, and Refine Edge. To find out more about Feather and Antialias, see the section "Applying Marquee options," earlier in this chapter. For the scoop on Refine Edge, see the section "Refining the edges of a selection," later in this chapter.

Here's how to make a selection with the Lasso tool:

1. **Select the Lasso tool from the Tools panel.**

   It's the tool that looks like a rope. You can also just press the L key. If the Lasso tool isn't visible, press L to cycle through the various Lasso flavors.

2. **Position the cursor anywhere along the edge of the object you want to select.**

   The leading point of the cursor is the protruding end of the rope, as shown in Figure 7-5. Don't be afraid to zoom in to your object, using the Zoom tool — or, more conveniently, pressing Control++ (⌘++ on the Mac) — if you need to see the edge more distinctly. In this figure, we started at the top of the tulip.

3. **Hold down the mouse button and trace around your desired object.**

   Try to include only what you want to select. While you trace around your object, an outline follows the mouse cursor.

Lasso cursor

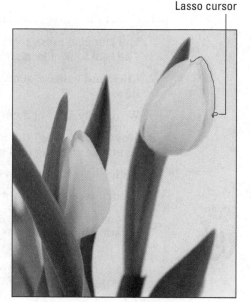

©istockphoto.com/jtyler Image #2723146

Figure 7-5: The Lasso tool makes freeform selections.

Try not to release the mouse button until you return to your starting point. When you release the mouse button, Elements assumes that you're done and closes the selection from wherever you released the mouse button to your starting point; if you release the button too early, Elements creates a straight line across your image.

4. **Continue tracing around the object and return to your starting point; release the mouse button to close the selection.**

   You see a selection border that matches your lasso line. Look for a small circle that appears next to your lasso cursor when you return to your starting point. This icon indicates that you're closing the selection at the proper spot.

## Getting straight with the Polygonal Lasso tool

The Polygonal Lasso tool has a specific mission in life: to select any element whose sides are straight. Think pyramids, stairways, skyscrapers, barns — you get the idea. It also works a tad differently from the Lasso tool. You don't drag around the element with the Polygonal Lasso. Instead, you click and release the mouse button at the corners of the element you're selecting. The Polygonal Lasso tool acts like a stretchy rubber band.

Follow these steps to select with the Polygonal Lasso tool:

1. **Select the Polygonal Lasso tool from the Tools panel.**

   You can also press the L key to cycle through the various Lasso tools. The tool looks like a straight-sided lasso rope.

2. **Click and release at any point to start the Polygonal Lasso selection line.**

   We usually start at a corner.

3. **Move (don't drag) the mouse and click at the next corner of the object. Continue clicking and moving to each corner of your element.**

   Notice how the line stretches out from each point you click.

4. **Return to your starting point and click to close the selection.**

   Be on the lookout for a small circle that appears next to your lasso cursor when you return to your starting point. This circle is an indication that you're indeed closing the selection at the right spot.

   *Note:* You can also double-click at any point, and Elements closes the selection from that point to the starting point.

   After you close the polygonal lasso line, a selection border appears, as shown in Figure 7-6.

Polygonal lasso selection border

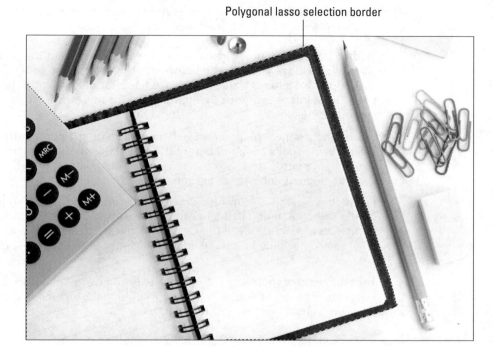

©istockhoto.com/fotostorm Image #17970388

**Figure 7-6:** After you close the polygonal lasso line, Elements creates a selection border.

## Snapping with the Magnetic Lasso tool

The third member of the Lasso team is the Magnetic Lasso. We aren't huge fans of this Lasso tool, which can sometimes be hard to work with. However, we show you how it works so that you can decide whether to use it. The Magnetic Lasso tool works by defining the areas of the most contrast in an image and then snapping to the edge between those areas, as though the edge has a magnetic pull.

You have the most success using the Magnetic Lasso tool on an image that has a well-defined foreground object and high contrast between that element and the background — for example, a dark mountain range against a light sky.

The Magnetic Lasso tool also has some unique settings, which you can adjust in the Tool Options before you start selecting:

- **Width:** Determines how close to the edge (between 1 and 256 pixels) you have to move your mouse before the Magnetic Lasso tool snaps to that edge. Use a lower value if the edge has a lot of detail or if the contrast in the image is low. Use a higher value for high-contrast images or smoother edges.

- **Contrast:** Specifies the percentage of contrast (from 1 percent to 100 percent) that's required before the Magnetic Lasso snaps to an edge. Use a higher percentage if your image has good contrast between your desired element and the background.

- **Frequency:** Specifies how many fastening points (from 1 to 100) to place on the selection line. The higher the value, the greater the number of points. As a general rule, if the element you want to select has a smooth edge, keep the value low. If the edge has a lot of detail, try a higher value.

- **Tablet Pressure (pen icon):** If you're the proud owner of a pressure-sensitive drawing tablet, select this option to make an increase in stylus pressure cause the edge width to decrease.

Follow these steps to use the Magnetic Lasso tool:

1. **Select the Magnetic Lasso tool from the Tools panel.**

   You can also press the L key to cycle through the various Lasso tools. The Magnetic Lasso tool looks like a straight-sided lasso with a little magnet on it.

2. **Click the edge of the object that you want to select to place the first fastening point.**

   *Fastening points* anchor the selection line, as shown in Figure 7-7. You can start anywhere; just be sure to click the edge between the element you want and the background you don't want.

3. **Continue to move your cursor around the object without clicking.**

   While the selection line gets pinned down with fastening points, only the newest portion of the selection line remains active.

   If the Magnetic Lasso tool starts veering off the desired edge of your object, back up your mouse and click to force down a fastening point. Conversely, if the Magnetic Lasso tool adds a fastening point where you don't want one, press Backspace (Delete on the Mac) to delete it. Successive presses of the Backspace or Delete key continue to remove the fastening points.

If the Magnetic Lasso isn't cooperating, you can temporarily switch to the other Lasso tools. To select the Lasso tool, hold down Alt (Option on the Mac), click the mouse button, and drag. To select the Polygonal Lasso tool, hold down Alt (Option on the Mac) and click.

4. **Return to your starting point and click the mouse button to close the selection.**

   You see a small circle next to your cursor, indicating that you're at the right spot to close the selection. You can also double-click, whereby Elements closes the selection from where you double-clicked to your starting point. The selection border appears when the selection is closed.

Magnetic Lasso anchor points

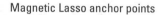

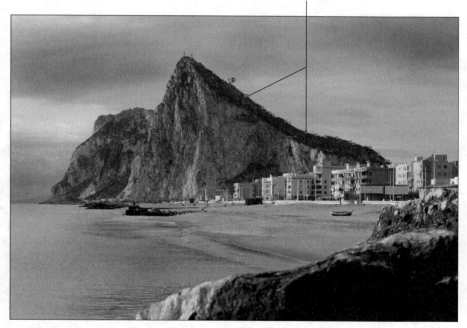

©istockphoto.com/swilmor Image #3160253

**Figure 7-7:** The Magnetic Lasso tool snaps to the edge of your element and places fastening points to anchor the selection.

# Working Wizardry with the Magic Wand

The Magic Wand tool is one of the oldest tools in the world of digital imaging. This beloved tool has been around since Photoshop was in its infancy and Elements was not yet a twinkle in Adobe's eye. It's extremely easy to use, but you'll have a somewhat harder time predicting what selection results it will present.

Here's how the Magic Wand tool works: You click inside the image, and the Magic Wand tool makes a selection. This selection is based on the color of the pixel you clicked. If other pixels are similar in color to your target pixel, Elements includes them in the selection. What's sometimes hard to predict, however, is how to determine *how* similar the color has to be to get the Magic Wand tool to select it. Fortunately, that's where the Tolerance setting comes in. In the sections that follow, we first introduce you to this setting and then explain how to put the Magic Wand to work.

## Talking about Tolerance

The Tolerance setting determines the range of color that the Magic Wand tool selects. The range of color is based on brightness levels, ranging from 0 to 255:

- Setting the Tolerance to 0 selects one color only.
- Setting the Tolerance to 255 selects all colors, or the whole image.

The default setting is 32, so whenever you click a pixel, Elements analyzes the value of that base color and then selects all pixels whose brightness levels are between 16 levels lighter and 16 levels darker.

What if an image contains a few shades of the same color? It's not a huge problem. You can make multiple clicks of the Magic Wand to pick up additional pixels that you want to include in the selection. You can find out how in the section "Modifying Your Selections," later in this chapter. Or you can try a higher Tolerance setting. Conversely, if your wand selects too much, you can also lower your Tolerance setting.

So you can see by our talk on tolerance that the Magic Wand tool works best when you have high-contrast images or images with a limited number of colors. For example, the optimum image for the Wand would be a solid black object on a white background. Skip the wand if the image has a ton of colors and no real definitive contrast between your desired element and the background.

## Wielding the Wand to select

To use the Magic Wand tool and adjust its Tolerance settings, follow these steps:

1. **Select the Magic Wand tool from the Tools panel.**

   It looks like a wand with a starburst on the end. You can also just press A to cycle through the Magic Wand, Quick Selection, and Selection Brush tools. Or you can choose any of the tools and then select your desired tool in the Tool Options.

2. **Click anywhere on your desired element, using the default Tolerance setting of 32.**

   The pixel you click determines the base color.

   If the Pixel Gods are with you and you selected everything you want on the first click, you're done. If your selection needs further tweaking, like the top image shown in Figure 7-8, continue to Step 3.

3. **Specify a new Tolerance setting in the Tool Options.**

   If the Magic Wand selects more than you want, lower the Tolerance setting. If the wand didn't select enough, increase the value. While you're poking around in the Tool Options, here are a couple more options to get familiar with:

   - *Sample All Layers:* If you have multiple layers and enable this option, the Magic Wand selects pixels from all visible layers. Without this option, the tool selects pixels from the active layer only. For more on layers, see Chapter 8.

   - *Contiguous:* Forces the Magic Wand to select only pixels that are adjacent to each other. Without this option, the tool selects all pixels within the range of tolerance, whether or not they're adjacent to each other.

REMEMBER

Tolerance 32

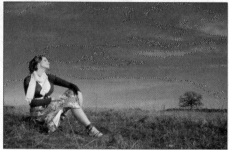

Tolerance 90

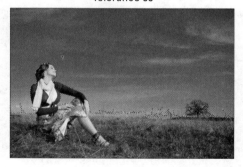

©istockphoto.com/bholland Image #5314427

**Figure 7-8:** The Magic Wand selects pixels based on a specified Tolerance setting.

- *Anti-aliasing:* Softens the edge of the selection by one row of pixels. See the section "Applying Marquee options," earlier in this chapter, for details.

- *Refine Edge:* Click the Refine Edge button. In the Refine Edge dialog box, clean up your selection by moving the Smooth slider to reduce the amount of jagginess in your edges. Feather works like the Feather option discussed in the "Applying Marquee options" section, earlier in the chapter. Move the Shift Edge slider to the left or right to decrease or increase the selected area, respectively. For even more details, see the section "Refining the edges of a selection," later in this chapter. We explain yet another way to refine edges (which you don't find in the Tool Options) in "Applying the Grow and Similar commands," also later in this chapter.

4. **Click your desired element again.**

   Unfortunately, the Magic Wand tool isn't magical enough to modify your first selection automatically. Instead, it deselects the current selection and makes a new selection based on your new Tolerance setting. If it still isn't right, you can adjust the Tolerance setting again. Try, try again.

## Modifying Your Selections

It's time for a seventh-inning stretch in this chapter on selection tools. In this section, you can find out how to refine that Marquee, Lasso, or Magic Wand selection to perfection.

You're not limited to the manual methods described in the following sections or even to keyboard shortcuts. You can also use the four selection option buttons on the left side of the Tool Options to create a new selection (the default), add to a selection, subtract from a selection, or intersect one selection with another. Just choose your desired selection tool, click the selection option button you want, and drag (or click if you're using the Magic Wand or Polygonal Lasso tool).

### Adding to, subtracting from, and intersecting a selection

Although the Marquee, Lasso, or Magic Wand tools do an okay job of capturing the bulk of your selection, if you take the time to add or subtract a bit from your selection border, you can ensure that you get only what you really want:

- **Add:** If your selection doesn't quite contain all the elements you want to capture, you need to add those portions to your current selection border. To add to a current Marquee selection, simply press the Shift key and drag around the area you want to include. If you're using the Polygonal Lasso, click around the area. And if you're wielding the Magic Wand, just press the Shift key and click the area you want.

You don't have to use the same tool to add to your selection that you used to create the original selection. Feel free to use whatever selection tool you think can get the job done. For example, it's very common to start off with the Magic Wand and fine-tune with the Lasso tool.

✔ **Subtract:** Got too much? To subtract from a current selection, press the Alt (Option on the Mac) key and drag the marquee around the pixels you want to subtract. With the Alt (Option on the Mac) key, use the same method for the Magic Wand and Polygonal Lasso as you do for adding to a selection.

✔ **Intersect two selections:** Get your fingers in shape. To intersect your existing selection with a second selection, press Shift+Alt (Shift+Option on the Mac) and drag with the Lasso or Marquee tools. Or, if you're using the Magic Wand or Polygonal Lasso, press those keys and click rather than drag. Your selection now includes only the area common to both selections.

## Avoiding key collisions

If you read the beginning of this chapter, you found out that by pressing the Shift key, you get a perfectly square or circular selection. We tell you in the section "Adding to, subtracting from, and intersecting a selection," earlier in this chapter, that if you want to add to a selection, you press the Shift key. What if you want to create a perfect square while adding to the selection? Or what if you want to delete part of a selection while also drawing from the center outward? Both require the use of the Alt (Option on the Mac) key. How in the heck does Elements know what you want? Here are a few tips to avoid keyboard collisions — grab your desired Marquee tool:

✔ **To add a square or circular selection, press Shift and drag.** While you drag, keep the mouse button pressed, release the Shift key for just a second, and then press it again. Your added selection area suddenly snaps into a square or circle. You must then release the mouse button and then release the Shift key.

✔ **To delete from an existing selection while drawing from the center outward, press Alt (Option on the Mac) and drag.** While you drag, keep the mouse button pressed, release the Alt (Option on the Mac) key for just a second, and then press it down again. You're now drawing from the center outward. Again, release the mouse button first and then release the Alt (Option on the Mac) key.

You can also use the selection option buttons in the Tool Options.

# Painting with the Selection Brush

If you like the organic feel of painting on a canvas, you'll appreciate the Selection Brush. Using two different modes, you can either paint over areas of an image that you want to select or paint over areas you don't want to select. This great tool also lets you first make a basic, rudimentary selection with another tool, such as the Lasso, and then fine-tune the selection by brushing additional pixels into or out of the selection.

Here's the step-by-step process of selecting with the Selection Brush:

1. **Select the Selection Brush from the Tools panel.**

   It looks like a paintbrush with a dotted oval around the tip. Or simply press the A key to cycle through the Selection Brush, Quick Selection, and Magic Wand tools. You can also select any of these tools and then choose your desired tool in the Tool Options.

   This tool works in either Expert or Quick mode.

2. **Specify your Selection Brush options in the Tool Options.**

   Here's the rundown on each option:

   - *Mode:* Choose Selection if you want to paint over what you *want* to select or Mask if you want to paint over what you *don't* want.

     If you choose Mask mode, you must choose some additional overlay options. An *overlay* is a layer of color (that shows onscreen only) that hovers over your image, indicating protected or unselected areas. You must also choose an overlay opacity between 1 and 100 percent (which we describe in the Tip at the end of these steps). You can change the overlay color from the default red to another color. This option can be helpful if your image contains a lot of red.

   - *Brush Presets Picker:* Choose a brush from the presets drop-down list. To load additional brushes, click the downward-pointing arrow to the left of Default Brushes and choose the preset library of your choice. You can select the Load Brushes command from the panel menu (top-right down-pointing arrow).

   - *Size:* Specify a brush size, from 1 to 2,500 pixels. Enter the value or drag the slider.

   - *Hardness:* Set the hardness of the brush tip, from 1 to 100 percent. A harder tip creates a crisper, more defined stroke.

3. **Paint the appropriate areas:**

   - *If your mode is set to Selection*: Paint over the areas you *want* to select.

You see a selection border. Each stroke adds to the selection. (The Add to Selection button in the Tool Options is selected automatically.) If you inadvertently add something you don't want, simply press the Alt (Option on the Mac) key and paint over the undesired area. You can also click the Subtract from Selection button in the Tool Options. After you finish painting what you want, your selection is ready to go.

- *If your mode is set to Mask:* Paint over the areas that you *don't* want to select.

When you're done painting your mask, choose Selection from the Selection/Mask drop-down list or simply choose another tool from the Tool Options, in order to convert your mask into a selection border. Remember that your selection is what you *don't* want.

While you paint, you see the color of your overlay. Each stroke adds more to the overlay area, as shown in Figure 7-9. In the example, the sky is masked (with a red overlay) to replace it with a different sky. When working in Mask mode, you're essentially covering up, or *masking,* the areas you want to protect from manipulation. That manipulation can be selecting, adjusting color, or performing any other Elements command. Again, if you want to remove parts of the masked area, press Alt (Option on the Mac) and paint.

If you painted your selection in Mask mode, your selection border is around what you *don't* want. To switch to what you do want, choose Select⇨Inverse.

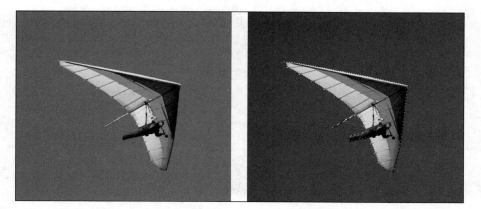

©istockphoto.com/Hanis Image #2054524

**Figure 7-9:** The Selection Brush allows you to make a selection (right) by creating a mask (left).

Which mode should you choose? Well, it's up to you. But one advantage to working in Mask mode is that you can partially select areas. By painting with soft brushes, you create soft-edged selections. These soft edges result in partially selected pixels. If you set the overlay opacity to a lower percentage, your pixels are even less opaque, or "less selected." If this partially selected business sounds vaguely familiar, it's because this is also what happens when you feather selections, as we discuss in the section "Applying Marquee options," earlier in this chapter.

## Painting with the Quick Selection Tool

Think of the Quick Selection tool as a combination Brush, Magic Wand, and Lasso tool. Good news — it lives up to its "quick" moniker. Better news — it's also easy to use. The best news? It gives pretty decent results, so give it a whirl.

Here's how to make short work of selecting with this tool:

1. **Select the Quick Selection tool from the Tools panel.**

   The tool looks like a wand with a marquee around the end. It shares the same Tools panel space with the Selection Brush tool and the Magic Wand tool. You can also press the A key to cycle through the Quick Selection, Selection Brush, and Magic Wand tools.

   This tool works in either Expert or Quick mode.

2. **Specify the options in the Tool Options.**

   Here's a description of the options:

   - *New Selection:* The default option enables you to create a new selection. There are also options to add to and subtract from your selection.

   - *Size:* Choose your desired brush size. Specify the diameter, from 1 to 2,500 pixels.

   - *Brush Settings:* With these settings, you can specify hardness, spacing, angle, and roundness. For details on these settings, see Chapter 12.

   - *Sample All Layers:* If your image has layers and you want to make a selection from all the layers, select this option. If you leave it deselected, you will select only from the active layer.

   - *Auto-Enhance:* Select this option to have Elements automatically refine your selection by implementing an algorithm.

3. **Drag or paint the desired areas of your image.**

   Your selection grows as you drag, as shown in Figure 7-10. If you stop dragging and click in another portion of your image, your selection includes that clicked area.

4. **Add to or delete from your selection, as desired:**

   - *To add to your selection,* press the Shift key while dragging across your desired image areas.

   - *To delete from your selection,* press the Alt (Option on the Mac) key while dragging across your unwanted image areas.

   You can also select the Add to Selection and Subtract from Selection options in the Tool Options.

5. **If you need to fine-tune your selection, click the Refine Edge option in the Tool Options and then change the settings, as desired.**

   The settings are explained in detail in the "Refining the edges of a selection" section, later in this chapter.

   *Note:* If your object is fairly detailed, you may even need to break out the Lasso or another selection tool to make some final cleanups. Eventually, you should arrive at a selection you're happy with.

The selected portion is surrounded by a border.

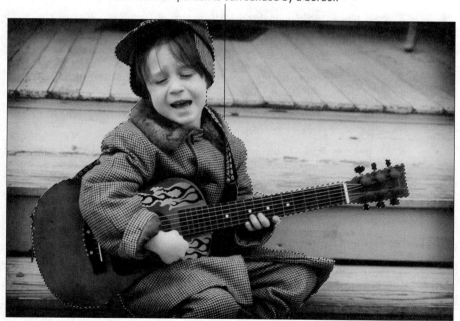

©istockphoto.com/ParkerDeen Image #6013582

**Figure 7-10:** Paint a selection with the Quick Selection tool.

# Fine-Tuning with the Refine Selection Brush

As we mention in the beginning of this chapter, being able to make selections quickly and accurately is a coveted skill. Luckily, Elements has introduced a new tool to make this skill easier to obtain. The Refine Selection Brush helps you to add or delete portions of your selection by automatically detecting edges of your desired element.

Here's how to refine your selections with this new tool:

1. **Make your selection using the Quick Selection tool, Selection Brush, or any other selection tool, for that matter.**

   Elements doesn't care how you make your initial selection, as long as you have one. Don't worry if it isn't perfect. That's where the Refine Selection Brush comes in.

2. **Select the Refine Selection Brush.**

   This tool shares a tool slot with the Quick Selection tool, Magic Wand, and Selection Brush.

   Your cursor appears as two concentric circles, as shown in Figure 7-11. The outer circle reflects the Tolerance setting to detect an edge. For more on tolerance, see "Talking about Tolerance," earlier in this chapter.

3. **Specify the settings in the Tool Options.**

   Here's a description of the options:

   - *Size:* Use the slider to adjust your brush diameter from 1 to 2,500 pixels.

   - *Snap Strength:* Use the slider to adjust your snap strength from 0 to 100%. *Snap Strength* indicates the intensity of the pull.

   - *Add/Subtract:* Choose this option to either add to or subtract from your selection.

   - *Push:* Place your cursor inside the selection to increase your selection within the diameter of the outer circle of your cursor. It will snap to the edge of the element closest to the cursor. Place your cursor outside the selection to decrease your selection within the diameter of the outer circle.

   - *Smooth:* If your selection border looks a little too jagged, use this option to smooth your selection edge.

4. **Continue to use the Refine Selection Brush to perfect your selection until you're satisfied.**

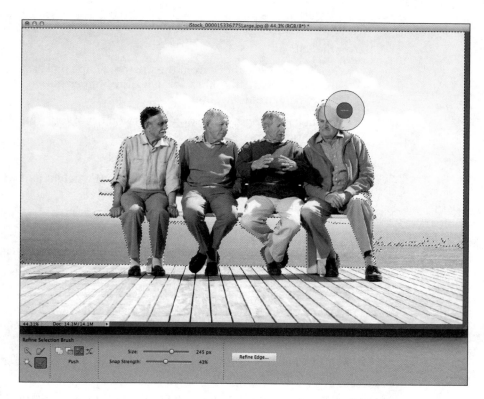

©istockphoto.com/Yuri #000015336775

**Figure 7-11:** Use the new Refine Selection Brush to fine-tune your selection.

# Working with the Cookie Cutter Tool

The Cookie Cutter tool is a cute name for a pretty powerful tool. You can think of it as a Custom Shape tool for images. But, whereas the Custom Shape tool creates a mask and just hides everything outside the shape, the Cookie Cutter tool cuts away everything outside the shape. The preset libraries offer you a large variety of interesting shapes, from talk bubbles to Swiss cheese. (We're not being funny here — check out the food library.)

Here's the lowdown on using the Cookie Cutter:

1. **Select the Cookie Cutter tool from the Tools panel.**

   There's no missing this tool; it looks like a flower. You can also press the C key. The Cookie Cutter lost its private space in the Tools panel and shares a space with the Crop tool. If you don't see it, press C a second time or select the Crop tool and then select the Cookie Cutter in the Tool Options.

2. **Specify your options in the Tool Options.**

   Here's the list:

   - *Shape:* Choose a shape from the Custom Shape picker preset library. To load other libraries, click the Shapes pop-up menu and choose one from the submenu.

   - *Geometry Options:* These options let you draw your shape with certain parameters:

   - *Unconstrained:* Enables you to draw freely.

   - *Defined Proportions:* Enables you to keep the height and width proportional.

   - *Defined Size:* Crops the image to the original, fixed size of the shape you choose. You can't make it bigger or smaller.

   - *Fixed Size:* Allows you to enter your desired width and height.

   - *From Center:* Allows you to draw the shape from the center outward.

   - *Feather:* This option creates a soft-edged selection. See the section "Applying Marquee options," earlier in this chapter, for more details.

   - *Crop:* Click this option to crop the image into the shape. The shape fills the image window.

3. **Drag your mouse on the image to create your desired shape, size the shape by dragging one of the handles of the bounding box, and position the shape by placing the mouse cursor inside the box and dragging.**

   You can also perform other types of transformations, such as rotating and skewing. You can use these functions by dragging the box manually or by entering values in the Tool Options. For more on transformations, see Chapter 9.

4. **Click the Commit button on the image or press Enter to finish the cutout.**

   See Figure 7-12 to see the image cut into a leaf shape. If you want to bail out of the bounding box and not cut out, you can always click the Cancel button on the image or press Esc.

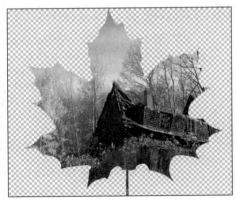

©istockphoto.com/buzbuzzer Image #2272088

**Figure 7-12:** Crop your photo into interesting shapes with the Cookie Cutter.

# Eliminating with the Eraser Tools

The Eraser tools let you erase areas of your image. Elements has three Eraser tools: the regular Eraser, the Magic Eraser, and the Background Eraser. The Eraser tools look like those pink erasers you used in grade school, so you can't miss them. If you can't locate them, you can always press E to cycle through the three tools.

When you erase pixels, those pixels are history — they're gone. So before using the Eraser tools, always have a backup of your image stored somewhere. Think of it as a cheap insurance policy in case things go awry.

## The Eraser tool

The Eraser tool enables you to erase areas on your image to either your background color or, if you're working on a layer, a transparent background, as shown in Figure 7-13. For more on layers, check out Chapter 8.

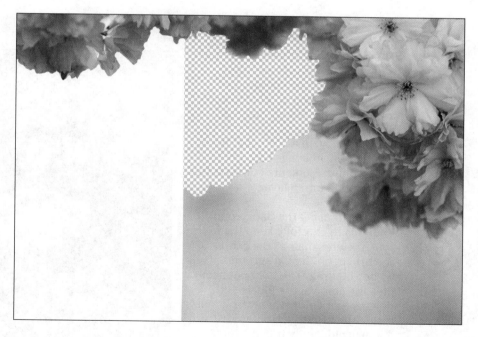

©istockphoto.com/samdiesel Image #6164396

**Figure 7-13:** Erase either to your background color (left) or to transparency (right).

To use this tool, simply select it and drag through the desired area on your image, and you're done. Because it isn't the most accurate tool on the planet, remember to zoom way in and use smaller brush tips to do some accurate erasing.

You have several Eraser options to specify in the Tool Options:

- **Brush Presets Picker:** Click the drop-down list to access the Brush presets. Choose a brush. Again, additional brush libraries are available on the Brush list. (Click the down-pointing arrow in the top-right corner.)

- **Size:** Slide the Size slider and choose a brush size between 1 and 2,500 pixels.

- **Opacity:** Specify a percentage of transparency for your erased areas. The lower the Opacity setting, the less it erases. Opacity isn't available in Block mode.

- **Type:** Select Brush, Pencil, or Block. When you select Block, you're stuck with one size (a 16-x-16-pixel tip) and can't select other preset brushes.

## The Background Eraser tool

The Background Eraser tool, which is savvier than the Eraser tool, erases the background from an image while being mindful of leaving the foreground untouched. The Background Eraser tool erases to transparency on a layer. If you use this tool on an image with only a background, Elements converts the background into a layer.

The key to using the Background Eraser is to carefully keep the *hot spot,* the crosshair at the center of the brush, on the background pixels while you drag. The hot spot samples the color of the pixels and deletes that color whenever it falls inside the brush circumference. But if you accidentally touch a foreground pixel with the hot spot, it's erased as well. And the tool isn't even sorry about it! This tool works better with images that have good contrast in color between the background and foreground objects, as shown in Figure 7-14. If your image

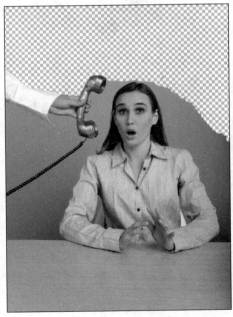

©istockphoto.com/Darkcloud Image #7909523

**Figure 7-14:** The Background Eraser erases similarly colored pixels sampled by the hot spot of your brush cursor.

has very detailed or wispy edges (such as hair or fur), and you're up for a challenge, layer masking can also provide good results. We describe layer masks in Chapter 8.

Here's the rundown on the Background Eraser options:

- **Brush Settings:** Click the Brush Settings button to bring up the settings to customize the Size, Hardness, Spacing, Roundness, and Angle of your brush tip. The Size and Tolerance settings at the bottom are for pressure-sensitive drawing tablets.

- **Limits:** *Discontiguous* erases all similarly colored pixels wherever they appear in the image. *Contiguous* erases all similarly colored pixels that are adjacent to those under the hot spot.

- **Tolerance:** The percentage determines how similar the colors have to be to the color under the hot spot before Elements erases them. A higher value picks up more colors, whereas a lower value picks up fewer colors. See the section "Talking about Tolerance," earlier in this chapter, for more details.

### The Magic Eraser tool

You can think of the Magic Eraser tool as a combination Eraser and Magic Wand tool. It selects *and* erases similarly colored pixels simultaneously. Unless you're working on a layer with the transparency locked (see Chapter 8 for more on locking layers), the pixels are erased to transparency. If you're working on an image with just a background, Elements converts the background into a layer.

Although the Magic Eraser shares most of the same options with the other erasers, it also offers unique options:

- **Sample All Layers:** Samples colors using data from all visible layers but erases pixels on the active layer only.

- **Contiguous:** Selects and erases all similarly colored pixels that are adjacent to those under the hot spot.

- **Anti-aliasing:** Creates a slightly soft edge around the transparent area.

## Using the Select Menu

In the following sections, we breeze through the Select menu. Along with the methods we describe in the "Modifying Your Selections" section, earlier in this chapter, you can use this menu to further modify selections by expanding, contracting, smoothing, softening, inversing, growing, and grabbing similarly colored pixels. If that doesn't satisfy your selection needs, nothing will.

## Selecting all or nothing

The Select All and Deselect commands are no-brainers. To select everything in your image, choose Select⇨All or press Ctrl+A (⌘+A on the Mac). To deselect everything, choose Select⇨Deselect or press Ctrl+D (⌘+D on the Mac). Remember that you usually don't have to Select All. If you don't have a selection border in your image, Elements assumes that the whole image is fair game for any manipulation.

## Reselecting a selection

If you sacrifice that second cup of coffee to steady your hand and take the time to carefully lasso around your desired object, you don't want to lose your selection before you have a chance to perform your next move. But all it takes is an inadvertent click of your mouse while you have an active selection border to obliterate your selection. Fortunately, Elements anticipated such a circumstance and offers a solution: If you choose Select⇨Reselect, Elements retrieves your last selection.

One caveat: The Reselect command works for only the last selection you made, so don't plan to reselect a selection you made last Tuesday or even just five minutes ago, if you selected something else after that selection. If you want to reuse a selection for the long term, save it as we explain in the section "Saving and loading selections," later in this chapter.

## Inversing a selection

You know the old song lyric: "If you can't be with the one you love, love the one you're with." Well, making selections in Elements is kind of like that. Sometimes it's just easier to select what you don't want rather than what you do want. For example, if you're trying to select your beloved in his senior photo, it's probably easier to just click the studio backdrop with the Magic Wand and then inverse the selection by choosing Select⇨Inverse.

## Feathering a selection

In the "Applying Marquee options" section earlier in this chapter, we describe how to feather a selection when using the Lasso and Marquee tools by entering a value in the Feather box in the Tool Options. Remember that this method of feathering requires that you set the Feather value *before* you create your selection. What we didn't tell you is that there's a way to apply a feather *after* you make a selection.

Choose Select➪Feather and enter your desired amount from 0.2 to 250 pixels. Your selection is subsequently softened around the edges.

This method is actually a better way to go. Make your selection and fine-tune it by using the methods we describe earlier in this chapter. Then apply your feather. The problem with applying the feather before you make a selection happens when you want to modify your initial selection. When you make a selection with a feather, the marquee outline of the selection adjusts to take into account the amount of the feathering. So the resulting marquee outline doesn't resemble your precise mouse movement, making it harder to modify that selection.

## Refining the edges of a selection

The Refine Edge option enables you to fine-tune the edges of your selection. It doesn't matter how you got the selection, just that you have one. You can find the command in the Tool Options of the Magic Wand, Lasso, and Quick Selection tools. And, of course, you can find it on the Select menu. Here's the scoop on each setting for this option, as shown in Figure 7-15:

- ✔ **View Mode:** Choose a mode from the pop-up menu to preview your selection. Hover your cursor over each mode to get a tooltip. For example, Marching Ants shows the selection border. Overlay lets you preview your selection with the edges hidden and a semi-opaque layer of color in your unselected area. On Black and On White show the selection against a black or white background. Show Original shows the image without a selection preview. Show Radius displays the size of the area in which the edge refinement is happening.

- ✔ **Smart Radius:** Select this option to have Elements automatically adjust the radius for hard and soft edges near your selection border. If your border is uniformly hard or soft, you may not want to select this option. This enables you to have more control over the radius setting.

- ✔ **Radius:** Specifies the size of the selection border you will refine. Increase the radius to improve the edge of areas with soft transitions or a lot of detail. Move the slider while looking at your selection to find a good setting.

- ✔ **Smooth:** Reduces jaggedness along your selection edges.

- ✔ **Feather:** Move the slider to the right to create an increasingly softer, more blurred edge.

- ✔ **Contrast:** Removes artifacts while tightening soft edges by increasing the contrast. Try using the Smart Radius option before playing with Contrast.

- **Shift Edge:** Decreases or increases your selected area. Slightly decreasing your selection border can help to *defringe* (eliminate undesirable background pixels) your selection edges.

- **Decontaminate Colors:** Replaces background fringe with the colors of your selected element. Because decontamination changes the colors of some of the pixels, you will have to output to, or create, another layer or document to preserve your current layer. To see the decontamination in action, choose Reveal Layer for your View mode. Chapter 8 explains how to work with layers.

- **Amount:** Changes the level of decontamination.

- **Output To:** Choose whether you want to output your refined, decontaminated selection to a selection on your current layer, layer mask, layer, layer with layer mask, new document, or new document with layer mask.

- **Refine Radius tool:** Select the Paintbrush tool on the left and brush around your border to adjust the area you're refining. To understand exactly what area is being included or excluded, change your View mode to Marching Ants. Use the right and left brackets to decrease and increase the brush size.

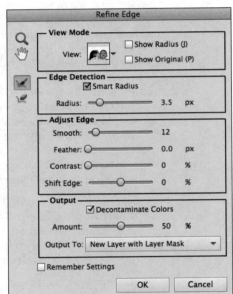

- **Erase Refinements tool:** Use this tool (which looks like an Eraser), also located on the left, to clean up any unwanted refinements made with the Refine Radius tool.

- **Zoom tool:** Allows you to zoom in to your image to see the effects of your settings.

- **Hand tool:** Enables you to pan around your image window to see the effects of your settings.

Figure 7-15: Fine-tune your selection with Refine Edge.

## Using the Modify commands

Although the commands on the Modify submenu definitely won't win any popularity contests, they may occasionally come in handy. Here's the scoop on each command:

- **Border:** Selects the area, from 1 to 200 pixels, around the edge of the selection border. By choosing Edit⇨Fill Selection, you can fill the border with color.

- **Smooth:** Rounds off any jagged, raggedy edges. Enter a value from 1 to 100 pixels, and Elements looks at each selected pixel and then includes or deselects the pixels in your selection based on your chosen value. Start with a low number, like 1, 2, or 3 pixels. Otherwise, your selection may be less accurate.

- **Expand:** Enables you to increase the size of your selection by a given number of pixels, from 1 to 100. This command is especially useful if you just barely missed getting the edge of an elliptical selection and need it to be a little larger.

- **Contract:** Decreases your selection border by 1 to 100 pixels. When you're compositing multiple images, you often benefit by slightly contracting your selection if you plan to apply a feather. That way, you avoid picking up a fringe of background pixels around your selection.

## Applying the Grow and Similar commands

The Grow and Similar commands are often used in tandem with the Magic Wand tool. If you made an initial selection with the Magic Wand but didn't quite get everything you want, try choosing Select⇨Grow. The Grow command increases the size of the selection by including adjacent pixels that fall within the range of tolerance. The Similar command is like Grow except that the pixels don't have to be adjacent to be selected. The command searches throughout the image and picks up pixels within the Tolerance range.

These commands don't have their own Tolerance options. They use whatever Tolerance value is displayed on the Tool Options when the Magic Wand tool is selected. You can adjust that Tolerance setting to include more or fewer colors.

## *Saving and loading selections*

At times, you toil so long over a complex selection that you really want to save it for future use. Saving it is not only possible but highly recommended. It's also a piece of cake. Here's how:

1. **After you perfect your selection, choose Select➪Save Selection.**

2. **In the Save Selection dialog box that appears, leave the Selection option set to New Selection and enter a name for your selection, as shown in Figure 7-16.**

   The operation is automatically set to New Selection.

3. **Click OK.**

4. **When you want to access the selection again, choose Select➪Load Selection and choose a selection from the Selection drop-down list.**

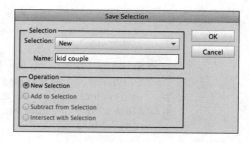

Figure 7-16: Save your selection for later use to save time and effort.

# 8

# Working with Layers

## In This Chapter

▶ Getting to know layers, the Layers panel, and the Layer menu
▶ Working with the Select menu
▶ Using different layer types
▶ Creating new layers
▶ Moving, merging, transforming, and flattening layers
▶ Adding layer masks

*U*sing Elements without ever using layers would be like typing a book on an old IBM Selectric typewriter: Sure, you could do it, but it wouldn't be fun. An even bigger issue would occur when it came time to edit that book and make changes. Correction tape, Wite-Out, and erasers would make that task downright tedious, not to mention messy. The benefit of using layers is that you have tremendous flexibility. You can make as many edits as you want for as long as you want, as long as you keep your composite image in layers. Layers make working in Elements a lot more productive. Don't give a darn about productivity? Well, let's just say that layers also make it a breeze for you to bring out your more artsy side.

This chapter explains the tools and techniques you need to start working with layers. After you give layers a try, you'll wonder how you ever lived without them.

## Getting to Know Layers

Think of layers as sheets of acetate or clear transparency film. You have drawings or photographs on individual sheets. What you place on each sheet doesn't affect any of the other sheets. Any area on the sheet that doesn't have an image on it is transparent. You can stack these sheets on top of the others to create a combined image, or *composite* (or *collage,* if you prefer). You can reshuffle the order of the sheets, add new sheets, and delete old sheets.

In Elements, *layers* are essentially digital versions of these clear acetate sheets. You can place elements, such as images, text, or shapes, on separate layers and create a composite, as shown in Figure 8-1. You can hide, add, delete, or rearrange layers. Because layers are digital, of course, they have added functionality. You can adjust how opaque or transparent the element on a layer is. You can also add special effects and change how the colors interact between layers.

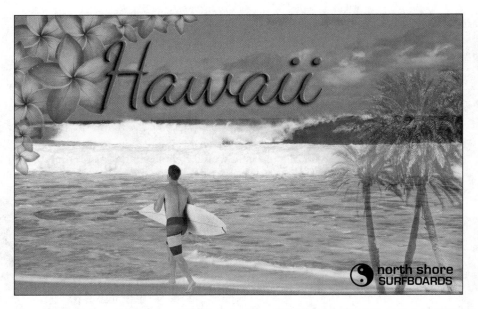

*istockphoto.com/ Kubrak78 Image #12642467, naomiwoods Image #9128343, 4x6, Image #20236672, goldhafen Image #1512452*

**Figure 8-1:** Layers enable you to easily create composite images.

To work with layers, you must be in the Photo Editor in Expert mode.

## Converting a background to a layer

When you create a new file with background contents of white or a background color, scan an image into Elements, or open a file from a CD or your digital camera, you basically have a file with just a *background.* There are no layers yet.

An image contains at most one background, and you can't do much to it besides paint on it and make basic adjustments. You can't move the background or change its transparency or blend mode. How do you get around all these limitations? Convert your background into a layer by following these easy steps:

1. **Choose Window⇨Layers to display the Layers panel.**

   The Layers panel is explained in detail in the following section.

2. **Double-click Background on the Layers panel.**

   Or choose Layer⇨New⇨Layer From Background.

3. **Name the layer or leave it at the default name of Layer 0.**

   You can also adjust the blend mode and opacity of the layer in the New Layer dialog box. Or you can do it via the Layers panel commands later.

4. **Click OK.**

   Elements converts your background into a layer, known also as an *image layer.*

   When you create a new image with transparent background contents, the image doesn't contain a background but instead is created with a single layer.

## Anatomy of the Layers panel

Elements keeps layers controlled with a panel named, not surprisingly, the *Layers panel.* To display the Layers panel, choose Window⇨Layers in the Photo Editor in Expert mode. (Figure 8-2 shows you what you can expect.)

The order of the layers on the Layers panel represents the order in the image. We refer to this concept in the computer graphics world as the *stacking order.* The top layer on the panel is the top layer in your image, and so on. Depending on what you're doing, you can work on a single layer or on multiple layers at one time. Here are some tips for working with the Layers panel:

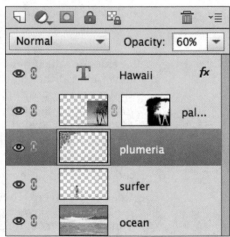

**Figure 8-2:** The Layers panel controls layers in your image.

- **Select a layer.** Click a layer name or its thumbnail. Elements highlights the *active layer* on the panel.

- **Select multiple contiguous layers.** Click your first layer and then Shift-click your last layer.

- **Select multiple noncontiguous layers.** Ctrl-click (⌘-click on the Mac) your desired layers.

- **View and hide layers.** To hide a layer, click the eye icon for that layer so that the eye disappears. To redisplay the layer, click the blank space in the eye column. You can also hide all the layers except one by selecting your desired layer and Alt-clicking (Option-clicking on the Mac) the eye icon for that layer. Redisplay all layers by Alt-clicking (Option-clicking on the Mac) the eye icon again. Hiding all the layers except the one you want to edit can be helpful in allowing you to focus without the distraction of all the other imagery.

Only layers that are visible are printed. This can be useful if you want to have several versions of an image (each on a separate layer) for a project within the same file.

- **Select the actual element (the nontransparent pixels) on the layer.** Ctrl-click (⌘-click on the Mac) the layer's thumbnail (not the name) on the panel.

- **Create a new blank layer.** Click the Create a New Layer icon at the top of the panel.

- **Add a layer mask.** Click the Add Layer Mask icon at the top of the panel. A layer mask enables you to selectively show and hide elements or adjustments on your layer, as well as creatively blend layers together. For more details, see "Adding Layer Masks," later in this chapter.

- **Create an Adjustment layer.** Click the Create a New Fill or Adjustment Layer icon at the top of the panel. *Adjustment layers* are special layers that modify contrast and color in your image. You can also add *fill layers* — layers containing color, gradients, or patterns — by using this command. We give you more details on adjustment and fill layers in the section "Working with Different Layer Types," later in this chapter.

- **Duplicate an existing layer.** Drag the layer to the Create a New Layer icon at the top of the panel.

- **Rearrange layers.** To move a layer to another position in the stacking order, drag the layer up or down on the Layers panel. While you drag, you see a fist icon. Release the mouse button when a highlighted line appears where you want to insert the layer.

If your image has a background, it always remains the bottommost layer. If you need to move the background, convert it to a layer by double-clicking the name on the Layers panel. Enter a name for the layer and click OK.

✔ **Rename a layer.** When you create a new layer, Elements provides default layer names (Layer 1, Layer 2, and so on). If you want to rename a layer, double-click the layer name on the Layers panel and enter the name directly on the Layers panel.

✔ **Adjust the interaction between colors on layers and adjust the transparency of layers.** You can use the blend modes and the opacity options at the top of the panel to mix the colors between layers and adjust the transparency of the layers, as shown in Figure 8-3.

✔ **Link layers.**
Sometimes you want your layers to stay grouped as a unit to make your editing tasks easier. If so, link your layers by selecting the layers on the panel and then clicking the Link Layers icon at the top of the panel. A link icon appears to the right of each layer name. To remove the link, click the Link Layers icon again.

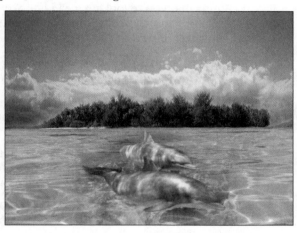

istockphoto/meltonmedia Image #1779174, tomh1000 Image #1281272

**Figure 8-3:** We created this effect by using blend modes and opacity options.

✔ **Lock layers.** Select your desired layer or layers and then click one of the two lock icons at the top of the panel. The *checkerboard square icon* locks all transparent areas of your layers. This lock prevents you from painting or editing any transparent areas on the layers. The *lock icon* locks your entire layer and prevents it from being changed in any way, including moving or transforming the elements on the layer. You can, however, still make selections on the layer. To unlock the layer, simply click the icon again to toggle off the lock.

By default, the background is locked and can't be unlocked until you convert it into a layer by choosing Layer➪New➪Layer from Background.

✔ **Delete a layer.** Drag it to the trash icon.

## Using the Layer and Select menus

As with many features in Elements, you usually have more than one way to do something. This is especially true when it comes to working with layers. Besides the commands on the Layers panel, you have two layer menus — the Layer menu and the Select menu — both of which you can find on the main menu bar at the top of the application window (top of the screen on the Mac).

### The Layer menu

Much of what you can do with the Layers panel icons you can also do by using the Layer menu on the menu bar and the Layers panel menu connected to the Layers panel. (Access the Layers panel menu by clicking the horizontally lined button in the upper-right corner of the Layers panel.) Commands, such as New, Duplicate, Delete, and Rename, are omnipresent throughout. But you find commands that are exclusive to the Layers panel, the main Layer menu, and the Layers panel menu, respectively. So if you can't find what you're looking for in one area, just go to another. Some commands require more explanation and are described in the sections that follow. However, here's a quick description of most of the commands:

- **Delete Linked Layers and Delete Hidden Layers:** These commands delete only those layers that have been linked or those hidden from display on the Layers panel.

- **Layer Style:** These commands manage the styles, or special effects, you apply to your layers.

- **Arrange:** This enables you to shuffle your layer stacking order with options, such as Bring to Front and Send to Back. Reverse switches the order of your layers if you have two or more layers selected.

- **Create Clipping Mask:** In a clipping mask, the bottommost layer (or *base* layer) acts as a mask for the layers above it. The layers above "clip" to the opaque areas of the base layer and don't show over the transparent areas of the base layer. Clipping masks work well when you want to fill a shape or type with different image layers.

- **Type:** The commands in the Type submenu control the display of type layers. For more on type, see Chapter 13.

- **Rename Layer:** This enables you to give a layer a new name. You can also simply double-click the name on the Layers panel.

- **Simplify Layer:** This converts a type layer, shape layer, or fill layer into a regular image layer. Briefly, a *shape layer* contains a vector object, and a *fill layer* contains a solid color, a gradient, or a pattern.

- **Merge and Flatten:** The various merge and flatten commands combine multiple layers into a single layer or, in the case of flattening, combine all your layers into a single background.

- **Panel Options:** You can select display options and choose to use a layer mask on your adjustment layers. Leave this option selected.

### The Select menu

Although the Select menu's main duties are to assist you in making and refining your selections, it offers a few handy layer commands. Here's a quick introduction to each command:

- ✔ **Select all layers.** Want to quickly get everything in your file? Choose Select⇨All Layers.

- ✔ **Select layers of similar type.** This command is helpful if you have different types of layers in your document, such as regular layers, type layers, shape layers, and adjustment layers, and you want to select just one type. Select one of your layers and then choose Select⇨Similar Layers. For details on different types of layers, see the following section.

- ✔ **Deselect all layers.** If you want to ensure that nothing is selected in your document, simply choose Select⇨Deselect Layers.

# Working with Different Layer Types

Layer life exists beyond just converting an existing background into a layer, which we describe in the section "Getting to Know Layers," earlier in this chapter. In fact, Elements offers five kinds of layers. You'll probably spend most of your time creating image layers, but just so that you're familiar with all types, the following sections describe each one.

## Image layers

The *image layer,* usually just referred to as a *layer,* is the type of layer we're referring to when we give the analogy of acetate sheets in the section "Getting to Know Layers," earlier in this chapter. You can create blank layers and add images to them, or you can create layers from images themselves. You can have as many image layers as your computer's memory allows.

The more layers you have, the larger your file size and the slower your computer speed.

Each layer in an image can be edited without affecting the other layers. You can move, paint, size, or apply a filter, for example, without disturbing a single pixel on any other layer or on the background, for that matter. And when an element is on a layer, you no longer have to make a selection to select it — just drag the element with the Move tool. If, however, you only want part of that layer, you need to make a selection. (See Chapter 7 for information on selections.)

## Adjustment layers

An *Adjustment layer* is a special kind of layer used for modifying color and contrast; Figure 8-4 shows an example. The advantage of using Adjustment layers for your corrections, rather than applying them directly on the image layer, is that you can apply the corrections without permanently affecting the pixels. This means that Adjustment layers are totally nondestructive. And because the correction is on a layer, you can edit, or even delete, the adjustment at any time. Adjustment layers apply the correction only to all the layers below them without affecting any of the layers above them.

Another unique feature of Adjustment layers is that when you create one, you also create a layer mask on that layer at the same time. If you're unfamiliar with layer masks, take a peek at the section "Adding Layer Masks," later in this chapter. The layer mask allows you to selectively and even partially apply the adjustment to the layers below it by applying shades of gray — from white to black — on the mask. By default, the mask is completely white (as shown in Figure 8-4), which allows the adjustment to be fully applied to the layers. If you paint on a layer mask with black, the areas under those black areas don't show the adjustment. If you paint with a shade of gray, those areas partially show the adjustment. ***Note:*** If you have an active selection border in your image before you add an Adjustment layer, the adjustment is applied only to that area within the selection border.

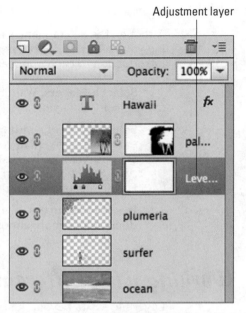

Adjustment layer

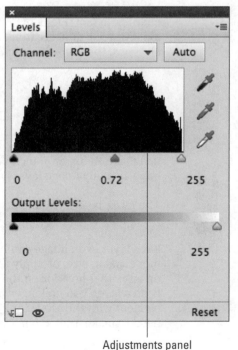

Adjustments panel

**Figure 8-4:** Adjustment layers correct color and contrast in your image.

Elements has eight kinds of Adjustment layers, and you can use as many as you want. These are the same adjustments that you find on the Enhance⇨Adjust Lighting, Enhance⇨Adjust Color, and Filter⇨Adjustments submenus. For specifics on each adjustment, see Chapters 9 and 10. Here's how to create an Adjustment layer:

1. **Open an image that needs a little contrast or color adjustment.**

   You don't need to convert your background into a layer to apply an Adjustment layer.

2. **Click the Create New Fill or Adjustment Layer icon at the top of the Layers panel, and from the drop-down list, choose your desired adjustment.**

   The Adjustment layer icon and a thumbnail appear on the adjustment layer. The thumbnail represents the layer mask. And the dialog box specific to your adjustment appears in the Adjustments panel.

3. **Make the necessary adjustments in the particular Adjustments panel.**

To selectively allow only portions of your image to receive the adjustment, you can paint on the layer mask using the Brush or Pencil tool. Or you can make a selection and fill that selection with any shade of gray, from white to black. Another technique is to use the Gradient tool on the mask to create a gradual application of the adjustment, as shown in Figure 8-5.

As with image layers, you can adjust the opacity and blend modes of an Adjustment layer. Reducing the opacity of an adjustment layer reduces the effect of the adjustment on the underlying layers.

Here are a few more tips on using adjustment layers:

✔ **To view your image without the adjustment,** click the eye icon in the left column of the Layers panel to hide the Adjustment layer.

✔ **To delete the Adjustment layer,** drag it to the trash icon on the Layers panel.

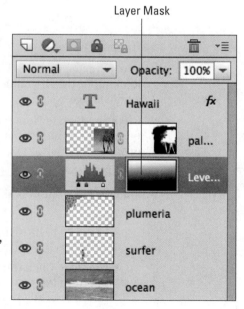

Figure 8-5: Layer masks control the amount of adjustment applied to your layers.

✔ **To edit an Adjustment layer,** simply double-click the Adjustment layer on the Layers panel. You can also choose Layer⇨Layer Content Options. In the Adjustments panel, make any desired edits. The only Adjustment layer that you can't edit is the Invert adjustment. It's either on or off.

✔ **To use the adjustment panel controls,** click an icon (shown in Figure 8-4). From left to right, here's what the icons do:

- *Have the Adjustment layer clip to the layer below.* (It will affect only the layer directly beneath it, not all the underlying layers in the stack.)

- *Toggle the Adjustment layer on and off.*

- *Reset the Adjustment layer settings back to the default.*

## Fill layers

A *fill layer* lets you add a layer of solid color, a gradient, or a pattern. Like Adjustment layers, fill layers also include layer masks. You can edit, rearrange, duplicate, delete, and merge fill layers similarly to adjustment layers. You can blend fill layers with other layers by using the opacity and blend mode options on the Layers panel. Finally, you can restrict the fill layer to just a portion of your image by either making a selection first or painting on the mask later.

Follow these steps to create a fill layer:

1. **Open an image.**

   Use an image that will look good with a frame or border of some kind. Remember that if you don't have a selection, the fill layer covers your whole image.

2. **Click the Create New Fill or Adjustment Layer icon on the Layers panel. From the drop-down list, choose a fill of a solid color, gradient, or pattern.**

   The dialog box specific to your type of fill appears.

3. **Specify your options, depending on the fill type you chose in Step 2:**

   - *Solid Color:* Choose your desired color from the Color Picker. See Chapter 12 for details on choosing colors and also gradients and patterns.

   - *Gradient:* Click the down-pointing arrow to choose a preset gradient from the drop-down panel, or click the gradient preview to display the Gradient Editor and create your own gradient.

- *Pattern:* Select a pattern from the drop-down panel. Enter a value to scale your pattern, if you want. Click Snap to Origin to make the origin of the pattern the same as the origin of the document. Select the Link with Layer option to specify that the pattern moves with the fill layer if you move that layer.

4. **Click OK.**

   The fill layer appears on the Layers panel, as shown in Figure 8-6. Notice the layer mask that was created on the fill layer. We filled our entire layer mask with black, with just the exception of the outside edge to create a frame around our image.

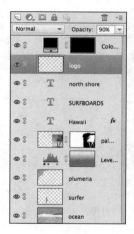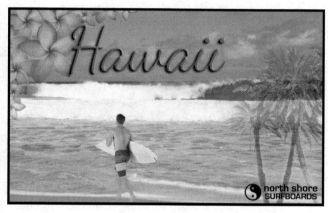

©istockphoto.com/ Kubrak78 Image #12642467, naomiwoods Image #9128343, 4x6, Image #20236672, goldhafen Image #1512452

**Figure 8-6:** Add a frame or border with a fill layer.

## Shape layers

If you haven't made your way to Chapter 12 yet, you may be surprised to discover that Elements also lets you draw shapes with seven different drawing tools. These shapes have the bonus of being *vector*-based. This means that the shapes are defined by mathematical equations, which consist of points and paths, instead of pixels. The advantage of vector-based objects is that you can freely resize these objects without causing degradation. In addition, they're always printed with smooth edges, not with the jaggies you're familiar with seeing in pixel-based elements.

To create a shape layer, grab a shape tool from the Tools panel and drag it on your canvas. When you create a shape, it resides on its own, unique shape layer, as shown by the yin-and-yang logo in the bottom-right corner of Figure 8-6. As with other types of layers, you can adjust the blend modes and opacity of a shape layer. You can also edit, move, and transform the actual shapes. However, to apply filters, you must first *simplify* the shape layer by choosing Layer⇨Simplify Layer. This process converts the vector paths to pixels.

### Type layers

To add words to your images (refer to Figure 8-6), click your canvas with the Type tool selected and just type. It's really as easy as that. Well, you can specify options, such as a font family and size, in the Tool Options, but when you click the Commit button on the image window, you create a type layer. On the Layers panel, the type layer displays a T icon. For details on working with type, check out Chapter 13.

## Tackling Layer Basics

Image layers are the heart and soul of the layering world. You can create multiple image layers within a single image. Even more fun is creating a composite from several different images. Add people you like; take out people you don't. Pluck people out of boring photo studios and put them in exotic locales. The creative possibilities are endless. In the following sections, we cover all the various ways to create image layers.

### Creating a new layer from scratch

If you're creating a new, blank file, you can select the Transparent option for your background contents. Your new file is created with a transparent layer and is ready to go. If you have an existing file and want to create a new, blank layer, here are the ways to do so:

- Click the Create a New Layer icon at the top of the Layers panel.
- Choose New Layer from the Layers panel menu.
- Choose Layer⇨New⇨Layer.

If you create a layer by using either of the menu commands, you're presented with a dialog box with options. In that dialog box, you can name your layer and specify options for grouping, blending, and adjusting opacity. Provide a name for your layer and click OK. You can always adjust the other options directly on the Layers panel later.

You can also use the Copy and Paste commands without even creating a blank layer first. When you copy and paste a selection without a blank layer, Elements automatically creates a new layer from the pasted selection. A better method of copying and pasting between multiple images, however, is to use the drag-and-drop method, which we describe in the section "Dragging and dropping layers," later in this chapter.

The Copy Merged command on the Edit menu creates a merged copy of all visible layers within the selection.

After you create your layer, you can put selections or other elements on that layer by doing one or more of the following:

- ✔ **Paint:** Grab a painting tool, such as the Brush or Pencil, and paint on the layer.

- ✔ **Copy a selection:** Make a selection on another layer or on the background within the same document, or from another image entirely, and then choose Edit➪Copy. Select your new, blank layer on the Layers panel and then choose Edit➪Paste.

- ✔ **Cut a selection:** Make a selection on another layer or on the background within the same document, or from another image, and then choose Edit➪Cut. Select your new, blank layer and then choose Edit➪Paste. Be aware that this action removes that selection from its original location and leaves a transparent hole, as shown in Figure 8-7.

If you cut a selection from a Background instead of an image layer, the space isn't a transparent hole; it's filled with the background color.

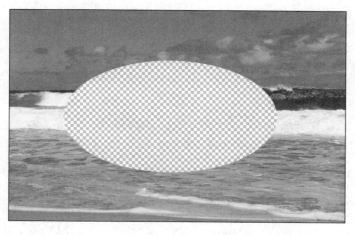

©istockphoto.com/Kubrak78 Image #12642467

**Figure 8-7:** When you cut a selection from a layer, take note of the resulting hole in the original location.

## Using Layer via Copy and Layer via Cut

Another way to create a layer is to use the Layer via Copy and Layer via Cut commands on the Layer menu's New submenu. Make a selection on a layer or background and choose Layer➪New➪Layer via Copy or Layer via Cut. Elements automatically creates a new layer and puts the copied or cut selection on the layer. Remember that if you use the Layer via Cut command, your selection is deleted from its original location layer, and you're left with a transparent hole when cutting from an image layer. If you use the background for the source, your background color fills the space. A reminder: You can use these two commands only within the same image. You can't use them among multiple images.

## Duplicating layers

Duplicating layers can be helpful if you want to protect your original image while experimenting with a technique. If you don't like the results, you can always delete the duplicate layer. No harm, no foul.

To duplicate an existing layer, select it on the Layers panel and do one of four things:

- Drag the layer to the Create a New Layer icon at the top of the panel. Elements creates a duplicate layer with *Copy* appended to the name of the layer.
- Choose Duplicate Layer from the Layers panel menu.
- Choose Layer➪Duplicate Layer.
- Choose Layer➪New➪Layer via Copy. (Make sure you don't have an active selection when choosing this command.)

If you use the menu methods, a dialog box appears, asking you to name your layer and specify other options. Provide a name for your layer and click OK. You can specify the other options later if you want.

## Dragging and dropping layers

The most efficient way to copy and paste layers between multiple images is to use the drag-and-drop method. Why? Because it bypasses your *Clipboard,* which is the temporary storage area on your computer for copied data. Storing data, especially large files, can bog down your system. By keeping your Clipboard clear of data, your system operates more efficiently.

If you already copied data and it's lounging on your Clipboard, choose Edit➪ Clear➪Clipboard Contents to empty your Clipboard.

Here's how to drag and drop layers from one file to another:

1. **Select your desired layer in the Layers panel.**

2. **Grab the Move tool (the four-headed arrow) from the Tools panel.**

3. **Drag and drop the layer onto your destination file.**

   The dropped layer pops in as a new layer above the active layer in the image. You don't need to have a selection border to copy the entire layer. But if you want to copy just a portion of the layer, make your selection before you drag and drop with the Move tool. If you want the selected element to be centered on the destination file, press the Shift key while you drag and drop.

If you have several elements (that aren't touching each other) on one layer and you want to select only one of the elements to drag and drop, use the Lasso tool to make a crude selection around the object without touching any of the other elements. Then press the Ctrl (⌘ on the Mac) key and press the up-arrow key once. The element then becomes perfectly selected. You can now drag and drop with the Move tool.

## Using the Paste into Selection command

The Paste into Selection command lets you put an image on a separate layer while also inserting that image into a selection border. For example, in Figure 8-8, we use this command to make it appear as though our surfer is in the water.

You can do the same by following these steps:

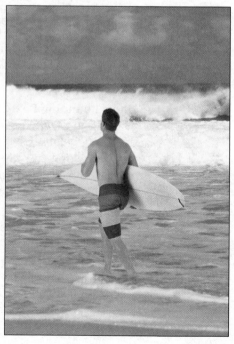

1. **Make your desired selection on the layer in your destination image.**

   In our figure, we selected the area in the water where the surfer would be positioned.

2. **Select the image that will fill that selection.**

   The image can be within the same file or from another file. Our surfer was in another file.

©istockphoto.com/Kubrak78 Image#12642467, 4x6 Image #20236672

**Figure 8-8:** Use the Paste into Selection command to make one element appear as though it's coming out of another element.

3. **Choose Edit➪Copy.**

4. **Return to the destination image layer and choose Edit➪Paste into Selection.**

   Elements converts the selection border on the layer into a layer mask. The pasted selection is visible only inside the selection border. In our example, the surfer shows only inside the selected area. His ankles and feet are outside the border and therefore are hidden.

# Moving a Layer's Content

Moving the content of a layer is a piece of cake: Grab the Move tool from the Tools panel, select your layer on the Layers panel, and drag the element on the canvas to your desired location. You can also move the layer in 1-pixel increments by using the keyboard arrow keys. Press Shift with the arrows to move in 10-pixel increments. *Note:* If you hold down the Alt (Option on the Mac) key while moving your element, you make a duplicate of that element.

The Auto Select Layer option in the Tool Options enables you to switch to a layer when you click any part of that layer's content with the Move tool. But be careful if you have a lot of overlapping layers because this technique can sometimes be more trouble than it's worth.

The Move tool has additional settings found in Tool Options. Here's the lowdown:

- ✔ **Show Bounding Box:** This option surrounds the contents of your layer with a dotted box that has handles, enabling you to easily transform your layer. Find details in the following section.

- ✔ **Show Highlight on Rollover:** Hover your mouse anywhere over the canvas to make an outline appear around the element on your layer. Click the highlighted layer to select it and then move it.

- ✔ **Arrange submenu:** This menu enables you to change your selected layer's position in the stacking order.

- ✔ **Link Layers:** This option, which resides not in the Tool Options, but in the Layers panel, connects the layers to make it easier to move (or transform) multiple layers simultaneously. Select a layer and then Ctrl-click (⌘-click on the Mac) to select more layers. Click the Link Layers icon (chain).

✔ **Align submenu:** Align your selected layers on the left, center, right, top, middle, and bottom. As with linking, select your first layer and then Shift-click to select more layers. Ctrl-click (⌘-click on the Mac) to select nonconsecutive layers. Choose an alignment option.

✔ **Distribute submenu:** Use this menu to evenly space your selected layers on the left, center, right, top, middle, and bottom. As with aligning, select your first layer and then Shift-click to select more layers. Ctrl-click (⌘-click on the Mac) to select nonconsecutive layers. Choose your desired distribution option.

# Transforming Layers

When working with layers, you may need to scale or rotate some of your images. You can do so easily by applying the Transform and Free Transform commands. The methods to transform layers and selections are identical.

Here's how to transform a layer:

1. **Select your desired layer.**

   You can also apply a transformation to multiple layers simultaneously by linking the layers first.

2. **Choose Image➪Transform➪Free Transform.**

   A bounding box surrounds the contents of your layer.

3. **Adjust (or transform) the bounding box.**

   - *Size the contents:* Drag a corner handle.

   - *Constrain the proportions:* Press Shift while dragging.

   - *Rotate the contents:* Move the mouse cursor just outside a corner handle until it turns into a curved arrow, and then drag. Or choose Image➪Rotate.

   - *Distort, skew, or apply perspective to the contents:* Right-click and choose the desired command from the context menu. You can also click the rotate, scale, and skew icons in the Tool Options, as well as enter your transform values numerically in the fields.

     If you want to apply just a single transformation, you can also choose the individual Distort, Skew, and Perspective commands from the Image➪Transform menu.

4. **When your layer is transformed to your liking, double-click inside the bounding box.**

Try to perform all your transformations in one execution. Each time you transform pixels, you put your image through the *interpolation process* (analyzing the colors of the original pixels and "manufacturing" new ones). Done to the extreme, this process can degrade the quality of your image. This is why it's prudent to use the Free Transform command rather than individual commands — so that all transformations can be executed in one fell swoop.

When the Move tool is active, you can transform a layer without choosing a command. Select the Show Bounding Box option in the Tool Options. This option surrounds the layer or selection with a box that has handles. Drag the handles to transform the layer or selection.

## Adding Layer Masks

One of the best creative tools Elements has to offer is layer masks. *Masking* is essentially just another way of making a selection. Instead of making a selection with a single selection outline — either it is selected or it isn't — masks enable you to define your selection with up to 256 levels of gray (from white to black). You can therefore have varying levels of a selection.

Here's how it works. First, think of a layer mask as a sheet of acetate that hovers over your layer. To add it to a layer, click the layer mask icon (dark rectangle with a light circle) at the top of the Layers panel. Then, with any of the painting tools (Brush tool, Gradient tool, and others), you apply black, white, or any shade of gray onto the layer mask. Where the mask is white, the image on the layer is selected and shows. Where the mask is black, the image is unselected and is hidden. And where the mask is gray, the image is partially selected; therefore, it partially shows. The lighter the gray, the more the image shows. By default, the mask starts out completely white so that everything is selected and shows.

Here are some things you can do with layer masks:

- **Creatively blend one layer into another.** If you want one image to gradually dissolve into another, using a layer mask is the way to go. Try using the Gradient tool with the black-to-white gradient selected to create a soft dissolve. You can use layer masks to blend images together in a realistic manner, as shown in Figure 8-9, where we combined a goldfish and a strange, bottled green beverage. In the figure, you can see where we painted with black to completely hide the original background of the fish image. We painted with gray on the fish to make it appear as if it is truly "swimming" in the green liquid. In other words, some of the liquid of the underlying bottle image shows through to the fish layer.

✔ **Adjust your layer mask to selectively show and hide the effects of the adjustment layer.** See the earlier section, "Adjustment layers."

✔ **Apply a filter to your layer mask to create an interesting special effect.** One of the best aspects of layer masks is that you can endlessly edit them. Unlike just making a feathered selection, you can keep adjusting how much of your current layer or underlying images show. Or you can adjust how gradually one image blends into another: Simply change the areas of white, black, and gray on the layer mask by painting with any of the painting tools. Just make sure you select the layer mask and not the image. When you select the layer mask thumbnail in the Layers panel, you see the appearance of an outline around the thumbnail.

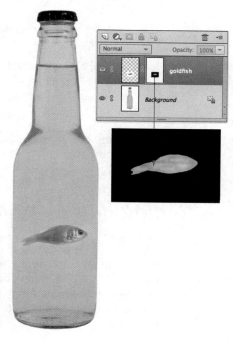

©istockphoto.com/joxxxxjo Image #2466705, Kameleon007 Image #2558590

**Figure 8-9:** Add a layer mask to blend one layer into another.

You can't add a layer mask to a background. You must convert the background into a layer first.

Here are some other things to keep in mind when you use layer masks:

✔ **To load the mask as a selection outline,** simply Ctrl-click (⌘-click on the Mac) the layer mask thumbnail in the Layers panel.

✔ **To temporarily hide a mask,** Shift-click the layer mask thumbnail in the Layers panel. Repeat to show the mask.

✔ **To view the mask without viewing the image,** Alt-click (Option-click on the Mac) the Layer Mask thumbnail in the Layers panel. This trick can be helpful when editing a layer mask.

✔ **To unlink a layer from its layer mask,** click the link icon in the Layers panel. Click again to reestablish the link. By default, Elements links a layer mask to the contents of the layer. This link enables them to move together.

✔ **To delete a layer mask,** drag its thumbnail to the trash icon in the Layers panel.

✔ **To apply a layer mask,** drag the mask thumbnail to the trash icon in the Layers panel and be sure to click Apply in the dialog box. When you apply a layer mask, you fuse the mask to the layer so editing is no longer possible.

*Note:* Many of the preceding commands are also available in the Layer⇨Layer Mask submenu.

## Flattening and Merging Layers

Layers are fun and fantastic, but they can quickly chew up your computer's RAM and bloat your file size. And sometimes, to be honest, having too many layers can start to make your file tedious to manage, thereby making you less productive. Whenever possible, you should merge your layers to save memory and space. *Merging* combines visible, linked, or adjacent layers into a single layer (not a Background). The intersection of all transparent areas is retained.

In addition, if you need to import your file into another program, certain programs don't support files with layers. Therefore, you may need to flatten your file before importing it. *Flattening* an image combines all visible layers into a Background, including type, shape, fill, and adjustment layers. You're prompted as to whether you want to discard hidden layers, and any transparent areas are filled with white. We recommend, however, that before you flatten your image, you make a copy of the file with all its layers intact and save it as a native Photoshop file. That way, if you ever need to make any edits, you have the added flexibility of having your layers.

By the way, the only file formats that support layers are native Photoshop (.psd); Tagged Image File Format, or TIFF (.tif); and Portable Document Format, or PDF (.pdf). If you save your file in any other format, Elements automatically flattens your layers into a background. See Chapter 2 for details on these file types.

## *Flattening layers*

To flatten an image, follow these steps:

1. **Make certain that all layers you want to retain are visible.**

   If you have any hidden layers, Elements asks whether you want to discard those hidden layers.

   It's always good insurance to save a copy of an image with layers while flattening another copy. You just never know — you may need to make edits at a later date.

2. **Choose Flatten Image from the Layers panel menu or the Layer menu.**

   All your layers are combined into a single background, as shown in Figure 8-10.

   If you mistakenly flatten your image, choose Edit⇨Undo or use your Undo History panel. (If you're not familiar with the History panel, see Chapter 1 for details.)

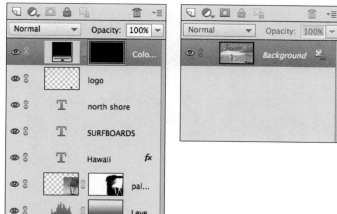

Figure 8-10: Flattening combines all your layers into a single background.

## *Merging layers*

Unlike flattening layers, where all layers get combined into a single Background, you can choose to merge just a few layers. Also, remember, when you do choose to merge all of your layers, they combine into a single layer versus a Background.

You can merge your layers in a few ways. Here's how:

- **Select only those layers you want to merge.** Choose Merge Layers from the Layers panel menu or the Layer menu.

- **Display only those layers you want to merge.** Click the eye icon on the Layers panel to hide those layers you don't want to merge. Choose Merge Visible from the Layers panel menu or the Layer menu.

- **Arrange the layers you want to merge so that they're adjacent on the Layers panel.** Select the topmost layer of that group and choose Merge Down from the Layers panel menu or the Layer menu. Merge Down merges your active layer with the layer directly below it.

# 9

# Simple Image Makeovers

## In This Chapter

▶ Cropping, straightening, and recomposing your images

▶ Using one-step auto fixes

▶ Editing with Quick mode

▶ Fixing small imperfections

*F*ixing images quickly, without pain or hassle, is probably one of the most desirable features you'll find in Elements and one that we're sure you'll embrace frequently. Whether you're an experienced photographer or an amateur shutterbug, cropping away unwanted background, tweaking the lighting or color of an image, and erasing the minor blemishes of a loved one's face are all editing tasks you'll most likely tackle. With the simple image-makeover tools in Elements, completing these tasks is as easy as clicking a single button or making a few swipes with a brush.

## Cropping and Straightening Images

Cropping a photo is probably one of the easiest things you can do to improve its composition. Getting rid of the unnecessary background around your subject creates a better focal point. Another dead giveaway of amateurish photography is crooked horizon lines. Not a problem. Elements gives you several ways to straighten those images after the fact. So after your next photo shoot, launch the Elements Photo Editor and then crop and straighten your images before you show them off.

### Cutting away with the Crop tool

The most common way to crop a photo is by using the Crop tool. Simple, quick, and easy, this tool gets the job done. Here's how to use it:

1. **In either Expert or Quick mode, select the Crop tool from the Tools panel.**

   You can also press the C key. The Crop tool looks like two intersecting "L" shapes. For details on the different editing modes, see Chapter 2. For full details on Quick mode, see the section "Editing in Quick Mode," later in this chapter.

2. **Optionally, choose one of the four cropping suggestions Elements provides for you. Simply hover your mouse over each of the crop suggestion thumbnails to get an idea of how it will frame your image. If you don't like any of the suggestions, proceed to step 3.**

3. **Specify your aspect ratio and resolution options in the Tool Options under the image window.**

   Here are your choices:

   - *No Restriction:* Allows you to freely crop the image at any size.

   - *Use Photo Ratio:* Retains the original aspect ratio of the image when you crop.

   - *Preset Sizes:* Offers a variety of common photographic sizes. When you crop, your image then becomes that specific dimension.

     When you crop an image, Elements retains the original resolution of the file (unless you specify otherwise in the resolution option). Therefore, to keep your image at the same image size while simultaneously eliminating portions of your image, Elements must resample the file. Consequently, your image must have sufficient resolution so that the effects of the resampling aren't too noticeable. This is especially true if you're choosing a larger preset size. If all this talk about resolution and resampling is fuzzy, be sure to check out Chapter 2.

   - *Width (W) and Height (H):* Enables you to specify a desired width and height to crop your image.

   - *Resolution:* Specify a desired resolution for your cropped image. Again, try to avoid resampling your image.

   - *Pixels/in or Pixels/cm:* Specify your desired unit of measurement.

   - *Grid Overlay:* Elements gives you an added tool to help you frame your image prior to cropping. Choose from the three options — None, Grid, or Rule of Thirds.

     *Grid:* Displays just that — a grid of intersecting horizontal and vertical lines — over the image.

     *Rule of Thirds:* This rule is a longtime photographic principle that encourages placing most interesting elements, or your intended focal point, at one of four intersecting points in your grid of two vertical and two horizontal lines, as shown in Figure 9-1. See Chapter 17 for additional information about the Rule of Thirds.

Rule of Thirds overlay    Handle                Shield

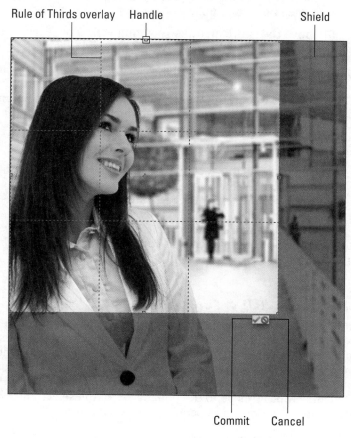

Commit    Cancel

©istockphoto.com/gehringj Image #9063164

**Figure 9-1:** The shield and Rule of Thirds overlay allow for easy framing of your image.

4. **Drag around the portion of the image you want to retain and release the mouse button.**

   When you drag, a crop marquee bounding box appears. Don't worry if your cropping marquee isn't exactly correct. You can adjust it in Step 5.

   The area outside the cropping marquee (called a *shield*) appears darker than the inside in order to better frame your image, as shown in Figure 9-1. If you want to change the color and opacity of the shield, or if you don't want it at all, change your Crop preferences by choosing Edit⇨Preferences⇨Display & Cursors. (On the Mac, choose Adobe Photoshop Elements Editor⇨Preferences⇨Display & Cursors.)

5. **Adjust the cropping marquee by dragging the handles of the crop marquee bounding box.**

   To move the entire marquee, position your mouse inside the marquee until you see a black arrowhead cursor, and then drag.

 If you move your mouse outside the marquee, your cursor changes to a curved arrow. Drag with this cursor to rotate the marquee. This action allows you to both rotate and crop your image simultaneously — handy for straightening a crooked image. Just be aware that rotation, unless it's in 90-degree increments, also resamples your image.

6. **Double-click inside the cropping marquee.**

   You can also just press Enter or click the green Commit button next to the marquee. Elements then discards the area outside the marquee. To cancel your crop, click the red Cancel button.

 If you're in the Organizer, and not the Photo Editor, click the Instant Fix button in the bottom-right corner. You can find the Crop tool in the Photo Fix Options panel.

## Cropping with a selection border

You can alternatively crop an image by choosing Image⇨Crop in either Expert or Quick mode. First, make a selection with any of the selection tools and then choose the command. You can use this technique with any selection border shape. That is, your selection doesn't have to be rectangular; it can be round or even freeform. Your cropped image doesn't take on that shape, but Elements crops as close to the boundaries of the selection border as it can. For details about making selections, see Chapter 7.

## Straightening images

There may be times when you just didn't quite get that horizon straight when you took a photo of the beach. Or maybe you scanned a photo and it wasn't quite centered in the middle of the scanning bed. It's not a big deal. Elements gives you several ways to straighten an image.

### Using the Straighten tool

This tool enables you to specify a new straight edge, and it then rotates the image accordingly. Here's how to use the Straighten tool:

1. **In Expert mode, select the Straighten tool from the Tools panel (or press the P key).**

   It looks like an analog level tool.

2. **Specify your desired setting from the Canvas Options in the Tool Options.**

   Here are your choices:

   - *Grow or Shrink* rotates the image and increases or decreases the size of the canvas to fit the image area.

   - *Remove Background* trims the background canvas outside the image area. This choice is helpful if you scan an image and white areas appear around your photo that you want removed.

   - *Original Size* rotates your image without trimming any background canvas.

     If you select either the Original Size or Remove Background option, you can select the Auto Fill Edges option. When selected, after you straighten the image, the edges that have missing pixels will fill using the content-aware algorithm. ***Note:*** You can also vertically straighten your image by pressing Ctrl (⌘ on a Mac) and dragging along a vertical edge.

3. **(Optional) Select Rotate All Layers.**

   If you have an image with layers and you want them all rotated, select this option.

4. **Draw a line in your image to represent the new straight edge.**

   Your image is then straightened and, if you chose any of the crop options in Step 2, also cropped.

## Using the Straighten menu commands

In addition to using the Straighten tool, you can straighten your images by using two commands on the Image menu, in either Expert or Quick mode:

- **To automatically straighten an image without cropping,** choose Image➪Rotate➪Straighten Image. This straightening technique leaves the canvas around the image.

- **To automatically straighten and crop the image simultaneously,** choose Image➪Rotate➪Straighten and Crop Image.

# Recomposing Images

This great tool actually allows you to resize, or as the name implies, *recompose,* your image without losing any vital content. For example, if you need to have people in your shot closer together because you need the final, cropped image to be more square than rectangular, this tool can help. Here's how it works:

1. **In Expert mode, select the Recompose tool from the Tools panel.**

   You can also press the W key. The tool looks like a square with a gear on it.

2. **In the Tool Options, select the Mark for Protection Brush (the brush with a plus sign icon) and brush over the areas in your image that you want to keep or protect.**

   You can specify your brush size with the Size option slider. You can erase any mistakes by using the Erase Highlights Marked for Protection tool (the eraser with a plus sign icon).

3. **With the Mark for Removal Brush (the brush with a minus sign icon), brush over the areas in your image that you want to remove or aren't vital to your final image, as shown in Figure 9-2.**

   You can specify your brush size with the Size option slider. You can erase any mistakes by using the Erase Highlights Marked for Removal tool (the eraser with a minus sign icon).

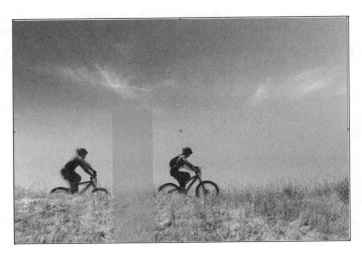

©istockphoto.com/alynst Image #11082865

**Figure 9-2:** Brush over areas you want to protect and remove in your image.

**4. Specify any other desired settings in the Tool Options.**

Here are the other options:

- *Threshold:* The slider determines how much recomposing appears in your adjustment. Selecting 100% totally recomposes your image. Experiment to get the results you want.

- *Preset Ratios:* Choose from preset aspect ratios to have your image framed to those dimensions. Or choose No Restriction to have free reign.

- *Width and Height:* This option resizes your image to your specified dimensions.

- *Highlight Skin Tones (green man icon):* Select this option to prevent skin tones from distorting when resizing.

**5. Resize, or recompose, your image by dragging the corner or side handles.**

The bikes are now closer together, as shown in Figure 9-3.

**6. Click the Commit button (green check-mark icon) when you have your desired composition.**

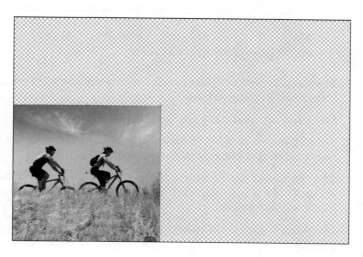

©istockphoto.com/alynst Image #11082865

**Figure 9-3:** Recompose your image to your desired size and aspect ratio without losing vital content.

# Employing One-Step Auto Fixes

Elements has seven automatic lighting-, contrast-, and color-correction tools that can improve the appearance of your images with just one menu command. These commands are available in either Expert or Quick mode, and they're all on the Enhance menu. For more on Quick mode, see the section "Editing in Quick Mode," later in this chapter.

The advantage of these one-step correctors is that they're extremely easy to use. You don't need to have one iota of knowledge about color or contrast to use them. The downside to using them is that sometimes the result isn't as good as you could get via a manual color-correction method. And sometimes these correctors may even make your image look worse than before by giving you weird color shifts. But because these correctors are quick and easy, you can try them on an image that needs help. Usually, you don't want to use more than one of the auto fixes. If one doesn't work on your image, undo the fix and try another. If you still don't like the result, move on to one of the manual methods we describe in Chapter 10.

## Auto Smart Tone

The Auto Smart Tone auto fix is designed to adjust the tonal values in your image.

Here are the steps to use this adjustment:

1.  **In either Expert or Quick mode, with your image open, choose Enhance⇨Auto Smart Tone.**

    Elements automatically applies a default correction.

2.  **Moving the controller "joystick" (double circle icon in the center of the image), fine-tune your correction.**

    The thumbnail previews in each corner, as shown in Figure 9-4, give you an idea of how the image will look when you move the joystick in that particular direction.

    Move the Before and After toggle to see the before-and-after adjustment previews.

3.  **Select the Learn from This Correction option (arrow with lines icon) in the lower-left corner of the dialog box to have Elements "learn" from this editing session.**

    If you select this option, Elements remembers the corrections you made on this image and positions the joystick on the basis of that correction on the next image you open and correct. The more images that are corrected, the smarter the Auto Smart Tone corrections become. This intelligent algorithm can distinguish between various image types (based on the tonal characteristics) and remembers the adjustment for that particular type of image.

If your adjustments are starting to get out of whack and you need to reset the learning archive, choose Edit⇨Preferences⇨General⇨Reset Auto Smart Tone Learning (on the Mac, Adobe Photoshop Elements Editor⇨Preferences⇨General⇨Reset Auto Smart Tone Learning).

**4. After you're satisfied with the adjustment, click OK.**

If you want to start over, click the Reset button.

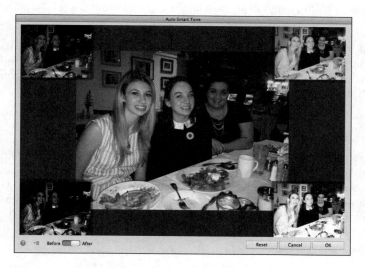

Figure 9-4: Apply Auto Smart Fix to quickly adjust the tonal values in an image.

## Auto Smart Fix

The Auto Smart Fix tool is an all-in-one command touted to adjust it all. It's designed to improve the details in shadow and highlight areas, and correct the color balance, as shown in Figure 9-5. The overexposed image on the left was improved quite nicely with the Auto Smart Fix command.

The Auto Smart Fix command, as well as the Auto Color, Auto Levels, Auto Contrast, Auto Sharpen, and Auto Red Eye Fix commands, are also available in the Organizer (in the Photo Fix Options pane), where you can apply the commands to several selected images simultaneously.

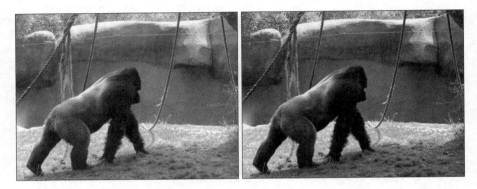

Figure 9-5: In a hurry? Apply the Auto Smart Fix command to quickly improve an image.

If the Auto Smart Fix was just too "auto" for you, you can crank it up a notch and try Adjust Smart Fix. This command is similar to Auto Smart Fix but gives you a slider that allows you, not Elements, to control the amount of correction applied to the image.

## Auto Levels

The Auto Levels command adjusts the overall contrast of an image. This command works best on images that have pretty good contrast (an even range of tones and detail in the shadow, highlight, and midtone areas) to begin with and need just a minor amount of adjustment. Auto Levels works by *mapping,* or converting, the lightest and darkest pixels in your image to black and white, thereby making highlights appear lighter and shadows appear darker, as shown in Figure 9-6.

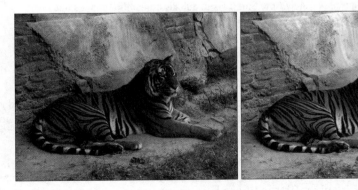

Figure 9-6: Auto Levels adjusts the overall contrast of an image.

Although the Auto Levels command can improve contrast, it may also produce an unwanted *color cast* (a slight trace of color). If this happens, undo the command and try the Auto Contrast command instead. If that still doesn't improve the contrast, it's time to bring out the big guns. Try the Levels command we describe in Chapter 10.

## Auto Contrast

The Auto Contrast command is designed to adjust the overall contrast in an image without adjusting its color. This command may not do as good a job of improving contrast as the Auto Levels command, but it does a better job of retaining the color balance of an image. Auto Contrast usually doesn't cause the funky color casts that can occur when you're using Auto Levels. This command works great on images with a haze, as shown in Figure 9-7.

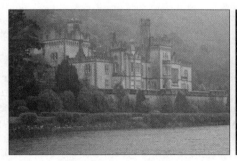 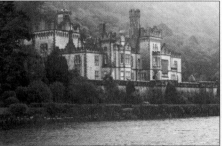

Figure 9-7: The Auto Contrast command works wonders on hazy images.

## Auto Color Correction

The Auto Color Correction command adjusts both the color and contrast of an image, based on the shadows, midtones, and highlights it finds in the image and a default set of values. These values adjust the amount of black and white pixels that Elements removes from the darkest and lightest areas of the image. You usually use this command to remove a color cast or to balance the color in your image, as shown in Figure 9-8. Occasionally, this command can also be useful in correcting oversaturated or undersaturated colors.

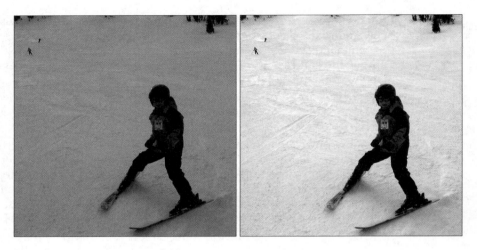

Figure 9-8: Use Auto Color Correction to remove a colorcast.

## Auto Sharpen

Photos taken with a digital camera or scanned on a flatbed scanner often suffer from a case of overly soft focus. Sharpening gives the illusion of increased focus by increasing the contrast between pixels. Auto Sharpen attempts to improve the focus, as shown in Figure 9-9, without overdoing it. What happens when you oversharpen? Your images go from soft to grainy and noisy. For more precise sharpening, check out the Unsharp Mask and Adjust Sharpness features we cover in Chapter 10.

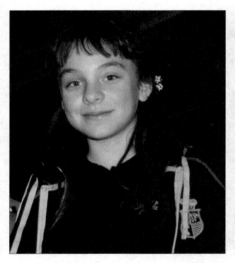
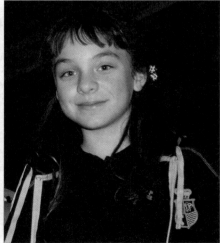

Figure 9-9: Use Auto Sharpen to improve focus.

Always make sharpening your last fix after you make all your other fixes and enhancements.

## Auto Red Eye Fix

The Auto Red Eye Fix command is self-explanatory. It automatically detects and eliminates red-eye in an image. Red-eye happens when a person or an animal (where red-eye can also be yellow-, green-, or even blue-eye) looks directly into the flash.

If for some reason the Auto Red Eye Fix doesn't quite do the trick, you can always reach for the Red Eye tool on the Tools panel. Here's how to remove red-eye manually:

1. **Select the Red Eye Removal tool from the Tools panel.**

   You can also press Y.

2. **Using the default settings, click the red portion of the eye in your image.**

   This one-click tool darkens the pupil while retaining the tonality and texture of the rest of the eye, as shown in Figure 9-10.

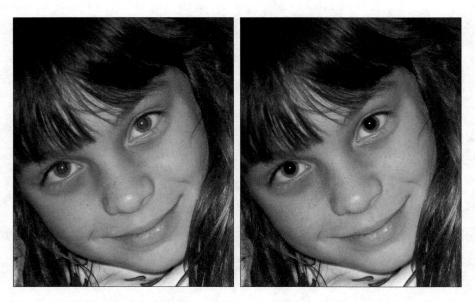

**Figure 9-10:** The Auto Red Eye Fix and the Red Eye tools detect and destroy dreaded red-eye.

3. **If you're unhappy with the fix, adjust one or both of these settings in the Tool Options:**

    - *Pupil Radius:* Use the slider to increase or decrease the size of the pupil.

    - *Darken:* Use the slider to darken or lighten the color of the pupil.

Pets can get white-, green-, blue- or yellow-eyes from the flash. Elements provides a Pet Eye option in Tool Options. If this option still doesn't do it, your best bet is to use the Color Replacement tool. See the section "Replacing one color with another," at the end of this chapter.

## Editing in Quick Mode

Quick mode is a pared-down version of Expert mode that conveniently provides basic fixing tools and tosses in a few unique features, such as a before-and-after preview of your image.

Here's a step-by-step workflow that you can follow in Quick mode to repair your photos:

1. **Select one or more photos in the Organizer, click the Editor button at the bottom of the workspace, and then click the Quick button at the top of the workspace.**

    Or, if you're in Expert mode, select your desired image(s) from the Photo Bin and then click the Quick button at the top of the workspace.

    *Note:* You can also open images by simply clicking the Open button and selecting your desired files.

2. **Specify your preview preference from the View drop-down list at the top of the workspace.**

    You can choose to view just your original image (Before Only), your fixed image (After Only), or both images side by side (Before & After) in either portrait (Vertical) or landscape (Horizontal) orientation, as shown in Figure 9-11.

3. **Use the Zoom and Hand tools to magnify and navigate around your image. (See Chapter 2 for more on these tools.)**

    You can also specify the Zoom percentage by using the Zoom slider in the Tool Options or in the top-right of the workspace.

4. **Choose your desired window view by clicking one of the following buttons located in the Tool Options: 1:1 (Actual Pixels), Fit Screen, Fill Screen (which zooms your image to fill your screen), or Print Size.**

    You also have another Zoom slider located in the Tool Options.

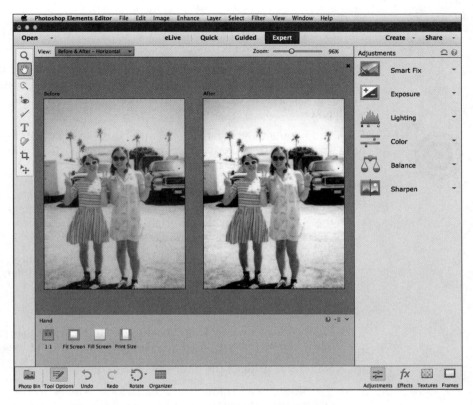

**Figure 9-11:** Quick mode enables you to view before-and-after previews of your image.

5. **Crop your image by using the Crop tool on the Tools panel.**

   You can also use any of the methods we describe in the "Cropping and Straightening Images" section, earlier in this chapter, except for the Straighten tool, which is exclusive to Expert mode.

6. **To rotate the image in 90-degree increments, click the Rotate Left or Rotate Right (accessed via the arrow next to Rotate Left) button in the left side of the workspace.**

7. **Apply any necessary auto fixes, such as Auto Smart Fix, Auto Levels, Auto Contrast, and Auto Color Correction.**

   All these commands are on the Enhance menu or in the Smart Fix, Lighting, and Color sections in the Adjustments pane of the workspace. If the commands aren't visible, click the Adjustments button in the bottom-right corner of the workspace.

   Each of these fixes is described in detail in the section "Employing One-Step Auto Fixes," earlier in this chapter. Remember that usually one of the fixes is enough. Don't stack them on top of each other. If one doesn't work, click the Reset button in the top-right corner of the image preview and try another. If you're not happy with the results, go to Step 8. If you are happy, skip to Step 9.

8. **If the auto fixes don't quite cut it, get more control by using the sliders, or clicking the thumbnails, available for Smart Fix, Exposure, Lighting, Color, and Balance located on the right side of the workspace.**

For all adjustments, you can hover your mouse over any of the thumbnails in the pane to get a dynamic preview of that particular adjustment. The slider automatically moves accordingly.

Here's a brief description of each available adjustment:

- *Exposure:* Adjusts the brightness or darkness of an image. Move the slider left to darken and right to lighten. The values are in increments of f-stops and range from –4 to 4.

- *Shadows:* When you drag the slider to the right, it lightens the darker areas of your image without adjusting the highlights.

- *Midtones:* Adjusts the contrast of the middle (gray) values and leaves the highlights and shadows as they are.

- *Highlights:* When you drag the slider to the right, it darkens the lighter areas of your image without adjusting the shadows.

- *Saturation:* Adjusts the intensity of the colors.

- *Hue:* Changes all colors in an image. Make a selection first to change the color of just one or more elements. Otherwise, use restraint with this adjustment.

- *Vibrance:* Adjusts the saturation of an image by increasing the saturation of less saturated colors more than those that are already saturated. This option tries to minimize *clipping* (or loss of color) as it increases saturation and preserves skin tones. Move the slider right to increase saturation. The values are in increments of f-stops and range from –1 to 1.

- *Temperature:* Adjusts the colors to make them warmer (red) or cooler (blue). You can use this adjustment to correct skin tones or to correct overly cool images (such as snowy winter photos) or overly warm images (such as photos shot at sunset or sunrise).

- *Tint:* Adjusts the tint after you adjust temperature to make the color more green or magenta.

If you still don't get the results you need, move on to one of the more manual adjustments that we describe in Chapter 10.

You can also apply fixes to just selected portions of your image. Quick mode offers the Quick Selection tool for your selection tasks. For details on using this tool, see Chapter 7.

9. **Add finishing fixes by using the remaining tools in the Tools panel.**

   Here's a description of each tool:

   - *Red Eye Removal tool:* Try the Auto Red Eye Fix to remove red-eye from your people's eyes. But if it doesn't work, try using the Red Eye tool. This method is described in the section "Auto Red Eye Fix," earlier in this chapter.

   - *Whiten Teeth:* This fix does what it says — it whitens teeth. Be sure to choose an appropriate brush size from the Size slider in the Tool Options. Click the Brush Settings option to specify Hardness, Spacing, Roundness, and Angle of the brush tip. (For more on brush options, see Chapter 12.) Using a brush diameter that's larger than the area of the teeth also whitens/brightens whatever else it touches — lips, chin, and so on. Click the teeth. (*Note:* This tool makes a selection and whitens simultaneously.) After your initial click, your selection option converts from New Selection to Add to Selection in the Tool Options. If you pick up too much in your dental selection, click the Subtract from Selection option and click the area you want to eliminate. When you're happy with the results of your whitening session, choose Select➪Deselect or press Ctrl+D (⌘+D on the Mac).

   - *Spot Healing Brush/Healing Brush:* These tools are great for fixing flaws, both big (Healing Brush) and small (Spot Healing Brush). For a detailed explanation on using these tools, see the upcoming sections "Retouching with the Healing Brush" and "Zeroing in with the Spot Healing Brush."

10. **(Optional) Add any desired text by clicking your image with the Text tool.**

    See Chapter 13 for details on working with text.

    Use the Move tool in Quick mode to fine-tune the positioning of your text.

11. **Sharpen your image automatically by clicking the Auto button under Sharpen in the right pane.**

    You can also choose Enhance➪Auto Sharpen. If automatically sharpening doesn't do the fix, you can manually drag the Sharpen slider.

    This fix should always be the last adjustment you make on your image.

The Quick mode sports additional panels. Click the Effects icon in the bottom-right corner of the workspace to access various effects, such as Toy Camera and Cross Process, that you can apply to your image. Click the Frames icon to apply borders, such as Scrapbook and Comic, to the perimeter of your photo. You can also click the Textures icon to access textures, such as Cracked Paint and Sunburst. Click the Adjustments icon to return to your default panel settings. To apply any effect, texture, or frame, simply click the appropriate thumbnail in the pane.

# Fixing Small Imperfections with Tools

Elements provides you with several handy tools to correct minor imperfections in your photos. You can use the Clone Stamp tool to clone parts of your image, heal blemishes with the Healing Brush or Spot Healing Brush tools, lighten or darken small areas with the Dodge and Burn tools, soften or sharpen the focus with the Blur or Sharpen tools, and fix color with the Sponge or Color Replacement tools.

## Cloning with the Clone Stamp tool

Elements enables you to clone elements without the hassle of genetically engineering DNA. In fact, the Clone Stamp tool works by just taking sampled pixels from one area and copying, or *cloning*, them onto another area. The advantage of cloning, rather than making a selection and then copying and pasting, is that it's easier to realistically retain soft-edged elements, such as shadows, as shown in Figure 9-12.

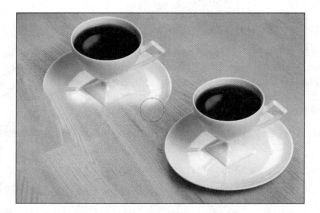

©istockphoto/Beano5 Image #14501558

**Figure 9-12:** The Clone Stamp tool enables you to realistically duplicate soft-edged elements, such as shadows.

The Clone Stamp doesn't stop there. You can also use this tool for fixing flaws, such as scratches, bruises, date/time stamp imprints from cameras, and other minor imperfections. Although the birth of the healing tools (discussed in the following sections) has somewhat pushed the Clone Stamp tool out of the retouching arena, it can still do a good repair job in many instances.

Here's how to use the Clone Stamp tool:

1. **In Expert mode, choose the Clone Stamp tool from the Tools panel.**

   It looks like an analog rubber stamp.

2. **In the Tool Options, choose a brush from the Brush Preset Picker panel and then use the brush as is or adjust its size with the Size slider.**

   Keep in mind that the size of the brush you specify should be appropriate for what you're trying to clone or retouch. If you're cloning a large object, use a large brush. For repairing small flaws, use a small brush. Cloning with a soft-edged brush usually produces more natural results. For details on brushes, see Chapter 12.

3. **Choose your desired Opacity and Blend Mode percentage.**

   For more on blend modes, see Chapter 11. To make your cloned image appear ghosted, use an Opacity percentage of less than 100 percent.

4. **Select or deselect the Aligned option.**

   With Aligned selected, the clone source moves when you move your cursor to a different location. If you want to clone multiple times from the same location, leave the Aligned option deselected.

5. **Select or deselect the Sample All Layers check box.**

   This option enables you to sample pixels from all visible layers for the clone. If this option is deselected, the Clone Stamp tool clones from only the active layer. Check out Chapter 8 for details about working with layers.

6. **Click the Clone Overlay button if you want to display an overlay.**

   Displaying an overlay can be helpful when what you're cloning needs to be in alignment with the underlying image. In the Clone Overlay dialog box, select the Show Overlay check box. Adjust the opacity for your overlay. If you select Auto Hide, when you release your mouse, you see a ghosted preview of how your cloned pixels will appear on the image. While you're cloning, however, the overlay is hidden. Select Clipped to have the overlay contained only within the boundaries of your brush. We think that this makes it easier to more precisely clone what you want. Finally, select Invert Overlay to reverse the colors and tones in your overlay.

7. **Alt-click (Option-click on the Mac) the area of your image that you want to clone to define the source of the clone.**

8. **Click or drag along the area where you want the clone to appear.**

   While you drag, Elements displays a crosshair cursor along with your Clone Stamp cursor. The crosshair is the source you're cloning from, and the Clone Stamp cursor is where the clone is being applied. While you move the mouse, the crosshair also moves, so you have a continuous reference to the area of your image that you're cloning. Watch the crosshair, or else you may clone something you don't want.

9. **Repeat Steps 7 and 8 until you've finished cloning your desired element.**

If you've selected the Aligned option when cloning an element, try to clone it without lifting your mouse. Also, when you're retouching a flaw, try not to overdo it. One or two clicks on each flaw is usually plenty. If you're heavy-handed with the Clone Stamp, you get a blotchy effect that's a telltale sign something has been retouched.

## Retouching with the Healing Brush

The Healing Brush tool is similar to the Clone Stamp tool in that you clone pixels from one area onto another area. But the Healing Brush is superior in that it takes into account the tonality (highlights, midtones, and shadows) of the flawed area. The Healing Brush clones by using the *texture* from the sampled area (the *source*) and then using the *colors* around the brush stroke while you paint over the flawed area (the *destination*). The highlights, midtones, and shadow areas remain intact, giving you a realistic and natural repair that isn't as blotchy or miscolored as the repair you get with the Clone Stamp tool.

Here are the steps to heal a photo:

1. **In Expert mode, open an image in need of a makeover and select the Healing Brush tool from the Tools panel.**

   The tool looks like a bandage. You can also press J to cycle between the Healing Brush and Spot Healing Brush tools. You can also select either of these tools and then choose the other tool from the Tool Options.

   You can also heal between two images, but be sure that they have the same color mode — for example, both RGB (red, green, blue). We chose a couple who are super photogenic but might appreciate a little tune-up, as shown in Figure 9-13.

2. **Specify a size for the Healing brush tool in the Tool Options.**

   You can also adjust the hardness, spacing, angle, and roundness in the Brush Settings. For details on these options, see Chapter 12. Don't be shy. Be sure to adjust the size of your brush as needed. Using the appropriate brush size for the flaw you're retouching is critical to creating a realistic effect.

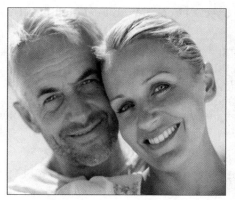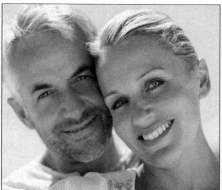

©istockphoto.com/Yuri_Arcurs Image #10297652

**Figure 9-13:** Wipe out ten years in two minutes with the Healing Brush tool.

3. **Choose your desired blend mode.**

   For most retouching jobs, you probably should leave the mode as Normal. Replace mode preserves textures, such as noise or film grain, around the edges of your strokes.

4. **Choose one of these Source options:**

   - *Sampled* uses the pixels from the image. You use this option for the majority of your repairs.

   - *Pattern* uses pixels from a pattern chosen from the Pattern Picker drop-down panel.

5. **Select or deselect the Aligned option.**

   For most retouching tasks, you probably should leave Aligned selected. Here are the details on each option:

   - *With Aligned selected:* When you click or drag with the Healing Brush, Elements displays a crosshair along with the Healing Brush cursor. The crosshair represents the sampling point, also known as the *source.* When you move the Healing Brush tool, the crosshair also moves, providing a constant reference to the area you're sampling.

   - *With Aligned deselected:* Elements applies the source pixels from your initial sampling point, no matter how many times you stop and start dragging.

6. **Select the Sample All Layers check box to heal an image by using all visible layers.**

   If this option is deselected, you heal from only the active layer.

   To ensure maximum editing flexibility later, select the Sample All Layers check box and add a new, blank layer above the image you want to heal. When you heal the image, the pixels appear on the new layer and not on the actual image, which means you can adjust opacity and blend modes and make other adjustments to the healed layer.

7. **(Optional) Click the Clone Overlay button.**

   See the earlier section, "Cloning with the Clone Stamp tool," for details on using an overlay.

8. **Establish the sampling point by Alt-clicking (Option-clicking on the Mac).**

   Make sure to click the area of your image that you want to clone from. In our example, we clicked a smooth area of the forehead when working on each person.

9. **Release the Alt (Option on the Mac) key and click or drag over a flawed area of your image.**

   Keep an eye on the crosshair because that's the area you're healing from. We brushed over the wrinkles under and around the eyes, mouth, and forehead. (Refer to Figure 9-13.) This couple never looked so good, and they endured absolutely no recovery time.

## Zeroing in with the Spot Healing Brush

Whereas the Healing Brush is designed to fix larger flawed areas, the Spot Healing Brush is designed for smaller imperfections, with one exception — the Content-Aware option, which we explain in Step 3 in the following steps. The Spot Healing Brush doesn't require you to specify a sampling source. It automatically takes a sample from around the area to be retouched. It's quick, easy, and often effective. But it doesn't give you control over the sampling source, so keep an eye out for less-than-desirable fixes.

Here's how to quickly fix flaws with the Spot Healing Brush tool:

1. **In Expert mode, open your image and grab the Spot Healing Brush tool.**

   The tool looks like a bandage with a dotted oval behind it. You can also press J to cycle between the Healing Brush and Spot Healing Brush tools. You can also select either of these tools and then choose the other tool from the Tool Options.

2. **In the Tool Options, click the Brush Preset Picker and select a brush tip. You can further adjust the diameter by dragging the Size slider.**

   Select a brush that's a little larger than the flawed area you're fixing.

3. **Choose a type in the Tool Options:**

   - *Proximity Match:* This type samples the pixels around the edge of the selection to fix the flawed area.

   - *Create Texture:* This type uses all the pixels in the selection to create a texture to fix the flaw.

   - *Content-Aware:* If you want to eliminate something larger than a mole or freckle, this is the option of choice where actual content from the image is used as a kind of patch for the flawed area. Large objects can be zapped away; Figure 9-14 shows how we eliminated the cannonballer. ***Note:*** You may have to paint over the offending object a couple of times to get your desired result. Also, a touch-up with the Clone Stamp or other healing tools may be needed.

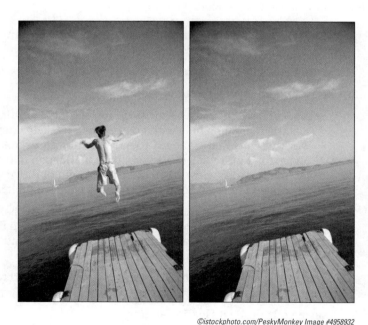

©istockphoto.com/PeskyMonkey Image #4958932

**Figure 9-14:** Eliminate cannonballers and other offending objects with the Content-Aware option.

Try Proximity Match first, and if it doesn't work, undo it and try Create Texture or Content-Aware.

4. **Select the Sample All Layers check box to heal an image by using all visible layers.**

   If you leave this check box deselected, you heal from only the active layer.

5. **Click, drag, or "paint" over the area you want to fix.**

   We painted over the cannonballer with the Spot Healing Brush and achieved realistic results, as shown in the after image in Figure 9-14.

## Repositioning with the Content-Aware Move tool

The Content-Aware Move tool enables you to select and move a portion of an image. The best thing is, however, that when you move that portion, the hole left behind is miraculously filled using content-aware technology. In other words, Elements analyzes the area surrounding the selected portion you're moving and then fills the hole with matched content.

Here's how to use this beneficial editing tool:

1. **In Expert mode, open your image and select the Content-Aware Move tool.**

   The tool looks like two arrows. You can also press the Q key.

2. **Choose either Move or Extend mode.**

   - *Move:* Elements moves your selection to a new location and then fills the remaining hole with content-aware pixels. The Move mode works great when you need to move an object, or objects, in your image for a more desirable composition. Keep in mind that this technique works best when the background of the new location of the object is similar to the background from which it was plucked.

   - *Extend:* Elements extends your selected area while maintaining any lines and structural elements and blending them into the existing object. This option works great for expanding or contracting objects such as hair, fur, trees, buildings and so on.

   For Figure 9-15, we chose the Move mode to move the girl to the right so we could add some type.

3. **Choose your desired Healing setting.**

   Healing controls the amount of flexibility Elements uses in determining how to shift pixels around and how strictly regions are preserved when determining the content-aware fill. The default setting is smack dab in the middle, which is what we stuck with.

   You can also select the Sample All Layers check box to use content from all your layers. If you leave this check box deselected, you use only content from the active layer.

4. **Drag around the area of your image that you want to move or extend.**

   If you need to fine-tune your selection, you can use the Path Operations options on the Options bar. Or you can press the Shift key to add to your selected area or press Alt (Option on the Mac) to delete from your selection.

5. **Move your selection to your desired location.**

6. **Touch up any areas that require it.**

   You can break out the Healing tools or the Clone Stamp tool to fix any mismatches or remaining flaws. We fixed a few spots along the girl that weren't quite matched up, as shown in Figure 9-15. We also spot-healed the ugly light fixture at the top of the image.

You now also have the option of filling any selected area with a Content-Aware option. Make a selection and choose Edit⇨Fill. Under Contents, choose Content-Aware from the Use pop-up menu.

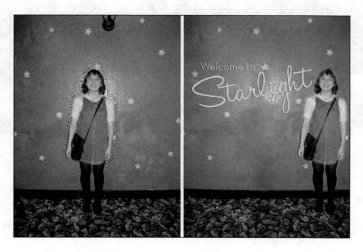

Figure 9-15: Recompose your image by using the Content-Aware Move tool.

## Lightening and darkening with Dodge and Burn tools

The techniques of dodging and burning originated in the darkroom, where photographers fixed negatives that had overly dark or light areas by adding or subtracting exposure, using holes and paddles as an enlarger made prints. The Dodge and Burn tools are even better than their analog ancestors because they're more flexible and much more precise. You can specify the size and softness of your tool by simply selecting from one of the many brush tips. You can also limit the correction to various tonal ranges in your image — shadows, midtones, or highlights. Finally, you can adjust the amount of correction that's applied by specifying an exposure percentage.

Use these tools only on small areas (such as the girl's face shown in Figure 9-16) and in moderation. You can even make a selection prior to dodging and burning to ensure that the adjustment is applied only to your specific area. Also, keep in mind that you can't add detail that isn't there to begin with. If you try to lighten extremely dark shadows that contain little detail, you get gray areas. If you try to darken overly light highlights, you just end up with white blobs.

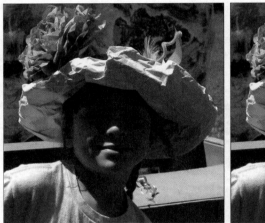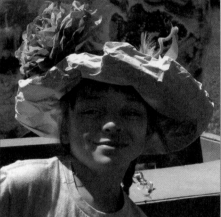

Figure 9-16: Use the Dodge and Burn tools to lighten and darken small areas.

Follow these steps to dodge or burn an image:

1. **In Expert mode, choose either the Dodge (to lighten) or Burn (to darken) tool from the Tools panel.**

   These tools look like a darkroom paddle and a hand making an "O," respectively. Press O to cycle through the Dodge and Burn tools. You can also select any of these tools and then choose your desired tool from the Tool Options.

2. **Select a brush from the Brush Preset Picker panel and also adjust the brush size if necessary.**

   Larger, softer brushes spread the dodging or burning effect over a larger area, making blending with the surrounding area easier.

3. **From the Range drop-down list, choose Shadows, Midtones, or Highlights.**

   Choose Shadows to darken or lighten the darker areas of your image. Choose Midtones to adjust the tones of average darkness. Choose Highlights to make the light areas lighter or darker.

   In Figure 9-16, the original image had mostly dark areas, so we dodged the shadows.

4. **Choose the amount of correction you want to apply with each stroke by adjusting the Exposure setting in the Tool Options.**

   Start with a lower percentage to better control the amount of darkening or lightening. Exposure is similar to the opacity setting that you use with the regular Brush tool. We used a setting of 10 percent.

5. **Paint over the areas you want to lighten or darken.**

   If you don't like the results, press Ctrl+Z (⌘+Z on the Mac) to undo.

## Smudging away rough spots

The Smudge tool, one of the focus tools, pushes your pixels around using the color that's under the cursor when you start to drag. Think of it as dragging a brush through wet paint. You can use this tool to create a variety of effects. When it's used to the extreme, you can create a warped effect. When it's used more subtly, you can soften the edges of objects in a more natural fashion than you can with the Blur tool. Or you can create images that take on a painterly effect, as shown in Figure 9-17. Keep an eye on your image while you paint, however, because you can start to eliminate detail and wreak havoc if you're not careful with the Smudge tool.

To use the Smudge tool, follow these steps:

1. **In Expert mode, select the Smudge tool from the Tools panel.**

   The tool looks like a finger. Press R to cycle through the Smudge, Blur, and Sharpen tools. You can also select any of these tools and then choose your desired tool from the Tool Options.

2. **Select a brush from the Brush Preset Picker panel. Use the Size slider to fine-tune your brush diameter.**

   Use a small brush for smudging tiny areas, such as edges. Larger brushes produce more extreme effects.

3. **Choose a blending mode from the Mode drop-down list.**

4. **Choose the strength of the smudging effect with the Strength slider or text box.**

   The lower the value, the lighter the effect.

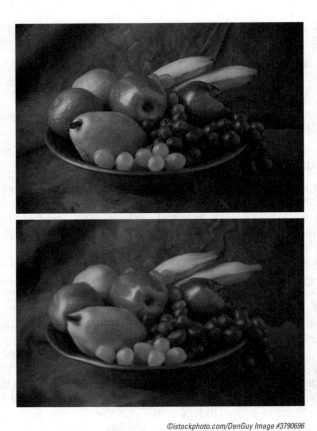

©istockphoto.com/DenGuy Image #3790696

Figure 9-17: The Smudge tool can make your images appear to be painted.

5. **If your image doesn't have layers, skip to step 6. If your image has multiple layers, select the Sample All Layers check box to make Elements use pixels from all the visible layers when it produces the effect.**

   The smudge still appears on only the active layer, but the look is a bit different, depending on the colors of the underlying layers.

6. **Use the Finger Painting option to begin the smudge by using the foreground color.**

   Rather than use the color under your cursor, this option smears your foreground color at the start of each stroke. If you want the best of both worlds, you can quickly switch into Finger Painting mode by pressing the Alt key while you drag. Release Alt to go back to Normal mode.

7. **Paint over the areas you want to smudge.**

   Pay attention to your strokes because this tool can radically change your image. If you don't like the results, press Ctrl+Z (⌘+Z on the Mac) to undo the changes and then lower the Strength percentage (discussed in the preceding Step 4) even more.

## Softening with the Blur tool

The Blur tool can be used to repair images, as well as for more artistic endeavors. You can use the Blur tool to soften a small flaw or part of a rough edge. You can add a little blur to an element to make it appear as though it was moving when photographed. You can also blur portions of your image to emphasize the focal point, as shown in Figure 9-18, where we blurred everything except the girl's face. The Blur tool works by decreasing the contrast among adjacent pixels in the blurred area.

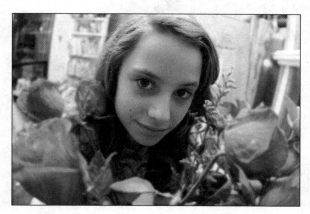

istockphoto.com/Meanttobe Image #13397598

**Figure 9-18:** The Blur tool can be used to emphasize a focal point.

The mechanics of using the Blur tool and its options are similar to those of the Smudge tool, as we describe in the preceding section. When you use the Blur tool, be sure to use a small brush for smaller areas of blur.

## Focusing with the Sharpen tool

If the Blur tool is yin, the Sharpen tool is yang. The Sharpen tool increases the contrast among adjacent pixels to give the illusion that things are sharper. You should use this tool with restraint, however. Sharpen can quickly give way to overly grainy and noisy images if you're not cautious.

Use a light hand and keep the areas you sharpen small. Sometimes, the eyes in a soft portrait can benefit from a little sharpening, as shown in Figure 9-19. You can also slightly sharpen an area to emphasize it against a less-than-sharp background.

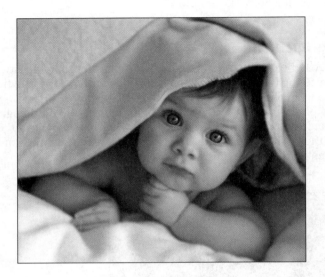

©istockphoto.com/ekinsdesigns Image #3158746

**Figure 9-19:** Reserve the Sharpen tool for small areas, such as eyes.

To use the Sharpen tool, grab the tool from the Tools panel and follow the steps provided for the Smudge tool in the section "Smudging away rough spots," earlier in this chapter. Here are some additional tips for using the Sharpen tool:

- ✔ Use a low value, around 25 percent or less.

- ✔ Remember that you want to gradually sharpen your element to avoid the nasty, noisy grain that can occur from oversharpening.

- ✔ Because sharpening increases contrast, if you use other contrast adjustments, such as Levels, you boost the contrast of the sharpened area even more.

- ✔ Select the Protect Detail option to enhance the details in the image and minimize artifacts. If you leave this option deselected, your sharpening is more pronounced.

If you need to sharpen your overall image, try choosing either Enhance⇨ Unsharp Mask or Enhance⇨Adjust Sharpness instead. These features offer more options and better control.

## Sponging color on and off

The Sponge tool soaks up color or squeezes it out. In more technical terms, this tool reduces or increases the intensity, or *saturation*, of color in both color and grayscale images. Yes, the Sponge tool also works in Grayscale mode by darkening or lightening the brightness value of those pixels.

As with the Blur and Sharpen tools, you can use the Sponge tool to reduce or increase the saturation in selected areas in order to draw attention to or away from those areas.

Follow these steps to sponge color on or off your image:

1. **In Expert mode, choose the Sponge tool from the Tools panel.**

   The tool looks like a sponge. Press O to cycle through the Sponge, Dodge, and Burn tools. You can also select any of these tools and then choose your desired tool from the Tool Options.

2. **Select a brush from the Brush Preset Picker panel. Further adjust the size of the brush tip if needed.**

   Use large, soft brushes to saturate or desaturate a larger area.

3. **Choose either Desaturate or Saturate from the Mode drop-down list to decrease or increase color intensity, respectively.**

4. **Choose a flow rate with the Flow slider or text box.**

   The *flow rate* is the speed with which the saturation or desaturation effect builds while you paint.

5. **Paint carefully over the areas you want to saturate or desaturate with color.**

   In the example shown in Figure 9-20, we used saturation to make one of the graduates a focal point and desaturated the others.

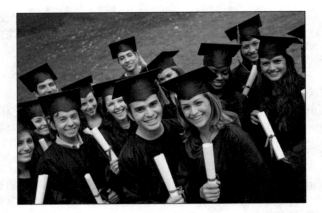

©istockphoto/Andresr Image #8312548

Figure 9-20: The Sponge tool increases or decreases the intensity of the color in your image.

## Replacing one color with another

The Color Replacement tool allows you to replace the original color of an image with the foreground color. You can use this tool in a multitude of ways:

- ✔ Colorize a grayscale image to create the look of a hand-painted photo.

- ✔ Completely change the color of an element, or elements, in your image, as shown in Figure 9-21, where we painted the field of pumpkins behind the girl with the Color Replacement tool using the color black.

- ✔ Eliminate red-eye (or yellow-eye in animals) if other, more automated methods don't work to your satisfaction.

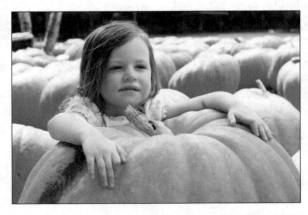

©istockphoto.com/killerb10 Image #4233667

Figure 9-21: The Color Replacement tool replaces the color in your image with the foreground color.

What we particularly like about the Color Replacement tool is that it preserves all the tones in the image. The color that's applied isn't like the opaque paint that's applied when you paint with the Brush tool. When you're replacing color, the midtones, shadows, and highlights are retained. The Color Replacement tool works by first sampling the original colors in the image and then replacing those colors with the foreground color. By specifying different sampling methods, limits, and Tolerance settings, you can control the range of colors that Elements replaces.

Follow these steps to replace existing color with your foreground color:

1. **In Expert mode, select the Color Replacement tool from the Tools panel.**

   The tool looks like a paintbrush with a small blue square next to it. Press B to cycle through the Brush, Impressionist Brush, and Color Replacement tools. You can also select any of these tools and then choose your desired tool from the Tool Options.

2. **In the Tool Options, choose your desired brush tip from the Brush Preset Picker panel. Further adjust your brush size as needed. Then adjust the hardness, spacing, roundness, and angle under Brush Settings.**

3. **Choose your desired blend mode.**

   Here's a brief rundown of each one:

   - *Color:* The default, this mode works well for most jobs. It will change the color without changing the brightness levels, thereby retaining your tonal range. This mode works great for eliminating red-eye.

   - *Hue:* Similar to color, this mode is less intense and provides a subtler effect.

   - *Saturation:* This mode is the one to use to convert the color in your image to grayscale. Set your foreground color to Black on the Tools panel.

   - *Luminosity:* This mode, the opposite of Color, doesn't provide much of an effect. It changes the brightness levels, with no regard to color.

4. **Select your Limits mode.**

   You have these options:

   - *Contiguous* replaces the color of adjacent pixels containing the sampled color.

   - *Discontiguous* replaces the color of the pixels containing the sampled color, whether or not they're adjacent.

5. **Set your Tolerance percentage.**

   *Tolerance* refers to a range of color. The higher the value, the broader the range of color that's sampled, and vice versa.

6. **Set your Sampling method.**

   You have these options:

   - *Continuous* allows you to sample and replace color continuously while you drag your mouse.

   - *Once* replaces color only in areas containing the color that you first sample.

   - *Background Swatch* replaces colors only in areas containing your current Background color.

7. **Select the Anti-aliasing option.**

   Antialiasing slightly softens the edges of the sampled areas.

8. **Click or drag your image.**

   The foreground color replaces the original colors of the sampled areas. Back in Figure 9-21, we used a black foreground color.

If you want to be very precise, make a selection before you replace your color. We did this with the girl in Figure 9-21 so we could avoid coloring outside the lines.

# Correcting Contrast, Color, and Clarity

## In This Chapter

▶ Editing your photos logically

▶ Adjusting lighting, color, and clarity

▶ Working with the Smart Brush tools

*I*f you've tried the quick and easy automatic fixes on your images and they didn't quite do the job, you've come to the right place. The great thing about Elements is that it offers multiple ways and multiple levels of repairing and enhancing your images. If an auto fix doesn't cut it, move on to a manual fix.

If you're still not happy, you can consider shooting in Camera Raw format, as long as your camera can do so. Elements has wonderful Camera Raw support, enabling you to process your images to your exact specifications. (Covering Camera Raw, however, is beyond the scope of this book, but you can find information about it in *Digital SLR Cameras & Photography For Dummies,* 5th Edition by David D. Busch. Chances are good that if you can't find the tools to correct and repair your images in Elements, those images are probably beyond salvaging.

This chapter covers the manual fixes you can make to your photos to correct lighting, contrast, color casts, artifacts, dust, scratches, sharpening, and blurring. We also cover using the Smart Brush tools to selectively apply an image adjustment.

# Editing Your Photos Using a Logical Workflow

With the information in Chapter 9 (where we explain quick fixes) and this chapter at your fingertips, you can develop a logical workflow when you tackle the correction and repair of your images. By performing steps in a particular order, you will be less likely to exacerbate the flaws and more able to accentuate what's good. For example, we use the following workflow when editing photos:

1. Crop, straighten, and resize your images, if necessary.

2. When you have the images in their proper physical state, correct the lighting and establish good tonal range for your shadows, highlights, and midtones to display the greatest detail possible.

   Often, just correcting the lighting solves minor color problems. If not, move on to adjusting the color balance.

3. Eliminate any color casts and adjust the saturation, if necessary.

4. Grab the retouching tools, such as the healing tools and filters, to retouch any flaws.

5. (Optional) Apply any enhancements or special effects.

6. Sharpen your image if you feel that it could use a boost in clarity and sharpness.

By following these steps and allocating a few minutes of your time, you can get all your images in shape to print, post, and share with family and friends.

# Adjusting Lighting

Elements has several simple, manual tools you can use to fix lighting if the Auto tools that we describe in Chapter 9 didn't work or were just too, well, automatic for you. The manual tools offer more control over adjusting overall contrast, as well as bringing out details in shadows, midtones, and highlight areas of your images. You can find all lighting adjustments in both Expert and Quick modes.

## Using touchscreen monitors

Elements supports touchscreen capability on both Windows and Mac platforms. Not only can you browse through images in the Organizer by flicking with your fingers, but you can even retouch and enhance your images by using all the tools in your Tools panel with your fingers. Talk about digital finger-painting!

## Fixing lighting with Shadows/Highlights

The Shadows/Highlights command offers a quick and easy method of correcting over- and underexposed areas, as shown on the left in Figure 10-1. This feature works especially well with images shot in bright, overhead light or in light coming from the back (*backlit*). These images usually suffer from having the subject partially or completely covered in shadows.

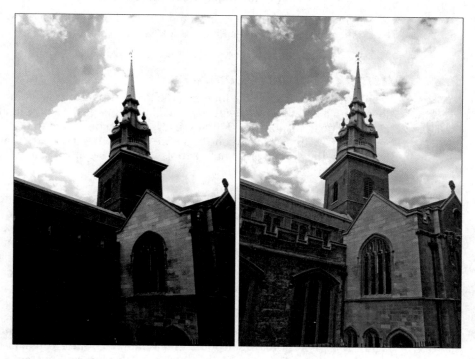

**Figure 10-1:** Correct the lighting in your images with the Shadows/Highlights adjustment.

To use the Shadows/Highlights adjustment, follow these steps:

1. **In Expert or Quick mode, choose Enhance⇨Adjust Lighting⇨Shadows/Highlights and make sure the Preview check box is selected.**

   When the dialog box appears, the default correction is applied automatically in your preview.

2. **If the default adjustment doesn't quite do the job, move the sliders (or enter a value) to adjust the amount of correction for your shadows (dark areas), highlights (light areas), and midtones (middle-toned areas).**

Your goal is to reveal more detail in the dark and light areas of your image. If, after you do so, your image still looks like it needs more correction, add or delete contrast in your midtone areas.

If only part of your image needs correcting, you can select just that portion before applying the adjustment. For more on selections, see Chapter 7.

3. **Click OK to apply the adjustment and close the dialog box.**

   If you want to start over, press the Alt (Option on the Mac) key, and the Cancel button becomes Reset. Click Reset to start again.

## Using Brightness/Contrast

Despite its aptly descriptive moniker, the Brightness/Contrast command doesn't do a great job of *brightening* (making an image darker or lighter) or adding or deleting contrast. Initially, users tend to be drawn to this command because of its appropriate name and ease of use. But after users realize its limitations, they move on to better tools with more control, such as Shadows/Highlights and Levels.

The problem with the Brightness/Contrast command is that it applies the adjustment equally to all areas of your image. For example, a photo's highlights may need darkening, but all the midtones and shadows are perfect. The Brightness slider isn't smart enough to recognize that, so when you darken the highlights in your image, the midtones and shadows also become darker. To compensate for the unwanted darkening, you try to adjust the contrast, which doesn't fix the problem.

The moral is, if you want to use the Brightness/Contrast command, select only the areas that need the correction, such as Alcatraz islands shown in Figure 10-2. (For more on selections, see Chapter 7.) After you make your selection, choose Enhance➪Adjust Lighting➪Brightness/Contrast.

## Pinpointing proper contrast with Levels

If you want real horsepower when it comes to correcting the brightness and contrast (and even the color) in your image, look no further than the Levels command. Granted, the dialog box is a tad more complex than what you find with the other lighting and color adjustment commands, but when you understand how the Levels dialog box works, it can be downright user-friendly.

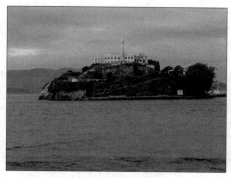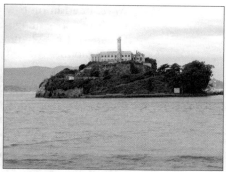

**Figure 10-2:** The Brightness/Contrast adjustment is best reserved for correcting selected areas (left) rather than the entire image (right).

You can get a taste of what Levels can do by using Auto Levels, detailed in Chapter 9. The Levels command, its manual cousin, offers much more control. And unlike the primitive Brightness/Contrast control, Levels enables you to darken or lighten 256 different tones. Keep in mind that you can use the Levels command on your entire image, a single layer, or a selected area. You can also apply the Levels command by using an adjustment layer, as we describe in Chapter 8.

If you're serious about image editing, the Levels command is one tool you want to know how to use. Here's how Levels works:

1. **In Expert or Quick mode, choose Enhance⇨Adjust Lighting⇨Levels.**

   We recommend using Expert mode for this command, where you'll have access to the Info panel in Step 2. If you're in Quick mode, skip to step 3.

   The Levels dialog box appears, displaying a *histogram,* as shown in Figure 10-3. This graph displays how the pixels of the image are distributed at each of the 256 available brightness levels. Shadows are shown on the left side of the histogram, midtones are in the middle, and highlights are on the right.

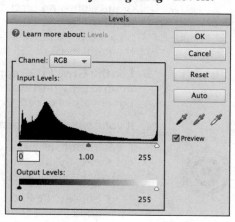

**Figure 10-3:** The Levels histogram displays the distribution of brightness levels.

*Note:* In addition to viewing the histogram of the composite RGB channel (the entire image), you can view the histogram of just the Red, Green, or Blue channel by selecting one of them from the Channel drop-down menu.

Although you generally make changes to the entire image by using the RGB channel, you can apply changes to any one of an image's component color channels by selecting the specific channel from the Channel drop-down menu. You can also make adjustments to just selected areas, which can be helpful when one area of your image needs adjusting and others don't.

2. **In Expert mode, choose Window⇨Info to open the Info panel.**

3. **Set the white point manually by using the eyedroppers in the dialog box:**

   a. *Select the White Eyedropper tool and then move the cursor over the image.*

   b. *Look at the Info panel, try to find the lightest white in the image, and then select that point by clicking it.*

   The lightest white has the highest RGB values.

4. **Repeat Step 3, using the Black Eyedropper tool and trying to find the darkest black in the image.**

   The darkest black has the lowest RGB values.

   When you set the pure black and pure white points, the remaining pixels are redistributed between those two points.

   You can also reset the white and black points by moving the position of the white and black triangles on the input sliders (just below the histogram). Or you can enter values in the Input Levels boxes. The three boxes represent the black, gray, and white triangles, respectively. Use the numbers 0 to 255 in the white and black boxes.

5. **Use the Gray Eyedropper tool to remove any color casts by selecting a neutral gray portion of your image, one in which the Info panel shows equal values of red, green, and blue.**

   If your image is grayscale, you can't use the Gray Eyedropper tool.

   If you're not sure where there's a neutral gray, you can also remove a color cast by choosing a color channel from the Channel drop-down list and doing one of the following:

   • Choose the Red channel and drag the midtone slider to the right to add cyan or to the left to add red.

   • Choose the Green channel and drag the midtone slider to the right to add magenta or to the left to add green.

   • Choose the Blue channel and drag the midtone slider to the right to add yellow or to the left to add blue.

6. **If your image requires a tweak in reducing contrast, adjust the output sliders at the bottom of the Levels dialog box.**

   Moving the black triangle to the right reduces the contrast in the shadows and lightens the image. Moving the white triangle to the left reduces the contrast in the highlights and darkens the image.

7. **Adjust the midtones (or *gamma values*) with the gray triangle input slider.**

   The default value for gamma is 1.0. Drag the triangle to the left to lighten midtones and drag to the right to darken them. You can also enter a value.

8. **Click OK to apply your settings and close the dialog box.**

   Your image should be greatly improved, as shown in Figure 10-4.

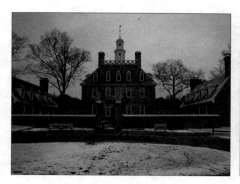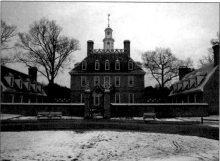

Figure 10-4: Improve the contrast of an image with the intelligent Levels command.

If you're not up to the task of manually adjusting your levels, you can opt to click the Auto button in the Levels dialog box. Elements applies the same adjustments as the Auto Levels command, as we explain in Chapter 9. Note the changes and subsequent pixel redistribution made to the histogram after you click this button.

# Adjusting Color

Getting the color you want can seem about as attainable as winning the state lottery. Sometimes an unexpected *color cast* (a shift in color) can be avoided at the shooting stage, for example, by using (or not using, in some cases) a flash or lens filter or by setting the camera's white balance for lighting conditions that aren't present. After the fact, you can usually do a pretty good job of correcting the color with one of the many Elements adjustments. Occasionally, you may want to change the color of your image to create a special effect. Conversely, you may want to strip out an image's color altogether to create a vintage feel. Remember that you can apply all these color adjustments to your entire image, a single layer, or just a selection. Whatever your color needs are, they'll no doubt be met in Elements.

You can find all color adjustments in either Expert or Quick mode, except for Defringe Layers, which is reserved for Expert mode only.

If you shoot your photos in the Camera Raw file format, you can open and fix your files in the Camera Raw dialog box. Remember that Camera Raw files haven't been processed by your camera. You're in total control of the color and the exposure.

## Removing color casts automatically

If you ever took a photo in an office or classroom and got a funky green tinge in your image, it was probably the result of the overhead fluorescent lighting. To eliminate this green color cast, you can apply the Remove Color Cast command. This feature is designed to adjust the image's overall color and remove the cast.

Follow these short steps to correct your image:

1. **In either Expert or Quick mode, choose Enhance⇨Adjust Color⇨Remove Color Cast.**

   The Remove Color Cast dialog box appears. Move the dialog box to better view your image.

2. **Click an area in your photo that should be white, black, or neutral gray, as shown in Figure 10-5.**

   In our example, we clicked the sky in the image on the left.

   The colors in the image are adjusted according to the color you choose. Which color should you choose? The answer depends on the subject matter of your image. Feel free to experiment. Your adjustment is merely a preview at this point and isn't applied until you click OK. If you goof up, click the Reset button, and your image reverts to its unadjusted state.

3. **If you're satisfied with the adjustment, click OK to accept it and close the dialog box.**

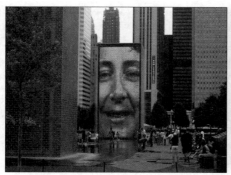 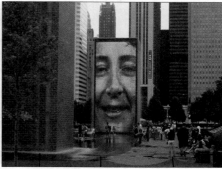

**Figure 10-5:** Get rid of nasty color shifts with the Remove Color Cast command.

If the Remove Color Cast command doesn't cut it, try applying a photo filter (as we describe in the section "Adjusting color temperature with photo filters," later in this chapter). For example, if your photo has too much green, try applying a magenta filter.

## Adjusting with Hue/Saturation

The Hue/Saturation command enables you to adjust the colors in your image based on their hue, saturation, and lightness. *Hue* is the color in your image. *Saturation* is the intensity, or richness, of that color. And *lightness* controls the brightness value.

Follow these steps to adjust color by using the Hue/Saturation command:

1. **In either Expert or Quick mode, choose Enhance⇨Adjust Color⇨Adjust Hue/Saturation.**

   The Hue/Saturation dialog box appears. Be sure to select the Preview check box so that you can view your adjustments. The Hue/Saturation command is also available in Guided mode.

2. **Choose Master from the Edit drop-down list to adjust all the colors or choose one color to adjust.**

3. **Drag the slider for one or more of the following attributes to adjust the colors as described:**

   - *Hue:* Shifts all the colors clockwise (drag right) or counterclockwise (drag left) around the color wheel.

   - *Saturation:* Increases (drag right) or decreases (drag left) the richness of the colors. ***Note:*** Dragging all the way to the left gives the photo the appearance of a grayscale image.

- *Lightness:* Increases the brightness values by adding white (drag right) or decreases the brightness values by adding black (drag left).

The top color bar at the bottom of the dialog box represents the colors in their order on the color wheel before you make any changes. The lower color bar displays the colors after you make your adjustments.

When you select an individual color to adjust, sliders appear between the color bars so that you can define the range of color to be adjusted. You can select, add, or subtract colors from the range by choosing one of the Eyedropper tools and clicking in the image.

The Hue/Saturation dialog box also lets you colorize images, a useful option for creating sepia-colored images.

4. **(Optional) Select the Colorize option to change the colors in your image to a new, single color. Drag the Hue slider to change the color to your desired hue.**

The pure white and black pixels remain unchanged, and the intermediate gray pixels are colorized.

5. **Click OK to apply your adjustments and exit the dialog box.**

Use the Hue/Saturation command, with the Colorize option, to create tinted photos, such as the one shown in Figure 10-6. You can also make selections in a grayscale image and apply a different tint to each selection. This can be especially fun with portraits. Tinted images can create a vintage or moody feel, and they can transform even mediocre photos into something special.

## Eliminating color with Remove Color

Despite all the talk in this chapter about color, we realize that there may be times when you don't want *any* color. With the Remove Color command, you can easily eliminate all the color from an image, a layer, or a selection. To use this one-step command, simply choose Enhance⇨Adjust Color⇨Remove Color.

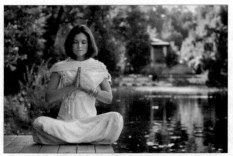

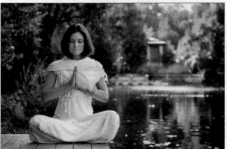

©istockphoto.com/NMaximova Image #17591577

**Figure 10-6:** Adjust the color, intensity, or brightness of your image with the Hue/Saturation command.

Sometimes, stripping away color with this command can leave your image *flat*, or low in contrast. If this is the case, adjust the contrast by using one of Elements' many lighting fixes, such as Auto Levels, Auto Contrast, or Levels.

If you want to convert a selection, a layer, or an entire image to grayscale, you can do that with the Convert to Black and White dialog box, as shown in Figure 10-7. (Choose Enhance➪Convert to Black and White.) But, rather than just arbitrarily strip color like the Remove Color command does, the Convert to Black and White command enables you to select a conversion method by first choosing an image style. To further tweak the results, you can add or subtract colors (red, green, or blue) or contrast by moving the Intensity sliders until your grayscale image looks the way you want. ***Note:*** You aren't really adding color; you're simply altering the amount of data in the color channels. For more information on channels, see Chapter 3.

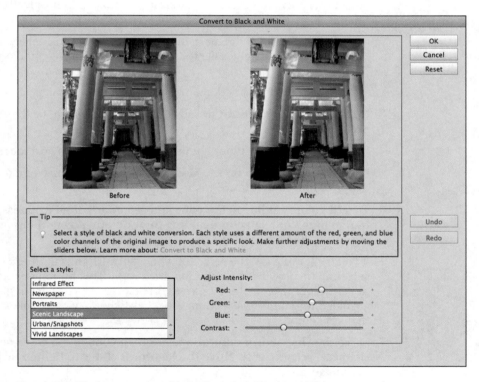

Figure 10-7: Wash away color with the Convert to Black and White command.

## Switching colors with Replace Color

The Replace Color command enables you to replace designated colors in your image with other colors. You first select the colors you want to replace by creating a *mask,* which is a selection made by designating white (selected), black (unselected), and gray (partially selected) areas. See Chapter 8 for more details on masks. You can then adjust the hue and/or saturation of those selected colors.

Follow these steps to get on your way to replacing color:

1. **In Expert or Quick mode, choose Enhance⇨Adjust Color⇨Replace Color.**

   The Replace Color dialog box appears.

2. **Select the Preview check box, and then choose either Selection or Image:**

   - *Selection* shows the mask in the Preview area. The deselected areas are black, partially selected areas are gray, and selected areas are white.

   - *Image* shows the actual image in the Preview area.

3. **Click the colors you want to select in either the image or the Preview area.**

4. **Shift-click or use the plus sign (+) Eyedropper tool to add more colors.**

5. **Press the Alt (Option on the Mac) key or use the minus sign (–) Eyedropper tool to delete colors.**

6. **To add colors similar to the ones you select, use the Fuzziness slider to fine-tune your selection, adding to or deleting from the selection based on the Fuzziness value.**

   If you can't quite get the selection you want with the Fuzziness slider, try selecting the Localized Color Clusters option. This option enables you to select multiple clusters, or areas, of color and can assist in getting a cleaner, more precise selection, especially when trying to select more than one color.

7. **Move the Hue and/or Saturation sliders to change the color or color richness, respectively. Move the Lightness slider to lighten or darken the image.**

   Be careful to use a light hand (no pun intended) with the Lightness slider. You can reduce the tonal range too much and end up with a mess.

8. **View the result in the image window.**

9. **If you're satisfied, click OK to apply the settings and close the dialog box.**

Figure 10-8 shows how we substituted the color of our tulips to change them from red to blue.

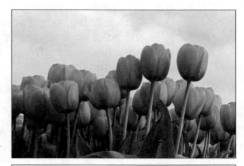

## Correcting with Color Curves

Elements borrowed a much-used feature from Photoshop named Curves. However, Elements adds the word *Color,* and Color Curves doesn't have all the sophistication of its Photoshop cousin. Nevertheless, the Color Curves adjustment attempts to improve the tonal range in color images by making adjustments to highlights, shadows, and midtones in each color channel. (For more on channels, see Chapter 3.) Try using this command on images in which the foreground elements appear overly dark due to backlighting. Conversely, the adjustment is designed to correct images that appear overexposed and washed out.

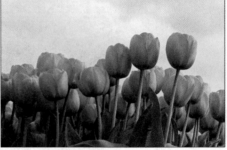

©istockphoto.com/toos Image #8696684

**Figure 10-8:** The Replace Color command enables you to replace one color with another.

Here's how to use this great adjustment on a selection, a layer, or an entire image:

1. **In Expert or Quick mode, choose Enhance⇨Adjust Color⇨Adjust Color Curves.**

The Adjust Color Curves dialog box appears.

2. **Select a curve adjustment style from the Select a Style area to make your desired adjustments while viewing your image in the After window.**

3. **Optionally, if you need greater precision, use the highlights, brightness, contrast, and shadows adjustment sliders, as shown in Figure 10-9, and then adjust the sliders as desired.**

   The graph in the lower right represents the distribution of tones in your image. When you first access the Color Curves dialog box, the tonal range of your image is represented by a straight line. While you drag the sliders, the straight line is altered, and the tonal range is adjusted accordingly.

   To start over, click the Reset button.

4. **Click OK when you've adjusted the image satisfactorily.**

   Check out Figure 10-10 for another before-and-after image.

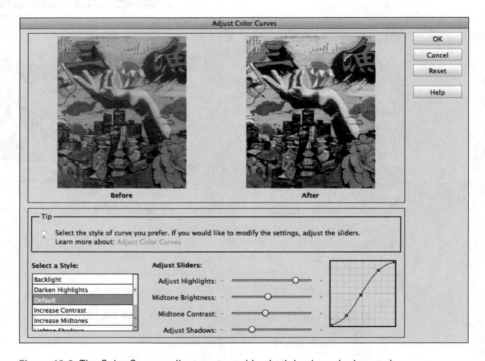

**Figure 10-9:** The Color Curves adjustment provides both basic and advanced adjustment controls.

Original                                      After the Color Curves adjustment

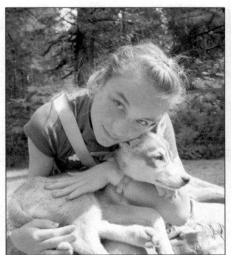 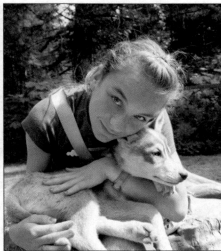

**Figure 10-10:** Color Curves improves tonal range in color images.

## Adjusting skin tones

Occasionally, you may find that the loved ones in your photos have taken on a rather sickly shade of green, red, or some other non-flesh-colored tone. To rectify that problem, Elements has the Adjust Color for Skin Tone command specifically designed to adjust the overall color in the image and get skin tones back to a natural shade.

Here's how to use this feature:

1. **Open your image in Expert or Quick mode, select the Preview check box, and do one or both of the following:**

   - *Select the layer that needs to be adjusted.* If you don't have any layers, your entire image is adjusted.

   - *Select the areas of skin that need to be adjusted.* Only the selected areas are adjusted. This is a good way to go if you're happy with the color of your other elements and just want to tweak the skin tones. For more on selection techniques, see Chapter 7.

2. **Choose Enhance⇨Adjust Color⇨Adjust Color for Skin Tone.**

   The Adjust Color for Skin Tone dialog box appears. This command is also found in Guided mode.

3. **In the image window, click the portion of skin that needs to be corrected.**

   The command adjusts the color of the skin tone, as well as the color in the overall image, layer, or selection, depending on what you selected in Step 1.

4. **If you're not satisfied with the results, click another area or fiddle with the Skin and Ambient Light sliders:**

   - *Tan* adds or removes the amount of brown in the skin.

   - *Blush* adds or removes the amount of red in the skin.

   - *Temperature* adjusts the overall color of the skin, making it warmer (right toward red) or cooler (left toward blue).

   To start anew, click the Reset button. And, of course, to bail out completely, click Cancel.

5. **When you're happy with the correction, click OK to apply the adjustment and close the dialog box.**

   The newly toned skin appears, as shown in Figure 10-11.

## Defringing layers

A telltale sign of haphazardly composited images is selections with fringe. We don't mean the cute kind hanging from your leather jacket or upholstery; we mean the unattractive kind that consists of background pixels that surround the edges of your selections, as shown in Figure 10-12.

Inevitably, when you move or paste a selection, some background pixels are bound to go along for the ride. These pixels are referred to as a *fringe* or *halo*. Luckily, the Defringe command replaces the color of the fringe pixels with the colors of neighboring pixels that don't contain the background color. In our example, we plucked the red flower out of a blue background and placed it on a white background. Some of the background pixels were included in our selection and appear as a blue fringe. When we apply the Defringe command, those blue fringe pixels are changed to colors of nearby pixels, such as red, as shown in Figure 10-12.

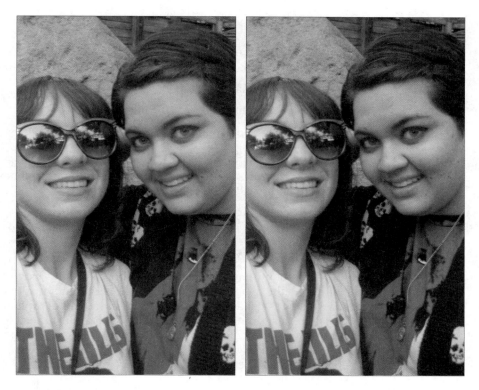

**Figure 10-11:** Give your friends and family a complexion makeover with the Adjust Color for Skin Tone command.

Fringe                    Defringed

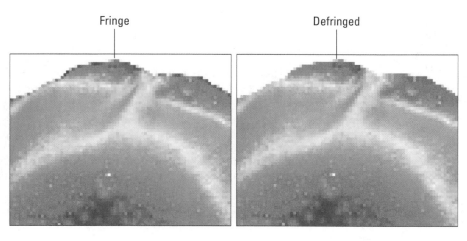

**Figure 10-12:** Remove the colored halo around your selections with the Defringe command.

Follow these steps to defringe your selection:

1. **In Expert or Quick mode, copy and paste a selection onto a new or existing layer, or drag and drop a selection onto a new document.**

   For more on selections, see Chapter 7.

2. **Choose Enhance⇨Adjust Color⇨Defringe Layer.**

   The Defringe dialog box appears.

3. **Enter a value for the number of pixels you want to convert.**

   Try entering 1 or 2 first to see whether that does the trick. If not, you may need to enter a slightly higher value.

4. **Click OK to accept the value and close the dialog box.**

## *Adjusting color temperature with photo filters*

Light has its own color temperature. A photo shot in a higher color temperature of light makes the image blue. Conversely, a photo shot in a lower color temperature makes the image yellow. In the old days, photographers placed colored glass filters in front of their camera lenses to adjust the color temperature of the light. They did this to either warm up or cool down photos or to just add a hint of color for subtle special effects. Elements gives you the digital version of these filters with the Photo Filter command.

To apply the Photo Filter adjustment, follow these steps:

1. **In Expert or Quick mode, choose Filter⇨Adjustments⇨Photo Filter.**

   The Photo Filter dialog box appears.

   You can also apply the photo filter to an individual layer by creating a photo-filter adjustment layer. For details, see Chapter 8.

2. **In the dialog box, select Filter to choose a preset filter from the drop-down list, or select Color to choose your own filter color from the Color Picker.**

   Here's a brief description of each of the preset filters:

   - *Warming Filter (85), (81), and (LBA):* These adjust the white balance in an image to make the colors warmer, or more yellow. Filter (81) is like (85) and (LBA), but it's best used for minor adjustments.

- *Cooling Filter (80), (82), and (LBB):* These also adjust the white balance that's shown, but instead of making the colors warmer, they make the colors cooler, or bluer. Filter (82) is like (80) and (LBB), but it's designed for slight adjustments.

- *Red, Orange, Yellow, and so on:* The various color filters adjust the hue, or color, of a photo. Choose a color filter to try to eliminate a color cast or to apply a special effect.

3. **Adjust the Density option to specify the amount of color applied to your image.**

4. **Select the Preserve Luminosity option to prevent the photo filter from darkening your image.**

5. **Click OK to apply your filter and close the dialog box.**

One way to minimize the need for color adjustments is to be sure you set your camera's white balance for your existing lighting conditions before shooting your photo.

## Mapping your colors

Elements provides color mapper commands that change the colors in your image by mapping them to other values. You find the color mappers on the Filter⇨Adjustments submenu. Figure 10-13 shows an example of each command; we explain all in the following list:

| Equalize | Gradient Map | Invert | Posterize | Threshold |

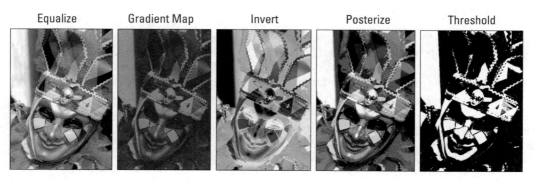

©istockphoto.com/raphotography Image #12799975

**Figure 10-13:** Change the colors in your image by remapping them to other values.

- **Equalize:** This mapper first locates the lightest and darkest pixels in the image and assigns them values of white and black. It then redistributes all the remaining pixels among the grayscale values. The exact effect depends on your individual image.

- **Gradient Map:** This command maps the tonal range of an image to the colors of your chosen gradient. For example, colors (such as orange, green, and purple) are mapped to the shadow, highlight, and midtone areas.

- **Invert:** This command reverses all the colors in your image, creating a kind of negative. Black reverses to white, and colors convert to their complementary hues. Complementary colors (which are opposite each other on the color wheel), when combined in the proper proportions, produce white, gray, or black. So blue goes to yellow, red goes to cyan, and so on.

- **Posterize:** This command reduces the number of brightness levels in your image. Choose a value between 2 and 255 levels. Lower values create an illustrative, poster-like look, and higher values produce a more photo-realistic image.

- **Threshold:** Threshold makes your image black and white, with all pixels that are brighter than a value you specify represented as white and all pixels that are darker than that value as black. You can change the threshold level to achieve different high-contrast effects.

## Adjusting Clarity

After your image has the right contrast and color, and you fix any flaws (as we describe in Chapter 9), you're ready to work on the overall clarity of that image. Although you may have fixed the nitpicky blemishes with the healing tools, if your image suffers from an overall problem, such as dust, scratches, or *artifacts* (blocky pixels or halos), you may need to employ the help of a filter. After you totally clean up your image, your last chore is to give it a good sharpening. Why wait until the bitter end to do so? Sometimes, while you're improving the contrast and color and getting rid of flaws, you can reduce the clarity and sharpness of an image. So you want to be sure that your image is as soft as it's going to get before you tackle your sharpening tasks.

Sharpening increases contrast, so depending on how much of your image you're sharpening, you may need to go back and fine-tune it by using the lighting adjustments described in the section "Adjusting Lighting," earlier in this chapter.

Finally, with all this talk about sharpening, we know that you may find it strange when we say that you may also need to occasionally blur your image. You can use blurring to eliminate unpleasant patterns that occur during scanning, to soften distracting backgrounds to give a better focal point, or even to create the illusion of motion.

## Removing noise, artifacts, dust, and scratches

Surprisingly, the tools you want to use to eliminate junk from your images are found on the Filter⇨Noise submenu in Expert or Quick mode. With the exception of the Add Noise filter, the others help to hide noise, dust, scratches, and artifacts. Here's the list of junk removers:

- **Despeckle:** Decreases the contrast, without affecting the edges, to make the dust in your image less pronounced. You may notice a slight blurring of your image (that's what's hiding the junk), but hopefully the edges are still sharp.

- **Dust & Scratches:** Hides dust and scratches by blurring those areas of your image that contain the nastiness. (It looks for harsh transitions in tone.) Specify your desired Radius value, which is the size of the area to be blurred. Also, specify the Threshold value, which determines how much contrast between pixels must be present before they're blurred.

    Use this filter with restraint because it can obliterate detail and make your image go from bad to worse.

- **Median:** Reduces contrast around dust spots. The process the filter goes through is rather technical, so suffice it to say that the light spots darken, the dark spots lighten, and the rest of the image isn't changed. Specify your desired radius, which is the size of the area to be adjusted.

- **Reduce Noise:** Designed to remove luminance noise and artifacts from your images. *Luminance noise* is grayscale noise that makes images look overly grainy. Specify these options to reduce the noise in your image:

    - *Strength:* Specify the amount of noise reduction.

    - *Preserve Details:* A higher percentage preserves edges and details but reduces the amount of noise that's removed.

    - *Reduce Color Noise:* Remove random colored pixels.

    - *Remove JPEG Artifact:* Remove the blocks and halos that can occur from low-quality JPEG compression.

### Blurring when you need to

It may sound odd that anyone would intentionally want to blur an image. But, if your photo is overly grainy or suffers from a nasty *moiré* (wavy) pattern (as described in the following list), you may need to blur the image to correct the problem. Often, you may even want to blur the background of an image to de-emphasize distractions or to make the foreground elements appear sharper and provide a better focal point.

All the blurring commands are found on the Filter⇨Blur menu in Expert or Quick mode, with the exception of the Blur tool itself, found in the Tools panel (explained in Chapter 9):

- **Average:** This one-step filter calculates the average value of the image or selection and fills the area with that average value. You can use it for smoothing overly noisy areas in your image.

- **Blur:** Another one-step filter, this one applies a fixed amount of blurring to the whole image.

- **Blur More:** This one-step blur filter gives the same effect as Blur, but more intensely.

- **Gaussian Blur:** This blur filter is probably the one you'll use most often. It offers a Radius setting to let you adjust the amount of blurring you desire.

Use the Gaussian Blur filter to camouflage moiré patterns on scanned images. A *moiré pattern* is caused when you scan halftone images. A *halftone* is created when a continuous-tone image, such as a photo, is digitized and converted into a screen pattern of repeating lines (usually between 85 and 150 lines per inch) and then printed. When you then scan that halftone, a second pattern results and is overlaid on the original pattern. These two different patterns bump heads and create a nasty moiré pattern. The Gaussian Blur filter doesn't eliminate the moiré — it simply merges the dots and reduces the appearance of the pattern. Play with the Radius slider until you get an acceptable trade-off between less moiré and less focus. If you happen to have a descreen filter (which attempts to remove the moiré pattern on scanned halftones) built into your scanning software, you can use that as well during the scanning of the halftone image.

✓ **Motion Blur:** This filter mimics the blur given off by moving objects. Specify the angle of motion and the distance of the blur. Make sure to select the Preview check box to see the effect while you enter your values.

✓ **Radial Blur:** Need to simulate a moving Ferris wheel or some other round object? This filter produces a circular blur effect. Specify the amount of blur you want. Choose the Spin method to blur along concentric circular lines, as shown in the thumbnail. Or choose Zoom to blur along radial lines and mimic the effect of zooming in to your image. Specify your desired Quality level. Because the Radial Blur filter is notoriously slow, Elements gives you the option of Draft (fast but grainy), Good, or Best (slow but smooth). The difference between Good and Best is evident only on large, high-resolution images. Finally, indicate where you want to place the center of your blur by moving the blur diagram thumbnail.

✓ **Smart Blur:** This filter provides several options to enable you to specify how the blur is applied. Specify a value for the radius and threshold, both defined in the following section. Start with a lower value for both and adjust from there. Choose a quality setting from the drop-down list. Choose a mode setting:

> *Normal* blurs the entire image or selection.

> *Edge Only* blurs only the edges of your elements and uses black and white in the blurred pixels.

> *Overlay Edge* also blurs just the edges, but it applies only white to the blurred pixels.

✓ **Surface Blur:** This filter blurs the surface or interior of the image instead of the edges. If you want to retain your edge details but blur everything else, use this filter.

If you've ever experimented with the aperture settings on a camera, you know that you can set how shallow or deep your depth of field is. Depth of field relates to the *plane of focus* (the areas in a photo that are in front of or behind the focal point and that remain in focus) or how in-focus the foreground elements are when you compare them with the background elements. The Lens Blur filter, as shown in Figure 10-14, enables you to give the effect of a shallower depth of field after you've already captured your image, thereby enabling you to take a fully focused image and create this selective focus.

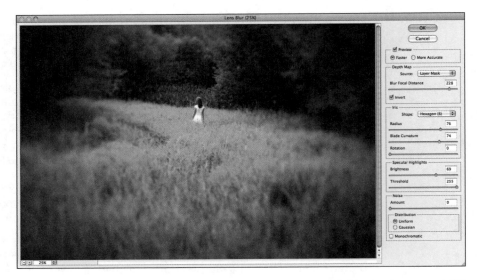

©istockphoto.com/TomFullum Image #15438998

**Figure 10-14:** Use the Lens Blur filter to create a shallow depth-of-field effect.

Here's how to use the Lens Blur filter:

**1. Choose Filter➪Blur➪Lens Blur.**

The Lens Blur Filter dialog box appears.

**2. Select your Preview mode.**

The Faster option gives you a quick preview, whereas More Accurate shows you the final rendered image.

**3. Choose a Source from the drop-down list for your depth map, if you have one.**

You can choose between a layer mask and a transparency. The filter uses a depth map to determine how the blur works.

A good way to create an image with this shallow depth-of-field effect is to create a layer mask on your image layer and fill it with a white-to-black gradient — black where you want the most focus, and white where you want the least focus or most blur. Choose Transparency to make an image blurrier and more transparent.

**4. Drag the Blur Focal Distance slider to specify how blurry or in focus an area of the image is. Or click the crosshair cursor on the part of the image that you want to be in full focus.**

Dragging the slider enables you to specify a value. You can also select Invert to invert, or reverse, the depth map source.

**5. Choose an Iris shape, such as triangle or octagon, from the Shape drop-down list.**

The Iris settings are meant to simulate a camera lens. Specify the shape of the lens, as well as the radius (size of the iris), blade curvature (how smooth are the iris edges), and rotation of that shape.

**6. Set the Brightness and Threshold values in the Specular Highlights area.**

The Lens Blur filter averages the highlights of an image, which, if left uncorrected, cause some highlights to appear grayish. The Specular Highlights controls help to retain Specular Highlights, or those highlights that should appear very white. Set the Threshold value to specify which highlights should be *specular* (remain white). Set a Brightness value to specify how much to relighten any blurred areas.

**7. Drag the Amount slider in the Noise area to add noise back into your image. Choose Monochromatic to add noise without affecting the color.**

Blurring obliterates any noise (or *film grain*) that an image may have. This absence of noise can cause the image to appear inconsistent or unrealistic, in many cases.

**8. Click OK to apply the Lens Blur and exit the dialog box.**

## Sharpening for better focus

Of course, if your images don't need any contrast, color, and flaw fixing, feel free to jump right into sharpening. Sometimes, images captured by a scanner or a digital camera are a little soft, and it's not due to any tonal adjustments. Occasionally, you may even want to sharpen a selected area in your image just so that it stands out more.

You can't really improve the focus of an image after it's captured. But you can do a pretty good job of faking it.

All sharpening tools work by increasing the contrast between adjacent pixels. This increased contrast causes the edges to appear more distinct, thereby giving the illusion that the focus is improved, as shown in Figure 10-15. Remember that you can also use the Sharpen tool for small areas, as described in Chapter 9. Here's a description of the two sharpening commands:

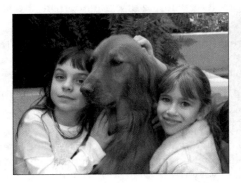 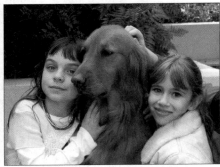

Figure 10-15: Sharpening mimics an increase in focus by increasing contrast between adjacent pixels.

✏ **Unsharp Mask:** Found on the Enhance menu in Expert or Quick mode, Unsharp Mask (which gets its odd name from a darkroom technique) is the sharpening tool of choice. It gives you several options that enable you to control the amount of sharpening and the width of the areas to be sharpened. Use them to pinpoint your desired sharpening:

- *Amount:* Specify an amount (from 1 to 500 percent) of edge sharpening. The higher the value, the more contrast between pixels around the edges. Start with a value of 100 percent (or less), which usually gives good contrast without appearing overly grainy.

- *Radius:* Specify the width (from 0.1 to 250 pixels) of the edges that the filter will sharpen. The higher the value, the wider the edge. The value you use is largely based on the resolution of your image. Low-resolution images require a smaller radius value. High-resolution images require a higher value.

  Be warned that specifying a value that's too high overemphasizes the edges of your image and makes it appear too "contrasty" or even "goopy" around the edges.

  A good guideline in selecting a starting radius value is to divide your image's resolution by 150. For example, if you have a 300 ppi image, set the radius at 2 and then use your eye to adjust from there.

- *Threshold:* Specify the difference in brightness (from 0 to 255) that must be present between adjacent pixels before the edge is sharpened. A lower value sharpens edges with very little contrast difference. Higher values sharpen only when adjacent pixels are very different in contrast. We recommend leaving Threshold set at 0 unless your image is very grainy. Setting the value too high can cause unnatural transitions between sharpened and unsharpened areas.

Occasionally, the values you enter for Amount and Radius may sharpen the image effectively but in turn create excess *grain,* or noise, in your image. You can sometimes reduce this noise by increasing the Threshold value.

✔ **Adjust Sharpness:** When you're looking for precision in your image sharpening, Unsharp Mask is one option. The Adjust Sharpness command, as shown in Figure 10-16, is the other. This feature enables you to control the amount of sharpening applied to shadow and highlight areas. It also allows you to select from various sharpening algorithms.

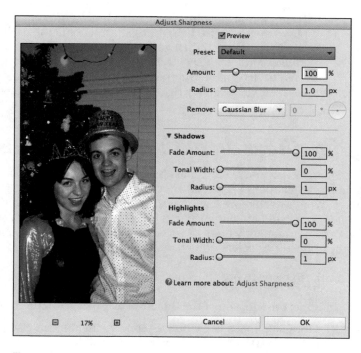

Figure 10-16: The Adjust Sharpness command.

Here are the various options you can specify:

- *Amount and Radius:* These work similar to the Unsharp Mask command; see the previous bullet.

- *Preset:* You can save your sharpening settings as a preset that you can load and use later.

- *Remove:* Choose your sharpening algorithm. Gaussian Blur is the algorithm used for the Unsharp Mask command. Lens Blur detects detail in the image and attempts to respect the details while reducing the nasty halos that can occur with sharpening. Motion Blur tries to sharpen the blurring that occurs when you move the camera (or if your subject doesn't sit still).

- *Angle:* Specify the direction of motion for the Motion Blur algorithm, described in the preceding bullet.

- *Shadows/Highlights:* You can now control the amount of sharpening in the Shadow and Highlight areas of your image. Determine the amount of sharpening with the *Fade Amount* setting. For the *Tonal Width* option, specify the range of tones you want to sharpen. Move the slider to the right to sharpen only the darker of the shadow areas and the lighter of the highlight areas. Finally, for the *Radius* setting, specify the amount of space around a pixel that's used to determine whether a pixel is in the shadow or the highlight area. Move the slider right to specify a greater area.

# Working Intelligently with the Smart Brush Tools

The Smart Brush and Detail Smart Brush tools enable you to selectively apply an image adjustment or special effect that appears on all or part of your image. What's even more exciting is that these adjustments and effects are applied via an adjustment layer, meaning that they hover over your layers and don't permanently alter the pixels in your image. It also means that you can flexibly edit or delete adjustments, if so desired.

Follow these steps to use the Smart Brush tool:

1. **In Expert mode, select the Smart Brush tool from the toolbar.**

   The tool icon looks like a house paintbrush. You can also press F, or Shift+F, if the Detail Smart Brush tool is visible.

2. **Select an adjustment category and then your particular preset adjustment from the Preset Picker drop-down list in the Tool Options.**

   In the Preset menu, you can find adjustments ranging from Photographic effects, such as a vintage Yellowed Photo, to Nature effects, such as Create a Sunset (which gives a warm, orange glow to your image).

   The Textures category has 13 presets, such as Broken Glass and Old Paper. Use these textures with your smart brushes to jazz up backgrounds and other elements in your images. For example, if that white wall in your shot is less than exciting, give it a Brick wall texture. If the drop cloth behind your portrait to reduce background clutter is a tad boring, give it a satin ripple.

3. **Choose your desired brush attributes, such as size, as shown in Figure 10-17. Or adjust attributes such as hardness, spacing, roundness, and angle from the Brush Settings drop-down panel.**

   For more on working with brushes, see Chapter 12.

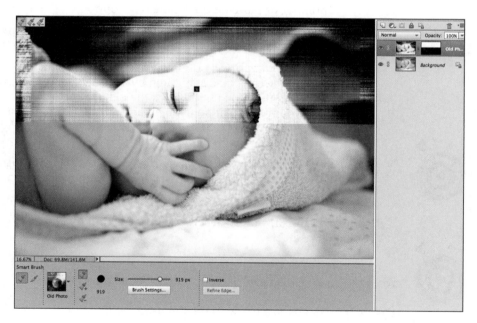

©istockphoto.com/KristinaGreke Image #17963386

**Figure 10-17:** The Smart Brush enables you to paint on adjustments.

4. **Paint an adjustment on the desired layer in your image.**

   While you paint, the Smart Brush tool attempts to detect edges in your image and snaps to those edges. In addition, while you brush, a selection border appears.

   A new adjustment layer is created automatically with your first paint stroke. The accompanying layer mask also appears on that adjustment layer. For more on adjustment layers, see Chapter 8.

5. **Using the Add and Subtract Smart Brush modes in the Tool Options, fine-tune your adjusted area by adding to and subtracting from it.**

   When you add to and subtract from your adjusted area, you're essentially modifying your layer mask. Adding to your adjusted area adds white to your layer mask, and subtracting from your adjusted area adds black to your layer mask. For more on layer masks, see Chapter 8.

6. **Make your necessary adjustments in the dialog box:**

   - *Refine your selected area.* Select the Refine Edge option in the Tool Options. For more on the Refine Edge option, see Chapter 7.

   - *Apply the adjustment to your unselected area.* Select the Inverse option in the Tool Options.

   - *Modify your adjustment.* Double-click the Adjustment Layer pin on your image. The pin is annotated by a small, square, black-and-red gear icon. After you double-click the pin, the dialog box corresponding to your particular adjustment appears. For example, if you double-click the Shoebox photo adjustment (under Photographic), you access the Hue/Saturation dialog box.

   You can also right-click and choose Change Adjustment Settings. Or you can choose Delete Adjustment and Hide Selection from the same menu.

7. **Click OK.**

8. **After you finish, simply deselect your selection by choosing Select➪Deselect.**

You can add multiple Smart Brush adjustments. After you apply one effect, reset the Smart Brush tool and apply additional adjustments.

Follow these steps to work with the Detail Smart Brush tool:

1. **In Expert mode, select the Detail Smart Brush tool in the toolbar.**

   This tool shares the flyout menu with the Smart Brush tool. The tool icon looks like an art paintbrush. You can also press F, or Shift+F, if the Smart Brush tool is visible.

2. **Select your desired adjustment category and then your particular preset adjustment from the Preset Picker drop-down list in the Tool Options.**

3. **Choose a brush tip from the Brush Preset Picker drop-down list Also choose your desired brush size.**

   Feel free to change your brush tip and size as needed for your desired effect. You can also choose other brush preset libraries from the Brush drop-down list in the Brush tip preset menu. For more on working with brushes, see Chapter 12.

   Several of the Special Effect adjustments are shown in Figure 10-18.

4. **Paint an adjustment on the desired layer in your image.**

   A new adjustment layer is created automatically with your first paint stroke, along with an accompanying layer mask. For details on adjustment layers and layer masks, see Chapter 8.

5. **Follow Steps 5 through 8 in the preceding list for the Smart Brush tool.**

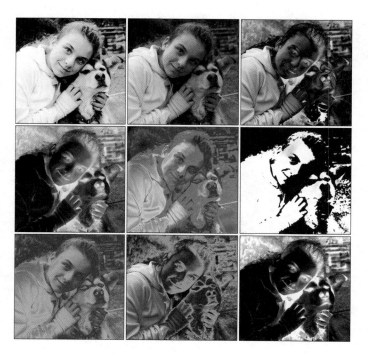

**Figure 10-18:** The Detail Smart Brush lets you paint on a variety of special effects.

# Part IV
# Exploring Your Inner Artist

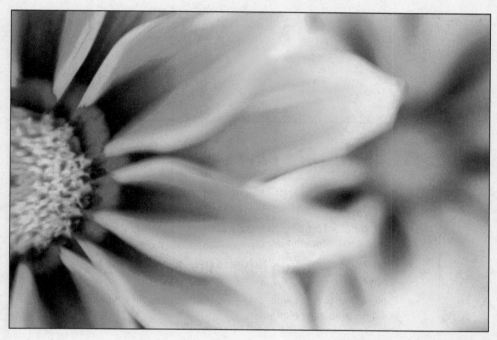

©istockphoto.com/OlsenMatt Image #2195921

At www.dummies.com/extras/photoshopelements, you can see examples of the five most useful blend modes in action.

## In this part . . .

- ✔ Use tools to draw and paint on existing photos. Or create new, blank documents and create your own drawings.

- ✔ Apply different artisitic effects by using many tools and customizing them for your own use.

- ✔ Discover tips for applying filters and styles to create dazzling images.

- ✔ Explore how to work with text — from setting headline type to creating special type effects.

# Playing with Filters, Effects, Styles, and More

## In This Chapter

▶ Fooling with filters and exploring the Filter Gallery

▶ Fixing camera distortion

▶ Exploring filters, or plug-ins

▶ Enhancing with effects

▶ Using layer styles

▶ Changing colors with blend modes

▶ Compositing images with Photomerge

After giving your images a makeover — edges cropped, color corrected, flaws repaired, focus sharpened — you may want to get them all gussied up for a night out on the town. You can do just that with filters, effects, layer styles, and blend modes. These features enable you to add that touch of emphasis, drama, whimsy, or just plain goofy fun. We're the first to admit that often the simplest art (and that includes photographs) is the best. That gorgeous landscape or the portrait that perfectly captures the expression on a child's happy face is something you may want to leave unembellished. But for the times when a little artistic experimentation is in order, turn to this chapter as your guide.

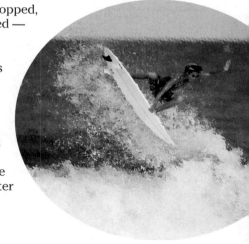

# Having Fun with Filters

Filters have been around since the early days of digital imaging, when Photoshop was just a little bitty program. *Filters,* also dubbed *plug-ins* because they can be installed or removed independently, change the look of your image in a variety of ways, as shown in Figure 11-1. They can correct less-than-perfect images by making them appear sharper or by covering up flaws, as we describe in Chapter 10. Or they can enhance your images by making them appear as though they're painted, tiled, photocopied, or lit by spotlights. The following sections give you the basics on how to apply a filter, as well as a few filtering tips.

| Original | Unsharp Mask Filter | Rough Pastels Filter |

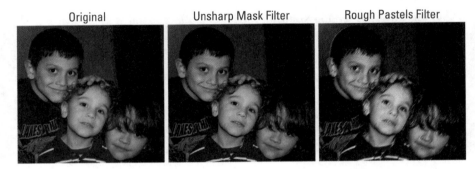

Figure 11-1: Use filters to correct image imperfections or to completely transform images.

You can't apply filters to images that are in Bitmap or Indexed Color mode. And some filters don't work on images in Grayscale mode. For a refresher on color modes, see Chapter 2.

## Applying filters

You can apply a filter in three ways:

- **The Filter menu:** In either Expert or Quick mode, from the Filter menu, choose your desired filter category and then select a specific filter.

- **The Effects panel:** In Expert mode, open the panel by choosing Window⇨ Effects or by clicking the Effects icon in the bottom right of the workspace. Click the Filters tab at the top of the panel. Choose your filter category from the drop-down list directly under the Filters tab. Double-click the thumbnail of your desired filter or drag the filter onto your image window.

✔ **The Filter Gallery:** In either Expert or Quick mode, choose Filter⇨Filter Gallery to apply one or more filters in a flexible editing environment. The Filter Gallery is described in the section "Working in the Filter Gallery," later in this chapter.

When you're using the Filter Gallery, make a backup copy of your image (or at least create a duplicate layer) before you apply filters. Filters change the pixels of an image permanently, and when you exit the Filter Gallery, the filters you apply can't be removed, except for using the Undo command or History panel. But when those options are exhausted, you're stuck with the image as is.

## Corrective or destructive filters

Although there are no hard-and-fast rules, most digital-imaging folks classify filters into two basic categories:

✔ **Corrective filters** usually fix some kind of image problem. They adjust color, improve focus, remove dust or artifacts, and so on. Don't get us wrong — pixels are still modified. It's just that the basic appearance of the image remains the same, albeit modified, we hope for the better. Two of the most popular corrective filters, Sharpen and Blur, are covered in Chapter 10.

✔ **Destructive filters** are used to create some kind of special effect. Pixels are also modified, but the image may look quite different from its original. These kinds of filters create effects, such as textures, brush strokes, mosaics, lights, and clouds. They can also distort an image with waves, spheres, and ripples.

## One-step or multistep filters

All corrective and destructive filters are one or the other:

✔ **One-step filters** have no options and no dialog boxes; select the filter and watch the magic happen.

✔ **Multistep filters** act almost like mini-applications. When you choose a multistep filter, you specify options in a dialog box. The options vary widely depending on the filter, but most come equipped with at least one option to control the intensity of the filter. A multistep filter appears on the menu with an ellipsis following its name, indicating that a dialog box opens when you choose the command.

## Fading a filter

Sometimes you don't want the full effect of a filter applied to your image. Fading a filter a bit softens the effect and can make it look less "computerish." Here's what you can do:

1. **Choose Layer⇨Duplicate Layer.**

   The Duplicate Layer dialog box appears.

2. **Click OK.**

3. **Apply your desired filter to the duplicate layer.**

   Applying your filter to a duplicate layer enables you to blend the filtered layer with the unfiltered and gives you much more control over the result (see Step 4). See the earlier "Applying filters" section for details.

4. **Use the blend modes and opacity settings located on the Layers panel to merge the filtered layer with the original unfiltered image.**

5. **(Optional) With the Eraser tool, selectively erase portions of your filtered image to enable the unfiltered image to show through.**

   For example, if you applied a Gaussian Blur filter to soften a harshly lit portrait, try erasing the blurred portion that covers the subject's eyes to let the unblurred eyes of the layer below show through. The sharply focused eyes provide a natural focal point.

Instead of erasing, you can also apply a layer mask to selectively show and hide portions of your filtered image. For details on layer masks, see Chapter 8.

## Selectively applying a filter

Up to this point in the book, we refer to applying filters to your *images*. But we use this word loosely. You don't necessarily have to apply filters to your entire image. You can apply filters to individual layers or even to selections. You can often get better effects when you apply a filter just to a portion of an image or layer. For example, you can blur a distracting background so that the person in your image gets due attention. Or, as shown in Figure 11-2, you can apply an Ocean Ripple or Wave filter to the ocean, leaving your surfer unfiltered to avoid that "overly Photoshopped" effect.

Exercising a little restraint in applying filters usually produces a more attractive image.

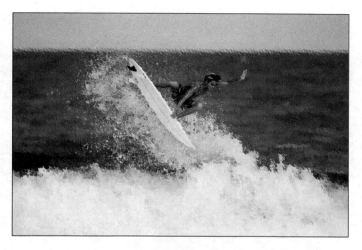

©istockphoto.com/schutzphoto Image #9642901

**Figure 11-2:** Selectively applying a filter can prevent an image from looking overly manipulated.

## Working in the Filter Gallery

When you apply a filter, don't be surprised if you're presented with a gargantuan dialog box. This *editing window,* as it's officially called, is the Filter Gallery. You can also access it by choosing Filter⇨Filter Gallery. In the flexible Filter Gallery, you can apply multiple filters, tweak their order, and edit them *ad nauseam*.

Follow these steps to work in the Filter Gallery:

1. **In either Expert or Quick mode, choose Filter⇨Filter Gallery.**

   The Filter Gallery editing window appears, as shown in Figure 11-3.

2. **In the center of the editing window, click your desired filter category folder.**

   The folder expands and shows the filters in that category. A thumbnail displays each filter's effect.

3. **Select your desired filter.**

   You get a large, dynamic preview of your image on the left side of the dialog box. To preview a different filter, just select it. Use the magnification controls to zoom in and out of the preview. To hide the Filter menu and get a larger preview box, click the arrow to the left of OK.

Show/Hide Applied Filter

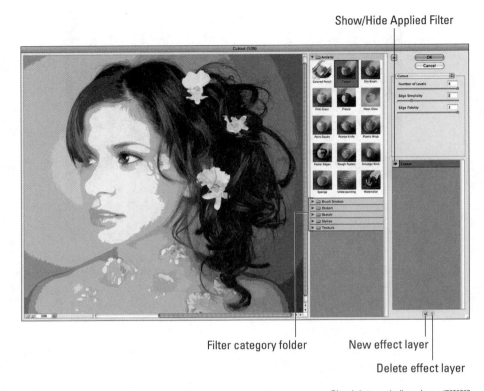

Filter category folder

New effect layer

Delete effect layer

©istockphoto.com/redhumv Image #7936392

Figure 11-3: Apply and edit multiple filters in the Filter Gallery.

**4. Specify any settings associated with the filter.**

The preview is updated accordingly.

**5. When you're happy with the results, click OK to apply the filter and close the editing window.**

**6. (Optional) If you want to apply another filter, click the New Effect Layer button at the bottom of the editing window.**

This step duplicates the existing filter.

**7. Choose your desired new filter, which then replaces the duplicate in the Applied Filters area of the dialog box.**

Each filter you apply is displayed in the lower-right area of the Filter Gallery dialog box.

You can make these changes to your filter:

- *Delete a filter.* Select it and click the Delete Effect Layer button.

- *Edit a filter's settings.* Select the filter from the list and make any changes. Keep in mind that when you edit a filter's settings, the edit may affect the look of any subsequent filters you've applied.

- *Rearrange the order of the applied filters.* Drag one of the filters above or below the other(s). Doing so changes the overall effect, however.

8. **When you're completely done, click OK to apply the filters and close the editing window.**

## Distorting with the Liquify filter

The Liquify filter is really much more than a filter. It's a distortion that allows you to manipulate an image as though it were warm taffy. You can interactively twist, pull, twirl, pinch, and bloat parts of your image. You can even put your image on a diet, as we did in Figure 11-4. In fact, most ads and magazine covers feature models and celebrities whose photos have "visited" the Liquify filter once or twice. You can apply this distortion filter on the entire image, on a layer, or on a selection. This *überfilter* comes equipped with a mega–dialog box that has its own set of tools and options, as shown in Figure 11-4.

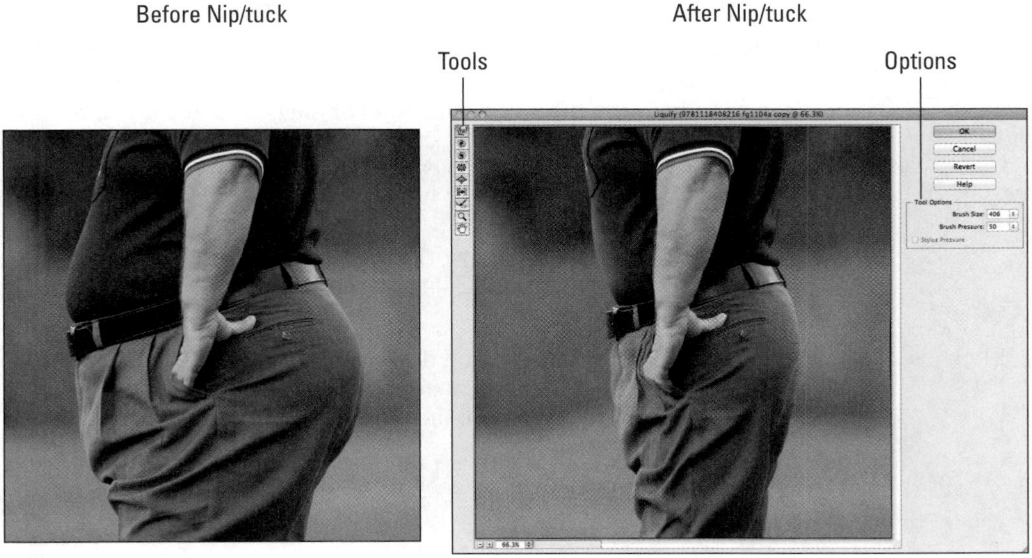

Before Nip/tuck                  After Nip/tuck

Tools            Options

©istockphoto.com/RBFried Image #1531763

**Figure 11-4:** The Liquify filter enables you to interactively distort your image.

Follow these steps to turn your image into a melted Dalí-esque wannabe:

1. **In either Expert or Quick mode, choose Filter⇨Distort⇨Liquify.**

   Your image appears in the preview area.

2. **Choose your distortion weapon of choice.**

   You also have a number of tools to help zoom and navigate around your image window.

   Here's a description of each tool to help you decide which to use. (The letter in parentheses is the keyboard shortcut.)

   - *Warp (W):* This tool pushes pixels forward while you drag, creating a stretched effect. Use short strokes or long pushes.

   - *Twirl Clockwise (R) and Twirl Counterclockwise (L):* These options rotate pixels either clockwise or counterclockwise. Place the cursor in one spot, hold down the mouse button, and watch the pixels under your brush rotate; or drag the cursor to create a moving twirl effect.

   - *Pucker (P):* Click and hold or drag to pinch your pixels toward the center of the area covered by the brush. To reverse the pucker direction *(bloat),* press the Alt (Option on the Mac) key while you hold or drag.

   - *Bloat (B):* Click and hold or drag to push pixels toward the edge of the brush area. To reverse the bloat direction *(pucker),* press the Alt (Option on the Mac) key while you hold or drag.

   - *Shift Pixels (S):* This tool moves pixels to the left when you drag the tool straight up. Drag down to move pixels to the right. Drag clockwise to increase the size of the object being distorted. Drag counterclockwise to decrease the size. To reverse any direction, press the Alt (Option on the Mac) key while you hold or drag.

   - *Reconstruct (E):* See Step 4 for an explanation of this tool's function.

   - *Zoom (Z):* This tool, which works like the Zoom tool on the Elements Tools panel, zooms the focus in and out so that you can better see your distortions.

   You can zoom out by holding down the Alt (Option on the Mac) key when you press Z. You can also zoom by selecting a magnification percentage from the pop-up menu in the lower-left corner of the dialog box.

- *Hand (H):* This tool works like the Hand tool on the Elements Tools panel. Drag with the Hand tool to move the image around the preview window.

3. **Specify your options in the Tool Options:**

   - *Brush Size:* Drag the pop-up slider or enter a value from 1 to 600 pixels to specify the width of your brush.

   - *Brush Pressure:* Drag the pop-up slider or enter a value from 1 to 100 to change the pressure. The higher the pressure, the faster the distortion effect is applied.

   - *Stylus Pressure:* If you're lucky enough to have a graphics tablet and stylus, click this option to select the pressure of your stylus.

4. **(Optional) If you get a little carried away, select the Reconstruct tool and then hold down or drag the mouse on the distorted portion of the image that you want to reverse or reconstruct.**

   *Reconstructing* enables you to undo portions of your distorted image back to a less distorted or original state. (The reconstruction occurs faster at the center of the brush's diameter.) To partially reconstruct your image, set a low brush pressure and watch closely while your mouse drags across the distorted areas.

5. **Click OK to apply the distortions and close the dialog box.**

   If you mucked things up and want to start again, click the Revert button to get your original, unaltered image back. This action also resets the tools to their previous settings.

## Correcting Camera Distortion

If you've ever tried to capture a looming skyscraper or cathedral in the lens of your camera, you know that it often involves tilting your camera and putting your neck in an unnatural position. And then, after all that, what you end up with is a distorted view of what was an impressive building in real life, as shown with the before image on the left in Figure 11-5. Fortunately, that's not a problem with Elements. The Correct Camera Distortion filter fixes the distorted perspective created by both vertical and horizontal tilting of the camera. As a bonus, this filter also corrects other kinds of distortions caused by lens snafus.

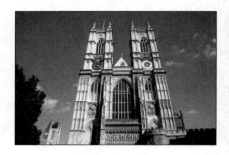 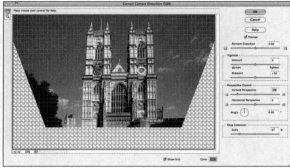

© istockphoto.com/veni Image #4193924

**Figure 11-5:** The Correct Camera Distortion filter fixes distortions caused by camera tilt and lens flaws.

Here's how to fix all:

1. **In either Expert or Quick mode, choose Filter⇨Correct Camera Distortion.**

2. **In the Correct Camera Distortion dialog box that appears, select the Preview option.**

3. **Specify your correction options:**

   - *Remove Distortion:* Corrects *lens barrel,* which causes your images to appear spherized or bloated. This distortion can occur when you're using wide-angle lenses. It also corrects *pincushion* distortion, which creates images that appear to be pinched in at the center, a flaw that's found when using telephoto or zoom lenses. Move the slider while keeping an eye on the preview. Use the handy grid as your guide for proper alignment.

   - *Vignette Amount:* Adjusts the amount of lightening or darkening around the edges of your photo that you can get sometimes from incorrect lens shading. Change the width of the adjustment by specifying a midpoint value. A lower midpoint value affects more of the image. Then move the Amount slider while viewing the preview.

   - *Vertical Perspective:* Corrects the distorted perspective created by tilting the camera up or down. Again, use the grid to assist in your correction. We used the vertical perspective to correct Westminster Abbey, as shown in Figure 11-5. It was a nice shot as is, but it could use a little tweaking.

- *Horizontal Perspective:* Also corrects the distorted perspective. Use the grid to make horizontal lines (real and implied) in your image parallel. For better results, set the angle of movement under the Angle option.

- *Angle:* Enables you to rotate the image to compensate for tilting the camera. You may also need to tweak the angle slightly after correcting the vertical or horizontal perspective.

- *Edge Extension Scale:* When you correct the perspective on your image, you may be left with blank areas on your canvas. You can scale your image up or down to crop into the image and eliminate these holes. Scaling up results in interpolating your image up to its original pixel dimensions. Basically, *interpolation* means Elements analyzes the colors of the original pixels in your image and creates new ones, which are then added to the existing ones. This often results in less than optimum quality. Therefore, if you do this, be sure to start with an image that has a high-enough pixel dimension, or *resolution,* to avoid severe degradation. For more on resolution, see Chapter 2.

- *Show Grid:* Shows and hides the grid, as needed. You can also choose the color of your grid lines by clicking on the Color option.

- *Zoom Tool:* Zooms in and out for your desired view. You can also use plus (+) and minus (–) icons and the Magnification pop-up menu in the bottom-left corner of the window.

- *Hand Tool:* Moves you around the image window when you're zoomed in.

4. **Click OK to apply the correction and close the dialog box.**

# Exploring Element's Unique Filters

Elements has a set of its very own filters. Prior to Elements 11, all the filters were hand-me-downs from Photoshop. You can find the three unique filters under the Filter⇨Sketch submenu. To really get a feel for the cool effects these filters can create, we invite you to open a couple of your favorite images and play with the various presets and settings.

Here are the general steps to apply any of these filters:

1. **In either Expert or Quick mode, choose Filter⇨Sketch⇨*Your Specific Filter.***

   For example, if you want to use the Comic filter, choose Filter⇨Sketch⇨ Comic.

2. **In the filter dialog box, choose from four presets.**

3. **Adjust any default settings.**

   You can find details about each filter's settings in the following sections outlining each filter.

   If you want to reset your sliders back to the default values for the preset, hold down the Alt (Option on the Mac) key, and the Cancel button in the dialog box changes to a Reset button.

4. **Adjust your view as needed by using the following controls:**

   • *Zoom:* Zoom in and out for your desired view. You can also use the 1:1 view (recommended) or Fit in Window view.

   • *Hand:* Moves you around the image window when you're zoomed in.

5. **Click OK to apply the filter and close the dialog box.**

## Creating a comic

The Comic filter takes your image and creates an effect that mimics a hand-drawn comic book illustration. In the Comic filter dialog box, you can choose from four presets, as shown in Figure 11-6:

✔ **Comic:** The default setting creates a basic comic book illustrative effect.

✔ **Grayscale:** Like comic, but converts all colors to grayscale.

✔ **Sunny Day:** Makes a high contrast, vivid effect.

✔ **Old Print:** Creates a more desaturated, old-newspaper effect.

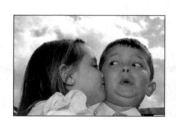
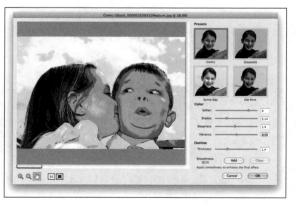

©istockphoto.com/ImagesbyTrista Image #1638352

Figure 11-6: The Comic filter turns a photo into an illustration.

Then using the sliders, you can adjust the default settings for the Color and Outline areas of the filtered image:

- **Soften:** Creates rounder or rougher areas of colors.
- **Shades:** A higher value adds more tonal levels.
- **Steepness:** A higher value makes the colored areas more defined and contrasty.
- **Vibrance:** Brightens the overall color of the image.
- **Thickness:** Affects the thickness and blackness of the outlined strokes.
- **Smoothness:** Fine-tunes your edges and enhances the overall filter effect.

## Getting graphic

The Graphic Novel filter might take a bit of experimentation to create the effect you want, at least it did for us. But after you get your settings established, the look is pretty fun and the result is like an illustration sketched for a graphic novel. *Note:* All the colors in your images convert to grayscale when you use this filter.

In the Graphic Novel filter dialog box, choose from four presets, as shown in Figure 11-7:

- **Painted Gray:** Creates an effect with a lot of midtone grays.
- **Fine Detail:** Results in an image with more white areas and an emphasis on retaining detail.
- **Hard Edges:** Like Fine Detail, but the overall look is more contrasty and the edges are more "sketchy" and less finely rendered.
- **Twisted Plot:** Creates a harsher effect with more dark areas.

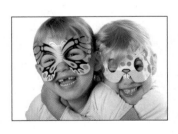
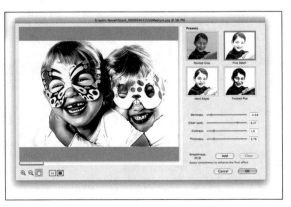

© istockphoto.com/pamspix Image #4431556

**Figure 11-7:** Create an image worthy of a graphic novel.

Then, using the sliders, you can adjust the default settings for the filtered image:

- **Darkness:** A higher value creates more areas of lightness.

- **Clean Look:** A higher value makes smoother, more refined strokes.

- **Contrast:** The higher the value, the more contrasty — and, overall, darker — an image appears. A lower value produces a lower-contrast, light-gray image.

- **Thickness:** Affects the thickness and blackness of the outlined strokes. A higher value produces a "goopier" stroke appearance.

- **Smoothness:** Fine-tunes your edges and enhances the overall filter effect.

## Using the Pen and Ink filter

The Pen and Ink filter creates an effect that looks like a hand-drawn pen-and-ink sketch.

In the Pen and Ink filter dialog box, choose from four presets, as shown in Figure 11-8. Each preset colors the image blue, purple, gray, or green respectively.

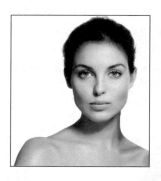
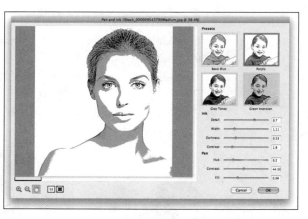

©istockphoto.com/iconogenic Image #9543790

**Figure 11-8:** Create a cartoon-like image with the Pen and Ink filter.

Then you can adjust the default setting of the sliders for the various settings for the Pen and Ink areas of the filtered image:

- **Detail:** A higher value creates finer, crisper edges.
- **Width:** A higher value creates thicker, goopier strokes, and a lower value creates crisper strokes.
- **Darkness:** A higher value creates more areas of darkness.
- **Contrast:** The higher the value, the more contrasty the image and more dark ink strokes are applied.
- **Hue:** Adjust the slider to select your desired color along the color ramp.
- **Contrast:** A higher value adds more contrast, darkness, and colored areas.
- **Fill:** Fills the image with more areas of color and less white.

# Dressing Up with Photo and Text Effects

In addition to the multitude of filters at your disposal, Elements provides a lot of effects that you can apply to enhance your photos, such as the Fluorescent Chalk effect we applied in Figure 11-9. *Note:* Some effects automatically create a duplicate of the selected layer, whereas other effects can work only on flattened images. (See Chapter 8 for details on layers.)

Unlike with filters, you can't preview how an effect will look on your image or type, nor do you have any options to specify.

Here are the steps to follow to apply an effect:

1. **In Expert mode, select your desired image layer in the Layers panel.**

   Or, if you're applying the effect to just a selection, make the selection before applying the effect.

2. **Choose Window⇨Effects or click the Effects icon in the bottom right of the workspace.**

3. **Select the Effects tab at the top of the panel.**

4. **Choose your desired category of effects from the drop-down list in the upper-right area of the panel.**

Elements 13 reorganized the categories of the effects and added about 20 new effects (at the writing of this book):

- *Frame:* Includes effects that enhance the edges of the layer or selection.

- *Faded Photo, Monotone Color, and Vintage:* This group of effects makes your image fade from color to grayscale, appear as a single color, or look like an old pencil sketch or a photo on old paper.

- *Glow:* This group adds a soft focus, and/or a white glow to your images.

- *Painting:* Makes your images look like paintings or chalk illustrations.

- *Panels:* These effects divide your image into paneled sections.

- *Seasons:* Includes effects to make your image appear snowy, rainy, sunny (bright and yellow), or wintery (white and overexposed).

- *Textures:* Gives your images a lizard skin or rubber stamped appearance.

Original

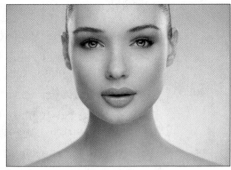

Flourescent Chalk effect

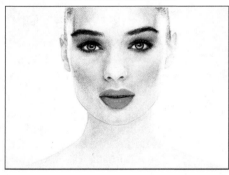

©istockphoto.com/Graffizone Image #5421076

**Figure 11-9:** Enhance your images by adding effects.

5. **On the Effects panel, double-click your desired effect or drag the effect onto the image.**

   You can view your styles and effects by thumbnails or by list. To change the view, click the down-pointing arrow in the upper-right corner of the panel to access the menu commands.

Quick mode sports its very own Effects panel. Click the Effects icon in the bottom-right corner of the workspace. To apply an effect, double-click it or drag it onto your image. Elements 13 added a bunch of new effects to Quick mode as well.

You may also want to check out the interesting effects found in Guided mode. Elements 13 even provides a few new effects — Black and White (converts image to grayscale), B&W Selection (paints selections grayscale), and B&W Color Pop (highlights your image with a colored tint) — that are worth a whirl.

You can also apply an effect to type. Select your type layer and follow Steps 2–5 in the preceding list. A dialog box alerts you that the type layer must be simplified before the effect can be applied. Simplifying that layer, of course, means you lose the ability to edit the text. Chapter 13 covers working with type in detail.

# Adding Shadows, Glows, and More

Layer styles go hand in hand with filters and photo effects. Also designed to enhance your image and type layers, layer styles range from simple shadows and bevels to the more complex styles, such as buttons and patterns.

The wonderful thing about layer styles is that they're completely nondestructive. Unlike filters, layer styles don't change your pixel data. You can edit them or even delete them if you're unhappy with the results.

Here are some important facts about layer styles:

- **Layer styles can be applied only to layers.** If your image is just a background, convert it to a layer first.

- **Layer styles are dynamically linked to the contents of a layer.** If you move or edit the contents of the layers, the results are updated.

- **When you apply a layer style to a layer, an fx symbol appears next to the layer's name on the Layers panel.** Double-click the fx icon to bring up the Style Settings dialog box and perform any editing that's necessary to get the look you want.

## Applying layer styles

Layer styles are stored in a few different libraries. You can add shadows, glows, beveled and embossed edges, and more complex styles, such as neon, plastic, chrome, and various other image effects. Figure 11-10 shows a sampling of styles.

Drop Shadow    Inner Shadow    Bevel

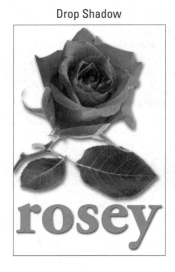 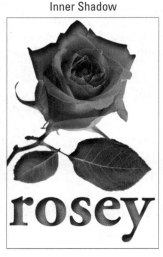 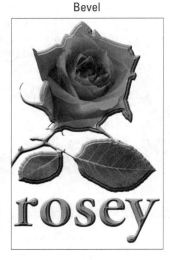

©istockphoto.com/skdonnell Image #1217074

**Figure 11-10:** Add dimension by applying shadows and bevels to your object or type.

Here are the steps to apply a style and a description of each style library:

1. **Select your desired image, shape, or type layer on the Layers panel.**

   You can apply layer styles to type layers, and the type layer doesn't need to be simplified.

2. **Choose Window⇨Effects or click the Effects icon in the bottom-right corner of the workspace.**

3. **Click the Styles button at the top of the Effects panel.**

4. **Select your desired library of styles from the drop-down list in the upper-right area of the panel:**

   • *Bevels:* Bevels add a three-dimensional edge on the outside or inside edges of the contents of a layer, giving the element some dimension. Emboss styles make elements appear as though they're raised off or punched into the page. You can change the appearance of these styles, depending on the type of bevel chosen. Adjust parameters, such as the lighting angle, distance (how close the shadow is to the layer contents), size, bevel direction, and opacity.

   • *Drop and Inner Shadows:* Add a soft drop or an inner shadow to a layer. Choose from the garden-variety shadow or one that includes noise, neon, or outlines. You can adjust the lighting angle, distance, size, and opacity as desired.

- *Outer and Inner Glows:* Add a soft halo that appears on the outside or inside edges of your layer contents. Adjust the appearance of the glow by changing the lighting angle, size, and opacity of the glow.

- *Strokes:* Add a stroke of varying width (size), opacity, and color to your selection or layer. You can position the stroke on the inside, center, or outside of your selection marquee.

- *Visibility:* Click Show, Hide, or Ghosted to display, hide, or partially show the layer contents. The layer style remains fully displayed.

- *Complex and others:* The remaining layer styles are a cornucopia of different effects ranging from simple glass buttons to the more exotic effects, such as Groovy and Rose Impressions. You can customize all these layer styles to a certain extent by adjusting the various settings, which are similar to those for other styles in this list.

5. **On the Layer Styles panel, double-click your desired effect or drag the effect onto the image.**

   The style, with its default settings, is applied to the layer. Layer styles are cumulative. You can apply multiple styles — specifically, one style from each library — to a single layer.

## Working with layer styles

Here are a few last tips for working with layer styles:

- ✔ **Edit the style's settings.** Either double-click the fx icon on the Layers panel, choose Layer⇨Layer Style⇨Style Settings, or click the gear icon located just below the Styles tab.

- ✔ **Delete a layer style or styles.** Choose Layer⇨Layer Style⇨Clear Layer Style, or drag the fx icon on the Layers panel to the trash icon.

- ✔ **Copy and paste layer styles onto other layers.** Select the layer containing the layer style and choose Layer⇨Layer Style⇨Copy Layer Style. Select the layer(s) on which you want to apply the effect and choose Layer⇨Layer Style⇨Paste Layer Style. If it's easier, you can also just drag and drop an effect from one layer to another while holding down the Alt (Option on the Mac) key.

- ✔ **Hide or show layer styles.** Choose Layer⇨Layer Style⇨Hide All Effects or Show All Effects.

- ✔ **Scale a layer style.** Choose Layer⇨Layer Style⇨Scale Effects. Select the Preview option and enter a value between 1 and 1,000 percent. This action allows you to scale the style without scaling the element.

If by chance you apply a layer style and nothing seems to happen, choose Layer⇨Layer Style⇨Show All Effects.

# Mixing It Up with Blend Modes

Elements sports a whopping 25 blend modes. *Blend modes* affect how colors interact between layers and also how colors interact when you apply paint to a layer. Not only do blend modes create interesting effects, but you can also easily apply, edit, or remove blend modes without touching your image pixels.

The various blend modes are located on a drop-down list at the top of your Layers panel in Expert mode. The best way to get a feel for the effect of blend modes is not to memorize the descriptions we give you in the following sections. Instead, grab an image with some layers and apply each of the blend modes to one or more of the layers to see what happens. The exact result varies, depending on the colors in your image layers.

## General blend modes

The Normal blend mode needs no introduction. It's the one you probably use the most. Dissolve is the next one on the list and, ironically, is probably the one you use the least.

Figure 11-11 shows both blend modes:

- ✔ **Normal:** The default mode displays each pixel unadjusted. You can't see the underlying layer at all with the Normal blend mode.

- ✔ **Dissolve:** This mode can be seen only on a layer with an opacity setting of less than 100 percent. It allows some pixels from lower layers, which are randomized, to show through the target (selected) layer.

Normal

Dissolve

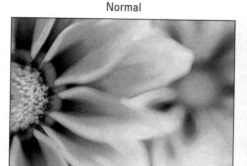

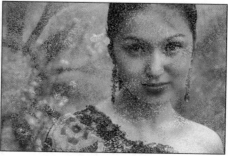

©istockphoto.com/OlsenMatt Image #2195921, Elpiniki Image #1861345

**Figure 11-11:** The Dissolve blend mode allows pixels from one layer to peek randomly through another.

## Darken blend modes

These blend modes produce effects that darken your image in various ways, as shown in Figure 11-12:

- **Darken:** Turns lighter pixels transparent if the pixels on the target layer are lighter than those below. If the pixels are darker, they're unchanged.

- **Multiply:** Burns the target layer onto the layers underneath, thereby darkening all colors where they mix. When you're painting with the Brush or Pencil tool, each stroke creates a darker color, as though you're drawing with markers.

- **Color Burn:** Darkens the layers underneath the target layer and burns them with color, creating a contrast effect, like applying a dark dye to your image.

- **Linear Burn:** Darkens the layers underneath the target layer by decreasing the brightness. This effect is similar to Multiply but often makes parts of your image black.

- **Darker Color:** When blending two layers, the darker color of the two colors is visible.

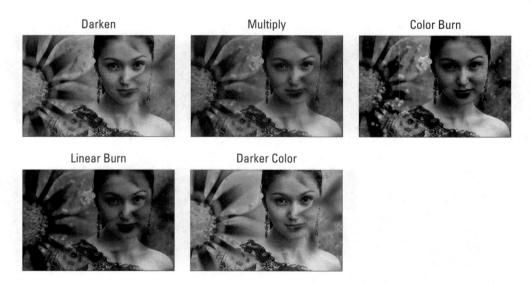

©istockphoto.com/OlsenMatt Image #2195921, Elpiniki Image #1861345

Figure 11-12: These blend modes darken your image layers.

## Lighten blend modes

The lighten blend modes are the opposite of the darken blend modes. All these blend modes create lightening effects on your image, as shown in Figure 11-13:

- **Lighten:** Turns darker pixels transparent if the pixels on the target layer are darker than those below. If the pixels are lighter, they're unchanged. This effect is the opposite of Darken.

- **Screen:** Lightens the target layer where it mixes with the layers underneath. This effect is the opposite of Multiply.

- **Color Dodge:** Lightens the pixels in the layers underneath the target layer and infuses them with colors from the top layer. This effect is similar to applying bleach to your image.

- **Linear Dodge:** Lightens the layers underneath the target layer by increasing the brightness. This effect is similar to Screen but often makes parts of your image white.

- **Lighter Color:** When blending two layers, the lighter color of the two colors is visible.

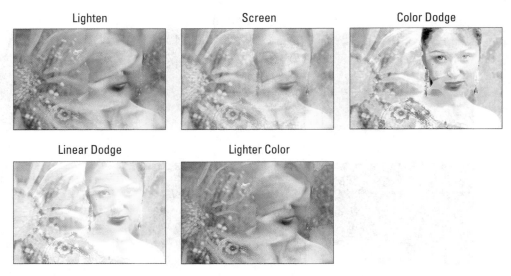

©istockphoto.com/OlsenMatt Image #2195921, Elpiniki Image #1861345

**Figure 11-13:** These blend modes lighten your image layers.

## Lighting blend modes

This group of blend modes plays with the lighting in your layers, as shown in Figure 11-14:

- **Overlay:** Overlay multiplies the dark pixels in the target layer and screens the light pixels in the underlying layers. It also enhances the contrast and saturation of colors.

- **Soft Light:** This mode darkens the dark (greater than 50-percent gray) pixels and lightens the light (less than 50-percent gray) pixels. The effect is like shining a soft spotlight on the image.

- **Hard Light:** This mode multiplies the dark (greater than 50-percent gray) pixels and screens the light (less than 50-percent gray) pixels. The effect is similar to shining a bright, hard spotlight on the image.

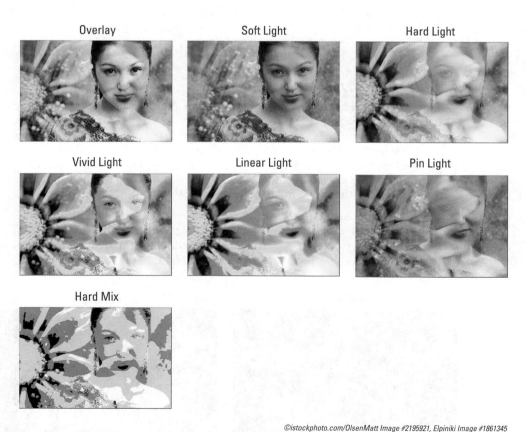

©istockphoto.com/OlsenMatt Image #2195921, Elpiniki Image #1861345

**Figure 11-14:** Some blend modes adjust the lighting between your image layers.

✔ **Vivid Light:** If the pixels on the top layer are darker than 50-percent gray, this mode darkens the colors by increasing the contrast. If the pixels on the top layer are lighter than 50-percent gray, the mode lightens the colors by decreasing the contrast.

✔ **Linear Light:** If the pixels on the top layer are darker than 50-percent gray, the mode darkens the colors by decreasing the brightness. If the pixels on the top layer are lighter than 50-percent gray, the mode lightens the colors by increasing the brightness.

✔ **Pin Light:** If the pixels on the top layer are darker than 50-percent gray, the mode replaces pixels darker than those on the top layer and doesn't change lighter pixels. If the pixels on the top layer are lighter than 50-percent gray, the mode replaces the pixels lighter than those on the top layer and doesn't change pixels that are darker. The mode is usually reserved for special effects.

✔ **Hard Mix:** This mode is similar to Vivid Light but reduces the colors to a total of eight: cyan, magenta, yellow, black, red, green, blue, and white. This mode creates a posterized effect.

## Inverter blend modes

The inverter blend modes invert your colors and tend to produce some radical effects, as shown in Figure 11-15:

✔ **Difference:** Produces a negative effect according to the brightness values on the top layers. If the pixels on the top layer are black, no change occurs in the underlying layers. If the pixels on the top layer are white, the mode inverts the colors of the underlying layers.

✔ **Exclusion:** Like Difference, but with less contrast and saturation. If the pixels on the top layer are black, no change occurs in the underlying layers. If the pixels on the top layer are white, this mode inverts the colors of the underlying layers. Medium colors blend to create shades of gray.

Difference

Exclusion

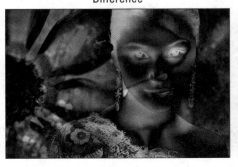 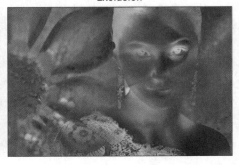

©istockphoto.com/OlsenMatt Image #2195921, Elpiniki Image #1861345

**Figure 11-15:** Difference and Exclusion blend modes invert colors.

## HSL blend modes

These blend modes use the HSL (hue, saturation, lightness) color model to mix colors, as shown in Figure 11-16:

- **Hue:** Blends the *luminance* (brightness) and *saturation* (intensity of the color) of the underlying layers with the *hue* (color) of the top layer.

- **Saturation:** Blends the luminance and hue of the underlying layers with the saturation of the top layer.

- **Color:** Blends the luminance of the underlying layers with the saturation and hue of the top layer. This mode enables you to paint color while preserving the shadows, highlights, and details of the underlying layers.

- **Luminosity:** The opposite of Color, this mode blends the hue and saturation of the underlying layers with the luminance of the top layer. This mode also preserves the shadows, highlights, and details from the top layer and mixes them with the colors of the underlying layers.

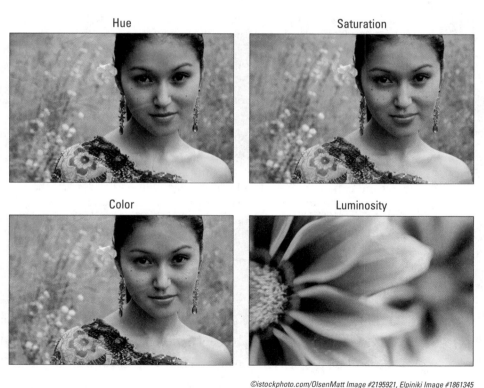

Hue

Saturation

Color

Luminosity

©istockphoto.com/OlsenMatt Image #2195921, Elpiniki Image #1861345

**Figure 11-16:** Some blend modes mix colors based on the actual hue, richness, and brightness of color.

## Using Photomerge

The awesome Photomerge features help you to create fabulous composites from multiple images. Whether it's creating the perfect shot of a group of friends or of your favorite vacation spot (without the passing cars and people), the Photomerge feature is the go-to tool to get it done. The following sections tell you how the Photomerge commands help to create the special type of composite image you need.

You can access all Photomerge commands in all three Photo Editor modes or in the Organizer.

### Photomerge Panorama

The Photomerge Panorama command enables you to combine multiple images into a single panoramic image. From skylines to mountain ranges, you can take several overlapping shots and stitch them together into one.

The following tips can help you start with good source files that will help you successfully merge photos into a panorama:

- Make sure that when you shoot your photos, you overlap your individual images by 15 to 40 percent, but no more than 50 percent.
- Avoid using distortion lenses (such as fish-eye) as well as your camera's zoom setting.
- Try to keep the same exposure settings for even lighting.
- Try to stay in the same position and keep your camera at the same level for each photo. If possible, using a tripod and moving both the tripod and camera along a level surface, taking the photos from the same distance and angle is best. However, if conditions don't allow for this, using a tripod and just rotating the head is the next best method. Be aware, however, that it can be harder to keep the lighting even, depending on the angle of your light source relative to the camera. You can also run into perspective-distortion issues with your shots.

Follow these steps to create a Photomerge Panorama image:

1. **In Expert mode, choose Enhance⇨Photomerge⇨Photomerge Panorama.**

   The Photomerge dialog box opens, as shown at the top in Figure 11-17.

2. **Choose Files or Folder from the Use drop-down list.**

3. **Click Add Open Files to use all open files, or click the Browse button and navigate to where your files or folder are located.**

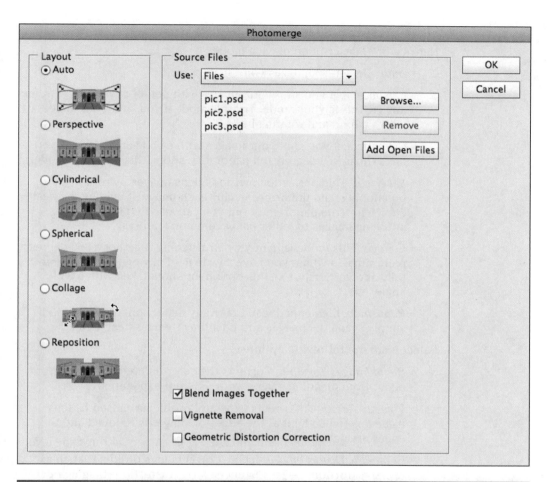

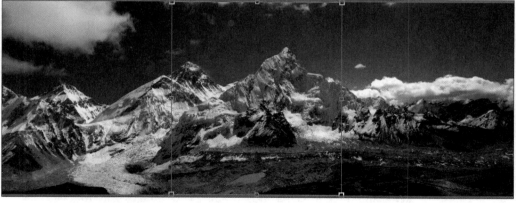

©istockphoto.com/weareadventurers Image #2375031

**Figure 11-17:** Combine multiple images into a single panorama with Photomerge.

**4. Choose your desired mode under Layout.**

Here's a brief description of each mode:

- *Auto:* Elements analyzes your images.

- *Perspective:* If you shot your images with perspective or at extreme angles, this is your mode. Try this mode if you shot your images with a tripod and rotating head.

- *Cylindrical:* If you shot your images with a wide-angle lens or you have those 360-degree, full-panoramic shots, this is a good mode.

- *Spherical:* This projection method aligns images by rotating, positioning, and uniformly scaling each image. It may be the best choice for true panoramas, but you can also find it useful for stitching images together using common features.

- *Collage:* This mode is handy when stitching together a 360-degree panorama, in which you have a wide field of view, both horizontally and vertically. Use this option for shots taken with a wide-angle lens.

- *Reposition:* Elements doesn't take any distortion into account; it simply scans the images and positions them as best it can.

**5. Select from the following options:**

- *Blend Images Together:* Corrects the color differences that can occur from blending images with different exposures.

- *Vignette Removal:* Corrects exposure problems caused by lens *vignetting* (when light at the edges of images is reduced and the edges are darkened).

- *Geometric Distortion Correction:* Corrects lens problems such as radial distortions — for instance, barrel distortion (bulging out) and pincushion distortion (pinching in).

**6. Click OK to create the panorama.**

Elements opens and automatically assembles the source files to create the composite panorama in a new file.

With any of the modes, Elements leaves your merged image in layers. You'll also notice that a layer mask has been added to each layer to better blend your panoramic image. You can edit your layer masks or move your layers to fine-tune the stitching of the images. For more on layer masks, see Chapter 8.

Elements alerts you if it can't composite your source files. If that happens, you may have to composite your images manually by creating a large canvas and then dragging and dropping your images onto that canvas.

## *Photomerge Group Shot*

We're sure you know how hard it is to get a group of people to all look great in one shot. Well, Photomerge Group Shot lets you take multiple group photos and merge the best of them to get that perfect shot.

Here are the steps to create a Photomerge Group Shot image:

1. **Select two or more photos from your Photo Bin.**

2. **Choose Enhance⇨Photomerge⇨Photomerge Group Shot in any of the edit modes.**

3. **Take your best overall group shot and drag it from the Photo Bin onto the Final window.**

4. **Select one of your other photos in the Photo Bin to use as your source image. Drag it to the Source window.**

5. **With the Pencil tool, draw a line around the portions of the source photo you want to merge into your final photo, as shown in Figure 11-18.**

   You can choose to show your pencil strokes and/or show your regions, which will be highlighted with an overlay.

6. **Repeat Steps 4 and 5 with any remaining photos.**

   If your photos aren't aligned, you can use the Alignment tool under the Advanced Options.

7. **With the Alignment tool, click your source image and position the three target markers on three key locations. Do the same on the final image and choose similar locations.**

8. **Click the Align Photos button.**

   As with Photomerge Panorama, the more alike in framing, size, and so on that your source and final images are, the better the merged result.

9. **(Optional) If you see any noticeable seams on your final image around the copied area, click the Pixel Blending button to help smooth over those flaws.**

   If you make a mess of things, click the Reset button.

10. **When you're satisfied with the result, click Done.**

    The file opens as a new file in Elements.

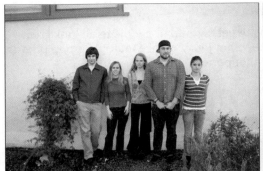
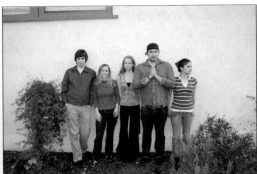

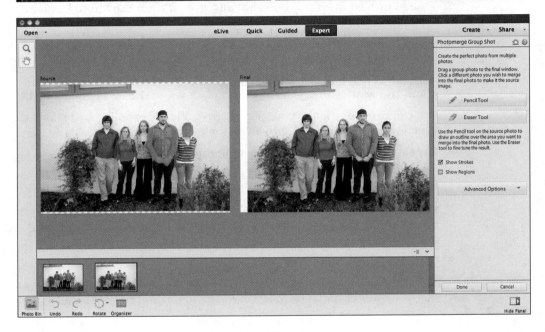

Figure 11-18: Get the perfect group shot from several images.

## Photomerge Faces

Photomerge Faces, a more-fun-than-useful tool, lets you blend features from multiple faces to get a kind of hybrid face. To create a hybrid human by using the Photomerge Faces feature, select two or more photos from your Photo Bin and choose File➪New➪Photomerge Faces in any of the edit modes. Use the Alignment and Pencil tools to choose how you want to merge the photos, similar to the steps described in the nearby section "Photomerge Group Shot."

## Photomerge Scene Cleaner

Photomerge Scene Cleaner (see Figure 11-19) sounds like a tool you might see in an episode of *CSI* to mop up a crime scene, but it isn't quite that gory. This member of the Photomerge commands family enables you to create the optimum image by allowing you to eliminate annoying distractions, such as cars, passersby, and so on.

To get the best source images for a clean scene, take multiple shots of your scene from the same angle and distance. It also works best when the elements you want to eliminate are moving.

Follow these steps to create a Photomerge Scene Cleaner composite:

1. **Select two or more photos from your Photo Bin.**

2. **Choose Enhance⇨Photomerge⇨Photomerge Scene Cleaner in any of the edit modes.**

   Elements attempts to auto-align your images the best it can.

3. **Take your best overall shot of the scene and drag it from the Photo Bin onto the Final window.**

4. **Select one of your other photos in the Photo Bin to use as your source image. Drag it to the Source window.**

5. **With the Pencil tool, draw a line around the elements in the final photo that you want to be replaced by content from the source photo.**

6. **Repeat Steps 4 and 5 with the remaining shots of the scene.**

   If your photos aren't aligned, you can use the Alignment tool under the Advanced Options.

7. **With the Alignment tool, click your source image and position the three target markers on three key locations. Do the same on the final image, choosing similar locations.**

8. **Click the Align Photos button in the Advanced Options section.**

   Again, as with the other Photomerge commands, the more similar your starting source images are (framing, angle), the better the merged result.

9. **(Optional) If you see any noticeable seams on your final image around the copied area, click the Pixel Blending button to help smooth over those flaws.**

   If you make a mess of things, click the Reset button and start over.

10. **When you're satisfied with the result, click Done.**

    The resulting image opens as a new file in Elements.

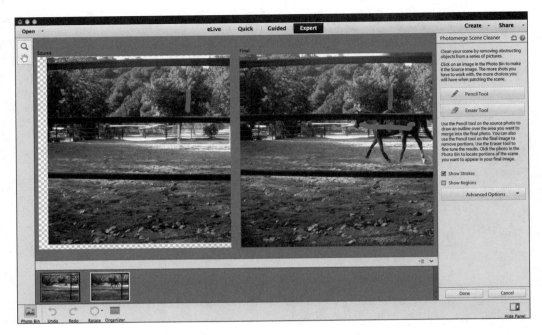

**Figure 11-19:** Eliminate annoying distractions with Photomerge Scene Cleaner.

## Photomerge Exposure

Sometimes you need to capture a shot that poses an exposure challenge — your foreground and background require different exposure settings. This dilemma often occurs in shots that are backlit. For example, suppose you have a person in front of an indoor window in the day or someone in front of a lit nighttime cityscape. With Photomerge Exposure, you can take shots with two different exposure settings and let the command blend them together for the perfect shot.

You can shoot your initial images using *exposure bracketing* (shooting at consecutive exposure camera settings) or with a flash and then without. Elements can detect all these camera settings. We recommend that you use a tripod, if possible, to keep your shots aligned. The added stability helps the blending algorithm do its job. Also, if your camera supports a timer, use it. That way, you don't accidentally bump the camera when pressing the shutter button.

Here's how to use this great command:

1. **Select two or more photos from your Photo Bin.**

2. **In any of the edit modes, choose Enhance⇨Photomerge⇨Photomerge Exposure.**

3. **Choose either Automatic or Manual mode.**

   If you've done a good job keeping your shots aligned, leave the mode on Automatic and go to Step 4.

   If you feel the need for even more control, click the Manual tab and go to Step 5.

4. **Select an option in Automatic mode and then skip to Step 11:**

   - *Simple Blending:* Elements automatically blends the two images.
   - *Smart Blending:* Access sliders to adjust the Highlights, Shadows, and Saturation settings for finer tuning of the resulting images.

   If you muck things up, click the Reset button.

5. **In Manual mode (as shown in Figure 11-20), choose your first shot from the Photo Bin and drag it to the Final window. If your other image isn't already the source image, drag it from the Photo Bin to the Source window.**

6. **With the Pencil tool, draw over the well-exposed areas you want to retain in the source image.**

   As you draw, your final image shows the incorporation of those drawn areas, as shown in Figure 11-20.

7. **If you mistakenly draw over something you don't want, grab the Eraser tool and erase the Pencil tool marks.**

   Choose the appropriate option to have your preview show strokes or regions.

8. **Control the blending by dragging the Transparency slider.**

   Dragging to the right blends less of the source areas into the final image. Select the Edge Blending option to get an even better blend of the two images.

9. **If your photos aren't aligning correctly, grab the Alignment tool under Advanced Options.**

   With the Alignment tool, click your source image and position the three target markers on three key locations.

   Do the same on the final image, choosing similar locations.

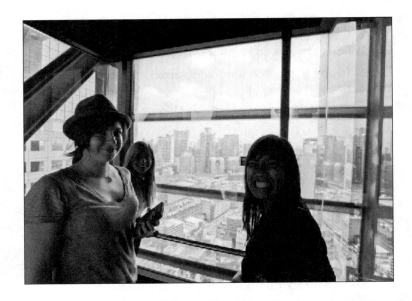

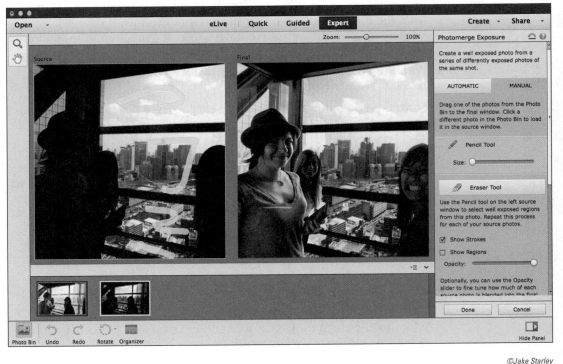

©Jake Starley

**Figure 11-20:** Combine images shot with two different exposures into a hero shot.

10. **Click the Align Photos button.**

    As with the other Photomerge commands, the more similar your starting source images are (framing, angle), the better the merged result.

    Again, if you make a mess of things, click the Reset button.

11. **When you're satisfied with the result, click Done.**

    The image opens as a new, layered file in Elements. The blended image appears on Layer 1. The background is your starting final image. You can either flatten the layered file, which keeps the appearance of Layer 1, or you can double-click your background to convert it to a layer and then delete it by dragging it to the trash icon in the Layers panel.

## Photomerge Compose

Although there are several methods to select and extract portions of images in Elements, the new Compose feature enables you to more easily extract one image and composite it into another.

Here's how to extract an element from one image and composite it into another:

1. **Open two photos in the Photo Bin.**

2. **In any of the edit modes, choose Enhance⇨Photomerge⇨Photomerge Compose.**

3. **From the Photo Bin, drag the image from which you want to extract an element onto the canvas.**

4. **Choose a Selection tool:**

   • *Quick Select:* Brush over to select your desired element, as shown in Figure 11-21. This tool works exactly like the regular Quick Select tool described in Chapter 7. Choose your selection mode — a new selection or add or subtract from an existing selection. You can also adjust the size of the diameter of your brush.

   • *Outline Select:* Trace around your desired element. After your initial trace, release your mouse. A red overlay appears over the unselected areas. Add or subtract from the red overlay, and then adjust the size of the diameter of your brush as needed.

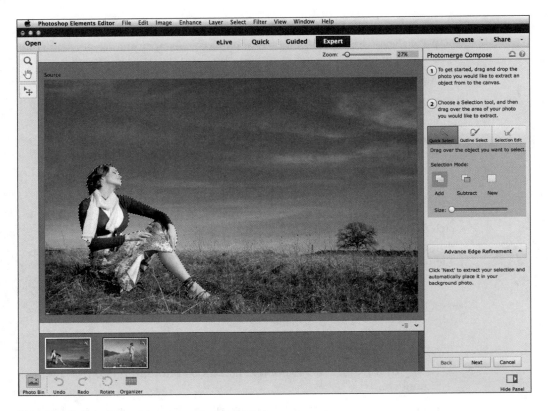

**Figure 11-21:** Select the element you want to extract.

5. **Further refine your selection using the Selection Edit tool.**

   In addition to the options found with the tools earlier, you can specify these additional settings:

   - *Snap:* Use the slider to adjust your snap strength from 0 to 100%. *Snap* is the intensity of the pull.

   - *Push:* Place your cursor inside the selection to increase your selection within the diameter of the outer circle of your cursor. It will snap to the edge of the element closest to the cursor. Place your cursor outside the selection to decrease your selection within the diameter of the outer circle.

   - *Smooth:* If your selection border looks a little too jagged, use this option to smooth your selection edge.

6. **Click Advance Edge Refinement.**

You can choose to set the background — in other words, the unselected portion of your current image — to Source Image (which leaves your image as is) or have it fill with transparency, black, white, or a red overlay.

You can also access the Refine Edge feature, which is described in detail in Chapter.7

7. **Click Next.**

Your extracted image is composited into your second image, as shown in Figure 11-22. Move and size your image as desired.

You can further refine your selection by using the Hide and Reveal tools to either add to, or delete from, your selection. You can adjust the size, opacity, and hardness of your brush to better fine-tune your extracted element.

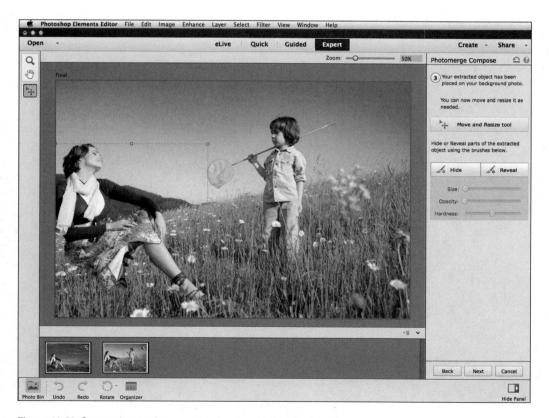

**Figure 11-22:** Composite two images seamlessly with Photomerge Compose.

# Drawing and Painting

## In This Chapter

▶ Choosing colors

▶ Drawing with the Pencil tool

▶ Painting with the Brush tool

▶ Filling and outlining your selections

▶ Pouring color with the Paint Bucket tool

▶ Creating gradients and patterns

▶ Creating and editing shapes of all sorts

*E*lements is such a deluxe, full-service image-editing program that it doesn't stop at giving you tools to select, repair, organize, and share your images. It figures that you may need to add a swash of color, either freeform with a brush or pencil, or in the form of a geometric or organic shape. Don't worry: This drawing and painting business isn't just for those with innate artistic talent. In fact, Elements gives you plenty of preset brushes and shapes to choose from. If you can pick a tool and drag your mouse, you can draw and paint.

## Choosing Color

Before you start drawing or painting, you may want to change your color to something other than the default color of black. If you read the earlier chapters in this book, you may have checked out the Elements Tools panel and noticed the two overlapping color swatches at the bottom of the panel. These two swatches represent two categories of color: *foreground* and *background*.

Here's a quick look at how they work with different tools:

✔ **Foreground:** When you add type, paint with the Brush tool, or create a shape, you're using the foreground color.

✔ **Background:** On the background layer of an image, when you use the Eraser tool, or when you increase the size of your canvas, you're accessing the background color.

✔ **Foreground and background:** When you drag with the Gradient tool, as long as your gradient is set to the default, you're laying down a blend of color from the foreground to the background.

Elements gives you three ways to choose your foreground and background colors: the Color Picker, the color swatches, and the Eyedropper tool, which samples color in an image. In the following sections, we explore each one.

## *Working with the Color Picker*

By default, Elements uses a black foreground color and a white background color. If you're experimenting with color and want to go back to the default colors, press the D key. If you want to swap between foreground and background colors, press the X key. If you want any color other than black and white, click your desired swatch (either foreground or background) at the bottom of the Tools panel. This action transports you to the Color Picker, as shown in Figure 12-1.

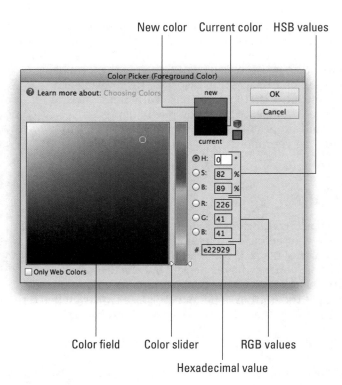

**Figure 12-1:** Choose your desired color from the Color Picker.

Here are the steps to choose your color via the Color Picker:

1. **Click either the foreground or background color swatch on the Tools panel.**

   The Color Picker appears.

2. **Drag the color slider or click the color bar to get close to the general color you desire.**

3. **Choose the exact color you want by clicking in the large square, or *color field*, on the left.**

   The circle cursor targets your selected color. The two swatches in the upper-right corner of the dialog box represent your newly selected color and the original foreground or background color.

   The numeric values on the right side of the dialog box also change according to the color you selected. If you happen to know the values of your desired color, you can enter them in the text boxes. RGB (red, green, blue) values are based on brightness levels from 0 (black) to 255 (white). You can also enter HSB (hue, saturation, brightness) values or the hexadecimal formula for web colors.

4. **When you're happy with your color, click OK.**

If you want to save your color for later use, do so by using the Color Swatches panel, described in the following section.

## Dipping into the Color Swatches panel

Elements enables you to select a foreground or background color by selecting a color on the Color Swatches panel. The Color Swatches panel is a digital version of the artist's paint palette. In addition to preset colors, you can mix and store your own colors for use now and later. You can have palettes for certain types of projects or images. For example, you may want a palette of skin tones for retouching portraits. Choose Window⇨Color Swatches to bring up the panel, as shown in Figure 12-2.

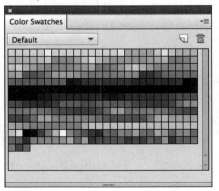

Figure 12-2: Choose and store colors in the Color Swatches panel.

To grab a color from the Color Swatches panel, click the color swatch you want. By the way, it doesn't matter which tool you have. As soon as you move the tool over the panel, it temporarily converts to an eyedropper that samples the color and makes it your new foreground or background color.

Although the Color Swatches panel is a breeze to use, here are a few tips to help you along:

- **Change the background color.** Either first click the background swatch on the Tools panel or Ctrl-click (⌘-click on the Mac) a swatch in the Color Swatches panel.

- **Use preset colors.** To load a particular preset swatch library, choose it from the drop-down list at the top of the Color Swatches panel. Elements offers libraries specific to web graphics, photo filters, and Windows and OS X systems.

- **Add a color to the Color Swatches panel.** Choose New Swatch from the panel menu. You can also simply click an empty portion of the panel. Name your swatch and click OK. Remember, it doesn't matter whether you created the color by using the Color Picker or by sampling with the Eyedropper tool — adding the color for later use is done the same way.

- **Save swatches.** Choose Save Swatches from the panel menu in the upper-right corner of the panel. We recommend saving the swatch library in the default Color Swatches folder in the Presets folder. If by chance this folder doesn't come up by default, just navigate to the Color Swatches folder by following this partial path: Program Files\Adobe\ `Photoshop Elements 13.0\Presets\Color Swatches` (Windows) or Applications\ `Adobe Photoshop Elements 13/Presets/Color Swatches` (Mac).

- **Save swatches for Exchange.** Choose this command from the panel menu to save your swatches for use in another Adobe program. Name the swatch set and save it in the same folder listed in the preceding bullet point.

- **Load swatches.** If you want to load a custom library created by you or someone else, choose Load Swatches from the panel menu. In the dialog box, select your desired library from the Color Swatches folder. The new library is added to your current library.

  You can also work with swatches by using the Preset Manager. For more on the Preset Manager, see Chapter 3.

- **Delete swatches.** To delete a swatch, drag it to the trash icon at the bottom of the panel or Alt-click (Option-click on the Mac) the swatch.

- **Change the panel's appearance.** Click the panel menu in the upper-right corner to choose Small or Large Thumbnail (swatch squares) or Small or Large List (swatch squares with a name).

- **Replace your current swatch library with a different library.** Choose Replace Swatches from the panel menu. Choose a library from the Color Swatches folder.

## Sampling with the Eyedropper tool

Another way that Elements enables you to choose color is via the Eyedropper tool. The Eyedropper tool comes in handy when you want to sample an existing color in an image and use it for another element. For example, you may want your text to be the same color as the green background in the image shown in Figure 12-3. Grab the Eyedropper tool (or press I) and click a shade of green in the background. The tool samples the color and makes it your new foreground color. You can then create the type with your new foreground color.

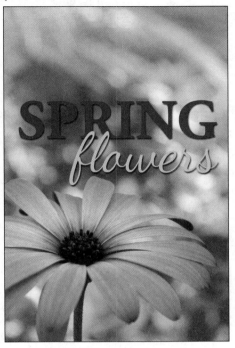

©istockphoto.com/miilerpd Image #3417360

**Figure 12-3:** The Eyedropper tool enables you to sample color from your image to use with other elements, such as type.

Here are a few things to remember when you're using the Eyedropper tool:

- **Sample a new foreground or background color.** Obviously, you can select either the foreground or background swatch on the Tools panel before you sample a color. But if the foreground color swatch is active, holding down the Alt (Option on the Mac) key samples a new background color, and vice versa.

- **Choose a color from any open image.** If you have multiple images open, you can even sample a color from an image that you're not working on!

- **Choose your sample size in the Tool Options.** You can select the color of just the single pixel you click (Point Sample), or Elements can average the colors of the pixels in a 3-x-3- or 5-x-5-pixel area.

- **Specify web colors.** If you right-click your image to bring up the contextual menu, you have a hidden option: Copy Color as HTML. This option provides the web hexadecimal color formula for that sampled color and copies it to the Clipboard. You can then paste that formula into an HTML file or grab the Type tool and choose Edit➪Paste to view the formula in your image. You can also choose Copy Color's Hex Code. This option also copies the web color but deletes the "color="" around the actual code. This is good for those writing their colors in CSS.

- **Choose to sample All Layers or just the Current Layer.** If you have multiple layers in your image, you can choose to sample from all those layers or just your currently active layer.

✔ **Toggle between the Eyedropper and other tools.** Elements, multitasker that it is, enables you to temporarily access the Eyedropper tool when you're using the Brush, Pencil, Color Replacement, Gradient, Paint Bucket, Cookie Cutter, or Shape tool. Simply press the Alt (Option on the Mac) key to access the Eyedropper tool. Release the Alt (Option on the Mac) key to go back to your original tool.

# Getting Artsy with the Pencil and Brush Tools

If you want to find out how to paint and draw with a color you've chosen, you've come to the right place. The Pencil and Brush tools give you the power to put your creative abilities to work, and the following sections show you how.

When you use these two tools, you benefit immensely from the use of a pressure-sensitive digital drawing tablet. The awkwardness of trying to draw or paint with a mouse or trackpad disappears and leaves you with tools that behave much closer to their analog ancestors.

## Drawing with the Pencil tool

Drawing with the Pencil tool creates hard edges. You can't get the soft, feathery edges that you can with the Brush tool. In fact, the edges of a pencil stroke can't even be *antialiased*. (For more on antialiasing, see the following section.) Keep in mind that if you draw anything other than vertical or horizontal lines, your lines will have some jaggies when they're viewed up close. But hey, don't diss the Pencil just yet. Those hard-edged strokes can be perfect for web graphics. What's more, the Pencil tool can erase itself, and it's great for digital sketches, as shown in Figure 12-4.

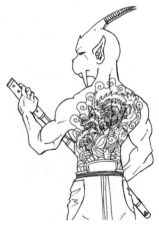

*Illustration by Chris Blair*

**Figure 12-4:** The Pencil tool can be used for digital drawings.

Follow these steps to become familiar with the Pencil tool:

1. **Select the Pencil tool from the Tools panel.**

   You can also press the N key. By default, the Pencil tool's brush tip is the 1-pixel brush. Yes, even though the Pencil tip is hard-edged, we still refer to it as a brush. In the next few steps, you customize the brush by setting various options.

2. **Click the arrow and select your desired brush from the Brush Preset Picker drop-down panel.**

3. **Optionally, to load another preset library, click the Brushes menu at the top of the panel.**

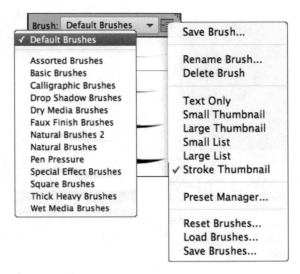

Figure 12-5: Choose from other brush libraries.

You aren't limited to the standard old brushes. Check out the Assorted and Special Effects brushes found in the Brush drop-down list at the top of the Brush Preset Picker panel, as shown in Figure 12-5. You'll be surprised by the interesting brushes lurking on these panels. Use them to create stand-alone images or to enhance your photographic creations.

Access the menu on the Brush Preset Picker panel menu to save, rename, or delete individual brushes and also save, load, and reset brush libraries. For more on these operations, see the following section.

4. **Choose your brush size, and optionally, if you want to change the size of that brush tip, drag the Size slider.**

5. **(Optional) If you want the background to show through your strokes, adjust the opacity by dragging the slider or entering an opacity percentage less than 100 percent.**

The lower the percentage, the more the background images show through.

Your strokes must be on a separate layer above your images for you to be able to adjust the opacity and blend modes after you draw them. For more on layers, see Chapter 8.

6. **Select a blend mode.**

*Blend modes* alter the way the color you're applying interacts with the color on your canvas. You can find more about blend modes in Chapter 11.

7. **(Optional) Select Auto Erase if you want to remove portions of your pencil strokes.**

For example, say that your foreground color is black and your background color is white, and you apply some black strokes. With Auto Erase enabled, you apply white if you drag back over the black strokes. If you drag over the white background, you apply black.

**8. Click and drag with the mouse to create your freeform lines.**

To draw straight lines, click at a starting point, release the mouse button, and then Shift-click at a second point.

## Painting with the Brush tool

The Brush tool creates soft-edged strokes. How soft those strokes are depends on which brush you use. By default, even the hardest brush has a slightly soft edge because it's antialiased. *Antialiasing* creates a single row of partially filled pixels along the edges to produce the illusion of a smooth edge. You can also get even softer brushes, which use feathering. For details on feathering, see Chapter 7.

The Brush tool shares most of the options found in the Pencil tool, except that the Auto Erase feature isn't available. Here's the lowdown on the unique Brush options:

- **Airbrush:** Click the Airbrush button in the Options panel to apply the Airbrush mode. In this mode, the longer you hold down the mouse button, the more paint the Brush pumps out and the wider the airbrush effect spreads.

- **Tablet Settings:** If you're using a pressure-sensitive digital drawing tablet, check the settings you want the tablet to control, including size, scatter, opacity, roundness, and hue jitter. The harder you press with the stylus, the greater the effect of these options.

- **Brush Settings:** These options, referred to as brush *dynamics,* change while you apply your stroke. See Figure 12-6 for an example of each one. These options include the following:

    - *Fade:* The lower the value, the more quickly the stroke fades. However, 0 creates no fade.

    - *Hue Jitter:* Vary the stroke between the foreground and background colors. The higher the value, the more frequent the variation.

    - *Scatter:* The higher the value, the higher the number of brush marks and the farther apart they are.

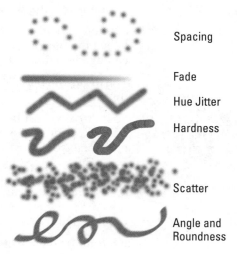

Spacing

Fade

Hue Jitter

Hardness

Scatter

Angle and Roundness

Figure 12-6: Change brush options to create a custom brush.

- *Spacing:* The higher the number, the more space between marks.

- *Hardness:* The higher the value, the harder the brush.

- *Roundness:* A setting of 100 percent is totally circular. The lower the percentage, the more elliptical your brush becomes.

- *Angle:* If you create an oval brush by adjusting the roundness, this option controls the angle of that oval brush stroke. It's so much easier to drag the points and the arrow on the diagram than to guesstimate values in the text boxes.

You can lock in these brush dynamics by selecting the Set This as a Default check box; this ensures that every brush you select adopts these settings.

As with the Pencil tool, you can load additional Brush libraries from the Brush drop-down list at the top of the Brush Preset Picker panel. Additional features for the Brush tool also appear in the menu on the Brush Preset Picker panel. Here's a quick description of each:

- ✔ **Save Brush:** Allows you to save a custom brush as a preset. See the following section for details.

- ✔ **Rename Brush:** Don't like your brush's moniker? Change it with this option.

- ✔ **Delete Brush:** Don't like your entire brush? Eliminate it with this option.

- ✔ **The display options:** Not a single command, but a set of commands that enable you to change the way your brush tips are displayed. The default view is Stroke Thumbnail, which displays the appearance of the stroke. These commands include Text Only, Small and Large Thumbnail, and Small and Large List.

- ✔ **Reset Brushes:** Reverts your current brush library to the default.

- ✔ **Save Brushes:** Saves custom brushes in a separate library.

- ✔ **Load Brushes:** Loads a preset or custom brush library.

You can also manage brush-tip libraries by using the Preset Manager. See Chapter 3 for information on using the Preset Manager.

## Using the Impressionist Brush

The Impressionist Brush is designed to paint over your photos in a way that makes them look like fine art paintings. You can set various options that change the style of the brush strokes.

Here's how to use this artistic brush:

**1. Select the Impressionist Brush from the Tools panel.**

It looks like a brush with a curlicue next to it. You can also press B to cycle through the brushes.

2. **Set your brush options.**

   The Brushes presets (Size, Opacity, and Mode options) are identical to those found with the Brush tool, described in the section "Painting with the Brush tool," earlier in this chapter. You can also find some unique options on the Advanced drop-down panel in the Tool Options:

   - *Style:* This drop-down list contains various brush stroke styles, such as Dab and Tight Curl.

   - *Area:* Controls the size of your brush stroke. The larger the value, the larger the area covered.

   - *Tolerance:* Controls how similar color pixels have to be before they're changed by the brush stroke.

3. **Drag on your image and paint with your brush strokes, as shown in Figure 12-7.**

   The best way to get a feel for what this tool does is to open your favorite image, grab the tool, and take it for a test drive.

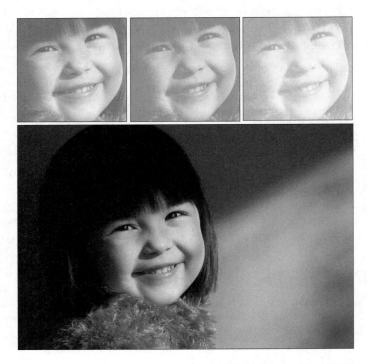

©istockphoto.com/agmit Image #1725665

Figure 12-7: The Impressionist Brush turns your photo into a painting.

## Creating your own brush

If you customize any brush to the point that you've created your own special Franken-brush that you'd love to use again, feel free to save it as a preset that you can access in the future. To do so:

1. **Choose Save Brush from the panel menu on the Brush Preset Picker panel.**

2. **Name the brush and click OK.**

   Your new custom brush shows up at the bottom of the Brush Preset Picker drop-down panel.

There's one additional way to create a brush. Elements allows you to create a brush from all or part of your image. The image can be a photograph or something you've painted or drawn.

Here's how to create a brush from your image:

1. **Select part of your image with any of the selection tools.**

   If you want to use the entire image or entire layer, deselect everything.

   For more on selections, see Chapter 7.

2. **Choose Edit⇨Define Brush or Edit⇨Define Brush from Selection.**

   You see one command or the other, depending on what you do in Step 1.

3. **Name the brush and click OK.**

   The new brush shows up at the bottom of your Brush Preset Picker drop-down panel. *Note:* Your brush is only a grayscale version of your image. When you use the brush, it automatically applies the color you've selected as your foreground color, as shown in Figure 12-8.

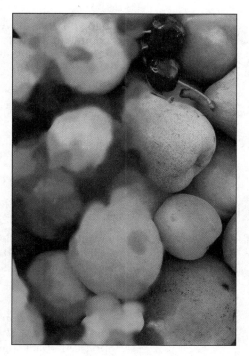

©istockphoto.com/ericmichaud Image #3173552

**Figure 12-8:** Create a custom brush from a portion of your image.

# Filling and Outlining Selections

At times, you may want to create an element on your canvas that can't quite be created with a brush or pencil stroke. Maybe it's a perfect circle or a five-point star. If you have a selection, you can fill or stroke that selection to create that element, rather than draw or paint it on. The Fill command adds a color or a pattern to the entire selection, whereas the Stroke command applies the color to only the edge of the selection border.

## Fill 'er up

You won't find a Fill tool on the Tools panel. Elements decided to avoid the over-populated panel and placed the Fill and Stroke commands on the Edit menu.

Here are the simple steps to fill a selection:

1. **Grab the selection tool of your choice and create your selection on a new layer.**

   Although you don't have to create a new layer to make a selection to fill, we recommend it. That way, if you don't like the filled selection, you can delete the layer, and your image or background below it remains safe. See Chapter 7 for more on selections and Chapter 8 for details on working with layers.

2. **Select either the foreground or background color, and then choose a fill color.**

   See the section "Choosing Color," earlier in this chapter, if you need a refresher.

3. **Choose Edit⇨Fill Selection.**

   The Fill Layer dialog box, as shown in Figure 12-9, appears.

   If you want to bypass the Fill Layer dialog box (and the rest of these steps), you can use these handy keyboard shortcuts instead:

   - *To fill the selection with the foreground color,* press Alt+Backspace (Option+Delete on the Mac).

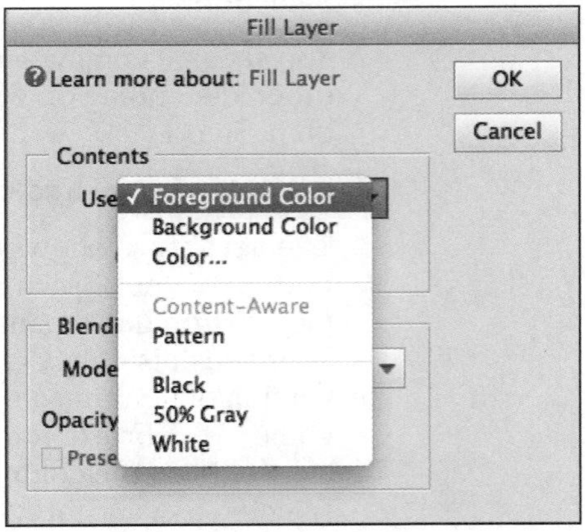

**Figure 12-9:** Fill your selection or layer with color or a pattern.

- *To fill the selection with the background color,* press Ctrl+Backspace (⌘+Delete on the Mac).

4. **Choose your desired fill from the Use drop-down list.**

   You can select whether to fill with the foreground or background color. You also can select Color, Pattern, Black, 50% Gray, or White. If you select Color, you're transported to the Color Picker. If you choose Pattern, you must then choose a pattern from the Custom Pattern drop-down panel. For more on patterns, see the section "Working with Patterns," later in this chapter.

   If you don't have an active selection border in your image, the command says Fill Layer and your entire layer is filled with your color or pattern.

   You can now also fill your selection using the Content-Aware option, which will fill your selection with pixels sampled from content nearby. For more details on this great new option, see Chapter 11.

5. **In the Blending area, specify whether to preserve transparency, which enables you to fill only the portions of the selection that contain pixels (the nontransparent areas).**

   Although you can also choose a *blend mode* (how the fill color interacts with colors below it) and opacity percentage, we urge you not to adjust your blend mode and opacity in the Fill Layer dialog box. Make those adjustments on your layer later, by using the Layers panel commands, where you have more flexibility for editing.

6. **Click OK.**

   The color or pattern fills the selection.

## Outlining with the Stroke command

Stroking a selection enables you to create colored outlines, or *borders,* of selections or layers. You can put this border inside, outside, or centered on the selection border. Here are the steps to stroke a selection:

1. **Choose a foreground color and create a selection.**

2. **Choose Edit⇨Stroke (Outline) Selection.**

   The Stroke dialog box opens.

3. **Select your desired settings.**

Many settings are the same as those found in the Fill Layer dialog box, as we explain in the preceding section. Here's a brief rundown of the options that are unique to strokes:

- *Width:* Enter a width of 1 to 250 pixels for the stroke.

- *Location:* Specify how Elements should apply the stroke: outside the selection, inside the selection, or centered on the selection border.

4. **Click OK to apply the stroke.**

We gave a 30-pixel centered stroke to our selection, as shown in Figure 12-10.

**Figure 12-10:** Stroke a selection to create a colored border.

# Splashing on Color with the Paint Bucket Tool

The Paint Bucket tool is a longtime occupant of the Tools panel. This tool, whose icon looks just like a bucket, behaves like a combination of the Fill command and the Magic Wand tool. (See Chapter 7.) The Paint Bucket tool makes a selection based on similarly colored pixels and then immediately fills that selection with color or a pattern. Like the Magic Wand tool, this tool is most successful when you have a limited number of colors, as shown in Figure 12-11.

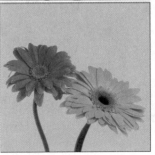

To use the Paint Bucket tool, simply click inside the selection you want to fill. Before you click, however, specify your settings in the Tool options:

- **Color:** Choose among paint, a fill of the foreground color, or a pattern.

- **Pattern:** If you select Pattern, choose a preset pattern from the drop-down panel. For more details on patterns, see the section "Working with Patterns," later in this chapter.

- **Opacity:** Adjust the opacity to make your fill more or less transparent.

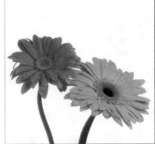

©istockphoto.com/nicolesy Image #2695305

**Figure 12-11:** The Paint Bucket tool makes a selection and fills it at the same time.

✔ **Tolerance:** Choose a tolerance level that specifies how similar in color a pixel must be before it's selected and then filled. The lower the value, the more similar the color must be. For more on tolerance, see the section on the Magic Wand in Chapter 7.

✔ **Mode:** Select a blending mode to change how your fill color interacts with the color below it.

✔ **Anti-aliasing:** Choose this option to smooth the edges between the filled and unfilled areas.

✔ **Contiguous:** If selected, this option selects and fills only pixels that are touching within your selection. If the option is deselected, pixels are selected and filled wherever they lie within your selection.

✔ **All Layers:** This option selects and fills pixels within the selection in all layers that are within your tolerance level.

# Working with Multicolored Gradients

If one color isn't enough for you, you'll be pleased to know that Elements enables you to fill a selection or layer with a gradient. A *gradient* is a blend of two or more colors that gradually dissolve from one to another. Elements provides a whole slew of preset gradients, but creating your own custom gradient is also fun and easy.

## Applying a preset gradient

Similar to colors, patterns, and brushes, gradients have a whole group of presets that you can apply to your selection and layers. You can also load other libraries of gradients from the Gradient panel menu.

Here's how to apply a preset gradient:

1. **Make the selection you want to fill with a gradient.**

   We recommend making the selection on a new layer so that you can edit the gradient later without harming the underlying image.

   If you don't make a selection, the gradient is applied to the entire layer or background.

2. **Select the Gradient tool from the Tools panel or press the G key.**

   It looks like a rectangle that goes from black on the left to white on the right.

3. **In the Tool Options, click the down-pointing arrow on the Gradient Picker swatch.**

   The Gradient Picker drop-down panel appears.

**4. Choose a preset gradient.**

Remember that you can choose other preset libraries from the Gradient panel menu. Libraries, such as Color Harmonies and Metals, contain interesting presets.

**5. Choose your desired gradient type by clicking one of the icons.**

See Figure 12-12 for an example of each type.

**6. Choose from the following options in the Tool Options:**

- *Mode:* Select a blending mode to change how the color of the gradient interacts with the colors below it.

- *Opacity:* Specify how opaque or transparent the gradient is.

- *Reverse:* Reverse the order in which the colors are applied.

- *Transparency:* Deselect this option to make Elements ignore any transparent areas in the gradient, making them opaque instead.

- *Dither:* Add *noise,* or random information, to produce a smoother gradient that prints with less *banding* (weird stripes caused by printing limitations).

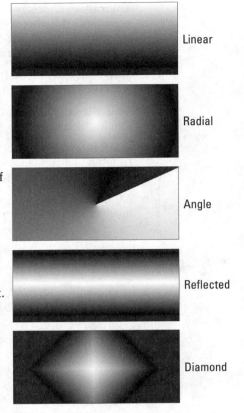

Linear

Radial

Angle

Reflected

Diamond

**Figure 12-12:** Choose one of five gradient types.

**7. Position your gradient cursor at your desired starting point within your selection or layer.**

**8. Drag in any direction to your desired end point for the gradient.**

Longer drags result in a subtler transition between colors, whereas shorter drags result in a more abrupt transition. Hold down the Shift key to restrain the direction of the gradient to multiples of a 45-degree angle.

**9. Release the mouse button to apply the gradient.**

We applied an Orange Yellow radial gradient from the Color Harmonies 2 preset library to a selection of a sun in Figure 12-13. We selected the Reverse option and dragged from the center of the sun to the tip of the top ray.

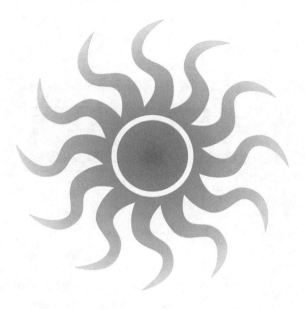

**Figure 12-13:** We filled our sun selection with a radial Orange Yellow gradient.

## Customizing gradients

If you can't find the exact gradient you need, you can easily create your own. The Gradient Editor lets you create your own custom gradient using as many colors as you want. After you create a custom gradient, you can save it as a preset to reuse in the future.

Follow these steps to create a custom gradient:

1. **Select the Gradient tool from the Tools panel.**

2. **Click the Edit button in the Tool Options.**

   The Gradient Editor dialog box opens, as shown in Figure 12-14.

3. **Pick an existing preset to use as the basis for your new gradient.**

   If you want to choose a gradient from a different preset library, choose that library from the Preset drop-down list.

4. **Choose your gradient type, either Solid or Noise, from the Type drop-down list.**

   A Noise gradient contains random colors. Interestingly, each time you create a Noise gradient, the result is different.

   As soon as you start to edit the existing gradient, the name of the gradient changes to Custom.

Opacity stop

Color stop        Midpoint slider

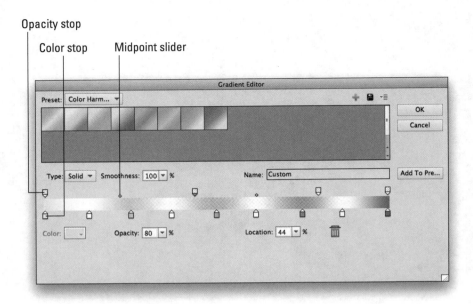

Figure 12-14: Use the Gradient Editor to edit and customize gradients.

5. **Choose your options for either a Solid or Noise gradient, depending on what you chose in Step 4:**

   • *If you chose Solid,* adjust the Smoothness percentage to determine how smoothly one color blends into another.

   • *If you chose Noise,* you can choose which Color Model to use to set the color range. You can also adjust the Roughness, which affects how smoothly or abruptly the color transitions from one to another. Click Restrict Colors to avoid oversaturated colors. The Add Transparency option adds transparency to random colors. Click the Randomize button to randomly generate a new gradient. You can then skip to Step 13 to finish the gradient-making process.

6. **If you're creating a solid gradient, choose the first color of your gradient by double-clicking the left color stop under the gradient bar. (Refer to Figure 12-14.)**

   The triangle on top of the stop turns black to indicate that you're working with the starting point of the gradient, and the Color Picker appears so that you can then choose your desired color.

   In the Stops area, you can also single-click the left color stop and then click the Color swatch to access the Color Picker. If you click the Color down-pointing arrow, you access the Color Swatches drop-down list, where you can choose from various preset Swatch libraries from the top of the panel.

7. **Select the ending color by double-clicking the right color stop. Repeat the process in Step 6 to define the color.**

8. **Change the percentage of one color versus the other by moving the starting or ending point's color stop to the left or right. Drag the midpoint slider (a diamond icon) to where the colors mix equally, 50/50.**

   You can also change the position of the midpoint by typing a value in the Location box.

9. **To add another color, click below the gradient bar at the position you want to add the color. Define a color in the same way you did in Steps 6 to 8.**

10. **Repeat Step 9 to add colors.**

11. **To add transparency to your gradient, select an opacity stop (refer to Figure 12-14) and adjust the Opacity slider to specify the amount of transparency you desire.**

    By default, a gradient has colors that are 100-percent opaque. You can fade a gradient to transparency so that the portion of the image under the gradient shows through.

    You can also add opacity stops in the same way you add color stops.

12. **Adjust your color and opacity stops and their midpoint sliders to vary the percentages of each color.**

    You can also redefine any of the colors. To delete a color stop, drag it up or down off the gradient bar.

13. **When you're done, name your gradient and click the New button.**

    Your gradient is added to the Presets menu.

 After all that work, you may want to consider saving your gradients for later use. To save a gradient, click the Save button in the Gradient Editor dialog box. Save the current presets, with your new gradient, under the current library's name or a new name altogether. You can later load that preset library. You can also manage your gradient presets with the Preset Manager, as we explain in Chapter 3.

# Working with Patterns

If you've ever seen someone wearing leopard-print pants with an argyle sweater and a plaid blazer, you're familiar with patterns. You can use patterns to occasionally fill selections or layers. (Don't go overboard, though — patterns aren't always pretty when used without restraint.) You can also stamp your image by using the Pattern Stamp tool. You can even retouch by using a pattern with the Healing Brush tool. Elements offers a lot of preset patterns to keep you happy. If you're not happy with Elements' selection, you can create your own, of course.

## Applying a preset pattern

Although you can apply patterns by using many different tools, this chapter sticks with applying patterns as fills. To fill a layer or selection with a preset pattern, follow these steps:

1. **Choose the layer or selection you want to fill with a pattern.**

   Again, we recommend making your selection on a new layer above your image for more flexible editing later on.

2. **Choose Edit⇨Fill Selection or Fill Layer and choose Pattern from the Use drop-down list.**

3. **Click the down-pointing arrow and choose a pattern from the Custom Pattern drop-down panel, as shown in Figure 12-15.**

   If you don't see a pattern to your liking, click the panel pop-up menu at the bottom of the submenu and choose another preset library.

4. **Choose any other fill options you want to apply, such as Mode, Opacity, or Preserve Transparency.**

   For details on these options, see the section "Filling and Outlining Selections," earlier in this chapter.

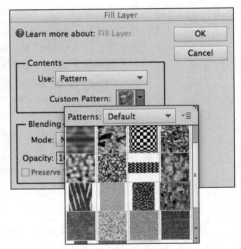

Figure 12-15: Fill your selection with one of the many Elements preset patterns.

5. **Click OK to fill the layer or selection with the chosen pattern.**

## Creating a new pattern

You may someday want to create your own pattern. Patterns can be easily created from any existing photo or painting you create in Elements. You can even scan your signature or logo, define it as a pattern, and use it with the Pattern Stamp tool to sign all your work.

To create your own pattern, follow these steps:

1. **Open the photographic, painted, or scanned image that contains the area you want to use as a pattern.**

2. **Use the Rectangular Marquee tool to select the area you want to convert into a pattern.**

Make sure that your Feather option is set to 0, or the pattern command won't be available.

If you don't make a selection, Elements uses your entire layer as a basis for the pattern.

3. **Choose Edit⇨Define Pattern from Selection or Edit⇨Define Pattern.**

   The Pattern Name dialog box appears.

4. **Enter a name for your pattern.**

   Your new pattern now appears in every Pattern panel, wherever it may lurk in Elements.

In addition to filling your selection with a pattern, you can stamp on a pattern with the Pattern Stamp tool. Press S to select the Pattern Stamp tool. If you get the Clone Stamp tool, press S again. Choose your desired pattern from the Pattern Picker drop-down list and your desired brush tip from the Brush Preset Picker drop-down list. Select your brush size, opacity, and mode and then brush your pattern on your image. You can also select the Impressionist option to have your pattern appear more "painterly."

# Creating Shapes of All Sorts

In this section, we leave the land of pixels and head into uncharted territory — Vectorville. Before we discuss the ins and outs of creating shapes, here's a little overview that explains the difference between pixels and vectors:

- ✔ **Pixel images describe a shape in terms of a grid of pixels.** When you increase the size of a pixel-based image, it loses quality and begins to look blocky, mushy, and otherwise nasty. For more details on resizing pixel-based images and the ramifications of doing so, see Chapter 2.

- ✔ **Vectors describe a shape mathematically.** The shapes comprise paths made up of lines, curves, and anchor points. Because vector shapes are math-based, you can resize them without any loss of quality whatsoever.

In Figure 12-16, you can see both types of images.

When you create a shape in Elements, you're creating a vector-based element. Shapes reside

**Figure 12-16:** Elements images can be vector-based (top) or pixel-based (bottom).

on a special kind of layer called, not surprisingly, a *shape layer.* Use shapes to create simple logos, web buttons, and other small spot illustrations.

## Drawing a shape

Elements offers an assortment of shape tools for you to choose from. Follow these steps to draw a shape in your document:

1. **Choose your desired shape tool from the Tools panel.**

   You can also press U to cycle through the shape tools. All the following tools have associated Geometry options, which are described in the section "Specifying Geometry options," later in this chapter. Here are the available tools:

   - *Rectangle and Ellipse:* As with their Marquee counterparts, you can hold down the Shift key while dragging to produce a square or circle; hold down the Alt (Option on the Mac) key to draw the shape from the center outward.

   - *Rounded Rectangle:* This tool works like the regular Rectangle but with the addition of a radius value used to round off the corners of the rectangle.

   - *Polygon:* This tool creates a polygon with a specified number of sides, from 3 to 100.

   - *Star:* This tool creates a polygon or star with a specified number of sides/vertices, from 3 to 100.

   - *Line:* This tool draws a line with a width from 1 to 1,000 pixels. You can also add arrowheads at either end.

   - *Custom:* Custom is the most varied shape tool. You have numerous preset custom shapes to choose from. As with any shape, hold down Shift to constrain proportions or the Alt (Option on the Mac) key to draw from the center out.

2. **In the Tool Options, click the down-pointing arrow to access Geometry options.**

   By default, the option is set to Unconstrained. For detailed explanations on the various Geometry options, see the upcoming sections.

3. **If you chose the Custom Shape tool in Step 1, click the Custom Shapes Preset Picker down-pointing arrow to access the pop-up Shapes panel and choose your desired shape.**

   You can access more preset shape libraries via the pop-up menu at the top of the panel.

4. **Choose your desired color from the Color drop-down list.**

   Click the color-wheel icon in the bottom-right corner to access the Color Picker for additional color choices.

**5. Choose a style from the Style Picker drop-down panel.**

To jazz up the shape with bevels and other fancy edges, choose a style from the panel. For more on styles, see Chapter 11.

**6. Drag in the document to draw the shape you defined.**

The shape appears in the image window on its own shape layer. Check out the Layers panel to see this phenomenon. Figure 12-17 shows our shape, a Japanese hairstyle, from the Dressup preset library, which we add to in the following section.

**Figure 12-17:** Custom shapes run the gamut from the ordinary to the exotic, such as this hairstyle.

## Drawing multiple shapes

After you create a shape layer, you can draw additional shapes on that layer. You can add, subtract, overlap, and intersect shapes in exactly the same way you do with selections. (See Chapter 7.) Just follow these steps:

**1. Select your desired state button in the Tool Options.**

You can choose from the following options:

- *New Shape Layer:* Creates your initial shape layer.

- *Add to Shape Area:* Combines and joins two or more shapes.

- *Subtract from Shape Area:* Subtracts one shape from another shape.

- *Intersect Shape Areas:* Creates a shape from only the areas that overlap.

- *Exclude Overlapping Shape Areas:* Creates a shape from only the areas that don't overlap.

**2. Choose your desired shape tool and draw the next shape.**

We completed the shape by adding the face, as shown in Figure 12-18.

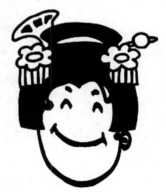

**Figure 12-18:** Add to your shape layer.

## Specifying Geometry options

Geometry options help define how your shapes look. Click the down-pointing arrow in the Tool Options to access the Geometry options described in the sections that follow.

### Rectangle and Rounded Rectangle Geometry options

Here are the Geometry options for the Rectangle and Rounded Rectangle shapes:

- ✔ **Unconstrained:** Enables you to have free rein to draw a rectangle at any size or proportion.
- ✔ **Square:** Constrains the shape to a perfect square.
- ✔ **Fixed Size:** Lets you draw rectangles in fixed sizes, as specified by your width and height values.
- ✔ **Proportional:** Allows you to define a proportion for the rectangle. For example, specifying 2W and 1H makes a rectangle twice as wide as it is high.
- ✔ **From Center:** Enables you to draw from the center out.
- ✔ **Snap:** Aligns the shape to the pixels on your screen.
- ✔ **Radius:** For Rounded Rectangles, applies the radius of a circle used to round off the corners. This option is found in the Tool Options itself, not in the Geometry Options pop-up menu.

### Ellipse geometry options

The Ellipse shape has the same options that are available for rectangles, except for the Snap option. The only difference is that, instead of being able to create a perfect square, you can create a perfect circle with the Circle option.

### Polygon Geometry options

The Geometry options for the Polygon shape are as follows:

- ✔ **Sides:** Specify the number of sides for your polygon.
- ✔ **Smooth: Corners:** Round off the corners.

### Star Geometry options

The Geometry options for the Star shape are as follows:

- ✔ **Sides:** Specify the number of points for your star.
- ✔ **Smooth: Corners:** Round off the inner corners of indented sides or round off the corners.
- ✔ **Smooth: Indents:** Determine the amount that the sides indent inward.

### Line Geometry options

The line's Geometry settings include whether to put arrowheads at the start or end of the line. You can also adjust the width, length, and concavity settings to change the arrowhead shapes.

### Custom Shape Geometry options

The Custom Shape options are similar to those you find for the other shapes, but with a couple unique options:

- **Defined Proportions:** Draws a shape based on the original proportions you used when you created it.

- **Defined Size:** Draws a shape based on its original size when you created it.

## Editing shapes

You can edit shapes that you create by using a variety of tools and techniques. Here's a list of the things you can do to modify your shapes:

- **Select:** Choose the Shape Selection tool to select one or more shapes in their layers. You can find this tool in the Tool Options along with the shapes tools.

- **Move:** Choose the Move tool (press V) to move the entire contents of the shape layer.

- **Delete:** Select a shape with the Shape Selection tool and press Delete to remove it.

- **Transform Shape:** Choose the Shape Selection tool and select your shape. Choose Image⇨Transform Shape and choose your desired transformation.

- **Change the color:** Double-click the thumbnail of the shape layer on the Layers panel. This action transports you to the Color Picker, where you can choose a new color.

- **Clone a shape:** Hold down the Alt (Option on the Mac) key and move the shape with the Move tool.

To convert your vector-based shape into a pixel-based shape, click the Simplify button in the Tool Options or choose Layer⇨Simplify Layer. You can't edit a shape after you simplify it except to modify the pixels. But you can now apply filters to the layer. See Chapter 11 for more on fun with filters.

# Working with Type

*In This Chapter*

▶ Understanding type basics

▶ Creating point, paragraph, and path type

▶ Setting type options

▶ Editing and simplifying (rasterizing) type

▶ Masking with type

▶ Stylizing and warping type

*A*lthough we spout on in this book about how a picture says a thousand words, we'd be terribly negligent if we didn't at least give a nod to the power of the written word as well. You may find that you never need to go near the type tools. That's fine. We won't be offended if you skip right past this chapter.

Then again, you may have an occasional need to add a caption, a headline, or maybe even a short paragraph to an image. Although it's by no means a word-processing or even page-layout program, Elements does give you ample tools for creating, editing, stylizing, and even distorting type.

## Understanding Type Basics

Elements has seven type tools. Two of them are for entering horizontally oriented type, and two are for entering vertically oriented type. Don't worry about the vertical type tools. Although you can use them, they're really designed for the Asian market so users can enter Chinese and Japanese characters. The remaining three tools are for creating type on a selection, shape, or *path* (which is a line, curved or straight, that doesn't appear in your actual image but that your text follows).

## Tools

The horizontal and vertical type tools are identical in their attributes, so we cover just the two horizontal type tools here. For the sake of simplicity, we call them the Type and Type Mask tools:

- ✐ **Type:** Use this tool to enter type. This type is created on its own type layer except when used in Bitmap mode or Indexed Color mode, neither of which supports layers.

  We refer to layers a lot in this chapter, so if your layer knowledge is rusty, check out Chapter 8.

- ✐ **Type Mask:** This tool doesn't create actual type; instead, it creates a selection border in the shape of the type you want to enter. The selection border is added to the active layer. You can do anything with a type selection that you can do with any other selection. (Chapter 7 is your one-stop guide to selections.)

The remaining three type tools all create type on a path in different ways:

- ✐ **Text On Selection:** This tool enables you to draw on your image to create a selection, similar to the Quick Selection tool. The selection converts into a path. When you add text, it follows the shape of the path.

- ✐ **Text On Shape:** This tool enables you to draw any chosen shape from your shapes menu. When you add text, it follows the shape.

- ✐ **Text On Custom Path:** This tool lets you draw any custom path that you desire on your image. Enter text on that custom path, and it adheres to that path.

  The three path type tools all create a type layer. Find out how to use these tools in the upcoming section, "Creating Path Type."

  A path has three components: anchor points, straight segments, and curved segments. The path essentially hovers above the image in its own "space," thereby not altering or marking the image in any way. The path in this context is merely a track upon which the text can flow. You can alter the path to your liking by using the Refine Path option. Find out more in the later "Creating Path Type" section.

## Modes

You can enter text in Elements in three different modes: point, paragraph, and path. Both the Type and Type Mask tools can enter either point or paragraph mode. Here's a brief description of each mode (for the step-by-step process of creating the text, see the following sections):

✔ **Point:** Use this mode if you want to enter only a few words. Select the Type tool, click in your image, and, well, type. The text appears while you type and continues to grow. In fact, it even continues past the boundary of your image!

Point type *never* wraps around to a new line. To wrap to the next line, you must press Enter (Return on a Mac).

✔ **Paragraph:** Use this mode to enter longer chunks (or constrained blocks) of text on an image. Click and drag your type tool to create a text bounding box and then type. All the text is entered in this resizable bounding box. If a line of text is too long, Elements automatically wraps it around to the next line.

✔ **Path:** Elements also offers the capability of placing text along a path via three unique type tools. Double-click the path and type; the text appears, adhering to the shape of the path.

## Formats

Elements can display and print type in two formats. Each format has its pros and cons, and which format you use depends on your needs. Here's the low-down on both of them:

✔ **Vector:** All text in Elements is initially created as vector type. *Vector* type provides scalable outlines that you can resize without producing jaggy edges in the diagonal strokes. Vector type remains fully editable and always prints with optimum quality, appearing crisp and clean. Vector type is the default type format in Elements, except for images in bitmap or Indexed color modes.

✔ **Raster:** When Elements converts vector type into pixels, the text is *rasterized.* Elements refers to this rasterization process as simplifying. When text is *simplified,* it's no longer editable as text but is converted into a raster image. You usually simplify your vector type when you want to apply filters to the type to produce a special effect or when you want to merge the type with the image. You can't resize simplified type without losing some quality or risking jagged edges. For more details, see the section "Simplifying Type," later in this chapter.

# Creating Point Type

The majority of your type entry will most likely be in *point type mode.* Point type is useful for short chunks of text, such as headlines, labels, logos, and headings for web pages.

Point type is so called because it contains a single *anchor point,* which marks the starting point of the line of type. Remember that point-type lines don't wrap automatically, as you can see in Figure 13-1.

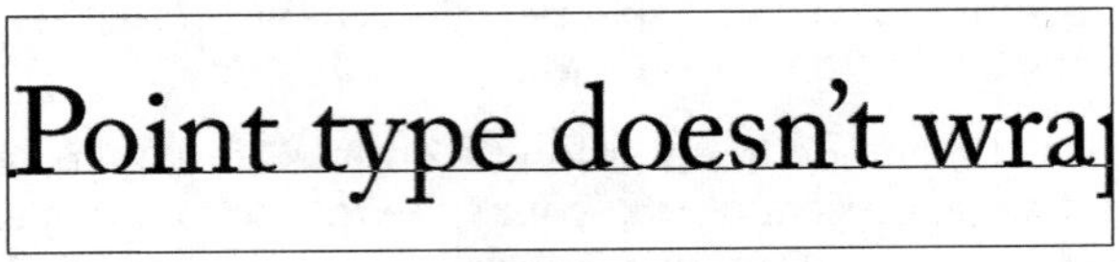

## Point type doesn't wra

**Figure 13-1:** Point type doesn't wrap automatically, but instead can run off your image into a type Neverland.

Follow these steps to create point type:

1. **Open the Photo Editor and choose Expert mode.**

2. **Open an image or create a new, blank Elements file by choosing File⇨New⇨Blank File.**

3. **Select the Horizontal Type tool from the Tools panel.**

   You can also press T to cycle through the various type tools. Additionally, you can also select the Horizontal Type tool from the Tool Options. It looks like a capital letter T.

4. **On the image, click where you want to insert your text.**

   Your cursor is called an *I-beam.* When you click, you make an insertion point.

   A small, horizontal line about one-third of the way up the I-beam shows the *baseline* (the line on which the text sits) for horizontal type.

5. **Specify your type options from the Tool Options.**

   All the options are described in detail in the section "Specifying Type Options," later in this chapter.

6. **Type your text and press Enter (Return on a Mac) to begin a new line.**

   When you press Enter (or Return), you insert a hard return that doesn't move.

7. **When you finish entering the text, click the Commit button (the green check-mark icon) near your text.**

   If you want to bail out, click the Cancel button (the red No icon).

   You can also commit the type by pressing Enter on the numeric keypad or by clicking any other tool on the Tools panel. A new type layer with your text is created. Type layers appear on your Layers panel and are indicated by the T icon.

# Creating Paragraph Type

If you have larger chunks of text, it's usually more practical to enter the text as paragraph type. Entering paragraph type is similar to entering text in a word-processing or page-layout program, except that the text is contained inside a bounding box. When you type and come to the end of the bounding box, Elements automatically wraps the text to the next line.

To enter paragraph type, follow these steps:

1. **Open the Photo Editor and choose Expert mode.**

2. **Open an image or create a new, blank Elements file by choosing File⇨New⇨Blank File.**

3. **Select the Horizontal Type tool from the Tools panel or press T to cycle through the various type tools.**

   You can also select the Horizontal Type tool from the Tool Options.

4. **On the image, insert and size the bounding box by using one of two methods:**

   • *Drag to create a bounding box close to your desired size.* After you release the mouse button, you can drag any of the handles at the corners and sides of the box to resize it.

   • *Hold down the Alt (Option on the Mac) key and click the image.* The Paragraph Text Size dialog box appears. Enter the exact dimensions of your desired bounding box. When you click OK, your specified box appears, complete with handles for resizing later.

5. **Specify your type options from the Tool Options.**

   Options are described in detail in the following section.

6. **Enter your text; to start a new paragraph, press Enter (Return on a Mac).**

   Each line wraps around to fit inside the bounding box, as shown in Figure 13-2.

   If you type more text than can squeeze into the text box, an overflow icon (a box with a plus sign inside) appears. Resize the text box by dragging a bounding box handle.

7. **Click the Commit button (the green check-mark icon) next to the text box or press Enter on the numeric keypad.**

   If you're not happy with the text, you can click the Cancel button (the red No icon) and start over.

   After you click Commit, Elements creates a new type layer.

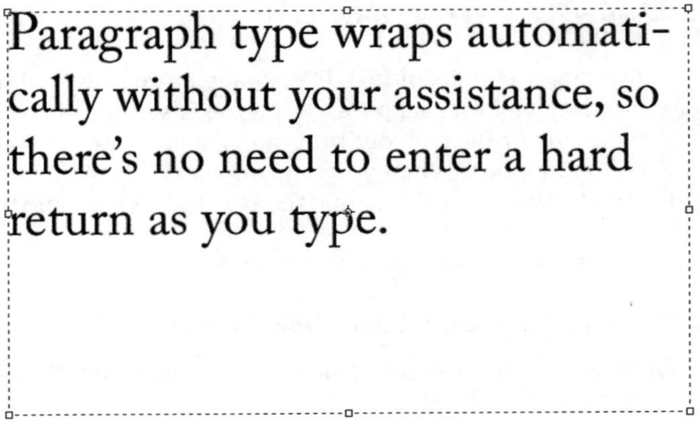

Paragraph type wraps automatically without your assistance, so
there's no need to enter a hard
return as you type.

Figure 13-2: Paragraph type automatically wraps to fit within your bounding box.

# Creating Path Type

If you want your type to flow in a circle, wave, stair step, or any other shape, you're in luck. Elements provides three type tools that enable you to do just that. The great thing is that path type is easy to create, totally editable, and the type resides on its very own layer.

## Using the Text On Selection tool

You can create path type by first creating a selection of your image, which is similar to the way you create a selection with the Quick Selection tool. Here's how:

1. **Open the Photo Editor and choose Expert mode.**

2. **Open an image or create a new, blank Elements file by choosing File⇨New⇨Blank File.**

3. **Select the Text On Selection tool from the Tools panel or press T to cycle through the various type tools.**

    You can also select the Text On Selection tool from the Tool Options. It looks like a capital letter T with a dotted square around it.

4. **On the image, "paint" (drag) over your desired selection.**

5. **Refine your selection by adding or subtracting from it in one of four ways:**

   - Press the Shift key and drag around the additional area that you want to include in your selection.

   - Press the Alt (Option on the Mac) key and drag around the area that you want to subtract from your selection.

   - Select the Add to Selection or Subtract from Selection buttons in the Tool Options and drag around your desired areas.

   - In the Tool Options, drag the Offset slider right to expand, or left to contract, your selection.

   You can specify additional options, which are common to all the type tools; these are described in detail in the later section, "Specifying Type Options."

6. **When your selection is complete, click the Commit button (the green check-mark icon) to convert your selection to a path.**

   If you want to start over, click the red Cancel (a slashed circle) icon to do so.

7. **Position your mouse pointer over the path and, when the cursor icon changes to an I-beam (a capital letter *I* with a crooked line crossing over), click the path and type your text.**

   The text wraps along the path. If you type more text than can fit on the path, an overflow icon appears. Resize the selection until all your text appears.

8. **When you're done entering your text, click the Commit button (the green check-mark icon).**

   Elements creates a new type layer. You can edit any attributes, such as font and size, just as you can with point or paragraph text. See the upcoming section "Editing Text" for details.

## Using the Text On Shape tool

The Text On Shape tool enables you to create type that flows along the perimeter of any shape. To do so, follow these steps:

1. **Open the Photo Editor and choose Expert mode.**

2. **Open an image or create a new, blank Elements file by choosing File➪New➪Blank File.**

3. **Select the Text On Shape tool from the Tools panel or press T to cycle through the various type tools.**

   You can also select the Text on Shape tool from the Tool Options. It looks like a capital letter T with a wavy box around it.

4. **Select your desired shape from the shape options in the Tool Options.**

5. **Drag your tool over the image to create the shape.**

   - *To constrain your proportions,* hold down the Shift key while dragging.

   - *To draw from the center outward,* hold down the Alt (Option on the Mac) key while dragging.

6. **(Optional) Transform your shape by choosing Image⇨Transform Shape and choosing your desired transformation.**

   You can specify additional options, which are common to all the type tools; these are described in detail in the upcoming section, "Specifying Type Options."

   For details on transformations, see Chapter 8.

7. **Position your mouse pointer over the path and, when the cursor icon changes to an I-beam (a capital letter *I* with a crooked line crossing over), click the path and type your text.**

   The text wraps along the shape's path, as shown in Figure 13-3.

   If you type more text than can fit on the path, an overflow icon appears. Adjust the path until all your text appears.

8. **When you're done entering your text, click the Commit button (the green check-mark icon).**

   If you want to start over, click the red Cancel icon.

   Elements creates a new type layer. You can edit any attributes, such as font and size, just as you can with point or paragraph text. See the section "Editing Text" for details.

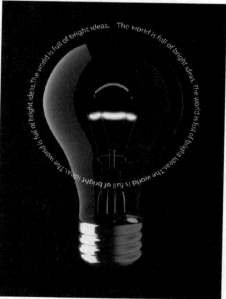

©istockphoto.com/fpm Image #6201684

**Figure 13-3:** Text can adhere to any path that you create.

TIP

You can also refine your shape path by using the Refine Path tool (labeled Modify), which appears in the Tool Options when the Text On Custom Path tool is selected. Just be sure that your type layer is selected in the Layers panel before working with this option.

### Using the Text On Custom Path tool

If you want to create your own path or shape as the basis for your type, the Text On Custom Path tool is for you. Here's how:

1. **Open the Photo Editor and choose Expert mode.**

2. **Open an image or create a new, blank Elements file by choosing File⇨New⇨Blank File.**

3. **Select the Text On Custom Path tool from the Tools panel or press T to cycle through the various type tools.**

   You can also select the Text On Custom Path tool from the Tool Options. It looks like a capital letter T on a line.

4. **Drag your tool over the image to create the custom path of your choice.**

5. **Refine your path by selecting the Refine Path option (labeled Modify) in the Tool Options. Drag the anchor points or path segments with the tool to get your desired shape.**

   You can also transform your custom path by choosing Image⇨Transform Shape. For details on transformations, see Chapter 8.

   You can specify additional options, which are common to all the type tools; these are described in detail in the following section, "Specifying Type Options."

6. **Position your mouse pointer over the path and, when the cursor icon changes to an I-beam (a capital letter *I* with a crooked line crossing over), click the path and type your text.**

   The text wraps along the shape's path.

   If you type more text than can fit on the path, an overflow icon appears. Adjust the path as needed so that all the text appears.

7. **When you're done entering your text, click the Commit button (the green check-mark icon) or click the red Cancel icon to start again.**

   Elements creates a new type layer. You can edit any attributes, such as font and size, just as you can with point or paragraph text. See the section "Editing Text" for details.

8. **To create a new custom path, select the background layer in the Layers panel and repeat Steps 3–7.**

## Specifying Type Options

When you're using a Type tool, the Tool Options (found at the bottom of the workspace) includes several character and paragraph type settings, as shown in Figure 13-4. These options enable you to specify your type to your liking and pair it with your images.

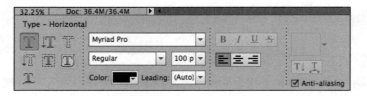

Figure 13-4: Specify your type options, such as font family and size, before you type.

Here's an explanation of each available option in the Tool Options:

- ✔ **Font Family:** Select the font you want from the drop-down list. Elements provides a WYSIWYG (What You See Is What You Get) font menu. After each font name, the word *Sample* is rendered in the actual font — no more selecting a font without knowing what it really looks like.

    You also find one of these abbreviations before each font name to let you know what type of font it is:

    - *a:* Adobe Type 1 (PostScript) fonts
    - *TT:* TrueType fonts
    - *O:* OpenType fonts

    Fonts with no abbreviation are bitmapped fonts.

- ✔ **Font Style:** Some font families have additional styles, such as light or condensed. Only the styles available for a particular font appear in the list. This is also a WYSIWYG menu.

- ✔ **Font Size:** Choose your type size from the drop-down list or just type a size in the text box. Type size is most commonly measured in points (in which 72 points equals about 1 inch at a resolution of 72 ppi). You can switch to millimeters or pixels by choosing Edit➪Preferences➪Units & Rulers (on the Mac, choose Adobe Photoshop Elements Editor➪ Preferences➪Units & Rulers).

- ✔ **Text Color:** Click the color swatch to select a color for your type from the Color Picker. You can also choose a color from the Swatches panel.

- ✔ **Leading:** Leading (pronounced *LED-ding*) is the amount of space between the baselines of lines of type. A *baseline* is the imaginary line on which a line of type sits. You can choose Auto Leading or specify the amount of leading to apply. When you choose Auto Leading, Elements uses a value of 120 percent of your type point size. Therefore 10-point type gets 12 points of leading. Elements adds that extra 20 percent so that the bottoms of the lowest letters don't crash into the tops of the tallest letters on the next line.

✔ **Text Alignment:** These three options align your horizontal text on the left or right, or in the center. If you happen to have vertical text, these options rotate 90 degrees clockwise and change into top, bottom, and center vertical settings.

✔ **Anti-aliasing:** Select this option to slightly smooth out the edges of your text. The Anti-aliasing option softens that edge by 1 pixel, as shown in Figure 13-5. For the most part, you want to keep this option turned on. The one occasion in which you may want it turned off is when you're creating small type to be displayed onscreen, such as on web pages. The soft edges can sometimes be tough to read.

Anti-aliased    Not anti-aliased

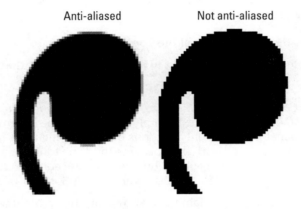

Figure 13-5: The Anti-aliasing option softens the edges of your type.

✔ **Faux Bold:** Use this option to create a fake bold style when a real bold style (which you'd choose under Font Style) doesn't exist. Be warned that, although the sky won't fall, applying faux styles can distort the proportions of a font. You should use fonts with real styles, and if they don't exist, oh well.

✔ **Faux Italic:** This option creates a phony oblique style and carries the same warning as the Faux Bold option.

✔ **Underline:** This setting (obviously) underlines your type, like <u>this</u>.

✔ **Strikethrough:** Choose this option to apply a ~~strikethrough~~ style to your text.

✔ **Style:** Click this option to access a drop-down panel of preset layer styles that you can apply to your type. This option is accessible after you have committed your type. For more on this option and the Create Warped Text option (described in the last bullet), see the section "Stylizing and Warping Type," later in this chapter.

  ✓ **Change the Text Orientation:** Select your type layer and then click this option to switch between vertical and horizontal type orientations.

  ✓ **Create Warped Text:** This fun option lets you distort type in more than a dozen ways.

You can apply type settings either before or after you enter your text.

## Editing Text

To correct typos, add and delete type, or change any of the type options, simply follow these steps:

1. **Select the Type tool from the Tools panel.**

2. **Double-click within the text to automatically select the type layer.**

3. **Make any changes to your text:**

   • *Change the font family, size, color, or other type option.* If you want to change all the text, simply select that type layer on the Layers panel. To select only portions of the text, highlight the text by dragging across it with the I-beam of the Type tool. Then select your changes in the Tool Options; see the preceding section "Specifying Type Options" for details about your options for the Type tool.

   • *Delete text.* Highlight the text by dragging across it with the I-beam of the Type tool. Then press the Backspace key (Delete on the Mac).

   • *Add text.* Make an insertion point by clicking your I-beam within the line of text. Then type your new text.

   *Note:* These editing steps apply to all types of text — point, paragraph, and path.

4. **When you're done editing your text, click the Commit button (the green check-mark icon).**

You may also occasionally need to transform your text. To do so, make sure that the type layer is selected on the Layers panel. Then choose Image➪Transform➪Free Transform. Grab a handle on the bounding box and drag to rotate or scale. Press Ctrl (⌘ on the Mac) and drag a handle to distort. When you're done, double-click inside the bounding box to commit the transformation. For more details on transformations, see Chapter 8.

For path type, applying the transformation command enables you to change the shape of your path but not the actual type itself. When you double-click the bounding box, the type will rewrap along the transformed path.

# Simplifying Type

As we explain in the section "Understanding Type Basics" earlier in this chapter, Elements can display and print type in two different formats: vector and raster.

As long as you keep type in a vector format on a type layer, you can edit and resize that type all day long.

Occasionally, however, you may need to *simplify* your type — to convert your type into pixels. After it's simplified, you can apply filters, paint on the type, and apply gradients and patterns. If you're working with layers and *flatten* your image (merge your layers into a single background image), your type layer is also simplified and merged with the other pixels in your image. By the way, if you try to apply a filter to a type layer, Elements barks at you that the type layer must be simplified before proceeding and gives you the opportunity to click OK (if you want to simplify) or Cancel.

To simplify your type, select the type layer on the Layers panel and choose Layer⇨Simplify Layer. Your type layer is then converted (the T icon disappears) into a regular layer on which your type is now displayed as pixels against a transparent background, as shown in Figure 13-6.

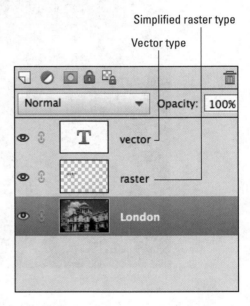

Figure 13-6: Simplifying your type layer converts vector type into pixels.

To avoid having to re-create your type from scratch, make all necessary edits before simplifying. This includes sizing your text. After you simplify your type, you can't resize your text without risking the dreaded jaggies. The other downside to remember about simplified type is that although it looks identical to vector type onscreen, it never prints as crisply and cleanly as vector type. Even at higher-resolution settings, a slight jagged edge always appears on simplified type. So, if you're experimenting with painting or filters on your type, just make a duplicate of your type layer before simplifying it and then hide that layer.

## Masking with Type

Using the Type Mask tool epitomizes the combination of type and image. Unlike the Type tool, the Type Mask tool doesn't create a new layer. Instead, it creates a selection on the active layer. Type Mask is the tool of choice for filling text with an image or cutting text out of an image so that the background shows through, as shown in Figure 13-7.

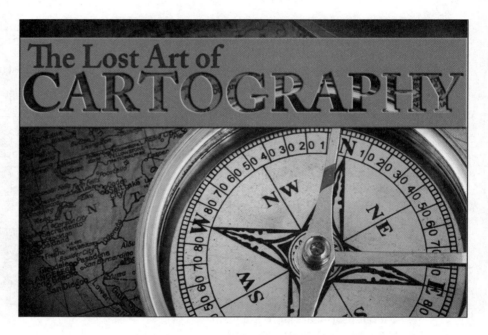

©istockphoto.com/Akirastock Image #8791096

**Figure 13-7:** The Type Mask tool enables you to cut type out of solid color or image layers.

A selection is a selection no matter how it was created. So, even though type mask selections look like letters, they act like selections. You can move, modify, and save them.

Here are the steps to create a type mask:

1. **In the Photo Editor in Expert mode, open the image of your choice.**

   We selected a stone texture.

2. **Convert your background into a layer by double-clicking the word** *Background* **on the Layers panel, and then click OK.**

   This step enables you to jazz up the type with styles later.

3. **Choose the Horizontal Type Mask tool from the Tools panel.**

4. **Specify your type options (such as Font Family, Style, and Size) in the Tool Options.**

5. **Click the image, and type your desired text. When you're done, click the Commit button (the green check-mark icon).**

   A selection border in the shape of your type appears on your image.

6. **Choose Select⇨Inverse, which deselects your letter selections and selects everything else.**

7. **Press the Backspace (Delete on a Mac) key to delete everything outside your selection border.**

   Your type is now filled with your image.

8. **Choose Select⇨Deselect.**

9. **Experiment with applying layer styles to your type.**

   a. *Choose Window⇨Effects or click the Effects button at the bottom of the workspace (assuming you're in Basic Workspace).*

      If you need to get back to the Basic Workspace, click the arrow on the More button in the bottom-right corner of the workspace and choose Basic Workspace from the submenu.

   b. *Click the Styles button located at the top of the Effects panel.*

   c. *Choose the type of layer styles you desire from the drop-down list at the top of the panel, such as Drop Shadows or Bevels.*

   d. *Double-click the exact style you want.*

      We used a drop shadow and a simple inner bevel in Figure 13-8. See Chapter 11 for more about layer styles.

If you want to admire your type against a solid background, as we did, create a new layer, choose Edit⇨Fill Layer, and then choose your desired color from the Use drop-down list.

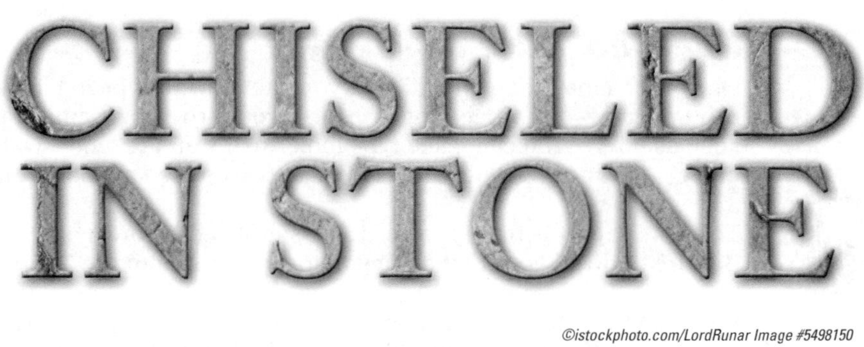

# CHISELED IN STONE

©istockphoto.com/LordRunar Image #5498150

**Figure 13-8:** Fill type with imagery by using the Type Mask tool.

# Stylizing and Warping Type

If you've tried your hand at creating a type mask, you know that Elements is capable of much more than just throwing a few black letters at the bottom of your image. With a few clicks here and there, you can warp, distort, enhance, and stylize your type. If you're not careful, your creative typography can outshine your image.

## Adjusting type opacity

If you checked out Chapter 8 before reading this chapter, you know that *layers* are a digital version of the old analog transparency sheets. You can change element opacity on layers to let the underlying layer show through in varying degrees. This is also possible on a type layer. Figure 13-9 shows how varying the opacity percentage of your type layer makes more of the underlying layer show through. In Figure 13-9, the underlying layer is an image of water.

To change the opacity of a type layer, simply select the layer on the Layers panel, click the arrow to the right of the Opacity percentage, and drag the slider. The lower the percentage, the less opaque the type (and the more the underlying layer shows through).

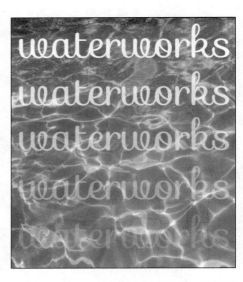

©istockphoto.com/Mikosch Image #2592893

**Figure 13-9:** You can vary the opacity of type layers to allow the underlying layer to peek through.

## Applying filters to your type

One of the most interesting things you can do with type in Elements that you can't do in a word-processing or page-layout program is apply special effects, such as filters. You can make type look like it's on fire, underwater, or on the move — as shown in Figure 13-10, where we applied a motion blur.

The only caveat is that type has to be simplified before a filter can be applied. Be sure to do all your text editing before you move to the filtering stage.

Applying the filter is as easy as selecting the simplified type layer on the Layers panel and choosing a filter from the Filter menu. For more on filters, see Chapter 11.

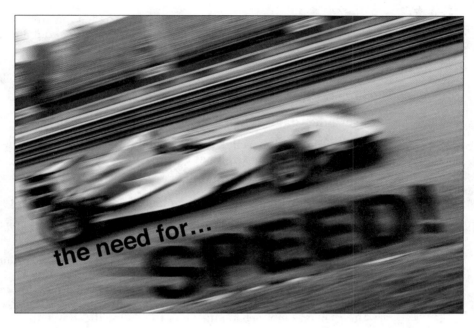

©istockphoto.com/EduLeite Image #13233892

**Figure 13-10:** Applying a motion blur to type can make it appear as fast as the car.

## *Painting your type with color and gradients*

Changing the color of text is as easy as high-lighting it and selecting a color from the Color Picker. But what if you want to do something a little less conventional, such as apply random brush strokes of paint across the type, as we did in the top image shown in Figure 13-11? It's really easier than it looks. Again, as with apply-ing filters to text, the only criterion is that the type has to be simplified first. After that's done, select a color, grab the Brush tool with set-tings of your choice, and paint. In our example, we used the Granite Flow brush, found in the Special Effect Brushes presets. We used a diam-eter of 39, 15, and 6 pixels and just swiped our type a few times.

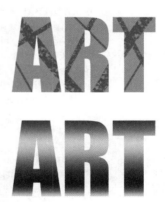

**Figure 13-11:** Bring your type to life with color (top) or a gradient (bottom).

If you want the color or gradient to be confined to the type area, select the text by either Ctrl-clicking (⌘-clicking on a Mac) the layer containing the text or locking the layer's transparency on the Layers panel.

You can also apply a gradient to your type. Here are the steps to follow after simplifying your type:

1. **Select the Gradient tool from the Tools panel.**

2. **In the Tool Options, click the down-pointing arrow next to the Gradient Picker to access the Gradient Picker panel.**

3. **Choose your desired gradient.**

   If you want to create a custom gradient, find out how in Chapter 12.

4. **Position your gradient cursor on the text where you want your gradient to start; drag to where you want your gradient to end.**

   Don't like the results? Drag again until you get the look you want. You can drag at any angle and to any length, even outside your type. In the bottom image shown in Figure 13-11, we used the copper gradient and just dragged from the top of the letters to the bottom. We also locked the transparent pixels on the layer to confine the gradient to just the type area.

## Warping your type

If horizontal or vertical text is just way too regimented for you, try the Warp feature. The best part about the distortions you apply is that the text remains fully editable. This feature is fun and easy to use. Click the Create Warped Text button at the far right of the Tool Options. (It's the T with a curved line below it.) This action opens the Warp Text dialog box, where you find a vast array of distortions on the Style drop-down list with descriptive names such as Bulge, Inflate, and Squeeze.

After selecting a warp style, you can adjust the orientation, amount of bend, and degree of distortion by dragging the sliders. The Bend setting affects the amount of warp, and the Horizontal and Vertical Distortions apply perspective to that warp. Luckily, you can also view the results while you adjust. We could give you technical explanations of these adjustments, but the best way to see what they do is to just play with them. See Figure 13-12 to get a quick look at a few warp styles. The names speak for themselves.

You can also use the Transform command, such as scale and skew, to manipulate text. See Chapter 8 for details on transforming.

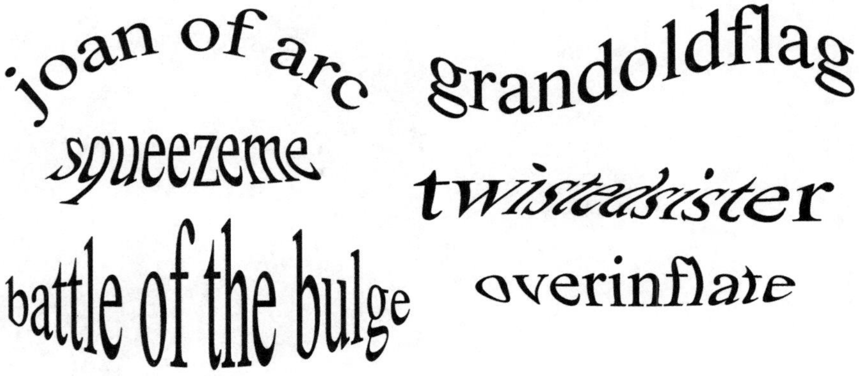

joan of arc    grandoldflag

squeezeme    twistedsister

battle of the bulge    overinflate

Figure 13-12: Text remains fully editable after you apply distortions with the Warp command.

# Part V
# Printing, Creating, and Sharing

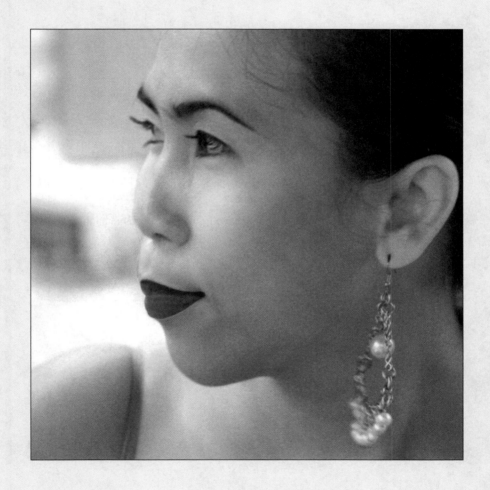

Check out www.dummies.com/extras/photoshopelements for details about saving photos to display online and creating photo calendars.

## *In this part . . .*

- ✔ Manage color, use color profiles, and get your output to closely match what you see onscreen.
- ✔ Print your pictures either at home or through an online service.
- ✔ Share your pictures with family and friends on social media and online sharing services.
- ✔ Display your photos in photo books, greeting cards, and slide shows.

# Getting It on Paper

*In This Chapter*

▶ Preparing files for printing

▶ Working with printer profiles

▶ Using the Print dialog box

*P*erhaps the greatest challenge when using programs such as Photoshop Elements (and even the professionals who use its granddaddy, Adobe Photoshop) is getting what you see on your monitor to render a reasonable facsimile on a printed page. You can find all sorts of books on color printing — how to get color right, how to calibrate your equipment, and how to create and use color profiles — all for the purpose of getting a good match among your computer monitor, your printer, and the paper used to print your output. It's downright discouraging to spend a lot of time tweaking an image so that all the brilliant blue colors jump out on your computer monitor, only to find that all those blues turn to murky purples when the photo is printed.

If you read Chapter 2, you're ahead of the game because you know a little bit about color management, color profiles, and printer resolutions. After you check out that chapter, your next step is to get to know your printer and understand how to print your pictures correctly.

In this chapter, we talk about options — many options — for setting print attributes for printing to your own color printer. If you need to, reread this chapter a few times just to be certain that you understand the process for printing good-quality images. A little time spent here will, we hope, save you some headaches down the road.

# Getting Pictures Ready for Printing

The first step toward getting your photos to your desktop printer is to prepare each image for optimum output. You have several considerations when you're preparing files, including the ones in this list:

- **Set resolution and size.** See your printer's documentation to find out what resolution the manufacturer recommends. As a general rule, 200 to 300 ppi (pixels per inch) works best for most desktop printers printing on high-quality paper. If you print on plain paper, you often find that lower resolutions work just as well or even better. Chapter 2 explains setting size and resolution in detail.

- **Make all brightness and color corrections before printing.** Make sure that your pictures appear their best before sending them to your printer. If you have your monitor properly calibrated, as we discuss in Chapter 2, you should see a fair representation of what your pictures will look like before you print them. Chapters 9 and 10 cover corrections.

- **Decide how color will be managed before you print.** You can color-manage output to your printer in three ways, as we discuss in the following section. Know your printer's profiles and how to use them before you start to print your files.

- **Get your printer ready.** When printing to desktop color printers, always be certain your ink cartridges have ink and the nozzles are clean. Make sure you use the proper settings for paper and ink when you send a file to your printer. Be sure to review the manual that came with your printer so you know how to perform all the steps required to make a quality print.

Various sources offer alternatives for purchasing inks. You can purchase third-party inks for your printer, use refillable ink cartridges, or have your printer modified to hold large ink tanks that last much longer than the manufacturer-supplied cartridges. These alternatives provide you with significant savings when purchasing inks.

However, using any inks other than manufacturer-recommended inks can produce color problems. Each developer provides printer profiles specific for their recommended inks. With third-party inks, you don't have the advantage of using color profiles that have been tested by a printer manufacturer. If getting the most accurate color on your prints is important to you, use only those inks and papers recommended by your printer manufacturer.

# Working with Color Printer Profiles

In Chapter 2, we talk about creating color profiles for your monitor and selecting a color workspace. The final leg in a color-managed workflow is to convert color from your color workspace profile to your printer's color profile. Basically, this conversion means that the colors you see on your monitor in your current workspace are accurately converted to the color that your printer can reproduce. To print accurate color, a color profile designed for your printer and the paper you use needs to be installed on your computer.

You can manage color in Photoshop Elements in three ways when it comes time to print your files:

✓ **Printer Manages Colors:** This method permits your desktop color printer to decide which profile to use when you print your photo. Your printer makes this decision according to the paper you select. If you choose Epson Premium Glossy Photo Paper, for example, your printer chooses the profile that goes along with that particular paper. If you choose another paper, your printer chooses a different color profile. This method is all automatic, and color profile selection is made when you print your file.

✓ **Photoshop Elements Manages Colors:** When you make this choice, color management is taken out of the hands of your printer and is controlled by Elements. You must choose the color profile. If color profiles are installed by your printer, you can choose a color profile from the list of profiles that match your printer and the paper source.

✓ **No Color Management:** You use this choice if you have a color profile embedded in one of your pictures. You'll probably rarely use this option. Unless you know how to embed profiles or receive files with embedded profiles from other users, don't make this choice in the Print dialog box. Because very few Elements users work with files with embedded profiles, we skip covering this method of printing your files.

Each of these three options requires you to decide how color is managed. You make choices (as we discuss later in this chapter when we walk you through the steps for printing) about whether to color-manage your output. These selections are unique to the Print dialog box and more specifically to the More Options dialog box for your individual printer.

Color profiles are also dependent upon the ink being used, and refilling cartridges with generic ink can (in some cases) result in colors shifting. Similarly, if the nozzles aren't clean and delivering ink consistently, you may see strange results.

## Printer color profiles

Color profiling has been developed quite well by the three top desktop color printer developers (Epson, HP, and Canon). You can find a wealth of information on the Internet for using color profiles with each of these printers. For starters, take a look at the following URLs for more information about printing using color profiles:

**Epson Printers (Windows)**

```
www.redrivercatalog.com/profiles/lightroom/how-to-use-icc-color-
printer-profiles-lightroom-epson-desktop-windows.html
```

**Epson Printers (Macintosh)**

```
www.redrivercatalog.com/profiles/lightroom/how-to-use-icc-color-
printer-profiles-lightroom-epson-mac.html
```

**HP Printers (Windows)**

```
http://h10025.www1.hp.com/ewfrf/wc/document?cc=us&lc=en&dlc=en&
docname=c00286904
```

**HP Printers (Macintosh;** a very nice PDF file that describes using color profiles for Mac and with HP Printers)

```
http://h10088.www1.hp.com/gap/Data/en/us/colormgmttb_
final_060901.pdf
```

**Canon Printers (Windows)**

```
www.redrivercatalog.com/profiles/lightroom/how-to-use-icc-color-
printer-profiles-lightroom-canon-desktop-windows.html
```

**Canon Printers (Macintosh)**

```
http://www.redrivercatalog.com/profiles/lightroom/how-to-use-
icc-color-printer-profiles-lightroom-canon-mac.html
```

Some of the descriptions on these websites show the initial Print command executed from Adobe Photoshop or Adobe Lightroom. Just follow the steps after the Print command is executed.

### Printing a photo with the printer managing color

Without going into all the settings you have to choose from in the Print and More Options dialog boxes, for now we look at printing a photo and letting the printer manage color. We explain more print options that are available later in this chapter in the section "Creating transfers, borders, and more with More Options."

Unless you want to print Picture Packages or Contact Sheets (Windows), use the Print dialog box from the Photo Editor. Color Management options offer you much better choices for managing color.

For the following example, we use an Epson printer. If you have a different printer, some of the dialog boxes and terms may be different. With a little careful examination of the Print dialog box, you can apply the following steps for any printer:

1. **With a photo open in the Photo Editor, choose File⇨Print or press Ctrl+P (⌘+P on the Mac).**

   The Print dialog box that opens contains all the settings you need to print a file, as shown in Figure 14-1.

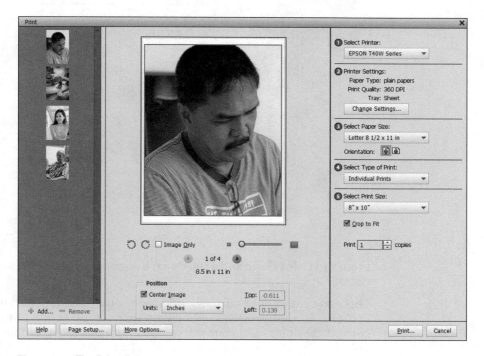

**Figure 14-1:** The Print dialog box.

2. **Click Page Setup at the bottom of the Print dialog box and select the orientation of your print. Click OK.**

   Your orientation choices are Portrait and Landscape. After you click OK, you return to the Print dialog box.

3. **In the upper right, choose your printer from the Select Printer drop-down list.**

4. **Set the print attributes.**

   Select the paper size, type of print, print size, and number of copies you want. (Note the items shown in Figure 14-1.)

5. **In the lower left, click the More Options button, and, in the More Options dialog box that appears, click Color Management from the list on the left.**

   In the Color Management area, as shown in Figure 14-2, you choose how to manage color when you print files.

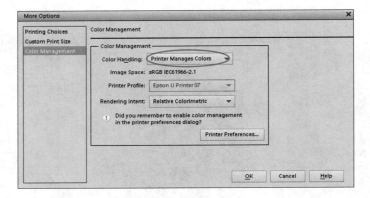

**Figure 14-2:** Look over the Color Management area in the More Options dialog box (when printing from the Photo Editor) for options on how to manage color.

6. **From the Color Handling drop-down list, choose Printer Manages Colors.**

   This choice uses your current workspace color — either sRGB or Adobe RGB (1998). Moreover, this option tells your computer and printer to convert the color from your workspace to the printer output file when you open the Print dialog box. (We introduce color workspaces in Chapter 2.)

7. **Set the printer preferences.**

   *Windows:* Click the Printer Preferences button in the More Options dialog box. The printing preferences dialog box for your printer driver opens, as shown in Figure 14-3. Proceed to Step 8.

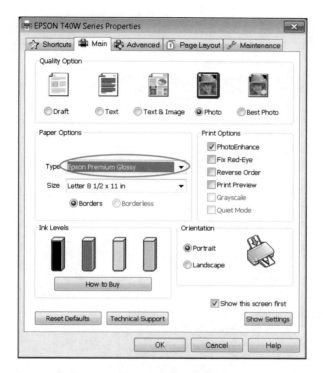

**Figure 14-3:** Click Preferences in the first dialog box that opens, and the selected printer preferences dialog box opens.

*Mac:* You don't have a Printer Preferences button in the More Options dialog box. On a Mac, follow these steps instead:

  a. *Click OK in the More Options dialog box.*

  b. *Click Print.*

   The OS X Print dialog box opens.

  c. *From the drop-down list below the Pages item in the Print dialog box, choose Print Settings, as shown in Figure 14-4.*

  d. *From the Media Type drop-down list, choose the paper for your output, also shown in Figure 14-4.*

  e. *To set color management, open the Print Settings drop-down list and choose Color Management, as shown in Figure 14-5.*

  f. *Make sure the default setting of Color Controls is selected, also shown in Figure 14-5.*

   This setting is used when the printer manages color.

  g. *Click Print.*

   Your Mac and your printer take it from here to print your image. Enjoy!

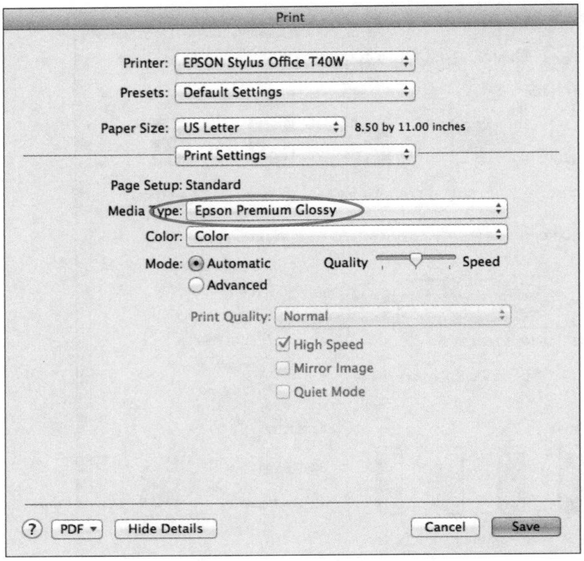

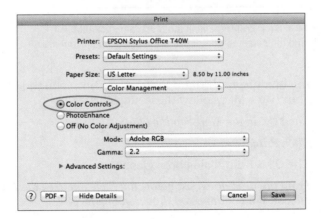

**Figure 14-4:** Choose Print Settings on the Mac and make a choice for the paper you use for the output.

**Figure 14-5:** Choose Color Management and make sure Color Controls is selected.

8. **(Windows only) Set print attributes from your printer's dialog box.**

   Select a paper type, such as Epson Premium Glossy (or another paper from the Type drop-down list that you may be using; refer to Figure 14-3). Then click the Best Photo radio button.

Now it's time to color-manage your file. This step is critical in your print-production workflow.

**9. (Windows only) Click the Advanced tab.**

The Printing Preferences dialog box opens, displaying advanced settings, as shown in Figure 14-6.

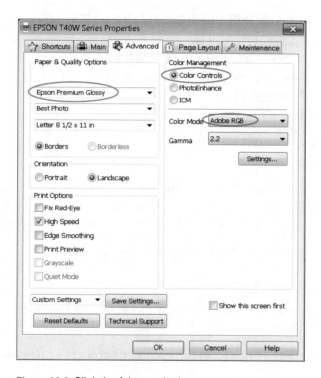

Figure 14-6: Click the Advanced tab.

**10. (Windows only) Make your choices in the advanced printing preferences dialog box.**

Here are the most important choices:

- *Select a paper type.* In this example, we printed a letter-size photo on Epson Premium Glossy paper, so we chose those settings in the Paper & Quality Options section of the dialog box. Choose the same paper here as you did in Step 8.

- *Turn on color management.* Because you're letting the printer driver determine the color, you need to be certain that the Color Controls radio button is active. This setting tells the printer driver to automatically select a printer profile for the paper type you selected.

- *Set the color mode.* Don't use Epson Vivid. This choice produces inferior results on photos. Choose Best Photo, the Epson Standard, or Adobe RGB, depending on your printer.

If you frequently print files using the same settings, you can save your settings by clicking the Save Setting button.

11. **(Windows only) To print the photo, click OK and then click OK again in the Print dialog box.**

Your file is sent to your printer. The color is converted automatically from your source workspace of sRGB or Adobe RGB (1998) to the profile that the printer driver automatically selects for you.

## Printing a photo with Elements managing color

Another method for managing color when you're printing files is to select a printer profile from the available list of color profiles installed with your printer. Whereas in the preceding section you used your printer to manage color, this time you let Photoshop Elements manage the color.

The steps in this section are the same as the ones described in the preceding section (for printing files for automatic profile selection) when you're setting up the page and selecting a printer. To let Elements handle the color conversion, follow these steps in the Print dialog box:

1. **Choose File⇨Print from the Photo Editor. In the Print dialog box, click More Options.**

   The More Options dialog box appears.

2. **Click Color Management in the left pane to display the color management options. Click Photoshop Elements Manages Colors, as shown in Figure 14-7.**

3. **From the Printer Profile drop-down list, choose the color profile designed for use with the paper you've chosen.**

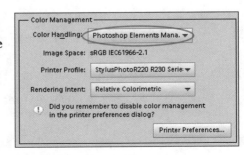

Figure 14-7: Choose a printer profile that matches the paper you use.

In this example, we use a profile designed for a specific printer, also shown in Figure 14-7. (Note that custom color profiles you acquire from a profiling service come with recommended color-rendering intents. For this paper, Relative Colorimetric is recommended and is selected on the Rendering Intent drop-down list, as shown in Figure 14-7.)

4. **Click the Printer Preferences button.**

   You arrive at the same dialog box shown in Figure 14-3. On the Mac, you arrive at the same dialog box shown in Figure 14-4.

5. **Choose a paper.**

   - *In Windows,* click the Best Photo radio button. From the Type drop-down list, choose the recommended paper choice.

   - *On the Mac,* make your paper choice, as shown in Figure 14-4.

   Custom color profiles are also shipped with guidelines for selecting proper paper.

6. **Go to the Advanced settings.**

   - *In Windows,* click the Advanced tab and click Continue to arrive at the same dialog box shown earlier in Figure 14-6.

   - *On the Mac,* choose Color Management from the pop-up menu to arrive at the same dialog box shown in Figure 14-5.

   The paper choice selection is automatically carried over from the previous Properties dialog box; refer to Figure 14-6. The one setting you change is in the Color Management section.

7. **Choose Color Management.**

   - *In Windows,* select the ICM (Image Color Management) radio button and select the Off (No Color Adjustment) check box, as shown in Figure 14-8.

   - *On the Mac,* select the Off (No Color Adjustment) radio button. (Refer to Figure 14-5.)

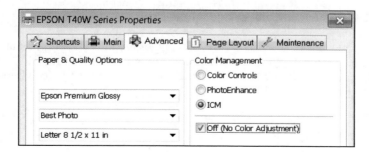

**Figure 14-8:** Select the ICM radio button and the Off (No Color Adjustment) check box.

8. **After making all the color management choices, click OK to return to the Print dialog box.**

9. **Click Print.**

   The file prints to your printer.

   Because you selected the color profile in Step 3 and you're letting Elements manage the color, be sure the Color Management feature is turned off. If you don't turn off Color Management, you end up double-profiling your print.

Deciding whether to manage color is simplified in Photoshop Elements. In the Color Management area of the dialog box, a message appears each time you make a selection from the Color Handling drop-down list. Right below the Rendering Intent drop-down list, you see a message asking whether you remembered to turn Color Management on or off. Each time you make a selection for the color handling, pause a moment and read the message (refer to Figure 14-7). This is your reminder that you need to follow the recommendation to properly handle color.

Each time you print a file — whether it be a single photo, a contact sheet, a photo package, or other type of print — you use the same steps for color management. In the upcoming section, "Getting Familiar with the Print Dialog Box," we talk about a number of options you have for printing photos, but remember that you need to manage the color for each type of print you want.

## Printing a picture package or contact sheet

Elements offers two additional printing options that are available in different places on Windows and the Mac:

- ✔ **Picture Package:** This option, as shown in Figure 14-9, enables you to arrange one or more images on a page, and print those images from a selection of standard-size prints.

- ✔ **Contact Sheet:** Choose this option to print samples of several images. (Before digital photography, the contact sheet format was how photographers initially evaluated their shots.)

If you want to print a picture package or a contact sheet, you must print from the Organizer (Windows) or choose a command (Picture Package or Contact Sheet) from the File menu in the Photo Editor on the Mac, where these options are available.

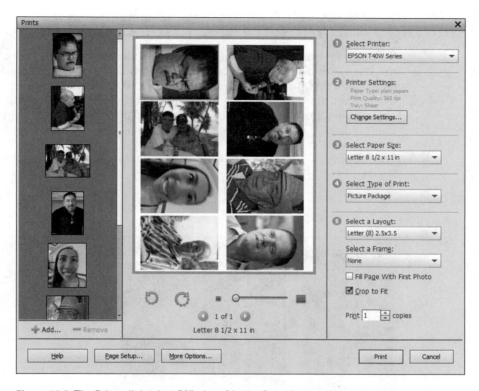

**Figure 14-9:** The Prints dialog box (Windows) in the Organizer enables you to set up a picture package or contact sheet.

All the steps for printing are basically the same as outlined in the the earlier section, "Printing a photo with the printer managing color." The key difference is the Color Management options you see. The Color Management options are limited to choosing a Print Space (such as sRGB or Adobe RGB). See the section "Printing a photo with Elements managing color" earlier in this chapter for selecting a color print space.

On a Windows computer, the Photo Editor offers better Color Management options. Always print your files from the Photo Editor unless you want to print a special print, such as a Picture Package, that requires you to print from the Organizer. Printing from the Photo Editor enables you to make use of all the Color Management options available in the More Options dialog box.

## Getting Familiar with the Print Dialog Box

Because the Print dialog box options are identical in the Organizer and the Photo Editor in Windows (with the exception for color profile management), you find the same menus and buttons when you choose File➪Print from either the Organizer or Photo Editor. On the Mac, inasmuch as you can choose File➪Print in the Organizer, the actual printing is available only in the Photo Editor.

The following are the individual items you find in either dialog box (see Figure 14-10):

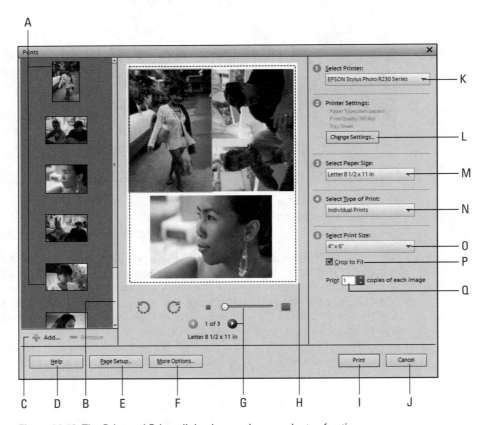

**Figure 14-10:** The Print and Prints dialog boxes give you plenty of options.

**A. Image Thumbnails:** When you select multiple images in the Organizer, all the selected images appear in a scrollable window on the left side of the dialog box.

**B. Scroll bar:** When so many photos are selected that they all cannot be viewed in the thumbnail list on the left side of the dialog box, you can use the scroll bar to see all images.

**C. Add/Remove:** If the Print dialog box is open and you want to add more photos to print, click the Add (+) icon to open the Add Photos dialog box. A list of thumbnails appears, showing all photos in the current open catalog. Select the check boxes next to the images that you want to add to your print queue. You can also choose an entire catalog, albums, photos marked with keyword tags, and photos that have a rating.

If you want to remove a photo from the list to be printed, click the photo in the scrollable list in the Print dialog box and click the Remove (–) icon.

**D. Help:** Click the Help button to open help information pertaining to printing photos.

**E. Page Setup:** Click this button to open the Page Setup dialog box. See "Using Page Setup," later in this chapter.

**F. More Options:** Click More Options to open another dialog box that allows you to choose additional options. (See the section "Creating transfers, borders, and more with More Options," later in this chapter.)

**G. Scroll Print Preview:** Click the arrows to go through a print preview for all images in the list. Move the slider to zoom photos in the Print Preview.

**H. Print Preview:** This image displays a preview of the image to be printed.

**I. Print:** Click Print after making all adjustments in the Print dialog box.

**J. Cancel:** Clicking Cancel dismisses the dialog box without sending a photo to the printer.

**K. Select Printer:** Choose a target printer from the drop-down list.

**L. Printer Settings (Windows only):** Click this button to open properties unique to the selected printer.

**M. Select Paper Size:** Choose from print sizes that your printer supports. This list may change when you choose a different printer from the Select Printer drop-down list.

**N. Select Type of Print:** In Windows, you have three options available — Print Individual Prints, Contact Sheets, and Picture Packages. On the Mac, these options appear as separate menu commands in the File menu in Expert mode. For more information on contact sheets and picture packages, see the section "Printing a picture package or contact sheet," earlier in this chapter.

**O. Select Print Size:** Select from the print size options that your printer supports.

**P. Crop to Fit:** Select this check box to crop an image to fit the selected paper size.

**Q. Print __ Copies of Each Image:** By default, one copy is printed. You can choose to print multiple copies by entering the number you want in the text box.

## Using Page Setup

When you click the Page Setup button in the Print dialog box, the Page Setup dialog box opens. In this dialog box, you can select print attributes that may be specific to your printer. However, you can control the options for most desktop printers in the Print dialog box.

## Creating transfers, borders, and more with More Options

If you want to add special features to your print, check out the More Options dialog box (refer to Figure 14-2).We explain the Color Management options you find here in the earlier section "Working with Color Printer Profiles." This section is about the fun stuff, available on the Printing Choices pane of the More Option dialog box. Here's a quick tour of what you find:

- **Photo Details:** Select the check boxes for the detail items you want printed as labels on your output.

- **Iron-On Transfer:** This option is used for heat-transfer material such as Mylar, LexJet, and other substrates that require *e-down* printing (*emulsion-down* printing, in which the negative and the image are flipped).

- **Border:** Select the check boxes to print a border on the photo prints.

  If you're looking for a border that's fancier than a basic line, check out these other options elsewhere in Elements:

  - The Picture Package options offer frames, such as antique ovals and more. See "Printing a picture package or contact sheet" earlier in this chapter for details.

  - You can fine-tune how a basic border appears with a fill layer, as we explain in Chapter 8.

  - Quick Mode offers graphical frames. Chapter 9 has the details.

  - And last but not least, Picture Effects (which we cover in Chapter 11) enable you to choose from a range of frames, too.

- **Trim Guidelines:** Select the Print Crop Marks check box to print crop marks.

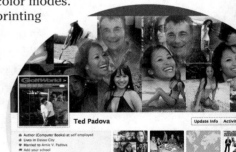

# Sharing Your Work

## In This Chapter

▶ Understanding packaging and sharing options

▶ Working with video

▶ Using Adobe Revel

▶ Sending email attachments

▶ Creating files for web viewing

*E*lements is a great packaging tool that can deploy your photos and projects for screen viewing — and not just on your computer monitor. You can edit photos or assemble creations that are exported for web viewing, and you can even prepare files to show on your television.

In Chapter 2, you can find out about resolutions and color modes. In Chapter 14, we cover the output requirements for printing files, which are much different from what you use for screen viewing.

In this chapter, we cover the options for web and screen viewing that get you started with the basics, including saving images for the web (or for screen viewing), as online slide shows, and sharing files on social networks such as Adobe Revel and Facebook.

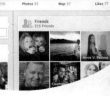

## Getting Familiar with the Elements Sharing Options

Before you delve into making creations for screen viewing in Chapter 16, you should be familiar with your available options for not only screen images but also sharing — particularly online sharing services. You also need to be familiar with the acceptable standards for online hosts, where you eventually expect to send your creations, and the kinds of devices people are likely to use to view your creations.

## *Planning ahead*

Before you choose a sharing activity and ultimately begin work on a creation, you need to ask a few questions:

- **What device(s) are going to display my creations?** When it comes to viewing photos and movies, you have choices that include computers (including desktops, notebooks, and netbooks), handheld devices such as cellphones and tablets (such as the Apple iPad and Samsung Galaxy), and TVs. If you want your creations to be viewable on all devices, you need to use different Elements tools and file formats than you would use for showing creations exclusively on a TV or on a computer.

  Consider two factors regarding devices and viewing your creations:

  - *Adobe Flash:* Some online hosts convert your video uploads to Adobe Flash. If you want to share photos with iPhone/iPod/iPad users (several hundred million and counting), stay away from any host that supports Flash-only conversions.

  - *Storage space:* Hosts vary greatly in terms of space allocated for storing content. If you want to share large video files, be certain the storage host you choose allocates enough storage space to permit you to upload your files.

- **What storage hosts are the most popular?** From within Photoshop Elements, you can export photos directly to Facebook, Flickr, Adobe Revel, or SmugMug. For videos, you have direct support for YouTube and Vimeo.

  As of Elements 12, you also have a direct link to Twitter. Twitter has increased its support for hosting photos.

- **What types of creations can I share?** Obviously, you can upload individual photos to any one of the online services. You can use the Share panel and choose to share directly to Flickr, Facebook, SmugMug, YouTube, Vimeo, Twitter, and Adobe Revel. In addition to uploading single photos to a service, some of the creations you might want to share include the following:

  - *Albums:* You can create photo albums and share the albums on many different sites.

  - *Slide shows:* In Windows, you can create a slide show and choose to export the slide show as a movie file (.wmv) or a PDF. On the Mac, you're limited to PDF only. If you use Windows, export to .wmv and upload your file to an online host. If you use Facebook, all devices show your creations. Slide shows have an additional benefit in supporting audio files. You can add audio to the creations, and the audio plays on all devices if you upload them to Facebook.

- *Videos:* If you want to host videos on your own website and make the videos available to iPhone/iPod/iPad users as well as computer users, you need a little help from Adobe Premiere Elements. In Premiere Elements, you can export video for mobile devices, and the resultant file can be viewed on an iPhone/iPod/iPad as well as a computer. Also, Premiere Elements supports some of the services on the Mac that you don't have available in Photoshop Elements, such as slide shows exported as movie files.

## Understanding photo sharing in Elements

Not all sharing providers are directly linked to Photoshop Elements. Many more social media sharing providers exist than those you find in the Elements Share panel. You can always make creations and manually upload creations, photos, and videos to many other services. A list of the more popular websites is shown in Table 15-1.

| Table 15-1 | Photo Sharing Providers | |
|---|---|---|
| *Source* | *URL* | *Description* |
| Adobe Revel | `www.adoberevel.com` | Free photo and video hosting for a maximum of 50 uploads monthly. |
| dotPhoto | `www.dotphoto.com` | Free unlimited photo uploads for one year. After one year, a paid subscription is required. |
| Facebook | `www.facebook.com` | Free unlimited photo and video uploads. Figure 15-1 shows a video shared on Facebook. |
| Flickr | `www.flickr.com` | Allows 300MB of photo uploads per month and two videos per month for free service. |
| Google+ | `https://plus.google.com` | Free unlimited photo and video uploads. |
| Photobucket | `http://photobucket.com` | Up to 2GB photo and video uploads per month. |
| Shutterfly | `www.shutterfly.com` | Concentrates on photo products – calendars, iPhone cases, cards, cushion covers, and so on – rather than photo storage. |

*(continued)*

**Table 15-1** *(continued)*

| Source | URL | Description |
|--------|-----|-------------|
| SlickPic | www.slickpic.com | Store 1000 size-limited images for the free account. For paid accounts, you can get 50GB of space and up with no size limits. |
| SmugMug | http://smugmug.com | Monthly fee of $5 per month to store photos and videos. Limits on photo size may apply. |
| Twitter | https://twitter.com | Allows up to 100 images, and most recent uploads are displayed. |
| Vimeo | https://vimeo.com | Free video uploads of 500MB per week. |
| YouTube | www.youtube.com | Free unlimited video uploads of up to 10 minutes and not exceeding 100MB. |

# Working with Adobe Revel

At the top of the Share panel in both the Organizer and the Photo Editor, you find Private Web Album.

Adobe Revel is a web-hosting service for storing your photos in the cloud, where you can view and share your photos on all your devices, such as computers, smartphones, tablets, notebooks, and so on. When you edit a photo, the photo is updated automatically on all devices.

As this book goes to press, Revel is a free service that lets you upload up to

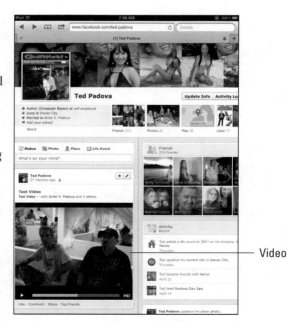

Video

Figure 15-1: Video on Facebook is shown on an Apple iPad.

50 photos per month. You can upgrade and get more storage space for a monthly service fee.

When you visit the Adobe Revel website at www.adoberevel.com and log in with your Adobe ID and password, you arrive at your Carousel, which displays all your photo uploads.

## Knowing what Adobe Revel offers you

Adobe Revel is more than just a hosting service. You can perform many tasks with Adobe Revel, such as the following:

- **Store photos and sync in the cloud:** Your photos are safely stored on the Adobe website, and you can sync the photos to all your devices such as computer, tablet, and phone.

- **Privacy:** As a default, all your photos are uploaded to your private account. Only you can see the photos you upload. When you want to share the photos, you can share them with the public or selected users.

- **Photo albums:** You can add photos to albums and view the photos within a given album in a Slideshow view.

- **Edit photos:** Adobe Revel is the only photo-sharing service that offers you Adobe Lightroom performance for editing photos. If you want this editing capability, though, you need to download the Revel app. See the following section for details.

## Downloading the Adobe Revel applications

In Photoshop Elements, you can upload and download photos through the link to Adobe Revel.

The Adobe Revel application — which you can download for free — enables you to edit photos. When you save the edited photos, you can view the updated photos on all your devices. Here's where you can find the Revel app for your computer and/or mobile devices:

- **For Desktop users:** The Adobe Revel application is available for Windows 8 users and Macintosh OS X users. You can download the application directly from the Windows App Store for Windows 8 or through iTunes for the Mac.

- **For iOS devices:** Adobe Revel can be downloaded to iOS devices for use on your iPhone, iPod touch, or iPad. These versions provide you with sharing and editing features. Your device needs to have iOS version 6 and greater.

✔ **For Android devices:** You can download Adobe Revel for Android devices. You can download Adobe Revel for Android from the Google Play Store, and the app requires Android version 2.2.

## Understanding the Adobe Revel interface

Regardless of whether you work on a desktop or an iOS device, the Revel app offers similar features, although there are some slight interface differences among the apps for various operating systems. Figure 15-2 shows the Revel interface on an iOS device.

When viewing an album, you have a few different options. The middle bar (from left to right) enables you to view the photos in the album as a slide show, display the photos in a grid, display photos individually where you can scroll through the album, and the fourth icon enables you to change the Album settings such as renaming and sharing options.

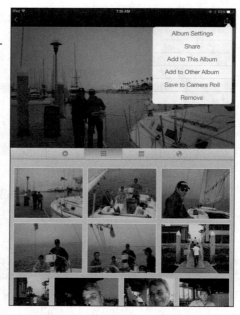

Figure 15-2: Adobe Revel application as shown on an iPad.

In the top-right corner of the screen, tap the icon to open a drop-down list of options.

## Editing a photo with Adobe Revel

To edit a photo using Adobe Revel on a Mac or iOS device, do the following:

1. **Log in to your Adobe Revel account.**

   Launch the application on your Mac or iOS device. Sign in using your email address and password. If you haven't created an Adobe ID, you can choose the option to create a new account. After you log in, you see the photos you have in your Carousel (library) or photos you imported from a Photoshop.com library.

## Moving from Photoshop.com to Revel

Your online Revel photos are comprised of two libraries: your Revel Carousel, which contains photos you upload to your Revel account, and a Photoshop.com library if you used Photoshop. com in an earlier version of Elements. The Photoshop.com library is added to your Revel account when you first log in from the Organizer.

2. **Tap a photo in iOS or click a photo on the desktop app.**

   The view changes to an editing view where the editing tools are available, as shown in Figure 15-3.

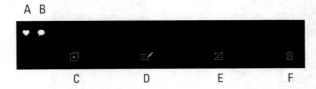

Figure 15-3: The Adobe Revel editing tools.

3. **Make photo edits.**

   The tools available include the following:

   A. *Favorites:* On iOS devices, the Favorites icon is represented with a heart. On desktops, the Favorites icon is a star. Tap or click the icon, and the photo you're viewing is added to your favorites.

   B. *Comment:* Tap the Comment icon, and a comments panel opens so that you can type a comment.

   C. *Slideshow view:* The first icon at the bottom left of the window is used to run a slide show. This icon works if you tap an album. If you have a single photo selected, tapping this icon prevents you from swiping to change photos. To exit the Slideshow view, tap anywhere outside a photo or press the Esc key on your keyboard.

   D. *Keyboard:* Tap this icon, and the keyboard pops up on iOS devices. You can type a caption that's added at the bottom of the photo. On the desktop version, a panel opens that provides a number of different sharing options.

   E. *Edit:* Tap this icon to enter editing mode. You have choices for making an auto fix, changing white balance, adjusting exposure and contrast, making red-eye corrections, and cropping and rotating a photo. The best way to familiarize yourself with the editing tools is to play with them and make changes for auto correction, exposure, contrast, cropping, and rotation if needed. Figure 15-4 shows a photo targeted for cropping.

*F. Delete:* Click the trash icon to delete a photo.

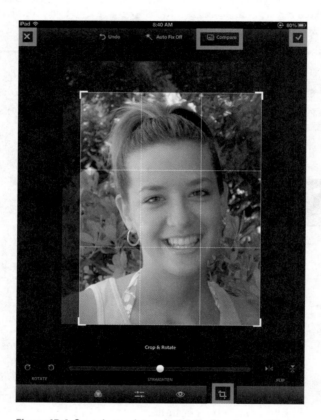

Figure 15-4: Cropping a picture in Adobe Revel on an iPad.

### 4. Compare your edits with the original photo.

To make a comparison between your edits and the original photo, keep your finger pressed on the Compare icon at the top of the window. While your finger is depressed on the icon, you see the original photo before any edits. When you release your finger from the icon, you see the photo as you have edited it.

### 5. Save your edits.

Tap the check mark at the top-right corner of the window, and your edits are saved and the file is updated. When updated, the new edited file appears the same on all your devices.

6. **Dismiss the editing mode.**

   Tap the left arrow at the top-left corner and you return to your library view. (Refer to Figure 15-2.)

## Sharing photos with Adobe Revel

After you make some edits on photos and update them, you can see the new edited photos on all your devices as long as they're connected to the cloud. However, the photos are secure, and only you can view them unless you decide to share them.

Share your photos with an iOS device using the following steps:

1. **Select a photo in your library.**

2. **Tap the Action icon (in the top-right corner) on your device to display the action menu, shown in Figure 15-5.**

   If you want to share your photo via Facebook, tap the Facebook icon. Other options exist for attaching the photo to a message, copying the photo, and attaching the photo to an email.

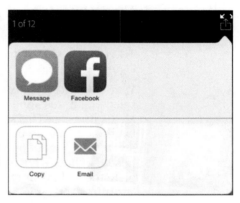

Figure 15-5: The action menu on an iOS device.

3. **Tap an option for where you want to send the file.**

   In our example, we share to Facebook.

4. **Add a title.**

   In the dialog that opens, you can type a title for your photo and, if desired, identify a location, as shown in Figure 15-6.

5. **Tap the Post link to upload the photo to your Facebook account.**

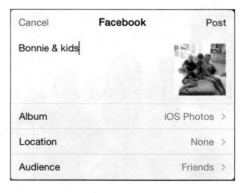

Figure 15-6: When you're uploading a photo or album to Facebook, a pop-up dialog opens.

## Downloading images from Adobe Revel

You can download selected photos or an entire library from your Revel account from your Carousel (or Photoshop.com libraries; see the earlier "Moving from Photoshop.com to Revel" sidebar in this chapter).

To sync photos from your Revel account to the Organizer, do the following:

1. **Click the + button next to the Mobile Albums link in the Import panel on the left side of the Organizer.**

   A login window for Adobe Revel opens.

2. **Type your email address and your Adobe ID password, and then click the Sign In button to access your Adobe Revel account.**

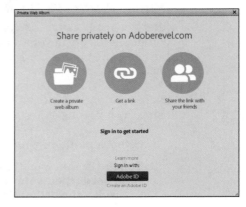

Figure 15-7: The Adobe revel login screen.

   Alternately, you can sign in to Adobe Revel by choosing File⇨Sign In to Adobe Revel. The window shown in Figure 15-7 opens.

   Your entire Revel library or the selected photos appear in the Media Browser. This step can take some time, so be patient if you have a lot of photos hosted online. When you complete the task, your media is synced and can be viewed in the Elements Organizer and on your devices.

You can choose how to sync your media in Photoshop Elements Preferences. In the Organizer, press Ctrl+K (Windows) or ⌘+K (Mac) and click Adobe Revel. You can turn the automatic sync on and off in this preference setting. When the Revel Agent is on, new and edited photos appear automatically in the Media Browser.

## Using the Share Panel

You choose an option in the Share panel by clicking one of the buttons, and then one of two interfaces appears:

- ✔ Some options lead you to more specific choices in the Share panel.
- ✔ Other choices open a window where you log in to an account for sharing photos. The choices for sharing photos with other services open windows for logging in to your account and proceeding through steps to prepare and upload images.

Figure 15-8 shows the Share panel as it appears in the Organizer (left) and in the Photo Editor (right). The Photo Editor share panel has a more abbreviated set of options.

Organizer                    Photo Editor

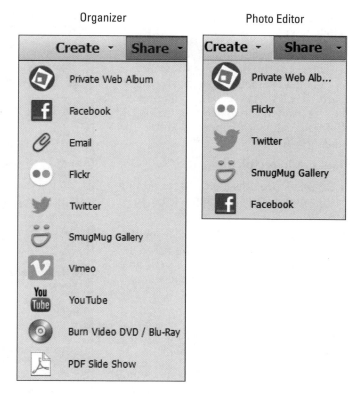

Figure 15-8: The Share panel as it appears in the Organizer (left) and Photo Editor (right).

To bring Elements together on the Mac and Windows Adobe has made the options in the Share panel identical on both platforms.

In the sections ahead, we explore using the Share panel in the Organizer and making choices for preparing photos for sharing.

## Emailing photos

Rather than save your file from Elements and then open your email client (such as Outlook or Apple Mail) and select the photo to attach to an email, you can use Elements to easily share photos via email with one click.

When you want to email a photo or a creation like some of those we talk about in Chapter 16, follow these steps:

1. **In the Organizer, select the photos you want to email to a friend.**

2. **Open the Share panel and select Email Attachments.**

3. **Choose a quality setting for the attachment and click Next.**

   Drag the Quality slider and observe the file size noted at the bottom of the panel where you see Estimated Size, as shown in Figure 15-9. If the file is large, you may need to resize it in the Image Size dialog box before emailing the photo. Chapter 2 explains how to resize images.

4. **(Optional) Add recipients.**

   The next panel provides settings for adding a message and adding recipients from an Address Book.

   You can bypass adding recipients from your Address Book. If no recipients are listed in the Select Recipients panel, you can add recipient email addresses in the new message window in your email client.

5. **Click Next.**

   The photo(s) are attached to a new email message in your default email client.

   Elements attaches the media to a new email message. You need to toggle to your email client in order to see the message and send the mail.

6. **Review the To, Subject, and Attach fields to be certain the information is correct. Then click the Send button.**

   By default, Elements uses your primary email client application, which may or may not be the email program you use. You can change the default email client by pressing Ctrl+K (⌘+K on the Macintosh) to open the Preferences dialog box when you're in the Organizer and then clicking Sharing in the left pane. From a drop-down list in the Sharing preferences, choose the email client application that you want Elements to use.

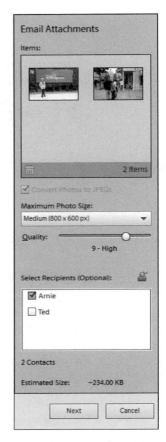

Figure 15-9: Set the Quality slider to a medium setting for faster uploads to your mail server.

Elements now supports using web based email clients. If you use Yahoo, Gmail, or even another account, you can send your photos using your existing mail client. If you choose Other in the Email Preferences, you need to supply your SMTP Server and the Port number. If you need help with setting up the mail for other accounts not listed in the Email Preferences, contact your ISP for assistance.

## Working with Adobe Premiere Elements

Several options in the Share and Create panels require that you use Adobe Premiere Elements. The items denoted as Burn Video DVD/BluRay, Online Video Sharing, and Mobile Phones and Players all require Adobe Premiere Elements.

If any of these items interest you, you can download a free trial of Adobe Premiere Elements and work with it for 30 days. If Premiere Elements is a tool you find worthwhile, you can purchase it from the Adobe Store. If you're perusing this book and have not yet purchased Elements 13, you can purchase the Adobe Photoshop Elements 13 and Adobe Premiere Elements 13 bundle. Buying the bundle purchase is much less expensive than buying the products separately.

For Adobe Premiere Elements trial versions, just click one of the options for video sharing in the Share panel, and you're prompted to download a trial version of Premiere Elements.

## Sharing your photos on social networks

You have a variety of options for sharing photos and placing orders on a number of service networks. We don't have enough space in this book to cover each and every service that Elements supports, so we walk through the more popular services (Flickr, Facebook, and Twitter) as an example for connecting with a service provider. If other services interest you, poke around and explore options for the services you use.

Previous users of Elements will immediately notice that services such as Flickr, Facebook, and SmugMug have been promoted from options nested in the More Options drop-down list found in earlier versions of Elements to buttons shown in the Share panel.

### Sharing photos on Flickr, Facebook, and Twitter

Whether you're uploading photos to Flickr, Facebook, or Twitter, you follow the same process in Elements. You first select photos, albums, or creations in the Organizer and then click the Flickr, Facebook, or Twitter button in the Share panel.

You need to authorize Elements to communicate with these social networks before uploading any content. Click the Authorize button and proceed to a login page, where you supply your account username and password information.

After you are logged in to a site, the process for uploading images is easy, as shown in Figure 15-10, where we logged in to Facebook.

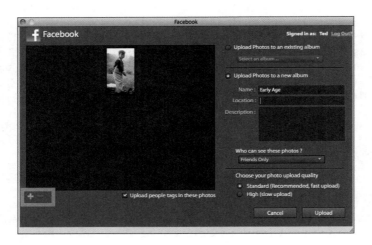

Figure 15-10: After authorizing Facebook, the Share to Facebook window permits you to upload selected photos to your Facebook account.

Attribute choices in the Share to Facebook window are straightforward and easy to follow. Here's what you find:

- **If you want to add more photos,** click the plus (+) button. Selecting a thumbnail in the window and clicking the minus (–) button deletes the photo.

- **You can choose to add photos to existing Facebook albums or create a new album** by selecting the respective radio button choice, as shown in Figure 15-11.

✔ **You have privacy options.** For Facebook, open the Who Can See These Photos? drop-down list and choose who can see your photos. In Flickr, you have choices for Private and Public. Within the Private option, you have choices for visibility to Friends or Family.

After a photo is uploaded, you see the photo on your timeline or in a photo collection (as shown in Figure 15-11).

### Using other online services

After you become familiar with uploading photos to a service, you can easily follow similar steps to upload photos to any of the services that are supported by Elements. You first encounter the window to authorize an account. When setting up a new account, you can log in to the service and create the new account.

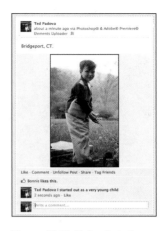

Figure 15-11: Uploaded photo as it appears on Facebook.

When you enter a site for sharing photos, printing photos, or creating items such as photo frames, follow the easy online steps that each service provides.

# 16

# Making Creations

*In This Chapter*

▶ Understanding creations

▶ Creating a Facebook Cover

▶ Understanding common creation assembly

▶ Creating slide shows

▶ Creating other projects, such as photo collages or photo calendars

*A*dobe Photoshop Elements offers you a number of creations that you can share onscreen or in print. From both the Create and Share panels in the Panel Bin in the Organizer and Photo Editor, you have a number of menu choices for making creations designed for sharing.

In this chapter, we talk about creations designed for print and sharing. It's all here in Photoshop Elements, for both Windows and Mac users. If you're looking for how to create files for screen and web viewing, flip back to Chapter 15.

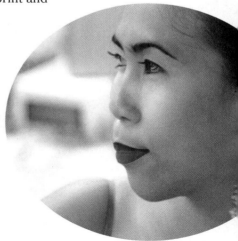

## Checking Out the Create Panel

To see the creations available on the Create panel, as shown in Figure 16-1, click the Create tab above the Panel Bin. Like the Share panel we introduced in Chapter 15, the Create panel is available from either the Organizer or the Photo Editor.

Macintosh users finally can create slide shows. Now, the Create panel offers identical options in Windows and the Mac. The Facebook Cover creation is also new in Elements 13. Using this Create option, you can create and upload images for a Facebook Cover and profile picture by following some simple guided steps. The magic of it all is that this feature permits you to precisely place the profile picture on top of the cover image, and the files are sized perfectly for display on your Facebook page.

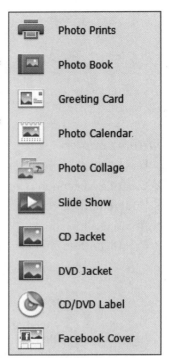

Figure 16-1: The Create panel is identical on Windows and the Mac.

# Creating Facebook Cover Images

You can select one or more images in the Organizer and open the files in the Editor. Open the Photo Bin so you can see your open files. To create a Facebook Cover and upload the file(s) to your Facebook account, do the following:

1. **Select photos in the Photo Bin.**

2. **Open the Create Panel and choose Facebook Cover.**

   The Facebook Cover Wizard opens.

3. **Choose a theme category and then a theme (see Figure 16-2).**

4. **Edit the images for position and size, and then click the green check mark when you have the image(s) sized to your liking.**

5. **(Optional) Click the Save button in the lower right, as shown in Figure 16-3, to save the file as a PSE file that you can reopen and rework if you decide to change your mind.**

6. **Click the Upload button to add the final image to your Facebook account.**

   The wizard shown in Figure 16-4 appears. Step through the wizard to authenticate your account and upload the photo.

7. **Click Next (see Figure 16-4) in the Facebook Cover Wizard and proceed through the guided steps to upload your new cover image.**

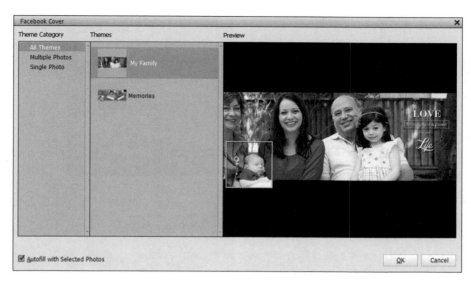

Figure 16-2: Choose a Theme for your Facebook Cover image.

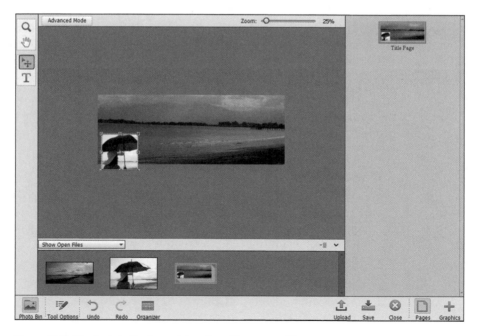

Figure 16-3: Manipulate the image(s) and position as you like.

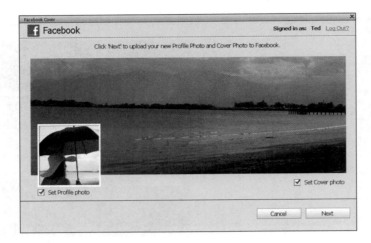

Figure 16-4: Click Next and proceed through the steps to upload the image.

# Grasping Creation-Assembly Basics

Creations such as photo books, greeting cards, photo calendars, and photo collages that you assemble from the Create panel (refer to Figure 16-1) are intended for output to either print or screen sharing.

Many creation options follow a similar set of steps to produce a file that is shared with other users or sent to an online printing service. In the Panel Bin, you can find all you need to make a new project by choosing layouts and producing a creation. Here are the common steps to follow when making a choice from the Create panel:

1. **Select photos.**

   In the Organizer or in the Photo Bin in the Photo Editor, select the photos you want to use for your creation. Sort photos or use keyword tags (as we explain in Chapters 5 and 6) to simplify finding and selecting photos you want to use for a creation.

2. **Click the Create tab.**

   The Create panel opens in the Panel Bin. The minute you click a creation you're switched automatically to the Photo Editor.

3. **Click an option for the type of creation you want.**

   You can click Photo Book, Photo Calendar, Greeting Card, Photo Collage, and so on.

   After you select the kind of creation you want to make, a wizard opens where you choose the options you want.

4. **Select a size for the output in the left column.**

   In Figure 16-5, we selected to make a photo book, and the sizes are displayed in the left column.

5. **Select a theme/layout.**

   Many of the creation options enable you to select a template. When you click a creation option on the Create panel, the panel changes to display choices for various themes, backgrounds, and borders. You make choices by clicking the theme or background. In Figure 16-5, you can see the Themes column for a photo book creation.

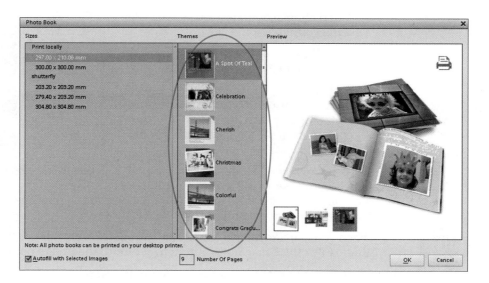

Figure 16-5: Select a theme for your creation.

Elements automatically creates the number of pages to accommodate the number of photos you selected in the Organizer or Photo Bin.

6. **Select your options in the Create panel. Click OK.**

   The Create panel changes to a wizard and displays three icons to the right of the Close icon at the bottom of the panel, as shown in Figure 16-6:

   - *Pages*: Add or delete pages.

   - *Layouts:* Choose a layout, as shown in Figure 16-7. You can click different layouts and view the results in the wizard.

   - *Graphics:* Add artwork and text with the Graphics panel. Explore each item and choose options available for editing your creation.

7. **(Optional) Select options in the creation's Advanced mode.**

   Up to this point, you couldn't make any changes to your photos (other than sizing and rotating) because the wizard interface is separate from the Organizer and Photo Editor.

   Click the Advanced Mode button in the upper-left corner of the wizard, and you have access to the Photo Editor Tools panel. You can now make edits on any photos in the creation, as shown in Figure 16-8.

   When you click Advanced Mode, the button name changes to Basic Mode. Click the Basic Mode button to return to the Create panel.

8. **Click the output option at the bottom of the wizard:**

   - *Save:* Save the file as a Photoshop Elements Project. You can return to the project and edit it at a later time.

   - *Print:* Before the output is generated, look over the preview of your creation. If you're using Advanced mode, click the Basic button at the top of the window and scroll through the pages to preview the creation.

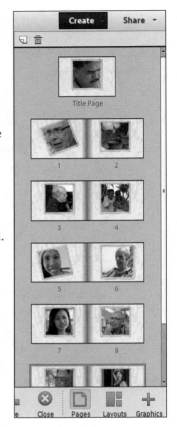

**Figure 16-6:** The Pages panel.

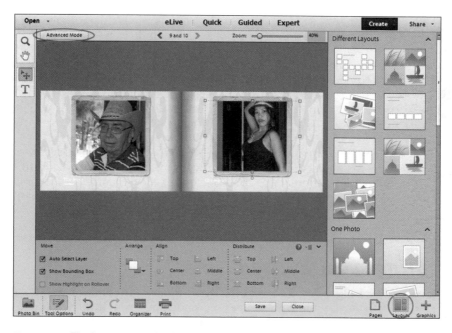

**Figure 16-7:** The Layouts panel offers choices for many layouts.

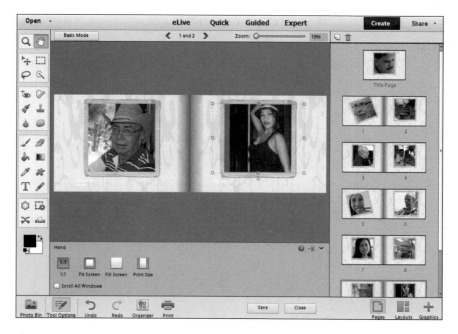

**Figure 16-8:** Advanced mode provides you with the Photo Editor tools to edit photos in your creation before saving or printing.

Whether you want to create a photo book, a calendar, or any one of the other first five options in the Create panel, you follow the same steps.

When you make a creation that will ultimately be shared with other users or sent to an online service for printing, you *must* first select the photos you want in your creation. For example, creating a photo book by clicking the Photo Book button on the Create panel first requires you to select photos.

The reason you must first select photos — in either the Organizer or Photo Bin — is because the creation process involves using a wizard to set the attributes for your creation. You leave either the Organizer or Photo Bin when you begin the process; Elements makes no provision for you to drag and drop photos from the Organizer or Photo Bin to the wizard.

## Creating a Slide Show

This *Million Dollar Baby* is no *Mystic River* — it's simply *Absolute Power!* Well, maybe you won't travel the same path from Rowdy Yates to multiple Academy Award–winning director and filmmaker Clint Eastwood, but even Mr. Eastwood might be impressed with the options for moviemaking with the Photoshop Elements slide show creations. When he's not rolling out his Panaflex camera, he may just want to take photos of the grandkids and do the directing and producing, as well as the editing, right in Photoshop Elements.

Everyone else can channel their own Clint Eastwood by using the powerful features of the Photoshop Elements Slideshow Editor to create PDF slide shows and movie files. It's so easy that Elements promises you won't be *Unforgiven*.

There are two options for creating slide shows and they appear in two different places in the Organizer/Photo Editor:

- ✔ One choice is found in the Create panel for creating a movie file of your slides by choosing Slide Show.
- ✔ The other option is found in the Share panel where you can create a PDF Slide Show.

Here's how to create a slide show in the Create panel:

1. **Select photos in the Organizer and choose Slide Show in the Create panel.**

   You see the Slideshow Wizard, shown in Figure 16-9.

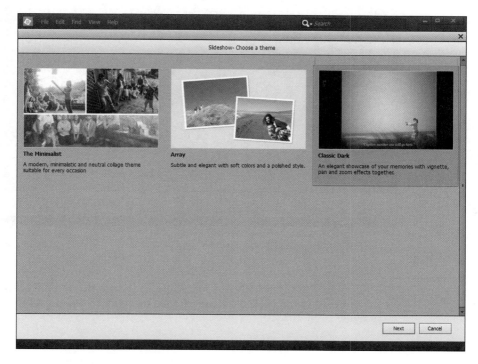

**Figure 16-9:** The Slideshow wizard.

2. **Select a theme for your photos and click the Next button.**

   The slide show begins to play.

3. **If you want to edit the slide show, click the Edit button.**

   The Slideshow Builder appears, which enables you to add or delete photos as shown in Figure 16-10. You can choose to use music by selecting options from the Speed menu, and you have a choice to save your slide show or export it.

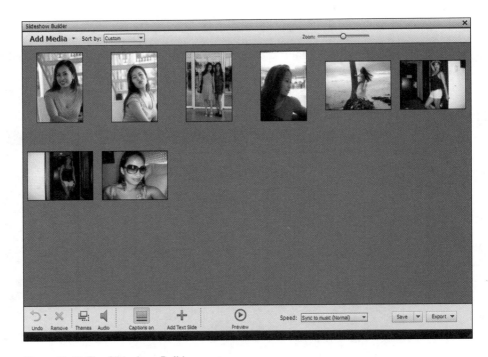

Figure 16-10: The Slideshow Builder.

4. **To export your slideshow to a movie file, from the Export menu choose Export to Local Disk. You can choose to export your file to the following sizes:**

   - *640x480* a size suited for web viewing

   - *720P* a lower high-definition resolution suited for both TVs and tablets.

   - *1080i* a higher high-definition resolution suited for TV Screens and tablets.

## Creating a PDF Slide Show

In the Share panel, you have the PDF Slide Show option. When you select photos in the Organizer and choose this option, the Share panel opens and provides the same options as you find when using Email (as described in Chapter 15). The only difference between this option and choosing to email your photos is the selected images are saved as a PDF and then emailed to the recipients you select in the Share panel.

# Making Additional Creations

Unfortunately, we don't have room in this book to cover each creation. If you want more detail on all the creation types, see *Photoshop Elements 13 All-in-One For Dummies* (John Wiley & Sons, Inc.). Fortunately, many of the other creation types are intuitive and easy to master. To create instant videos, you need Adobe Premiere Elements. Other readily available items include photo books, greeting cards, photo stamps, calendars, and CD/DVDs that you burn (Windows only). For each creation type, Elements provides you with many editing options. Explore each of the creations available to you and consult the online Help file for steps you can follow.

# Part VI
# The Part of Tens

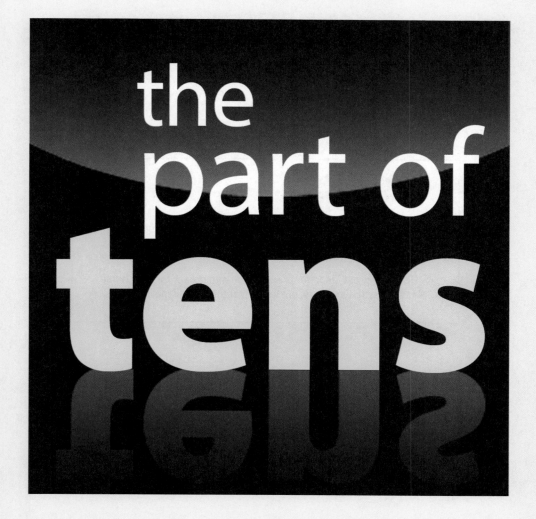

Find out how to add attractive flair to your images by checking out the Web Extras at www.dummies.com/extras/photoshopelements.

## In this part . . .

- Find our top ten tips for composing better photos, such as the Rule of Thirds, framing, and other simple tricks that can make your photos look better than ever.

- Discover great ideas for projects you can create for your home or work, such as flyers, posters, inventories, and more.

# Ten Tips for Composing Better Photos

*In This Chapter*

▶ Finding a focal point and using the Rule of Thirds

▶ Cutting the clutter and framing your shot

▶ Employing contrast, leading lines, and viewpoints

▶ Using light and giving direction

▶ Considering direction of movement

*W*e can help you take photographs that are interesting and well composed. Some of these tips overlap and contain common concepts, but they're all free; they don't require any extra money or equipment.

## Find a Focal Point

One of the most important tools for properly composing a photo is establishing a *focal point* — a main point of interest. The eye wants to be drawn to a subject.

Keep these tips in mind to help find your focal point:

✔ Pick your subject and then get close to it.

✔ Include something of interest in scenic shots.

✔ When it's appropriate, try to include an element in the foreground, middle ground, or background to add depth and a sense of scale.

## Use the Rule of Thirds

When you're composing your shot, mentally divide your frame into vertical and horizontal thirds and position your most important visual element at any intersecting point; see Figure 17-1. When you're shooting landscapes, remember that a low horizon creates a dreamy and spacious feeling and that a high horizon gives an earthy and intimate feeling. For close-up portraits, try putting the face or eyes of a person at one of those points.

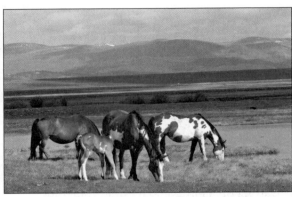

©istockphoto.com/cgbaldauf Image #7047812

**Figure 17-1:** Position your subject at one of the intersecting points on the Rule-of-Thirds grid.

If you have an autofocus camera, you need to lock the focus when you're moving from center.

## Cut the Clutter

Here are some ways you can cut the clutter from your background:

- Try to fill the frame with your subject.

- Shoot at a different angle.

- Move around your subject.

- Move your subject.

- Use background elements to enhance your subject.

- Use space around a subject to evoke a certain mood.

- If you're stuck with a distracting background, use a wider aperture (such as f/4).

# Frame Your Shot

When it's appropriate, use foreground elements to frame your subject. Frames lead you into a photograph. You can use tree branches, windows, archways, and doorways, as shown in Figure 17-2. Your framing elements don't always have to be sharply focused. Sometimes, if they're too sharp, they distract from the focal point.

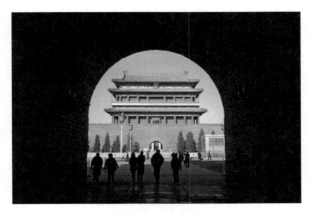

©istockphoto.com/Photomorphic Image #3125827

**Figure 17-2:** Use elements that frame your subject.

# Employ Contrast

"Light on dark, dark on light." A light subject has more impact and emphasis if it's shot against a dark background, and vice versa, as shown in Figure 17-3. Keep in mind, however, that contrast needs to be used carefully. Sometimes it can be distracting, especially if the high-contrast elements aren't your main point of interest.

# Experiment with Viewpoints

Not much in the world looks fascinating when photographed from a height of 5 to 6 feet off the ground. Try to break out of this common mode by taking photos from another vantage point. Experiment with taking a photo from above the subject *(bird's-eye view)* or below it *(worm's-eye view)*. A different angle may provide a more interesting image.

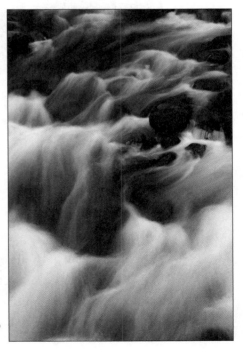

©istockphoto.com/cpshell Image #9056415

**Figure 17-3:** High-contrast shots demand attention.

## Use Leading Lines

*Leading lines* are lines that lead the eye into the picture and, hopefully, to a point of interest. The best leading lines enter the image from the lower-left corner. Roads, walls, fences, rivers, shadows, skyscrapers, and bridges provide natural leading lines, especially in scenic or landscape photos. The photo shown in Figure 17-4 of the Great Wall of China is an example of curved leading lines.

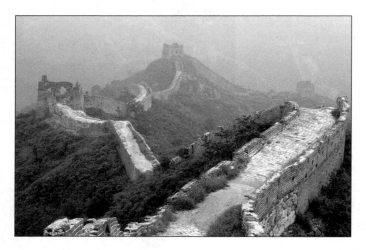

©istockphoto.com/stray_cat Image #2188656

**Figure 17-4:** You don't have to trek to China to find leading lines, although you may not find a longer unbroken curve than the Great Wall.

## Use Light

Here are a few tips about light:

- The best light is in early morning and later afternoon.
- Avoid taking portraits at midday.
- Overcast days can be great for photographing, especially portraits.
- *Backlighting* can produce dramatic results. See Figure 17-5.
- Ensure that the brightest light source isn't directed into the lens to avoid *lens flare*.

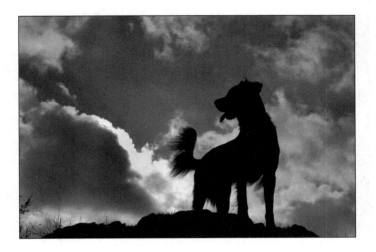

©istockphoto.com/helicefoto Image #16473327

**Figure 17-5:** Backlighting can yield dramatic images.

✔ Use a flash in low light. For portraits especially, positioning your flash so the light comes from above at a 30- to 45-degree angle gives better depth and eliminates the risk of red-eye.

✔ Get creative. Look for interesting patterns and effects created by the light.

## Give Direction

Don't be afraid to play photo stylist:

✔ Get someone to help direct.

✔ Give directions about where you want people to stand, look, and so on. See Figure 17-6.

✔ Designate the location.

✔ Arrange people around props, such as trees or cars.

✔ Use a variety of poses.

✔ Try to get people to relax.

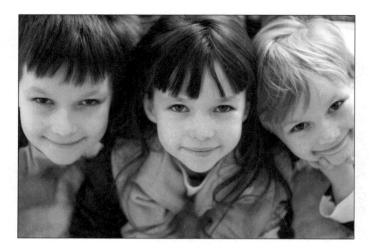

©istockphoto.com/MaszaS Image #2575210

**Figure 17-6:** Provide direction to the people you're photographing while also trying to capture their personalities.

# Consider Direction of Movement

When the subject is capable of movement, such as a car, a person, or an animal, make sure that you leave more space in front of the subject than behind it, as shown in Figure 17-7. Likewise, if a person is looking out onto a vista, make sure that you include that vista.

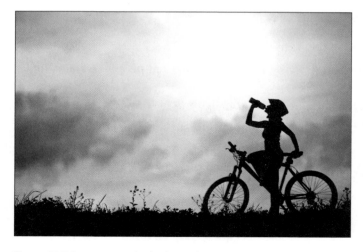

**Figure 17-7:** Leave space in the frame for your subject to move into.

# Ten More Project Ideas

**In This Chapter**

▶ Embellishing your computer screen

▶ Advertising in flyers and online auctions

▶ Decorating your duds

▶ Going big with posters

▶ Creating a household inventory or project documentation

▶ Sprucing up your homework

▶ Working with blogs

*E*ven though Elements already gives you a wide array of creations to make — from photo books to greeting cards to slide shows — you can easily do even more with the program. In this chapter, you find ideas for using your inventory of digital images to make your life more productive, more organized, and more fun. This chapter just scratches the surface. Before you know it, your photos will be a part of every aspect of your life, from your clothing to the art on your walls.

## Screen Savers

If you have two or more photos you want to use, you can create a screen saver in Windows or OS X. Follow these steps in Windows 7:

1. **Select the desired photos from the Organizer.**

2. **Choose File⇨Export as New File(s). In the Export New Files dialog box that appears, choose JPEG as the file type.**

3. **Select your photo size and choose a quality setting.**

    We recommend using a size that matches the resolution setting you're using for your monitor. Use a quality setting of 12 for maximum quality.

4. **Click the Browse button.**

5. **Click the Make New Folder button, save the photos as JPEGs to that folder, and name the folder something appropriate, such as *Screen Saver.* Click OK.**

6. **Choose whether to use the original names of your files or a common base name, such as screen 1, screen 2, and so on.**

7. **Click Export.**

    If all goes well, Elements informs you that it has executed the command.

8. **Click OK.**

9. **Right-click your desktop and choose Personalize. Then select Screen Saver from the window's bottom-right corner.**

10. **Click the downward-pointing arrow in the Screen Saver box and select a screen saver.**

11. **Specify your other options, such as wait time, power settings, and so on.**

12. **Click OK to close the window.**

Mac users can create custom screen savers even more easily:

1. **Choose System Preferences from the Apple menu.**

2. **Click Desktop & Screen Saver and then click the Screen Saver tab.**

3. **To choose one of your photos, click the plus sign, and choose Add Folder of Pictures. Find the folder with your images and choose the photo.**

4. **Specify options.**

5. **Click Test to see a preview. If you're happy, click the Close button in the top-left corner.**

## Flyers, Ads, and Online Auctions

Whether you're selling puppies or advertising an open house, adding a photo to an ad or flyer really helps to drive home your message. Here are the abbreviated steps to quickly create an ad or a flyer:

1. **In Expert mode, choose File⇨New⇨Blank File.**

2. **In the New dialog box, enter your specs and then click OK.**

Enter the final dimensions and resolution for your desired output. If you want to print your ad or flyer on your desktop printer or at a service bureau, a good guideline for resolution is 300 pixels per inch (ppi). Leave the color mode as RGB and the Background Contents as White.

To fill your background with color, as shown in Figure 18-1, choose Edit➪Fill Layer and then choose Color from the Contents pop-up menu. Choose your desired color in the Color Picker and then click OK.

3. **Open your photos and then drag and drop them onto your new canvas with the Move tool.**

Each image is on a separate layer.

Choose Window➪Images➪Cascade or Tile to view all your canvases at the same time.

4. **Select the Type tool, click the canvas, add your desired text, and then position your type with the Move tool.**

Figure 18-1 shows a drop shadow on the type. If you want to add a drop shadow as well, select your Type layer and in the Styles panel of the Effects panel (Window➪Effects), choose Drop Shadows from the pop-up menu. Double-click the shadow of your choice.

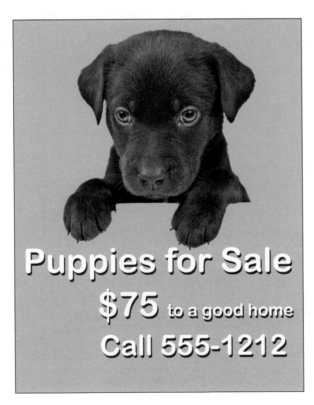

©istockphoto.com/WebSubstance Image #13474004

**Figure 18-1:** Quickly put together ads and flyers.

5. **When you're done, choose File⇨Save.**

6. **Name your file, choose Photoshop (.PSD) from the Format drop-down list, and make sure that the Layers and Color check boxes are selected.**

   If you're taking your document to a copy shop, save your document as a Photoshop PDF (.pdf) file.

7. **(Optional) To save a copy of your ad or flyer in the Organizer, select the Include in the Elements Organizer check box. In addition, select the Layers, ICC Profile (Embed Color Profile on the Mac), and Use Lower Case Extension (Windows only) options.**

8. **Click Save.**

## Clothes, Hats, and More

Buy plain white T-shirts at your local discount store or plain aprons and tote bags at a craft or fabric store. Then buy special transfer paper at your office supply, big-box, or computer store. Print your photos on the transfer paper (be sure to flip the images horizontally first) and iron the print onto the fabric. When you're done, you have a personalized gift for very little cash.

## Posters

You can get posters and large prints at many copy shops and even your local Costco. Call and talk to a knowledgeable rep so you know exactly how to prepare your file. Here are a few questions to ask:

✐ What file format and resolution should the file be?

✐ What print sizes do you offer?

✐ Do you provide mounting and lamination services?

## Household and Business Inventories

Shoot pictures of your items. In the Organizer, select the image and choose Edit⇨Add Caption to include makes, models, purchase dates, and dollar values of each piece. Then create a single PDF document from those multiple files by creating a slide show. Chapter 15 explains how to create the slide show PDF. After the PDF is finished, you can upload it to a *cloud* (online) storage site or save it to an external drive that's stored somewhere else (in a safety deposit box or other secure location).

# Project Documentation

If you're taking a class or workshop, take your camera to class (if the instructor doesn't mind). Documenting the positions or steps of that new yoga, pottery, or gardening class can help you practice or re-create it on your own. Import your desired photos into the Organizer and create notes on each step of the project in the caption area. When you're done, output the images to a PDF slide show. For details on creating PDF slide shows, see Chapter 15.

# School Reports and Projects

Have to write a paper on the habits of the lemurs of Madagascar? Trek down to your local zoo and have a photo shoot. Create a simple collage of lemurs eating, sleeping, and doing the other things that lemurs do. You can use the Photo Collage command on the Create panel or create a custom collage by making selections (see Chapter 7) and dragging and dropping them onto a blank canvas.

# Blogs

Creating a simple blog is a great way to share not only your latest and greatest photos but also recent news about family and friends. Some of the most popular free blogging platforms are `http://blogger.com`, `http://wordpress.com`, `www.tumblr.com`, and `www.livejournal.com`.

# Wait — There's More

Before you start taking your photos to the next dimension, consider a few extra ideas: Make fun place cards for dinner party guests; create your own business cards or letterhead; design your own bookmarks, bookplates, and notepads; or label storage boxes with photos of their contents. Check out `www.pinterest.com`, and other sites for a slew of projects to do with photos.

# Index

## • *Symbols and Numerics* •

16-bit support, 1
" (quote marks), 76

## • *A* •

Actions panel, 67–68
Adjust Smart Fix, 202
adjustment layers, 174, 178–180
Adjustments panel, 9, 68
Adobe Flash, 364
Adobe InDesign, 46
Adobe Partner Services, 76
Adobe Premiere Elements, 365, 375
Adobe Reader, 45
Adobe Revel
  applications for, 367–368
  downloading images from, 371–372
  editing images in, 368–371
  interface, 368
  overview, 365, 366–367
  sharing images from, 371
Adobe RGB profile, 22, 52–53
aging, removing, 213
Airbrush option, 306
albums
  creating, 112–113
  deleting, 114
  editing, 114
  overview, 111
  saving images from Photo Bin as, 70
  sharing, 114
  using as temporary space, 113–114
  viewing in Organizer, 101
algorithm, defined, 36
Alt (Option) key, 144, 155, 211, 214, 217
anchor point, 328
AND keyword, 130, 132

Android, 368
angle gradients, 314
antialiasing
  for Brush tool, 306
  for Color Replacement tool, 226
  defined, 145
  for Magic Eraser tool, 165
  for Pencil tool, 304
  for selections, 154
  for text, 335
Apple Mail, 373. *See also* Mac OS X
artifacts, 246–247
Asian characters, 76
aspect ratio
  cropping using, 194
  recomposing images, 199
  for selections, 145–146
attributes, document, 15–16
audio formats, 49
auto fixes
  Auto Color Correction, 201, 203–204
  Auto Contrast, 201, 203
  Auto Levels, 201, 202–203
  Auto Red Eye Fix, 201, 205–206
  Auto Sharpen, 201, 204–205
  Auto Smart Fix, 201–202
  Auto Smart Tone, 200–201
  in Organizer, 201
  in Quick mode, 207–208
Auto Select Layer option, 186

## • *B* •

background
  converting to layer, 172–173
  erasing, 163, 164–165
  flattening, 190
  foreground color versus, 299–300
  removing, 164–165

background *(continued)*
  specifying for new document, 16
  straightening, 197
backlighting, 229, 396
backup
  catalog, 124–125
  eraser tools and, 163
  full versus incremental, 124
baseline, 328, 334
before and after views, Quick mode, 10
bevel layer style, 278
Bicubic resampling, 33
Bilinear resampling, 33
bird's-eye view, 395
bit depth
  defined, 43
  formats and, 42
  scanning images, 91
bitmap format, 43, 48
Bitmap mode, 36–38
black-and-white
  Bitmap mode, 37
  Color Replacement tool, 224
  Colorize option, 236
  Convert to Black and White command,
    41–42, 237
  converting image to, 38–39
  converting part of photo to, 71–72
  desaturating layer, 39–41
  Levels command, 232
  pixels and grayscale, 26
  Remove Color command, 236–237
  resampling methods, 33
  scanning images, 91
  Sponge tool, 223
blend modes
  Color, 285
  Color Burn, 281
  Color Dodge, 282
  Darken, 281
  Darker Color, 281
  Difference, 284
  Dissolve, 280
  Exclusion, 284
  Hard Light, 283
  Hard Mix, 284
  HSL s, 285
  Hue, 285
  inverter s, 284

  Lighten, 282
  Lighter Color, 282
  Linear Burn, 281
  Linear Dodge, 282
  Linear Light, 284
  Luminosity, 285
  Multiply, 281
  Normal, 280
  Overlay, 283
  overview, 280
  Pin Light, 284
  Saturation, 285
  Screen, 282
  Soft Light, 283
  Vivid Light, 284
Bloat tool, 268
Blogger, 403
blogs, 403
Blue channel, 232
blue-eye, 206
Bluetooth, 95
blur filters, 248–251
Blur tool, 65, 221
BluRay, 375
.bmp format (Windows), 37, 43
books, photo, 382–386
Boolean expressions in search, 130, 132
borders, 311–312, 362
brightness
  Brightness/Contrast command, 230
  Color Curves, 239–241
  Levels command, 230–233
  maintaining by changing saturation, 41
Brush tool
  accessing Eyedropper tool
    temporarily, 304
  custom brushes, 309
  drawing with, 306–307
  in Tools panel, 65

● *C* ●

calendars, 382–386
calibrating monitor, 51–52
Camera Connection Kit, 97
Camera Raw, 43, 227, 234
cameras
  contrast, 395
  correcting distortion, 269–271

direction of movement, 398
downloading images from, 85–87
focal point, 393
framing shot, 395
leading lines, 396
lighting, 396–397
Rule of Thirds, 394
viewpoints, 395
Canon printers, 350
captions, searching, 130–131
card readers, 97
Cascading Style Sheets (CSS), 303
cast, color, 233–235
Catalog Manager, 122–123
catalogs
backing up, 124–125
corrupted, 124
importing free music files into, 122
managing, 122–123
overview, 121–122
performance of, 124
planning creating of, 123
switching between, 123
categories, tag, 109
CD (Compact Disc), 124–126
cellphones, 95–97
channels, color, 49–50
cheat sheet for book, 3
circular selections, 143–144, 155
clarity
blur filters, 248–251
general discussion, 246–247
removing artifacts, 247
sharpening filters, 251–254
Clipboard
clearing, 18, 184
creating new document from, 16
drag-and-drop, 184
clipping mask, 176
Clone Stamp tool, 65, 210–212
CMYK (cyan, magenta, yellow, and
    black), 36
Collage mode, 288
collages, 382–386
color
adjusting in Quick mode, 208
adjustment layers, 178
Auto Color Correction, 203–204
background, 299–300

cast of, 233–235
channels, 49–50
Color Curves, 239–241
defringing layers, 242–244
foreground, 299–300
Hex code for, 303
hue, 235–236
Levels command, 230–233
Magic Wand tool, 152
matching output, 51
monitor calibration, 51–52
photo filters, 244–245
Picker for, 300–301
preparing images for printing, 348
profiles for, 22, 349, 350
remapping, 245–246
removing, 236–237
replacing, 238–239
RGB, 49–50
sampling with Eyedropper tool, 303–304
saturation, 235–236
selecting, 300–304
skin tones, 241–243
specifying mode for document, 16
Swatches panel, 301–302
text, 334
workflow for editing, 228
workspace for, 52–53
Color blend mode, 285
Color Burn blend mode, 281
Color Dodge blend mode, 282
color management for printing
by Elements, 356–358
overview, 349
by printer, 350–356
color modes
bitmap format, 43
Bitmap mode, 36–38
combining images and, 36
defined, 25
formats, 42
general discussion, 35–36
grayscale, 38–42
Healing Brush tool, 212
in image window, 61
Indexed Color mode, 42
Photoshop format, 43
PNG, 46
scanning images, 91

Color Picker tool, 65
color profiles, monitor, 53
Color Replacement tool
  accessing Eyedropper tool
    temporarily, 304
  pet eyes, 206
  using, 224–226
Color Swatches panel, 68
color temperature, 208, 244–245
Colorize option, 236
ColorVision Spyder2express, 52
Comic filter, 272–273
Compact Disc (CD), 124–126
Compose feature, 295–297
composing photos
  contrast, 395
  direction of movement, 398
  focal point, 393
  framing shot, 395
  leading lines, 396
  lighting, 396–397
  Rule of Thirds, 394
  viewpoints, 395
composite images, 172, 295–297
compression, TIFF, 46–47
CompuServe GIF. *See* GIF
constraining proportions, 32
contact sheet, 358–359
Content tab, Organizer, 112
Content-Aware Move tool, 65, 216–217
Content-Aware option, 215, 311
contextual menus, 63
contiguous pixels, 153, 165
contrast
  adjusting in Quick mode, 208
  adjustment layers, 178
  Auto Color Correction, 203–204
  Auto Contrast, 203
  Auto Levels, 202
  Brightness/Contrast command, 230
  Color Curves, 239–241
  composing better photos, 395
  Levels command, 230–233
  Magic Wand tool, 152
  Magnetic Lasso tool, 149
  refining edges, 167
  Remove Color command, 237
  sharpening, 246, 252
Convert to Black and White command, 237

Cookie Cutter tool, 161–162, 304
Cooling Filter, 245
Copy Merged command, 183
corrective filters, 263
cover images, Facebook, 380–382
Create/Share panel, 69
creations, 382–386
Crop tool, 65, 193–196
cropping
  with Cookie Cutter tool, 161–162
  overview, 193–196
  preferences for, 196
  in Quick mode, 11, 207
  resampling, 31
  from selection, 196
  version 13 enhancements, 1
  when printing, 362
  workflow for editing, 228
CSS (Cascading Style Sheets), 303
Custom Shape tool, 161
custom tags, 106–108
Custom Workspace, 69
cyan, magenta, yellow, and black
    (CMYK), 36
Cylindrical mode, 288

Darken blend mode, 281
Darker Color blend mode, 281
decontaminating colors, 168
defringing layers, 242–244
defringing selection, 168
deleting
  albums, 114
  Clipboard contents, 184
  images from stack, 137
  layers, 175, 176
  masks, 190
  shapes, 323
depth-of-field, 249–251
desaturating layer, 39–41
Deselect command, 166
destructive filters, 263
Detail Smart Brush tool, 256–257
Details view, 126
diamond gradients, 314
.dib files, 43
Difference blend mode, 284

Digital Video Disc. *See* DVD
dimensions, image
    general discussion, 30
    in image window, 62
    resampling image, 31–32
    resolution, 30
    specifying for new document, 15–16
    units for, 31
direction of movement, 398
discontiguous pixels, 165
Display & Cursors preferences, 76
display resolution, 27
Dissolve blend mode, 280
distortion
    constraining proportions and, 32
    correcting, 269–271
    layer objects, 187
    for text, 336, 342–343
    warped effect, 219
dither, 314
Divide Scanned Photos command, 94–95
documents, Elements, 14–16
Dodge tool, 217–219
dotPhoto, 365
dots per inch (dpi), 16
Downloader, 85–87
downsampling
    defined, 30
    example of, 34
    resampling methods, 33
dpi (dots per inch), 16
drag-and-drop, 184–185
drawing
    Brush tool, 306–307
    custom brushes, 309
    filling selections, 310–311
    gradients, 313–317
    hand-drawn effect, 274–275
    Impressionist Brush tool, 307–308
    outlining with stroke, 311–312
    Paint Bucket tool, 312–313
    patterns, 317–319
    Pencil tool, 304–306
    shapes, 319–323
drawing tablets, 147, 150, 306
drop shadow, 278
duplicate items, finding, 133–134
duplicating layers, 184
dust, 247

DVD (Digital Video Disc)
    backup to, 124–126
    creating video on, 375

## • *E* •

editing images
    accepting changes, 11
    artifacts, removing, 247
    Auto Color Correction, 203–204
    Auto Contrast, 203
    Auto Levels, 202–203
    Auto Red Eye Fix, 205–206
    Auto Sharpen, 204–205
    Auto Smart Fix, 201–202
    Auto Smart Tone, 200–201
    Bitmap mode, 36–38
    blur filters, 248–251
    Blur tool, 221
    brightness, 230
    Burn tool, 217–219
    camera distortion, correcting, 269–271
    canceling changes, 11
    clarity, 246–247
    Clone Stamp tool, 210–212
    color casts, 233–235
    Color Curves, 239–241
    color mappers, 245–246
    Color Replacement tool, 224–226
    color temperature, 244–245
    Content-Aware Move tool, 216–217
    contrast, 230
    cropping, 11, 193–196
    defringing layers, 242–244
    Dodge tool, 217–219
    edit history, 17–18
    effects, applying, 275–277
    Facebook, preparing for, 12–14
    filters, applying, 262–263, 271–272
    Healing Brush tool, 212–214
    highlights, 229–230
    image window, 59
    Levels command, 230–233
    lighting, 229–233
    noise, 247
    Photo Filter adjustment, 244–245
    printing, preparing for, 348
    in Quick mode, 206–209
    recomposing, 198–199

editing images *(continued)*
remapping colors, 245–246
removing colors, 236–237
replacing color, 238–239
resizing, 12–13
reverting to last save, 18
saturation, 235–236
saving image, 12, 22
shadows, 229–230
shallow depth-of-field effect, 249–251
Sharpen tool, 221–223
sharpening filters, 251–254
skin tones, 241–243
Smart Brush tools, 254–257
Smart Fix, 10–11
Smudge tool, 219–221
Sponge tool, 223–224
Spot Healing Brush tool, 214–216
straightening, 196–197
workflow for, 228
e-down (emulsion-down) printing, 362
effects
applying, 275–277
panel for, 67, 262
in Quick mode, 209
shallow depth-of-field, 249–251
Smart Brush tools, 254–257
for text, 277
workflow for editing, 228
Elements Downloader, 85–87. *See also*
Photoshop Elements
eLive tab, 20–21
ellipse shape, 320, 322
elliptical selections, 143
email
JPEG, 44
sharing images via, 373–375
emulsion-down (e-down)
printing, 362
Epson printers, 350, 353–356
Epson Vivid color mode, 356
Equalize color mapper, 245–246
Erase Highlights Marked for Protection
tool, 198
Eraser tool, 65, 163–164
erasing
Background Eraser tool, 164–165
filtered image, 264
general discussion, 163

Magic Eraser tool, 165
overview, 163–164
events
adding in Organizer, 102
assigning images to, 118–119
tab in Organizer, 101
Exclusion blend mode, 284
Expert mode
applying filters from Effects panel, 262
blend modes, 280
Blur tool, 221
Burn tool, 217–219
Clone Stamp tool, 210–212
Color Replacement tool, 224–226
Content-Aware Move tool, 216–217
Defringe Layers command, 234, 242–244
desaturating layer, 39–41
Detail Smart Brush tool, 256–257
Dodge tool, 217–219
Healing Brush tool, 212–214
history, 17
in Photo Editor, 56
recomposing images, 198–199
saving images for web, 23–24
selections, 142
Sharpen tool, 221–223
Sponge tool, 223–224
Spot Healing Brush tool, 214–216
exposure
adjusting in Quick mode, 208
bracketing, 292
for Dodge and Burn tools, 219
merging images with different, 292–295
panorama best practices, 286
Shadows/Highlights command, 229–230
eXtensible Markup Language (XML), 107
eyedropper
choosing color using tool, 303–304
from Levels command, 232
from Replace Color command, 238

• *F* •

Facebook
authenticating account, 13
creating cover images for, 380–382
photo sharing providers, 365
preparing images for, 12–14
sharing images on, 375–377

Faces command, 290
fastening points, 150
Favorites panel, 67
feathering
    after creating selection, 144, 166–167
    with Cookie Cutter tool, 162
    marquee settings, using, 144–145
    refining edges, 167
    with Selection Brush tool, 158
File Names view, 126
fill layers
    creating, 174
    defined, 176
    using, 180–181
film grain, 251
filters
    applying, 262–263, 271–272, 340–341
    blur, 248–251
    camera distortion, correcting, 269–271
    color mappers, 245–246
    Comic, 272–273
    corrective, 263
    destructive, 263
    fading effect of, 264
    gallery for, 263, 265–267
    Graphic Novel, 273–274
    layer masks, 189
    Liquify, 267–269
    multistep, 263
    noise, 247
    overview, 262
    Pen and Ink, 274–275
    Photo Filter adjustment, 235, 244–245
    selectively applying, 264–265
    sharpening, 251–254
    simplifying shape layers and, 182
    text, applying to, 340–341
Find Offline Drives dialog box, 122
finding images. *See* searching
Finger Painting option, 220
FireWire, 77, 90
fish-eye, 286
Flash, Adobe, 364
flattening layers, 190–191
flattening stacks, 136–137
Flickr, 365, 375–377
flow rate for Sponge tool, 223
Fluorescent Chalk effect, 276
flyers, 400–402

focal point, 393
folders
    importing only new images from, 87–88
    organizing images in, 82
    view in Organizer, 102
fonts, 76, 334
foreground color, 299–300
formats
    audio, 49
    bitmap, 43
    changing versus saving in same, 21
    choosing when saving, 22
    comparison list, 47–48
    general discussion, 42–43
    GIF, 44
    JPEG, 44–45
    layer support, 190
    PDF, 45
    Photo Project, 44
    Photoshop, 43
    Pixar, 46
    PNG, 46
    TIFF, 46–47
    video, 49
forums, 19
Free Transform command, 187–188
freeform selections
    cropping from, 196
    Lasso tool, 147–148
    Magnetic Lasso tool, 149–151
    overview, 146–147
    Polygonal Lasso tool, 148–149
fringe, 242
full backup, 124
Fuzziness value, Replace Color
        command, 238
fx button, 277

● *G* ●

gamma, 51, 233
Gaussian Blur filter, 248
General preferences pane, 75
Get Files from Folders command, 83–85
GIF (Graphics Interchange Format)
    formats comparison, 48
    Indexed Color mode, 42
    overview, 44
glow layer style, 279

Gmail, 375
Google Maps, 117
Google+, 365
Gradient Map color mapper, 245–246
Gradient tool, 65, 304
gradients
  custom, 315–317
  default, 313–315
  defined, 313
  fill layers using, 180
  filling text with, 341–342
grainy images, 222
Granite Flow brush, 341
Graphic Novel filter, 273–274
Graphics Interchange Format. *See* GIF
Graphics panel, 67
grayscale
  Color Replacement tool, 224
  Colorize option, 236
  Convert to Black and White command,
    41–42
  converting image to, 37, 38–39, 237
  desaturating layer, 39–41
  Levels command, 232
  pixels, 26
  Remove Color command, 236–237
  resampling methods, 33
  scanning images, 91
  Sponge tool, 223
Green channel, 232
green-eye, 206
greeting cards, 382–386
grid, 71, 76, 194
group shots, 289–290
Grow command, 169
Guided mode
  effects in, 277
  overview, 71–73
  in Photo Editor, 56
  version 13 enhancements, 1
guidelines, 76
Guides & Grid preferences, 76

handheld devices, 95–97
Hard Light blend mode, 283
Hard Mix blend mode, 284
hardness, brush tip, 156
Healing Brush tool, 209, 212–214
help
  eLive tab, 20–21
  menu options, 19
  tooltips, 20
Hex code for color, 303
hidden files, 126, 135
highlights
  adjusting in Quick mode, 208
  Auto Color Correction command, 203
  Color Curves, 239–241
  Healing Brush tool, 212
  Levels command, 231
  Shadows/Highlights command, 229–230
  workflow for editing, 228
histogram, defined, 231
Histogram panel, 68
history
  clearing, 18
  panel for, 68
  in Photo Editor, 17–18
  searching, 131
hot spot, 164
HP printers, 350
HSL blend modes, 285
HTML (Hypertext Markup Language), 303
hue
  adjusting in Quick mode, 208
  Color Replacement tool, 225
  HSL blend modes, 285
  Hue/Saturation command, 40, 235–236
  Replace Color command, 238
Hue blend mode, 285
Hypertext Markup Language (HTML), 303

I-beam, 328
ICC (International Color Consortium), 22
Image Capture application (Mac), 93
image layers, 177
Image Size dialog box, 31–32
image window
  elements in, 60–62
  opening image in, 59

halftone images, 248
halo, 242
Hand tool, 65
hand-drawn effect, 274–275

importing images
  from iPhoto, 88–89
  only new images, 87–88
  overview, 83–85
Impressionist Brush tool, 307–308
incremental backup, 124
InDesign, Adobe, 46
Indexed Color mode, 42
Info panel, 69
inkjet printers, 35
inner glow, 279
inner shadow, 278
Instant Fix
  cropping images, 196
  in Organizer, 102
  version sets, 137
International Color Consortium (ICC), 22
interpolation process, 188
intersecting selections, 155
Inverse command, 166
Invert color mapper, 245–246
inverter blend modes, 284
iPad/iPhone/iPod, 95–97, 367
iPhoto, 88–89
iron-on transfers, 362, 402
iTunes, 97

### • J •

JPEG (Joint Photographic Experts Group)
  formats comparison, 48
  overview, 44–45
  saving image as, 13
  saving images for web, 23
  scanning images on Mac, 93
  TIFF compression, 47

### • K •

Key Concepts help option, 19

### • L •

laser printers, 35
Lasso tools
  intersecting selections, 155
  Magnetic Lasso tool, 149–151
  overview, 146–148
  Polygonal Lasso tool, 148–149
  in Tools panel, 65
Layer via Copy command, 184
Layer via Cut command, 184
layers
  adjustment, 174, 178–180
  arranging, 176
  blend modes, 280–285
  clipping mask, creating, 174, 176
  Clone Stamp tool, 211
  converting background to, 172–173
  copy/paste, 183
  creating, 182–184
  currently selected, 62
  cut and copy, creating via, 184
  defined, 39
  deleting, 175, 176
  desaturating, 39–41
  drag-and-drop using, 184–185
  duplicating, 39, 174, 184
  erasing on, 163
  fill, 174, 176, 180–181
  filtering duplicate, 263–264
  flattening, 176, 190–191
  formats supporting, 42, 190
  Healing Brush tool, 214
  hiding, 174
  image, 177
  linking, 175
  locking, 175
  Magic Wand tool, 153
  masks, 188–190
  menu for, 176
  merging, 176, 190, 192
  moving content in, 186–187
  nondestructive, 178
  overview, 171–172
  panel for, 66, 173–175
  Paste into Selection command, 185–186
  preserving when saving, 22
  renaming, 175, 176
  Select menu, 177
  selecting, 174, 177
  shape, 176, 181–182, 320
  showing, 174
  Spot Healing Brush tool, 216
  stacking order for, 173

layers *(continued)*
  straightening, 197
  styles for, 277–279
  transforming, 187–188
  turning off, 40
  type, 182, 337
LCD monitors, 52
leading (text), 334
leading lines, 396
Learn from This Correction option, 200
LED monitors, 52
lens barrel, 270
Lens Blur filter, 249–251
lens flare, 396
Levels command, 230–233
LexJet, 362
Lighten blend mode, 282
Lighter Color blend mode, 282
lighting
  blend modes for, 282–284
  Brightness/Contrast command, 230
  composing better photos, 396–397
  Levels command, 230–233
  Shadows/Highlights command,
    229–230
line art, 33, 91
Linear Burn blend mode, 281
Linear Dodge blend mode, 282
linear gradients, 314
Linear Light blend mode, 284
lines, drawing, 320, 322
Liquify filter, 267–269
List view, Media Browser, 89
LiveJournal, 403
locations, assigning images to, 117
Lomo effect, 72
luminosity
  Color Replacement tool, 225
  HSL blend modes, 285
  photo filters, 245
Luminosity blend mode, 285
LZW compression, 47

**• M •**

Mac OS X
  displaying scroll bars, 61
  importing images from iPhoto, 88–89

launching Photo Editor, 8
  PDFs, 45
  printing on, 360
  scanning images, 93
Magic Eraser tool, 165
Magic Wand tool
  adding to selection, 155
  Grow command, 169
  intersecting selections, 155
  overview, 152–154
  Similar command, 169
  subtracting from selection, 155
Magnetic Lasso tool, 149–151
Mail, Apple, 373
mapping pixels, 202
maps, placing images on, 116–118
Mark Face command, 116
Mark for Protection Brush tool, 198
Mark for Removal Brush tool, 198
Marquee tools
  adding to selection, 154–155
  creating selections using, 142–144
  intersecting selections, 155
  options for, 144–146
  subtracting from selection, 155
  in Tools panel, 65
masks
  adjustment layers, 178
  creating, 174
  deleting, 190
  fill layers, 180
  Replace Color command, 238
  with Selection Brush tool, 157–158
  unlinking from layer, 190
  using, 188–190
Media Browser
  adding events in, 118–119
  adding people in, 115–116
  overview, 89–90
  placing images on maps, 116–118
  rating images, 110
  searching in, 129–134
  stacks in, 135–137
  versions in, 137–138
  viewing photos by tag, 109–110
  views in, 126–127
media cards, 85–87, 97
Media tab, Organizer, 101
Media Types view, 126

memory
  albums, 113
  opening images, 59
  scratch disk space, 62, 77
merging layers, 190, 192
merging photos
  Compose command, 295–297
  Exposure command, 292–295
  Faces command, 290
  general discussion, 286
  Group Shot command, 289–290
  Panorama command, 286–288
  Scene Cleaner command, 291–292
  version 13 enhancements, 1
metadata, 131–133
Microsoft Office, 36
Microsoft Outlook, 373
Microsoft Windows
  Adobe Revel for, 367
  backup to CD/DVD, 124–126
  Bitmap mode versus .bmp format, 37
  color management options, 359
  creating movie from slide show, 364
  launching Photo Editor, 8
  printer settings, 361
  saving thumbnail with image, 23
  scanning images, 92–93
  64-bit support, 1
midtones
  adjusting in Quick mode, 208
  Auto Color Correction command, 203
  Color Curves, 239–241
  Healing Brush tool, 212
  Levels command, 231
  workflow for editing, 228
*moiré* pattern, 248
monitors
  calibrating, 51–52
  color profiles, 53
  touchscreen, 228
Motion Blur filter, 249
Move tool
  Content-Aware Move tool, 65, 216–217
  moving layer contents, 186–187
  in Tools panel, 65
movement, direction of in photo, 398
movie, creating from slide show, 128, 364,
    388. *See also* video
MP3 format, 49

Multiply blend mode, 281
music, 122
Mylar, 362

● *N* ●

Navigator panel, 69
Nearest Neighbor resampling, 33
New dialog box, 15
Noir Edit effect, 71
noise, 247, 251, 315–316
nondestructive layers, 178
Normal blend mode, 280
NOT keyword, 130
notes, searching, 130–131

● *O* ●

objects, searching within images, 134
Office, Microsoft, 36
offset press, 35
Old Fashioned Photo effect, 72
online content for book, 3
onscreen resolution, 27–30, 34–35
opacity
  for Clone Stamp tool, 211
  for custom gradients, 317
  for Eraser tool, 164
  of filtered layers, 264
  for text, 340
opening images
  in image window, 59
  in Quick mode, 9–10
Option key (Mac), 144, 155, 211, 214, 217
OR keyword, 130, 132
Organizer
  accessing from Photo Editor, 58
  adding images automatically when
    saving, 22
  albums in, 111–114
  auto fixes in, 201
  backing up files, 124–126
  catalogs for, 121–126
  cropping in, 196
  defined, 7
  eLive tab, 20–21
  events in, 118–119
  hard drive for images, 82
  hiding images, 135

Organizer *(continued)*
  importing images from iPhoto, 88–89
  importing images, overview, 83–85
  importing only new images, 87–88
  Media Browser, 89–90
  operating system import options, 83
  panels in, 69
  people in, 115–116
  Photo Downloader, 85–87
  Photo Fix Options pane, 201
  places in, 116–118
  portable device images, 95–97
  preferences for, 97
  rating images, 110–111
  scanning images, 90–95
  searching in, 129–134
  Share panel in, 373
  slide shows, 127–129
  stacks in, 135–137
  tags, categories for, 109
  tags, creating, 103–105
  tags, custom, 106–108
  tags, default, 108
  tags, icons for, 105–106
  tags, overview, 103
  tags, viewing photos by, 109–110
  versions in, 137–138
  views in, 126–127
  workspace for, 100–103
outer glow, 279
outlines, 142, 311–312
Outlook, Microsoft, 373
overexposure, 229
Overlay blend mode, 283

Paint Bucket tool, 65, 304, 312–313
painting
  Brush tool, 306–307
  custom brushes, 309
  filling selections, 310–311
  gradients, 313–317
  Impressionist Brush tool, 307–308
  outlining with stroke, 311–312
  patterns, 317–319
Panel Bin
  albums, creating, 112
  color modes, 25

  in Organizer, 101
  in Photo Editor, 56
panels
  Color Swatches, 301–302
  Create, 379–380
  docking/undocking, 69
  Effects, 67
  enabling additional, 67
  Favorites, 67
  Graphics, 67
  hiding, 102
  Layers, 66, 173–175
  Share, 372–373
panoramas, 286–288
Pantone huey Pro, 52
Paragraph mode, 327, 329–330
Partner Services, Adobe, 76
Paste into Selection command, 185–186
path, for text
  creating, 333
  defined, 325
  tools for creating text on, 326, 327
Pattern Stamp tool, 318
patterns
  applying, 318
  custom, 318–319
  fill layers using, 181
  overview, 317
.pdd files, 43
PDF (Portable Document Format)
  formats comparison, 48
  layer support, 190
  overview, 45
  scanning images on Mac, 93
  as slide show output, 388
.pdp files, 45
Pen and Ink filter, 274–275
Pencil tool, 65, 304–306
people
  adding in Media Browser, 115–116
  adding in Organizer, 102
  tab in Organizer, 101
Perfect Portrait effect, 73
performance
  of catalogs, 124
  history, 18
  preferences for, 76
  version 13 enhancements, 1

personalized gifts, 402
perspective, correcting, 270–271
Perspective mode, 288
Pet Eye option, 206
Photo Bin
  actions in, 70–71
  creating different views of image, 69–70
  dividing scanned photos, 94–95
  in Photo Editor, 57
  thumbnails in, 60
  viewing filenames, 70
photo books, 382–386
photo calendars, 382–386
photo collages, 382–386
Photo Downloader, 85–87
Photo Editor. *See also* editing images
  accessing from Organizer, 103
  contextual menus, 63
  converting to Bitmap mode, 37–38
  creating documents, 14–16
  defined, 8
  eLive tab, 20–21
  Guided mode, 71–73
  help in, 19–21
  history in, 17–18
  image window in, 59–62
  launching, 8
  modes in, 56
  Panel Bin, 56
  panels in, 66–69
  Photo Bin, 57, 69–71
  preferences, 73–77
  presets, 77–78
  Print dialog box, 351
  reverting to last save, 18
  Share panel in, 373
  Tool Options area, 66
  Tools panel, 57, 63–66
  workspace, 9, 55–59
Photo Filter adjustment, 235, 244–245
Photo Fix Options pane, Organizer, 201
photo lab printers, 35
Photo Project format, 44
Photobucket, 365
photography
  contrast, 395
  direction of movement, 398
  distortion, correcting, 269–271
  downloading images, 85–87

focal point, 393
framing shot, 395
leading lines, 396
lighting, 396–397
Rule of Thirds, 394
viewpoints, 395
Photomerge
  Compose, 295–297
  Exposure, 292–295
  Faces, 290
  general discussion, 286
  Group Shot, 289–290
  Panorama, 286–288
  Scene Cleaner, 291–292
  version 13 enhancements, 1
Photoshop Elements
  as default image editing application, 9
  help in, 19–21
  launching, 8
  version 13 enhancements, 1, 71, 276,
    311, 380
  Welcome screen, 8
Photoshop format
  formats comparison, 48
  layer support, 190
  overview, 43
Photoshop.com, 369
picas, 31
picture package, 358–359
Picture Stack effect, 72
Pin Light blend mode, 284
pincushion distortion, 270
Pinterest, 403
Pixar format, 46, 48
pixels
  color, 49
  defined, 25
  eraser tools, 163
  general discussion, 26
  Magic Wand tool, 152
  selecting partial, 142
  shapes using, 319
pixels per inch. *See* ppi
places
  adding in Organizer, 102
  placing images on maps,
    116–118
  tab in Organizer, 101
plane of focus, 249

plug-ins. *See also* filters
  defined, 262
  preferences for, 76
  for scanners, 92–93
PNG (Portable Network Graphics)
  formats comparison, 48
  Indexed Color mode, 42
  overview, 46
  scanning images on Mac, 93
Point mode, 327–328
points, 31
polygon shape, 320, 322
Polygonal Lasso tool
  adding to selection, 155
  intersecting selections, 155
  overview, 148–149
  subtracting from selection, 155
portable device images, 95–97
Portable Document Format. *See* PDF
Portable Network Graphics. *See* PNG
portraits, 73, 115–116
Posterize color mapper, 245–246
posters, 402
ppi (pixels per inch)
  calculating, 27
  for printing, 12, 35
  for screen viewing, 12, 35
  specifying for new document, 16
preferences
  for cropping, 196
  defined, 73
  opening, 74–75
  Organizer, 97
  panes in, 75–77
  Photo Editor versus Organizer, 74
  resetting Auto Smart Tone learning, 201
Premiere Elements, Adobe, 365, 375
presets, Photo Editor, 77–78
Preview application (Mac), 45
printing
  borders, 362
  color management by Elements, 356–358
  color management by printer, 350–356
  color management overview, 53, 349, 350
  contact sheet, 358–359
  iron-on transfers, 362
  Page Setup, 362
  from Photo Bin, 70
  picture package, 358–359

ppi for, 12
preparing images for, 348
Print dialog box, 360–362
resolution for, 27, 34–35
white color, 35
process color, 36
profiles, color
  choosing when saving, 22
  online resources, 350
  options for, 349
proportions, constraining, 32
.psd files, 43, 190
Pucker tool, 268
pupil radius, 206
Puzzle effect, 73
.pxr files, 46

QuarkXPress, 46
Quick mode
  before and after views in, 10
  cropping images, 11
  editing images in, 206–209
  opening images, 9–10
  in Photo Editor, 56
  purpose of, 7
  saving image, 12
  saving version set with image, 22
  Smart Fix, applying, 10–11
  tab for, 8
Quick Selection tool, 65, 158–159
QuickLook feature (Mac), 45
QuickTime format, 49
quote marks, 76

## • R •

Radial Blur filter, 249
radial gradients, 314
radius, 167, 206
RAM (random access memory), 77
rasterizing, 26, 327. *See also* simplifying
rating images, 110–111
Reader, Adobe, 45
Recompose tool, 65
recomposing images, 198–199
rectangle shape, 320, 322

Rectangle tool, 65
rectangular selections, 142
red, green, and blue. *See* RGB
Red channel, 232
red-eye
    Auto Red Eye Fix, 205–206
    Color Replacement tool, 224
    in Quick mode, 209
    tool for, 65
Refine Selection Brush tool, 160–161
refining edges, 146, 154, 167–168
reflected gradients, 314
remapping colors, 245–246
Remove Color Cast command, 234–235
Remove Color command, 236–237
Replace Color command, 238–239
Reposition mode, 288
resampling
    changing image size and resolution, 31–32
    data loss, 31
    with Image Size dialog box, 12–13
    methods for, 33
    overview, 30
    results from, 33–34
Reselect command, 166
resizing images, 12–13, 228
resolution, image
    changing, 12–13
    cropping, 194
    defined, 25
    general discussion, 27
    for onscreen viewing, 34–35
    for printing, 34–35, 348
    resampling image, 31–32
    scanning images, 91
    setting when converting color mode, 38
    specifying for new document, 16
    zooming, 28–30
Revel, Adobe
    applications for, 367–368
    downloading images from, 371–372
    editing images in, 368–371
    interface, 368
    overview, 365, 366–367
    sharing images from, 371
reverting to last save, 18
RGB (red, green, and blue)
    converting to Bitmap mode, 37–38
    as default color mode, 16

    general discussion, 35–36
    Levels command, 232
    overview, 49–50
    scanning images, 91
RGB profile, Adobe, 22, 52–53
.rle files, 43
rotating
    layer objects, 187
    in Photo Editor, 58
    in Quick mode, 207
rounded rectangle shape, 320, 322
Rule of Thirds, 194–195, 394

• *S* •

sample images, 59
Saturated Slide Film effect, 72
saturation
    adjusting, 40, 208
    Color Replacement tool, 225
    HSL blend modes, 285
    Hue/Saturation command,
        235–236
    Quick mode, adjusting in, 208
    Replace Color command, 238
    Sponge tool, 223
    workflow for editing, 228
Saturation blend mode, 285
Save As dialog box, 21–23
saving images
    bitmap format, 43
    comparison list, 47–48
    before editing, 22
    formats, 42–43
    general discussion, 21
    GIF, 44
    JPEG, 13, 44–45
    naming, 12
    PDF, 45
    Photo Project format, 44
    Photoshop format, 43
    Pixar format, 46
    PNG, 46
    preferences for, 75
    Save As dialog box, 21–23
    TIFF, 46–47
    in version set, 138
    video formats, 49
    for web, 23–24

scanning images
  color modes, 91
  on Mac, 93
  multiple, 94–95
  resolutions, 91
  on Windows, 92–93
Scene Cleaner, Photomerge, 291–292
scratch disk space, 62, 77
scratches, removing, 247
Screen blend mode, 282
screen savers, 399–400
screen-viewing, 27, 53
scroll bars, displaying on Mac, 61
SD cards, 97
searching
  Boolean expressions for, 130, 132
  captions, 130–131
  duplicate items, 133–134
  history, 131
  metadata, 131–133
  moved items, 122
  notes, 130–131
  objects within images, 134
  in Organizer, 101, 130
  untagged items, 130
  visually similar images, 133
Select menu, 177
Selection Brush tool, 156–158
selections
  adding to, 154–155
  Alt (Option) key, using with, 144
  Auto Select Layer option, 186
  border of, 142, 169
  Brightness/Contrast command, 230
  circular, 143–144
  contracting, 169
  Cookie Cutter tool, 161–162
  creating, 142–143
  cropping from, 196
  defining, 141
  deselecting, 166
  drawing from center, 144
  elliptical, 143
  expanding, 169
  filling, 310–311
  filters, applying to, 264–265
  freeform, 146–151
  Grow command, 169
  intersecting, 155

inversing, 166
key collisions when making, 155
Lasso tool, 147–148
layers, 174, 184
loading, 170
Magic Wand tool, 152–154
Magnetic Lasso tool, 149–151
marquee settings, 144–146
moving while creating, 143
Paste into Selection command, 185–186
pixels, 26
Polygonal Lasso tool, 148–149
Quick Selection tool, 158–159
rectangular, 142
Refine Selection Brush tool, 160–161
refining edges, 167–168
reselecting last, 166
saving, 170
selecting everything, 166
Selection Brush tool, 156–158
Shift key, using with, 143–144
Similar command, 169
smoothing edges, 169
square, 143–144
stroke for, 311–312
subtracting from, 155
as text path, 326, 330–331
version 13 enhancements, 1
shadows
  adjusting in Quick mode, 208
  applying style to layers, 278
  Auto Color Correction command, 203
  Color Curves, 239–241
  Dodge tool, 217–219
  Healing Brush tool, 212
  Levels command, 231
  Shadows/Highlights command, 229–230
  workflow for editing, 228
shallow depth-of-field effect, 249–251
shapes
  deleting, 323
  drawing, 320–321
  editing, 323
  geometry options for, 321–323
  layers for, 181–182, 320
  multiple, on layer, 321
  overview, 319–320
  simplifying, 323
  as text path, 326, 331–332

sharing images
  on Adobe Revel, 365, 366–372
  albums, 114
  on dotPhoto, 365
  by email, 373–375
  on Facebook, 365, 375–377
  on Flickr, 365, 375–377
  on Google+, 365
  movie, creating from slide show, 128
  online providers, 365–366
  Photo Editor menu for, 57
  on Photobucket, 365
  preparing images for, 12–14,
    364–365
  Share panel, 372–373
  on Shutterfly, 365
  on SlickPic, 366
  on SmugMug, 366
  on Twitter, 366, 375–377
  on Vimeo, 366
  on YouTube, 366
Sharpen tool, 221–223
sharpness
  adjusting in Quick mode, 209
  Auto Sharpen, 204–205
  blur filters, 248–251
  filters for, 251–254
  general discussion, 246–247
  removing artifacts, 247
  resampling, 33
  workflow for editing, 228
shield, defined, 195
Shift key, 64, 143–144, 154–155
shifting selection edge, 168
shortcut keys, 65
Shutterfly, 365
Similar command, 169
similar images, finding, 133
simplifying
  shape layers, 182, 323
  text, 327, 337, 340
single lens reflex (SLR), 30
size, image
  in image window, 61
  physical, 30
  resampling image, 31–32
  saving images for web, 23
  scanning images, 91
  specifying for new document, 15–16

sketch effect, 274–275
skew, 187
skin tones, 199, 241–243
SlickPic, 366
slide shows
  creating, 386–388
  movie, creating from, 128, 364, 388
  PDF output, 388
  Slideshow Builder, 127–129
  viewing from Organizer, 102
SLR (single lens reflex), 30
Smart Blur filter, 249
Smart Brush tool, 65, 254–257
Smart Fix, 10–11
smartphones, 27, 35, 95–97
smoothing selection edges, 169
Smudge tool, 219–221
SmugMug, 366
snap strength, 160
social networks
  preparing images for, 12–14
  sharing images on, 375–377
soft edges
  feathering, 144–145
  radius for, 167
  for selections, 158, 162
Soft Focus effect, 73
Soft Light blend mode, 283
sorting images
  by event, 119
  by location, 118
  by star rating, 110
  by tag, 109–110
spacebar, 143
specular, defined, 251
Spherical mode, 288
Sponge tool, 65, 223–224
Spot Healing Brush tool, 65, 209,
    214–216
Spyder2express, 52
square selections, 143–144, 155
sRGB profile, 22, 52–53
stacking order, layer, 173, 178
stacks, 135–137
star shape, 320, 322
stars, rating images with, 110–111
Straighten tool, 65
straightening images, 196–197, 228
Stroke command, 311–312

styles
  layer, 277–279
  resizing with image, 32
  for shapes, 321
  for text, 339
subcategories, tag, 107, 109
support, 19
Surface Blur filter, 249
swatches, color, 302

• T •

tablets, 27, 35
Tagged Image File Format. *See* TIFF
tags
  categories for, 109
  creating, 103–105
  custom, 106–108
  default, 108
  events, 101, 102, 118–119
  finding untagged items, 130
  icons for, 105–106
  importing from XML, 107
  overview, 103
  people, 101, 102, 115–116
  viewing photos by, 109–110
teeth, whitening, 209
temperature, color, 208, 244–245
temporary space, albums as, 113–114
text
  adding in Quick mode, 209
  adding on path, 330–333
  alignment, 335
  color, 334
  editing, 336
  effects for, 277
  filters, applying to, 340–341
  font, 334
  general discussion, 325
  gradients for, 341–342
  layer styles, applying, 277–279
  as mask, 338–339
  modes for, 326–327
  opacity, 340
  options for, 334–336
  orientation, 336
  Paragraph mode, 329–330
  Point mode, 327–328
  preferences for, 76

rasterized, 327
shortcut keys, 66
simplifying, 337
style, 335, 339
tools for, 326
transforming, 336
as vector object, 26
warped, 342–343
Text On Custom Path tool, 326, 333
Text On Selection tool, 326, 330–331
Text On Shape tool, 326, 331–332
textures, 212
Threshold color mapper, 245–246
thumbnails
  in Photo Bin, 60
  in Print dialog box, 361
  saving with image, 23
Thunderbolt, 77
TIFF (Tagged Image File Format)
  formats comparison, 48
  layer support, 190
  overview, 46–47
  scanning images on Mac, 93
Timeline view, 127
tint, 208
tolerance, 152, 165, 169, 226
tonal range, 239–241
Tool Options area, 63, 66
Tools panel
  color modes, 25
  overview, 63–66
  in Photo Editor, 57
  shortcut keys, 64–65
tooltips, 20
touchscreen monitors, 228
transformations
  layer, 187–188
  shape, 323
  text, 336
transparency
  in custom gradients, 317
  erasing on layer, 163
  locking layer areas, 175
  PNG, 46
  preferences for, 76
  for text, 340
Tree view, Media Browser, 90
Tumblr, 403
Twirl tools, 268

Twitter, 366, 375–377
type layers, 337
Type Mask tool, 326, 338–339
Type tool. *See also* text
  layers from, 182
  modes for, 326–327
  options for, 334–336
  overview, 326
  Paragraph mode, 329–330
  Point mode, 327–328
  shortcut keys, 66
  in Tools panel, 65
  as vector object, 26

### • U •

underexposure, 229
undo/redo, 58
Units & Rulers preferences, 76
Unsharp Mask command, 252–253
untagged items, 130
upsampling
  defined, 30
  example of, 34
  resampling methods, 33
USB devices, 77, 82, 83, 90, 96

### • V •

vector objects/images, 26, 181, 319, 327
version sets, 22, 137–138
vibrance, 208
video
  Adobe Premiere Elements, 375
  creating for mobile devices, 365
  creating from slide show, 128, 364, 388
  formats for, 49
  tutorials for Elements, 19
views, Organizer, 126–127
Vimeo, 366
visually similar images, 133
Vivid Light blend mode, 284

### • W •

Warming Filter, 244
Warp tool, 268

warped effect, 219
warped text, 336, 342–343
WAV format, 49
web, saving images for, 23–24, 44–45
web-based email, 375
Welcome screen, 8
white-eye, 206
Whiten Teeth fix, 209
Windows. *See* Microsoft Windows
WMA format, 49
WMV format, 49, 364
WordPress, 403
workflow for editing, 228
workspaces
  color, 52–53
  custom, 69
  Organizer, 100–103
  Photo Editor, 9
  preview preference in Quick mode, 206
worm's-eye view, 395
wrinkles, removing, 213

### • X •

XML (eXtensible Markup Language), 107

### • Y •

Yahoo email, 375
yellow-eye, 206
YouTube, 366

### • Z •

ZIP compression, 47
zooming
  magnification box in image window, 61
  in Organizer, 103
  resolution when, 28–30
  in Save for Web dialog box, 24
  tool for, 65
  while creating selection, 147

# About the Authors

**Barbara Obermeier** is the principal of Obermeier Design, a graphic design studio in Ventura, California. She is the author of *Photoshop All-in-One For Dummies* series and has contributed as author or co-author on over two dozen books on Photoshop, Photoshop Elements, Illustrator, PowerPoint, and digital photography for John Wiley & Sons, Peachpit Press, and Adobe Press. She is currently the interim Program Director of the Graphic Design Department in the School of Film and Communication at Brooks Institute.

**Ted Padova** is the former chief executive officer and managing partner of The Image Source Digital Imaging and Photo Finishing Centers of Ventura and Thousand Oaks, California. He has been involved in digital imaging since founding a service bureau in 1990. He retired from his company in 2005 and now spends his time writing and speaking on Acrobat, PDF forms, LiveCycle Designer forms, and Adobe Design Premium Suite applications.

Ted has written 60 computer books and is the world's leading author on Adobe Acrobat. He has written books on Adobe Acrobat, Adobe Photoshop, Adobe Photoshop Elements, Adobe Reader, Microsoft PowerPoint, and Adobe Illustrator. Recent books published by John Wiley & Sons include *Adobe Acrobat PDF Bible* (versions 4, 5, 6, 7, 8, 9, and X), *Acrobat and LiveCycle Designer Forms Bible, Adobe Creative Suite Bible* (versions CS, CS2, CS3, CS4, and CS5), *Color Correction for Digital Photographers Only, Microsoft PowerPoint 2007 For Dummies: Just the Steps, Creating Adobe Acrobat PDF Forms, Teach Yourself Visually Acrobat 5,* and *Adobe Acrobat 6.0 Complete Course*. He also coauthored *Adobe Illustrator Master Class — Illustrator Illuminated* and wrote *Adobe Reader Revealed* for Peachpit/Adobe Press.

# Authors' Acknowledgments

We would like to thank our excellent project editor, Rebecca Huehls, who kept us on track throughout the development of this work; Steve Hayes, our executive editor; Andy Cummings, *For Dummies* royalty; Richard Wentk, technical editing wizard, who made what we wrote sound better; and all the dedicated production staff at Wiley.

**Barbara Obermeier:** A special thanks to Ted Padova, my co-author and friend, who always reminds me there is still a 1 in 53 million chance that we can win the lottery.

**Ted Padova:** As always, I'd like to thank Barbara Obermeier for her continued collaborations and lasting friendship. Also, a special thanks to Regis and Malou Pelletier; Curtis and Grace Cooper; Irene Windley; Mike Bindi; and my bridge buddies Stefan, George, and Richard for all their special modeling assistance. A very special thank you to my friend Giuseppe Morisco of Master Chef Season 2 fame and host of www.foodloversretreats.com for posing in many photos and offering me some of his great cooking secrets.

## Publisher's Acknowledgments

**Executive Editor:** Steve Hayes

**Senior Project Editor:** Rebecca Huehls

**Copy Editor:** Jen Riggs

**Technical Editor:** Richard Wentk

**Editorial Assistant:** Claire Johnson

**Sr. Editorial Assistant:** Cherie Case

**Project Coordinator:** Lauren Buroker

**Cover Image:** ©iStock.com/IS_ImageSource

## le & Mac

d For Dummies,
Edition
-1-118-72306-7

ne For Dummies,
Edition
-1-118-69083-3

s All-in-One
Dummies, 4th Edition
-1-118-82210-4

X Mavericks
Dummies
-1-118-69188-5

## gging & Social Media

ebook For Dummies,
Edition
-1-118-63312-0

ial Media Engagement
Dummies
-1-118-53019-1

rdPress For Dummies,
Edition
-1-118-79161-5

## siness

ck Investing
Dummies, 4th Edition
-1-118-37678-2

esting For Dummies,
Edition
-0-470-90545-6

## Personal Finance
For Dummies, 7th Edition
978-1-118-11785-9

QuickBooks 2014
For Dummies
978-1-118-72005-9

Small Business Marketing
Kit For Dummies,
3rd Edition
978-1-118-31183-7

## Careers

Job Interviews
For Dummies, 4th Edition
978-1-118-11290-8

Job Searching with Social
Media For Dummies,
2nd Edition
978-1-118-67856-5

Personal Branding
For Dummies
978-1-118-11792-7

Resumes For Dummies,
6th Edition
978-0-470-87361-8

Starting an Etsy Business
For Dummies, 2nd Edition
978-1-118-59024-9

## Diet & Nutrition

Belly Fat Diet For Dummies
978-1-118-34585-6

## Mediterranean Diet
For Dummies
978-1-118-71525-3

Nutrition For Dummies,
5th Edition
978-0-470-93231-5

## Digital Photography

Digital SLR Photography
All-in-One For Dummies,
2nd Edition
978-1-118-59082-9

Digital SLR Video &
Filmmaking For Dummies
978-1-118-36598-4

Photoshop Elements 12
For Dummies
978-1-118-72714-0

## Gardening

Herb Gardening
For Dummies, 2nd Edition
978-0-470-61778-6

Gardening with Free-Range
Chickens For Dummies
978-1-118-54754-0

## Health

Boosting Your Immunity
For Dummies
978-1-118-40200-9

## Diabetes For Dummies,
4th Edition
978-1-118-29447-5

Living Paleo For Dummies
978-1-118-29405-5

## Big Data

Big Data For Dummies
978-1-118-50422-2

Data Visualization
For Dummies
978-1-118-50289-1

Hadoop For Dummies
978-1-118-60755-8

## Language &
## Foreign Language

500 Spanish Verbs
For Dummies
978-1-118-02382-2

English Grammar
For Dummies, 2nd Edition
978-0-470-54664-2

French All-in-One
For Dummies
978-1-118-22815-9

German Essentials
For Dummies
978-1-118-18422-6

Italian For Dummies,
2nd Edition
978-1-118-00465-4

**e Available in print and e-book formats.**

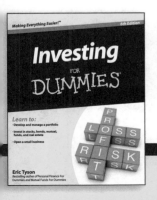

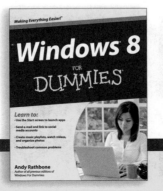

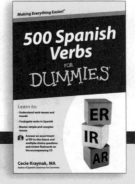

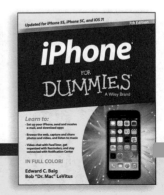

Available wherever books are sold. **For more information or to order direct visit www.dummies.com**

## Math & Science

Algebra I For Dummies,
2nd Edition
978-0-470-55964-2

Anatomy and Physiology
For Dummies, 2nd Edition
978-0-470-92326-9

Astronomy For Dummies,
3rd Edition
978-1-118-37697-3

Biology For Dummies,
2nd Edition
978-0-470-59875-7

Chemistry For Dummies,
2nd Edition
978-1-118-00730-3

1001 Algebra II Practice
Problems For Dummies
978-1-118-44662-1

## Microsoft Office

Excel 2013 For Dummies
978-1-118-51012-4

Office 2013 All-in-One
For Dummies
978-1-118-51636-2

PowerPoint 2013
For Dummies
978-1-118-50253-2

Word 2013 For Dummies
978-1-118-49123-2

## Music

Blues Harmonica
For Dummies
978-1-118-25269-7

Guitar For Dummies,
3rd Edition
978-1-118-11554-1

iPod & iTunes
For Dummies, 10th Edition
978-1-118-50864-0

## Programming

Beginning Programming
with C For Dummies
978-1-118-73763-7

Excel VBA Programming
For Dummies, 3rd Edition
978-1-118-49037-2

Java For Dummies,
6th Edition
978-1-118-40780-6

## Religion & Inspiration

The Bible For Dummies
978-0-7645-5296-0

Buddhism For Dummies,
2nd Edition
978-1-118-02379-2

Catholicism For Dummies,
2nd Edition
978-1-118-07778-8

## Self-Help & Relationships

Beating Sugar Addiction
For Dummies
978-1-118-54645-1

Meditation For Dummies,
3rd Edition
978-1-118-29144-3

## Seniors

Laptops For Seniors
For Dummies, 3rd Edition
978-1-118-71105-7

Computers For Seniors
For Dummies, 3rd Edition
978-1-118-11553-4

iPad For Seniors
For Dummies, 6th Edition
978-1-118-72826-0

Social Security
For Dummies
978-1-118-20573-0

## Smartphones & Tablets

Android Phones
For Dummies, 2nd Edition
978-1-118-72030-1

Nexus Tablets
For Dummies
978-1-118-77243-0

Samsung Galaxy S 4
For Dummies
978-1-118-64222-1

Samsung Galaxy Tabs
For Dummies
978-1-118-77294-2

## Test Prep

ACT For Dummies,
5th Edition
978-1-118-01259-8

ASVAB For Dummies,
3rd Edition
978-0-470-63760-9

GRE For Dummies,
7th Edition
978-0-470-88921-3

Officer Candidate Tests
For Dummies
978-0-470-59876-4

Physician's Assistant Exa
For Dummies
978-1-118-11556-5

Series 7 Exam For Dumm
978-0-470-09932-2

## Windows 8

Windows 8.1 All-in-One
For Dummies
978-1-118-82087-2

Windows 8.1 For Dumm
978-1-118-82121-3

Windows 8.1 For Dumm
Book + DVD Bundle
978-1-118-82107-7

**ℯ Available in print and e-book formats.**

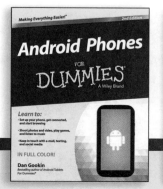 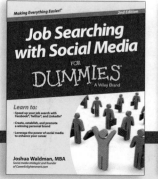 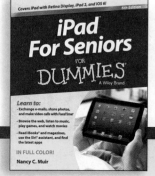 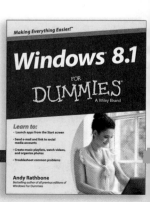

Available wherever books are sold. **For more information or to order direct visit www.dummies.com**

# Take Dummies with you everywhere you go!

Whether you are excited about e-books, want more from the web, must have your mobile apps, or are swept up in social media, Dummies makes everything easier.

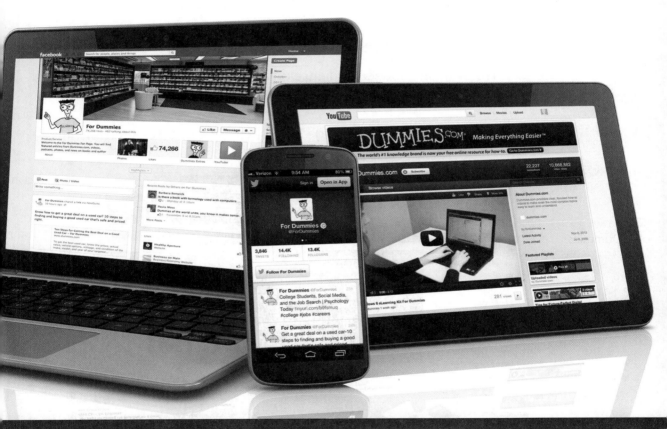

**Visit Us**

bit.ly/JE0O

**Join Us**

nkd.in/1gurkMm

**Like Us**

on.fb.me/1f1ThNu

**Pin Us**

bit.ly/16caOLd

**Follow Us**

bit.ly/ZDytkR

**Circle Us**

bit.ly/1aQTuDQ

**Watch Us**

bit.ly/gbOQHn

**Shop Us**

bit.ly/4dEp9

For Dummies is the global leader in the reference category and one of the most trusted and highly regarded brands in the world. No longer just focused on books, customers now have access to the For Dummies content they need in the format they want. Let us help you develop a solution that will fit your brand and help you connect with your customers.

## Advertising & Sponsorships

Connect with an engaged audience on a powerful multimedia site, and position your message alongside expert how-to content.

Targeted ads • Video • Email marketing • Microsites • Sweepstakes sponsorship

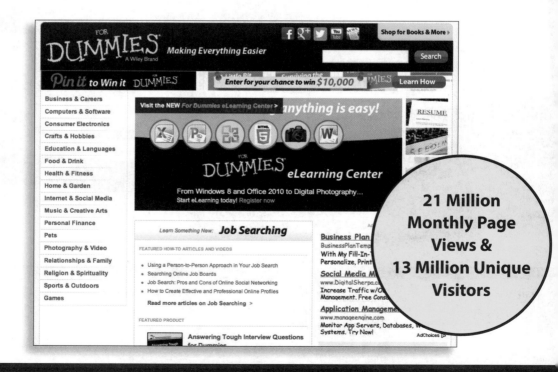

For Dummies is a registered trademark of John Wiley & Sons, Inc.

# Custom Publishing

Reach a global audience in any language by creating a solution that will differentiate you from competitors, amplify your message, and encourage customers to make a buying decision.

Apps • Books • eBooks • Video • Audio • Webinars

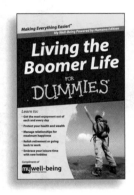
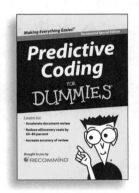
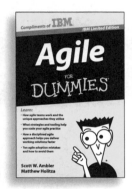
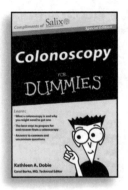

# Brand Licensing & Content

Leverage the strength of the world's most popular reference brand to reach new audiences and channels of distribution.

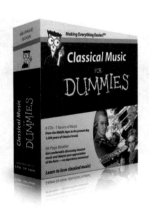
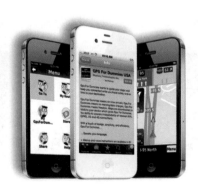
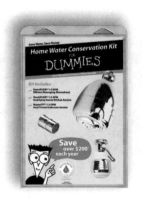
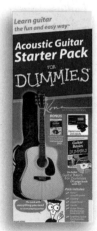

## For more information, visit www.Dummies.com/biz

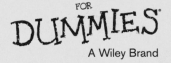

# Dummies products make life easier

- DIY
- Consumer Electronics
- Crafts
- Software
- Cookware
- Hobbies
- Videos
- Music
- Games
- and More!

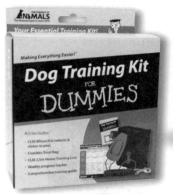

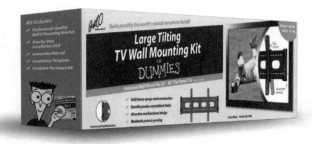

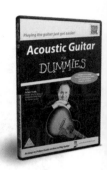

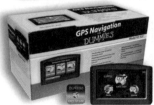

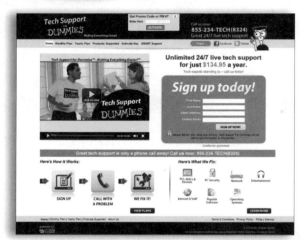

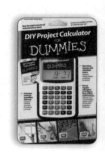

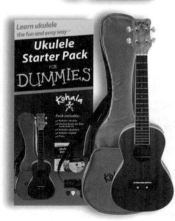

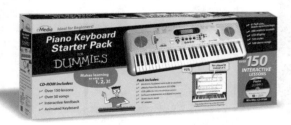

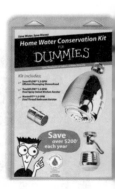

For more information, go to **Dummies.com** and search the store by category.

For Dummies is a registered trademark of John Wiley & Sons, Inc.

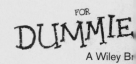

FOR
DUMMIE

A Wiley Br